UNIVERSITY RECORDS
AND LIFE in the Middle Ages

RECORDS OF CIVILIZATION
IN NORTON PAPERBACK EDITIONS

UNIVERSITY RECORDS AND LIFE in the Middle Ages

By LYNN THORNDIKE, PROFESSOR OF HISTORY IN COLUMBIA UNIVERSITY

The Norton Library

W·W·NORTON & COMPANY·INC·

NEW YORK

First published in this editon 1975
by arrangement with Columbia University Press

Books That Live
The Norton imprint on a book means that in the publisher's
estimation it is a book not for a single season but for the years.
W. W. Norton & Company, Inc.

Library of Congress Cataloging in Publication Data
Thorndike, Lynn, 1882-1965.
    University records and life in the Middle Ages.
    Reprint of the 1971 ed. published by Octagon Books,
New York, which was a reprint of the 1944 ed. published
by Columbia University Press, New York, as no. 38 of
Records of civilization—sources and studies.
    Includes bibliographical references.
    1. Universities and colleges—Europe. 2. Education,
Medieval. I. Title. II. Series: Records of civiliza-
tion—sources and studies ; no. 38.
LA627.T45   1975   378.4   75-8950
ISBN 0-393-09216-X

Printed in the United States of America
1 2 3 4 5 6 7 8 9 0

TABLE OF CONTENTS

PLAN

INTRODUCTION

A chronological arrangement of the passages here translated from university records and other sources has been adopted as the most convenient, cumulative, and historically illuminating, although it involves a separation and scattering of those concerned with a common topic. On the other hand, there are many documents of a more general nature, where any such single topic is inextricably merged with others. The geographical distribution of our material is not a matter of much consequence, since the medieval universities were international and universal rather than local or national, and also a good deal alike. I have, however, made a fairly wide selection in an effort to introduce as much variety and local interest as possible. But inasmuch as the records for the university of Paris, especially for the earlier centuries, are better preserved than those of Bologna or any other university, and are ready to hand in the volumes of the *Chartularium,* I have made this rather the backbone of the treatment, although seeking selections from various other sources, both documentary and literary.

Of 176 items in all, 78 are from the *Chartularium,* 21 from Fournier's edition of the statutes and privileges of other French universities. Of these last, five concern Toulouse; four, Montpellier; three, Avignon; two each, Angers, Orléans, Perpignan, and Caen; one, Valence. There are ten extracts from the *Urkundenbuch* for the university of Heidelberg; seven, from Borsetti's work on the university of Ferrara; eight, from Malagola's edition of the Bologna statutes; five, from the *Codice diplomatico* of the university of Pavia; single selections, from the Montpellier *Cartulaire,* Dallari's edition of the Bologna faculty rolls, and Anstey's *Munimenta.* This does not mean that these are the only universities treated, since Salamanca, Padua, Erfurt, Ingolstadt, Leipzig, Cracow, Wittenberg, Tübingen, and Hesse-Schaumburg are the themes of other selections.

From contemporary writers, as distinct from university records and official documents, some twenty-five selections are taken from those whose works have been printed. Of these John of Salisbury and Antonino, archbishop of Florence (1440–1459), are used most frequently, while Pierre Dubois is quoted at most length. Aside from these published authors, five hitherto unpublished manuscripts have been utilized, one for the longest passage of all. Four more selections are from articles in learned periodicals based upon manuscript materials. Yet other passages are drawn from old printed works which are inaccessible in this country.

The medieval universities and their scholastic mode of instruction survived with little change into early modern times. I have accordingly included a few selections regarding teachers, students and lectures in the sixteenth and seventeenth centuries. Approximately the same number, eleven, are devoted to the twelfth century; 45 to the thirteenth, and 46 to the fourteenth century; 63—many of which, however, are very brief—to the fifteenth century. The longest single selection, *On Commendation of the Clerk,* coming as it does apparently soon after the Black Death and William of Ockham, constitutes a sort of landmark or watershed, dividing our period and volume roughly into two halves. The Latin text of this hitherto unpublished educational treatise is reproduced as an appendix, and another is devoted to some account of the colleges at Paris in the later middle ages.

Since our selections are presented in chronological order, it may be well to preface them here by a topical summary, noting some of the chief subjects treated and the passages bearing upon each of these.

While the translations deal primarily with the records of the medieval universities and with the life and thought of those attending them, some attention has been given to preparatory schools and to the study of grammar which, although sometimes taught at universities, was normally acquired in grammar schools and by boys of an age when, as in the case of the pupils of Bernard of Chartres (Selection 2), corporal punishment was considered appropriate and necessary. As Rashdall has pointed out, it was seldom or never resorted to in the case of candidates for university degrees. But it is difficult to draw any hard and fast line between university instruction and previous preparation for it, as the treatise, *On Commendation of the Clerk* (Selection 81) well illustrates, and either is illuminated by the other, as that treatise also attests. Both are included in university records as they have reached us and as they have been published in modern editions. Both figure in the educational scheme of Pierre Dubois (Selection 59). I have therefore included here the decree of the Third Lateran Council, passages on the study and teaching of grammar at Toulouse, regulations as to school teachers in Paris, Angers and Ferrara, a grant of traveling expenses to grammar-school boys who hoped to enter Montpellier, the excluding of teachers of grammar from examinations in medicine at Bologna, and the hiring of a teacher of grammar at Treviso (Selections 9, 45, 68, 84, 89, 106, 124, 144, 146, 164).

Humanism and the humanities are further considered in four passages (6, 132, 163, 171), reflecting humanistic sentiment in the twelfth century and classical scholarship of the sixteenth, as well as Italian and German humanism of the fifteenth century. Four selections illustrate the medieval interest in Greek and oriental languages from the thirteenth to the fifteenth century (31, 55, 60, 120). Flemish masters and students appear in two extracts (35, 54), and the French language in one (161). Of eight passages relating to theology (13, 42, 56, 57, 63, 139, 157, 167), one concerns a dean, two are about professors, two about the faculty of theology at Paris as a whole and its relation to Arnald of Villanova and to the Templars, two concerning theological students at the Sorbonne, and one regarding Bible study at Heidelberg. Also closely related to theology are ten items bearing upon the enforcement of orthodoxy and the condemnation of errors (14, 20, 23, 24, 38, 41, 78, 97, 101, 154), including the lists of errors of 1210, 1241, and 1270 at Paris, the enforcement of orthodoxy there, the recantation of Blasius of Parma at Pavia, the expurgation of the Aristotelian works of natural philosophy, the action taken against the *Talmud*, against Occamist errors, and against the magic arts and magic books. Of eleven selections in the field of law (21, 22, 29, 63, 64, 74, 77, 115, 116, 118, 152), seven have to do with canon law, three with civil, one with both; three concern Bologna and three, Paris. Medicine and the related fields of surgery and pharmacy are the theme of fifteen items (3, 39, 40, 62, 82, 91, 107, 109, 110, 113, 121, 131, 134, 136, 170). These present faculty regulations, texts, lectures and classrooms, dissections and vacations, control of surgeons and apothecaries by the medical faculties, proceedings against illicit practitioners, fatherly advice as to one's health. Universities concerned are Montpellier, Paris, Toulouse, Bologna, Pavia, Padua and Caen. The rivalry between faculties of law and medicine is illustrated by Selection 103. Three items deal with the curriculum in arts for the A.B. degree (28, 107, 119). Aside from the errors already mentioned, five passages illustrate scholastic philosophy (126, 150, 158, 165, 168): two treat of *Quodlibeta*, the others, of nominalism, *via antiqua et via moderna*, and courses in ethics. Five more have to do with Aristotle, alchemy, astrology and astronomy (14, 20, 67, 108, 175). Nine selections may be said to cover the general field of education (1, 4, 5, 7, 53, 59, 81, 169, 172), illuminated by glimpses of the educational experience of Abelard and John of Salisbury in the twelfth century and of Cureus and Meuer in the sixteenth, as well as by the more theoretical schemes of Pierre Dubois and the author on *De commendatione cleri* in the fourteenth century. Four extracts are devoted to criticism of contemporary learning and education (11, 34, 70, 71) from the pens of Stephen of Tournai, Humbert de Romans, and Alvarus Pelagius.

To university statutes and academic regulations in general five selections are given over (15, 19, 69, 87, 133), while the following are concerned with the more specific aspects indicated: administration (50), determinations (26), inception (46), disputations (80, 102, 112), lectures (176), repetitions (116), points and examinations (111, 125, 153), degrees (92, 128), professorial salaries (159), student fees (105), scholarships (90), officials such as the rector, dean and bedell respectively (65, 130, 139, 33). Nine passages have to do with houses and colleges, their foundation, regulation and reform (10, 17, 36, 42, 48, 79, 80, 104, 167). Four deal with classrooms (25, 103, 115, 152); others, with the university buildings in general (166), the library (135), and the famous Street of Straw (85). There are six items about the hours of classes and mode of lecturing (74, 83, 88, 92, 117, 155) at Montpellier, Paris, Perpignan, Avignon, and Heidelberg. Five extracts are respectively devoted to the university calendar, vacations, religious holidays, postponements, and absences of professors (72, 131, 73, 117, 123). Five passages treat of booksellers, stationers and copying manuscripts (44, 49, 52, 66, 98). Two are concerned with academic costume (61, 75), but the subject is touched upon in several others. This, however, is more or less true of all particular topics, which are included also in the more general accounts.

Twenty-one selections are occupied with varied aspects of student life, good or bad, religion, recreation, dissipation and violence (37, 47, 51, 76, 93, 99, 100, 114, 122, 127, 137, 141, 145, 147, 148, 149, 151, 156, 162, 173, 174). Five items are about calls or migrations to new places and universities (12, 18, 96, 129, 143). Four are papal (8, 19, 21, 30). Of eight passages concerned with religious orders (16,

27, 32, 57, 67, 79, 86, 140), the majority have to do with the mendicant friars, the others with Cluniacs, Servites and Templars.

It should have already become clear that our records and selections are not merely or even mainly institutional and impersonal. Many a great name and well-known personality moves and speaks or is spoken of in them: Abelard, Anselm of Havelberg, Bernard of Chartres, John of Salisbury, Peter of Blois, Buoncompagni, Odofredus, Robert of Sorbonne, William of Auvergne, William of St. Amour, Humbert de Romans, Alvarus Pelagius, Augustinus Triumphus of Ancona, Pierre Dubois, Thomas Aquinas, Arnald of Villanova, William of Ockham, Jean Buridan, Blasius of Parma, Antonino of Florence, Conrad Celtes, Falloppia the anatomist, and yet others. Besides the errors of individuals, the experiences of individuals, the schemes of individuals, and the criticisms by individuals which have already been mentioned, the selections comprise students' jottings and records of their activities (58, 122, 138), and personal letters (6, 7, 62, 139, 160).

In lieu of further introductory statement as to educational conditions in general in the middle ages and the history of the universities, the following reading may be suggested to those desiring so to orient themselves: my "Elementary and Secondary Education in the Middle Ages," *Speculum*, XV (October, 1940), 400–408, and Professor Charles Homer Haskins' little book on *The Rise of the Universities*, New York, 1923. For fuller reference as to technical terms or the historical setting of particular events and documents the indices to Hastings Rashdall's three volume work, *The Universities of Europe in the Middle Ages*,[1] will usually prove helpful.

[1] Original edition, Oxford, 1895; posthumous new edition by F. M. Powicke and A. B. Emden, 1936.

UNIVERSITY RECORDS
AND LIFE in the Middle Ages

RIVALRY OF TEACHERS

Petri Abaelardi Historia calamitatum, Migne, *Patrologia latina,* vol. 178, cols. 114–26.

There is no more familiar, and perhaps no more important, figure in the intellectual history of the twelfth century than Abelard (1079–1142). His name has often been connected both with the origin of universities in western Europe and with the development of scholastic method in Latin. In the following extract from a letter telling the story of his misfortunes he gives details as to his own early studies and teaching which illustrate the rivalry between individual teachers that preceded the formation of scholastic gilds and university faculties.

. . . Moreover I had a father who had some training in letters before he put on the trappings of war. Wherefore later he grew so fond of literature that he was disposed to have all his sons instructed in letters before they were trained in arms. And so 'twas done. As therefore he held me his firstborn the more dear, so much the more pains did he take with my education. For my part, the more extensively and readily I progressed in literary studies, the more ardent became my devotion to them, and I was allured into such a passion for them that, surrendering to my brothers the pomp of military glory and my hereditary prerogative as firstborn, I totally abdicated the court of Mars to be received into the bosom of Minerva. And since I preferred the panoply of dialectical arguments to all the documents of philosophy, I exchanged other arms for these and esteemed the conflict of disputation more than the trophies of war. Whereupon traversing various provinces, disputing wherever I had heard that the pursuit of this art was flourishing, I became an emulator of the Peripatetics.

Finally I came to Paris, where already this discipline was accustomed to flourish most, to William forsooth of Champeaux as my teacher, who was then prominent in this field actually and by reputation. Tarrying with him a time I was at first welcomed but later cordially disliked, when I tried to refute some of his opinions and often ventured to argue against him and sometimes seemed superior in disputation. Which indeed those who were esteemed chief among our fellow scholars received with so much the greater indignation as I was considered their junior in years and time of study. Hence the first beginnings of my calamities which have lasted until now, and envy of others has multiplied against me, the more my fame has been extended. Finally it came about that presuming upon my ability beyond the strength of my years I, a mere youth, aspired to instruct classes and selected as a place where I should do so the then celebrated town of Melun and royal seat. My aforesaid teacher got wind of this and tried to remove my classes from his as far as he could and schemed secretly in every way he could to carry off my classes and the place provided for me before I should leave his. But since he had there some enemies among the powers that be, relying on their aid I stuck by my purpose, and his manifest jealousy won me the support of many.

From the very beginning of my teaching my name began to be so magnified in the dialectical art that not only the reputation of my fellow students but even of the master himself gradually contracted and was extinguished. Hence it came about that, becoming more confident of myself, I transferred my classes to Corbeil which is nearer Paris and so gave opportunity for more frequent assaults of disputation. But not long afterwards I had a breakdown from overstudy and had to go home, and, for some years removed from France, I was desired the more ardently by those whom the study of dialectic attracted. Moreover after a few years, when finally I had recovered my health, that teacher of mine, William, archdeacon of Paris, had changed his former habit and joined the order of regular clergy with this intention, as they said, that as he was believed more religious he would be promoted to a higher degree of prelacy, as soon happened, he being made bishop of Châlons. But this changed mode of life recalled him neither from the city of Paris nor from his accustomed study of philosophy, but in the monastery too, to which he had betaken himself for religion's sake, he straightway instituted public classes in the wonted manner. Then I, returned to him in order to hear rhetoric from him, among other aims of our disputations compelled him by the clearest line of argument to alter, nay to destroy, his old view as to universals. Moreover, he was of such opinion concerning the community of universals that he held that the same whole thing essentially was at once present in its single individuals, of which there would be no diversity in essence but variety only in the multitude of accidents. Then he so corrected his opinion that he said henceforth the same thing not essentially but indifferently. And since the main question among dialecticians regarding universals has always been on this very point—so that even Porphyry in his *Isagogae*, when he wrote of universals, did not venture to define it, saying, "For this is a very difficult business,"—when William had corrected, nay rather abandoned, this opinion, his lectures became so neglected that he was hardly permitted to lecture on logic, as if the whole sum of that art consisted in this opinion as to universals. As a consequence my teaching acquired such strength and authority that those who before were violent adherents of that master of ours and who most attacked my teaching poured into my classes, and the successor of our master in the schools of Paris offered his place to me, in order that there with others he might sit under my teaching, where once his master and my master had flourished.

Therefore within a few days after I began to teach dialectic there, with what envy our master began to grow green, with what grief to rage, is not easy to express in words. And not long enduring the tide of woe, he cannily set about to get rid of me even then. And because he had nothing which he could bring openly against me, by advancing most disgraceful charges he plotted to take away the classes from him who had yielded his teaching to me, substituting in his place another person hostile to me. Then I went back to Melun and held classes there as before, and the more clearly his envy had me as its object, so much the more authority it conferred upon me, according to the line of the poet:

Spite aims at the lofty, winds blow over the mountains.[1]

Moreover not long after, when he understood that almost all his disciples were much in doubt as to his religion and murmured loud as to his conversion, because forsooth he had not withdrawn from the city, he transferred himself and the convent of brothers with his classes to a town far from the city. Immediately I returned from Melun to Paris, hoping for peace from him henceforth. But since, as we have said, he had caused our place to be occupied by our rival, I pitched the camp of my classes outside the city on Mount Sainte Geneviève, as it

[1] Ovid, *De remediis amoris*, I, 369.

were to lay siege to him who had occupied my place. Hearing of this, our master, straightway impudently returning to the city, reestablished such classes as he could get and the convent of the brothers at the original monastery, as if to relieve from our siege his ally whom he had deserted. But although he intended to help him, he greatly harmed him. For that one had earlier had some students, such as they were, because of lectures on Priscian at which he was thought to excel. But after the master came back, he lost them all and so was compelled to give up teaching. Not long after, as it were despairing of further worldly glory, he too entered the monastery. But, after the return of our master to the city, what conflicts of disputations my students had both with him and his students and what success fortune gave mine in these conflicts and to me myself the event itself has long since informed you. But I may modestly repeat and boldly utter that saying of Ajax:

> . . . if you seek to know the outcome
> Of this fight, I was not overcome by him.[2]

But should I keep silence, the affair itself shouts and indicates its outcome.

But while these things were going on, my dearest mother Lucia forced me to return home. For she, after the conversion of my father Berengar to the monastic life, was arranging to do the same. When this was over, I returned to France, primarily to study theology at a time when our oft-mentioned master William had been raised to the bishopric of Châlons. Moreover, in lectures on theology his master, Anselm of Laon, then held from of yore the highest authority. I therefore went to this old man for whom long practice rather than ingenuity or memory had made a name. To whom if anyone went uncertain as to any question, he came away even more puzzled. He was indeed a wonder in the eyes of his auditors but of no account in the sight of those who asked him questions. He had a wonderful command of language but contemptible sense and no reasoning power. When he lit the fire, he filled the house with smoke, not with light. . . .

[2] Ovid, *Metamorphoses*, XIII, 89–90.

2

HOW BERNARD DRILLED THE BOYS IN GRAMMAR AT CHARTRES

Ioannis Saresberiensis episcopi Carnotensis Metalogicon, ed. C. C. I. Webb, Oxford, 1929, lib. I, cap. 24 (in part); Migne, *Patrologia latina,* vol. 199, cols. 854–55.

John of Salisbury, who died in 1180, completed the *Metalogicon* (or, *Metalogicus,* as it is less correctly called), from which the following extract is drawn, in 1159. It describes the much earlier teaching of Bernard of Chartres, who was perhaps dead by 1130. As the previous selection by Abelard depicted lectures in logic and theology, so John tells of more elementary instruction in the rudiments of Latin grammar, literature, and composition in the early twelfth century. Bernard of Chartres is no longer identified with the poet, Bernard Silvester, whose *De mundi universitate* was written later in the century during the pontificate of Eugenius III (1145–1153). Bernard of Chartres seems to have left no writings and to have been first and foremost a teacher. John of Salisbury seems to have learned of his methods of teaching only at second hand and after the event.

Bernard of Chartres, the most copious fount of letters in Gaul in modern times, followed this method and in the reading of authors pointed out what was simple and in accordance with the rules. Grammatical figures, rhetorical embellishments, the cavils of sophistry, and the bearings of the passage assigned for reading upon other disciplines he set forth as he went along, not however trying to teach everything at once but dispensing gradually a measured amount of learning according to the capacity of his hearers. And because a brilliant style comes either from *propriety,* that is, when adjective or verb is elegantly united with its substantive, or from *translation,* that is, when a word for good reason is altered to another meaning, he inculcated these points as occasion offered in the minds of his hearers. And because memory is strengthened and talent is sharpened by exercise, he urged some by admonitions to imitate what they heard and others by blows and penalties.[1] Each was obliged to review on the following

---

[1] This illustrates the fact that in medieval and early modern schools corporal punishment was inflicted for failure in lessons and not merely for infractions of discipline. It also shows that the school of Bernard of Chartres was below university grade. As

day something of what he had heard on the preceding day, some more, others less; for the day after was with them the disciple of the day before. The evening exercise, which was called *declinatio*, was so stuffed with grammar that if anyone took it for a full year, unless he was duller than the average, he would have in hand the principles of speaking and writing and could not remain ignorant of the meaning of words that are in common use.

But since neither school nor any day should be without religion, such material was set before them as would edify faith and morals, and by which those who had assembled, as if for some collation, should be stimulated to good deeds. So the last part of this *declinatio*, or rather philosophical collation, preferred the paths of piety and commended the souls of the dead to their Redeemer by devout repetition of the sixth Psalm in the Penitentials and the Lord's Prayer. As for the boys' preceding exercises, he assigned poets or orators whom they should imitate in prose or poems, bidding them follow in their footsteps, and he showed how to join statements together and how to end them elegantly. If anyone to improve his own work sewed on foreign cloth, he would call attention to the theft but usually would inflict no punishment. Rather if the inept composition merited this, he would with gracious indulgence order and make the person who had been thus detected set to work imitating authors, so that he who imitated the men of the past might come to deserve the imitation of posterity. This, too, he taught among the first rudiments and fixed in their minds, what virtue there is in economy, what in the adornment of things, what words are praiseworthy; when speech should be bare and, as it were, lean; when abundant, when fulsome, when moderate in all respects. He advised them to read over histories and poems carefully, not as if impelled by spurs to flight; and he was always demanding that from each reading one should daily commit something to memory. Yet he said to avoid what was superfluous and that the writings of illustrious authors were sufficient, since "to busy oneself with what any worthless man has ever written is either too wretched a task or a mat-

---

Rashdall writes (*The Universities of Europe in the Middle Ages*, III, 1936, 358–59): "It is only in reference to the grammar school that we meet with any allusion to flogging; it is the grammar-master who was presented with the birch as the symbol of his office. . . . In all the university records of the Middle Ages there is not a single hint or allusion to corporal punishment until the fifteenth century."

ter of empty boasting, and detains and wastes ability that might better be occupied otherwise. For that which takes the place of something better is in that respect disadvantageous and cannot be held of good repute. For to open every volume and turn over every leaf, even those not worth reading, is no more necessary than to attend to old wives' tales. For as Augustine says in the book *De ordine*, 'Who says that a man appears uneducated because he has not heard of Daedalus's flying? Does not he seem to be a liar who told the story; and he stupid who believes it; and he impudent who asks about it? Or take a case in which I am accustomed to pity my friends greatly, who, if they cannot tell the name of the mother of Euryalus, are accused of ignorance, although they dare not call those who question them curious and idle triflers.' " [2] Such were his words, spoken elegantly and truly. Wherefore it was justly held by the ancients to be a virtue in a grammarian *to be ignorant of some things*.

And since in every exercise for pupils nothing is more useful than to become accustomed to that which should be done by the art, they daily wrote prose and poems and drilled themselves in mutual collations, an exercise than which indeed there is nothing more useful for eloquence, nothing more expeditious toward science; and it is a great help in life, if only charity rules this industry and if humility is maintained in this literary progress. By no means "is it for the same man to serve letters and carnal vices." [3]

After the standards of this master my teachers in grammar, William of Conches and Richard Bishop,[4] now archdeacon at Coutances, a man of good life and conversation, for some time trained their students. But afterwards, because opinion made prejudice to the truth, and men preferred to seem rather than be philosophers, and professors of the arts promised to transmit all philosophy to their hearers in less than three or two years' time, they ceased teaching, overcome by the onslaught of the unskilled multitude. And from that time on less time

[2] Augustine, *De ordine*, II, 12, 37, Migne, *Patrologia latina*, 32, 1012–13.

[3] Jerome, *Epistolae*, 125, 11, Migne, *Patrologia latina*, 22, 1078.

[4] John seems to have studied under William and Richard from about 1138 to 1141. William later entered the service of Geoffrey Plantagenet, to whom as duke of Normandy he addressed his *Dragmaticon*, a revision of *Philosophia*, between 1144 and 1150, while he prepared for the future Henry II of England a collection of moral extracts from classical Latin authors. Richard Bishop became bishop of Avranches in 1171, dying only in 1182, but one infers that William was no longer living in 1159 when John wrote.

and pains have been spent on the study of grammar. The result is that those who profess all arts, both liberal and mechanical, do not know even the first, without which one vainly advances to the others. It may be, 'tis true, that other subjects are of assistance to literature, but it is the peculiar prerogative of this study to make men lettered. . . .

3

AN EARLY REFERENCE TO A MEDICAL SCHOOL AT MONTPELLIER

Anselmi Havelbergensis Vita Adelberti Moguntiae episcopi, ed. Jaffé, *Bibliotheca rerum germanicarum*, III, 592–93; reprinted in *Cartulaire de l'université de Montpellier*, I (1890), 758, and from it by Fournier, *Les statuts et privilèges*, II (1891), 1.

The selection is from the life by Anselm, bishop of Havelberg, of Adelbert II of Saarbrücken, elected bishop of Mainz in August 1137, consecrated May 29, 1138, and deceased at Erfurt July 17, 1141. It describes Adelbert's studies at Montpellier, which he visited after attending classes in Reims and Paris. Fournier gives a false impression that the lines apply to Anselm: "Anselm de Havelberg, avant son retour à Mayence, suit les cours de médecine à Montpellier." Anselm was sent in 1136 by the emperor Lothair to Constantinople where he disputed theological questions with Nicetas of Nicomedia, in the presence of the Byzantine emperor, John Comnenus, and such learned westerners and translators from the Greek as James of Venice, Burgundio of Pisa, and Moses of Bergamo, the last-named acting as interpreter. Anselm became archbishop of Ravenna in 1155 and died in 1158. In translating the leonine hexameters I have endeavored to keep the internal rhymes and something of the general effect.

Here an adolescent arrived to find the town pleasant,
Dear old Montpellier, whose real middle name is Live-well-aye,
Where medical science is granted a seat and appliance.
Here, too, sound doctrine, practical precepts of medicine,
By doctors are stated who have truly meditated
On giving advice to the well, to the sick a poultice.
He learned, while there dwelling, in brief what medicine is telling,
The causes perceiving of nature, things occult believing,

Not wealth to importune, nor seeking after a large fortune,
But because of Nature he would learn the true nomenclature.

4

THE EDUCATION OF JOHN OF SALISBURY

Metalogicon, ed. Webb, 1929, lib. II, cap. 10; Migne, *Patrologia latina,* vol. 199, cols. 867–69.

Concerning John of Salisbury see the introduction to Selection 2. His recollections as to his teachers and the time spent with them do not seem to be in exact chronological order, or at least are sometimes hard to reconcile with dates which are derived from other sources.

When first as a mere lad I went to Gaul for an education in the year after the illustrious king of the Angles, Henry, the lion of justice, departed from human affairs, I betook me to the Peripatetic of Palais [1] who at that time presided on the hill of Sainte Geneviève as a doctor celebrated and admired by all. There at his feet I received the first rudiments of the art of logic and as far as my small talents permitted I received with all the avidity of my mind whatever fell from his lips. Then after his departure, which seemed to me all too soon, I attached myself to master Alberic, who shone forth as the dialectian most esteemed among the rest and was indeed the sharpest opponent of the nominalists. Thus, spending almost the whole of two years on the hill, I had as my teachers in this art Alberic and master Robert of Melun —to use the name that he earned in the school system, although he was of English birth. One of them, very exact in everything, found room for questioning everywhere, so that no matter how polished the surface he could find some flaw in it and, as they say, a rush would not have been without knots for him, for even in it he would have shown where there ought to be knots! The other, on the other hand, very quick in his answers, never dodged any question by means of subterfuges, nay he would take either side of a contradiction, or by bringing out the manifold arguments he would teach that there was no one answer. So one was subtle and prolific in questions; the other, clear-

---

[1] Abelard is meant.

headed, brief, and apt in his answers. If the qualities of these two had all been combined in any one man, his equal as a disputant would not have been found in our age. For both were sharp-witted and hard students and in my opinion would have become great and famous men in physical studies, if they had built on the great foundation of literature, if they had devoted as much attention to the remains of the ancients as they gave applause to their own inventions. So much for the time in which I heard them. For afterwards one of them going to Bologna unlearned what he used to teach and on his return untaught it—whether for the better, let those judge who heard him both before and after. The other forsooth becoming proficient in divine letters won the glory of an even higher philosophy and of a more celebrated name.[2] Drilled by them for all of two years, I became so accustomed to allotting places, and to rules, and to the other elementary rudiments with which the minds of boys are instructed and in which the aforesaid doctors were most capable and expeditious, that it seemed to me that I knew all these things as well as my own nails and fingers. Evidently I had learned this: to account my knowledge with youthful levity as of more importance than it was. I thought myself an adept because I was quick in those things that I had heard.

Then coming to myself and measuring my powers, thanks to the kindness of my teachers I straightway betook me to the grammarian of Conches and heard him lecture for three years. Meanwhile I did a great deal of reading, nor shall I ever regret that time. Later on I followed Richard Bishop, a man ignorant of scarcely any science, who had more heart than mouth, more learning than facility, truth than vanity, virtue than ostentation; and what I had heard from others received all again from him and I learned some things which I had not heard pertaining to the quadrivium, on which to some extent I had previously heard Hardewin the Teuton. I reviewed rhetoric too, which before I had understood little of, when with some others I heard it scantily discussed by master Theodoric. But later I received

[2] R. L. Poole, *Illustrations of the History of Medieval Thought*, p. 205, commenting upon this passage, says: "Of Robert of Melun he could not now foretell the future, when as bishop of Hereford, twenty-five years later, he proved a prelate after Henry the Second's own heart and a sturdy combatant against the archbishop's party. At present John knows only his achievements as a theologian, in which quality he was greatly esteemed as a systematic and most orthodox writer."

it more fully from Peter Helias. And inasmuch as I had become the tutor of some nobles' children, who supplied me with a livelihood, destitute as I was of aid from friends and relatives, God relieving my poverty, I was stimulated by the requirements of my position and the urging of the boys to recall more frequently to mind what I had heard. Wherefore I struck up a closer friendship with master Adam, a man of keenest wit and, whatever others may think, of much learning, who applied himself to Aristotle more than the rest. So that, although he was not my master, he kindly gave me the benefit of his learning and showed himself very open with me, which he did to no one else or to very few. For he was thought to be of a jealous disposition.

Meanwhile William of Soissons—who later made an engine to lay siege, as his adherents say, to old-fashioned logic and reach unexpected consequences and destroy the opinions of the ancients—was teaching the first elements of logic, and finally I added him to the preceptor already mentioned. There perhaps he learned that the same is from contradiction, when Aristotle is maligned, because the same when it is and when it is not is not necessarily the same. And also when something is, it is not necessary that it be the same and not be. For nothing comes from contradiction, and it is impossible that contradiction come from anything. Wherefore I could not be induced by the impelling engine of my friend to believe that all impossibles come from one impossible. From this I was withdrawn by the scantiness of my income, the request of my associates, and the advice of friends, to assume the position of a teacher. I obeyed.

Returning at the end of three years I found master Gilbert [3] and heard him lecture on logic and theology, but all too soon he was removed. Robert Pullus succeeded, praiseworthy alike in life and learning. Then Simon of Poissy received me, a conscientious lecturer but

---

[3] Gilbert de la Porrée left Paris for Poitiers in 1141–1142 and died in 1154. He composed a standard work, *The Book of Six Principles* (*Liber sex principiorum*) which treated of the last six of the ten categories, of which Aristotle had discussed only the first four. It was printed accurately in 1479, 1481, and 1484, but in 1496 appeared in a garbled humanistic edition by Hermolaus Barbarus in which the sense of the original was often lost in the attempt to paraphrase it in more elegant Latin. This garbled version came to prevail in most subsequent editions and citations, and was even regarded as a translation from a Greek original. See Hauréau, *Notices et Extraits*, I (1890), 298–301. A recent edition of the *Liber de sex principiis* is by A. Heysee, O.M., Munich, 1929.

dull disputant. But I had these two teachers in theology exclusively. Thus well nigh twelve years slipped by, as I was occupied with varied studies.

So I thought it would be pleasant to revisit the old classmates whom I had left and whom dialectic still detained on the Mount, to confer with them concerning the old problems, and, by comparing notes, measure our respective progress. I found the same men and just where they were, for they neither seemed to have advanced an inch towards solving the old problems, nor had they added a single new one. As teachers they drove with the same goads that drove them as students. In only one respect had they grown proficient: they had unlearned moderation, they knew no modesty, to such a degree that one despaired of their reformation. Thus I learned by experience an evident lesson, that, just as dialectic facilitates other disciplines, so, if studied alone, it remains lifeless and sterile, nor does it stimulate the soul to bear fruits of Philosophy, unless it conceives elsewhere.

5

THE YOUTH MOVEMENT

John of Salisbury, *Entheticus*, lines 42–54, Migne, *Patrologia latina*, 199, 966.

In these lines John of Salisbury satirizes the self-confidence and presumption of the young scholars and teachers of his time.

On all sides they shout: "Where is this old donkey going?
Why speaks he to us of the sayings or deeds of the ancients?
We have inside information; our youth is self-taught.
Our band does not accept the dogmas of the ancients.
We do not bother ourselves to follow the utterances
Of those authors whom Greece has and Rome cherishes.

I am a resident of the Petit-Pont,[1] a new author in arts,
And glory that previous discoveries are my own.
What the elders taught, but dear youth knows not yet,

---

[1] The bridge at the foot of Rue S. Jacques connecting the Latin quarter of Paris with l'Ile de la Cité and opening on Place du Parvis Notre-Dame.

I swear was the invention of my own bosom.
A worshipping crowd of youth surrounds me, and thinks
That when I make grandiloquent boasts, I merely speak the truth."

6

LITERATURE VERSUS LOGIC

A LETTER WRITTEN ABOUT 1160 BY PETER OF BLOIS, CONCERNING TWO BOYS WHOM HE IS TUTORING

Chartularium universitatis Parisiensis, I, 27–29.

Peter of Blois was a disciple of John of Salisbury and maintained much the same views as his master with regard to the classics and contemporary education. He was on intimate terms with both Henry II of England and William II of Sicily and held high offices in both countries and in the church, but is noted especially as an elegant letter-writer. He did not die until the end of the twelfth century or beginning of the next.

To his dearest lord and friend R., archdeacon of Nantes, Pierre de Blois greeting and anything better. The day before yesterday you entrusted two of your nephews to me to educate, the one still a child, the other already past the age of puberty. Now by letter you strongly extol and commend the talent of the older and you assert that you have never found a man of subtler vein. So you beg and urge that timely magisterial vigilance center upon him, for you deem it light to put the finishing touches on that edifice to which another's care has given increment. But the thing really goes the other way. For I hope better things of the education of him who comes to me rude and unformed than from another whose character has already begun to harden and has as it were impressed on itself the stamp of another teacher. Wax and clay and things which are susceptible to moulding are shaped more easily and faithfully to the moulder's will if they have never received the lineaments of form before. Indeed Quintilian says in the book *On the Training of the Orator* [1] that Timotheus, a famous artist with the flute, was wont to ask double pay from those who had had a previous teacher. . . .

[1] Lib. II, cap. 3.

You regard William as of subtler vein and acuter genius because omitting grammar and literature he has hastened to the cunning of logic, where he learns dialectic not in books as is customary but in schedules and notebooks. In these there is no foundation for literature, and that subtlety which you extol is harmful to many. For Seneca says: "Naught is more hateful than subtlety, where subtlety is alone." [2] For what good does it do them to spend their days on these things which are of no advantage to anyone at home or in the camp or in the forum or in the cloister or at court or in the church, but only in the schools?

. . . Some before they are imbued with elementary disciplines are taught to inquire about the point, the line, the surface, the quantity of the soul, fate, the inclination of nature, chance and free will, matter and motion, the principles of bodies, the progress of multitude and section of magnitude, what time is, what empty space, what place, *de eodem et diverso*, of the divisible and individual, of the substance and form of the voice, of the essence of universals, of the origin, use, and end of virtues, of the causes of things, of the tides of ocean, of the source of the Nile, of various secrets of latent nature, of various figures of cases which occur in contracts or quasi-contracts, in criminal or quasi-criminal actions, of the first beginnings of things, and many other matters which require a foundation of fuller science and more eminent intellects.

Tender years should first be instructed in rules of the art of grammar, in analogies, in barbarisms, in solecisms, in tropes and schemata. These were the studies on which Donatus, Servius, Priscian, Isidore, Bede and Cassiodorus expended much diligence, which rest assured they would not have done if the foundation of science could be laid without these. For Quintilian, too, who transmits this discipline and asserts it should be transmitted, extols it with such praises that he openly protests that without it the name of science cannot exist. Caius Caesar published books on analogy, knowing that without this science neither prudence, in which he was most perfect, nor eloquence, in which he was most potent, could easily be obtained by anyone. Marcus Tullius, as is plain from his frequent letters, diligently invites his son to study grammar which he cherished most tenderly. And what use is it to evolve schedules, to found verbose *Summae* and invert cunning *sophismata*, to damn the writings of the ancients, and to reprove everything

[2] Epist. 88.

not found in the syllabi of their masters. It is written, that science is in the ancients. Nor is Jeremiah rescued from the lake till old and worn garments are let down to him by ropes. For one does not ascend from ignorance to the light of science, unless the writings of the ancients are pored over zealously. Jerome glories that he spent much time on the writings of Origen. Horace, too, boasts that he had read and re-read Homer,

> Who tells what's beautiful, what shameful, what useful,
> What not, more plainly and better than Chrisippus and Crantor.[3]

I know that it was of great use to me that, when as a boy I was trained in the art of versification, at the suggestion of the master I took my material not from fables but true history. It was of advantage to me that as an adolescent I was forced to memorize the letters of Hildebert of Le Mans, noted for their elegant style and suave urbanity. Besides certain other books which are celebrated in the schools, it was advantageous to me to inspect frequently Trogus Pompeius, Josephus, Suetonius, Egesippus, Quintus Curtius, Cornelius Tacitus, Titus Livius, who all insert in their histories much for the edification of morals and the perfecting of literary style. I read others too who do not deal with history, whose number is legion, in all whom the diligence of moderns can pluck flowers as it were in a fragrant garden and make for itself the honey of suave urbane speech.

Do not therefore allege further the subtle genius of your nephew William nor impute to me the fault if he does not attain perfection shortly. For a patient is purged before he diets, and according to the opinion of Timotheus, who required double pay for his labor from the disciples of others, what is useless must first be torn up before what is useful is planted. For in her marriage with Mercury, Philology vomits up books of useless science before she merits to be raised to the eminence of desired dignity.[4] Indeed I fear lest the saying of Timotheus be too true, for John now is ahead of William in a certain textbook, the head is turned towards the tail, and if John perseveres in purpose, the junior will supplant the firstborn, and Jacob, Esau.

[3] Horace, *lib*. I, *ep*. 2.
[4] Martianus Capella, *De nuptiis Philologiae et Mercurii*, lib. II.

7

JOHN OF SALISBURY AT PARIS, 1164

EXTRACTS FROM A LETTER BY HIM TO THOMAS BECKET

Chartularium universitatis Parisiensis, I, 16–19.

The letter, both from the joy expressed by John on his arrival and his extreme reluctance to leave, attests the attractions of Paris, especially to a former student there.

Since crossing the channel I have seemed to myself to sense the air of a softer clime, and, after the swelling gales of tempests, I have joyfully admired the abundance that prevails on every side, the quiet and happiness of the population. . . .

John goes on to tell of being well received by servants of the count of Guines, when he disembarked, and of proceeding to Paris by way of St. Omer, Arras and Noyon.

When I saw the abundance of victuals there, the cheerfulness of the people, the reverence of the clergy, the majesty of the entire Church, and the glory and varied occupations of those philosophizing, like Jacob admiring the ladder whose top touched the sky and which was ascended and descended by angels, under the spur of pleasant travel I was compelled to assert that truly God is in this place and I was unaware of it. . . .[1]

After a few days spent in hiring lodgings and unpacking luggage, I visited the king of France and set forth your case to him in order. . . .

John proceeds to explain that he has not gone on to Rome because, when he left England, Becket instructed him not to do so but to remain in Paris as a student.

So, therefore, I departed, instructed by you that I fix my seat at Paris and strive in all things to conform myself to the scholars there. God is my witness that, when I left you, I did not have tenpence in the whole world, nor anyone, so far as I could see, to help me out. I had, it is true, a few vessels worth about five marks, well known to

[1] *Genesis*, XXVIII, 16.

all associates of our house, and I was deeply in debt, as many are aware. So I borrowed twelve marks. But before leaving Kent I spent three of these on luggage and servants. Then from the hand of William, son of Paganus, I had seven marks of your generosity, with three more yet to come, as you had ordered. That I received less is not your fault.

Coming, then, to Paris, according to your instructions I engaged a commodious lodging, temporarily, as it seemed, and before I entered it, I had spent some twelve pounds. Nor could I get into it without advancing a whole year's rent. Therefore I let the horses go and made my arrangements for residence rather than traveling. So I am unprepared to make the circuits which you now suggest and which cannot be undertaken without expense, especially by a man holding ecclesiastical office and with many acquaintances. . . .[2]

8

PAPAL DEFENSE OF STUDENT PRIVILEGES, 1170–1172

Chartularium universitatis Parisiensis, I, 5–6.

It will be noted that this early example of papal support of student privileges is associated with schools at Reims, not with the university of Paris. Similarly, early in the century, Adelbert II of Mainz had studied at Reims before proceeding to Paris and Montpellier.

Alexander, bishop, servant of the servants of God, to Peter, abbot of St. Remy, and Fulco, dean of Reims, greeting. We have heard from a complaint sent us of certain scholars who live in the burg St. Remy that, when J. a priest of the burg St. Remy on a Sunday in the pres-

---

[2] On the other hand, Petrus Cellensis, an abbot at Reims, wrote warning John of the perils of Paris and setting forth the superior attractions of religion as follows: "There in the book of life you would discern, not figures and elements, but divinity as it is and truth face to face, without the trouble of reading, without aching sight, without fallacy or error of understanding, without trying to remember, without fear of forgetting. O blessed school, where Christ teaches our hearts by the word of His virtue, where without study and reading we learn how we should live happily to eternity! No book is bought there, no writing master is hired, no circumvention of disputations, no intricacy of sophisms, plain discussion of all questions, full apprehension of all reasons and arguments. There life is more than lectures, simpleness than tortuous reasoning." (*Chartularium*, I, 24.)

ence of clergy and laymen led dances, casting aside clerical modesty, and the same scholars in consequence reproached and derided the same priest, he with the support of some persons made a furious onslaught upon the front door and windows of the schools with rash daring and laid violent hands on certain of the same scholars. Not content with these injuries, without the knowledge of our venerable brother Henry, archbishop of Reims, and his officials, on the very next day he launched a sentence of excommunication upon them, although they had neither been cited nor had confessed, which excommunication the said archbishop caused to be removed, as he should. In which affair the same scholars submit that their liberty was grievously violated, since they assert that they possess the liberty that no one shall dare to lay violent hands upon them or to promulgate an ecclesiastical sentence so long as they wish to remain under the jurisdiction of their own master. Provoked by this and other injuries, the aforesaid scholars, as they assert, summoned the same priest to our presence, but he has not presented himself to our sight either in person or by proxy. Since therefore in this, if it be true, the same priest seems to have sinned in many ways, we, as indeed we should, not wishing to leave his sins unpunished, command your discretion by apostolic writings that, convoking the parties before your presence, you studiously inquire from them the truth of the matter, and, if you shall find that the said priest led dances in the sight of clergy and laymen, and for such reason so great injury was done the said scholars, or that he thus incautiously subjected them to the anathema, you shall punish him hard and well by our authority without possibility of appeal for such levity, presumption, and audacity. And if it shall seem clear to you that he or his accomplices laid violent hands on any of the said scholars who were clergy, you shall, relying on apostolic authority and refusing all contradiction and appeal, publicly denounce them excommunicate and you shall see to it that they are shunned as excommunicate, until they render due satisfaction to those injured and present themselves to the apostolic sight with the testimony of your letters. And you shall forbid anyone to dare to molest the said scholars against their liberty in any way, so long as they are prepared to submit to the jurisdiction of their master. Given at Tusculum the eighth of November.

9

DECREE OF THE THIRD LATERAN COUNCIL, 1179

Chartularium universitatis Parisiensis, I, 10.

Since the church of God as a kindly mother is held to provide for those needs which pertain to physical welfare and those which contribute to the progress of souls, lest the opportunity of reading and education be denied poor children who cannot be aided by the resources of their parents, let some sufficient benefice be set aside in every cathedral church for a master who shall teach the clergy of the same church and poor scholars gratis,[1] whereby the need for a teacher shall be met and the way to knowledge opened to learners. In other churches, too, and monasteries, if in time past any provision has been made for this purpose, let it be reestablished. And for the permission to teach let no one demand any fee whatever, or ask anything from teachers under the cover of some custom, or forbid any fit person to teach if he seeks permission. Moreover, whoever presumes to contravene this, let him be deprived of ecclesiastical benefice, since he seems to deserve deprivation of the fruits of his labor in the church of God who from cupidity of mind, while he sells the license to teach, strives to impede the progress of the church.

10

FOUNDATION OF THE COLLÈGE DE DIX-HUIT, 1180

Chartularium universitatis Parisiensis, I, 49.

This is the oldest record of the foundation of a college at Paris or any other European university. The eighteen scholars were for a time lodged in a house opposite the Hôtel-Dieu on the island but later were moved south of the Seine, where the college was located in Rue des Poirées next to the Sorbonne. Just before the French Revolution the chapter of Notre-Dame

[1] It would seem a fair inference from this that well-to-do laymen paid fees to schoolmasters to educate their sons.

still possessed the right of inspection, but the house had disappeared and its place was taken by the garden of the Sorbonne, while the number of pensioners had shrunk from eighteen to eight.

I, Barbe-d'Or, dean of the church of Paris and the entire chapter of the same church. We wish it made known to all, present or to come, that when Sir Jocius de Londoniis returned from Jerusalem and inspected with extreme zeal of devotion the administration of the hospice of the blessed Mary at Paris for the poor and sick, he saw there a certain room, in which by an old custom poor clerks were lodged. He acquired it in perpetuity from the proctors of the same house for use of the said clerks at a cost of 52 pounds, by our advice and that of master Hilduin, chancellor of Paris, then a proctor of the same place, on this condition, that the proctors of the same house forever provide sufficient beds for eighteen scholars and clerks and each month twelve *nummi* from the alms collected in the hospital chest. The said clerks should take turns in carrying the cross and holy water before the bodies of those who die in the same house and each night celebrate seven penitential psalms and the due prayers instituted of old. Moreover, that this remain firm and stable, said Jocius ordered this charter of our constitution to be drawn up for the said clerks and demanded that it be confirmed by the mark of our seal. Done publicly at Paris in our Chapter, the year from the Incarnation of the Lord 1180. . . .

[The names of the members of the Chapter follow.]

II

AN INVECTIVE AGAINST THE NEW LEARNING

STEPHEN OF TOURNAI TO THE POPE, 1192–1203

Chartularium universitatis Parisiensis, I, 47–48.

Stephen, who had previously been abbot of Sainte Geneviève, became bishop of Tournai in 1192 and died in 1203, but it is not known if this letter is addressed to Celestine III or Innocent III.

Having obtained indulgence, let us speak to our lord, whose gentleness emboldens us, whose prudence sustains our inexperience, whose patience promises impunity. To this the authority of our ancestors compels us and a disease gradually insinuating whose ills, if not met at the start, will be incurable in the end. Nor do we say this, father, as if we wished to be censors of morals, or judges of doctors, or debaters of doctrines. This load requires stouter shoulders, and this battle awaits the robust frames of spiritual athletes. We merely wish to indicate the sore spot to your holy paternity, to whom God has given both the power to uproot errors and the knowledge to correct them.

The studies of sacred letters among us are fallen into the workshop of confusion, while both disciples applaud novelties alone and masters watch out for glory rather than learning. They everywhere compose new and recent *summulae* and commentaries, by which they attract, detain, and deceive their hearers, as if the works of the holy fathers were not still sufficient, who, we read, expounded holy scripture in the same spirit in which we believe the apostles and prophets composed it. They prepare strange and exotic courses for their banquet, when at the nuptials of the son of the king of Taurus his own flesh and blood are killed and all prepared, and the wedding guests have only to take and eat what is set before them. Contrary to the sacred canons there is public disputation as to the incomprehensible deity; concerning the incarnation of the Word, verbose flesh and blood irreverently litigates. The indivisible Trinity is cut up and wrangled over in the trivia, so that now there are as many errors as doctors, as many scandals as classrooms, as many blasphemies as squares. Again, if a case comes up which should be settled by canon law either under your jurisdiction or within that of the ordinary judges, there is produced from the vendors an inextricable forest of decretals presumably under the name of pope Alexander of sacred memory, and older canons are cast aside, rejected, expunged. When this plunder has been unrolled before us, those things which were wholesomely instituted in councils of holy fathers neither impose form on councils nor an end to cases, since letters prevail which perchance advocates for hire invented and forged in their shops or cubicles under the name of Roman pontiffs. A new volume composed of these is solemnly read in the schools and offered for sale in the forum to the applause of a horde of notaries, who rejoice that in copying suspect opuscula both their labor is lessened and their pay increased. Two woes are the aforesaid, and lo, a third remains: faculties called liberal having lost their pristine liberty are sunk in such servitude that adolescents with long hair impudently usurp their professorships, and beardless youths sit in the seat of their seniors, and those who don't yet know how to be disciples strive to be named masters. And they write their *summulae* moistened with drool and dribble but unseasoned with the salt of philosophers. Omitting the rules of the arts and discarding the authentic books of the artificers, they seize the flies of empty words in their sophisms like the claws of spiders. Philosophy cries that her garments are torn and disordered and, modestly concealing her nudity by a few specific tatters, neither is consulted nor consoles as of old. All these things, father, call for the hand of apostolic correction, that the disorder in teaching, learning and disputing may be reduced to due form by your authority, that the divine word be not cheapened by vulgar handling, that it be not said on the street corners, "Lo Christ is here or lo He is there," lest what is holy be given to dogs and pearls be trodden under foot by swine.

12

A CALL TO CONSTANTINOPLE, 1205

INNOCENT III URGES MASTERS AND SCHOLARS OF PARIS TO GO TO THE AID OF THE NEW LATIN EM-PEROR OF CONSTANTINOPLE IN REESTABLISH-ING THE STUDY OF LETTERS THERE AFTER THE FOURTH CRUSADE

Chartularium universitatis Parisiensis, I, 62–63.

To all masters and scholars of Paris. Divine clemency excites us multi-fariously and in many ways to awake from the sleep of death to life and from the slough of despond to breathe the hope of eternal glory. We indeed exult, and the entire church of the saints may justly exult, that there has visited us a visitor arising from on high, so that a great part of the eastern church, almost all Greece forsooth, which for a long time past has scorned to follow the footsteps of its mother the holy Roman church, in our time has changed from disobedience to obedience and from contempt to devotion. To greater affluence of joys contributes the fact that the most Christian man, our dearest son in Christ, Baldwin, illustrious emperor of Constantinople, is working with all his powers at means by which the Christian religion can and should be propagated, and is laboring zealously and diligently that the edifice already in large part constructed may not sink in ruin. Recently in fact, diffusing the devotion planted in his breast to the branches of good works, he humbly begged us to see fit to induce and warn you by apostolic letters to come to Greece and work for the reform of the study of letters there, where it is known to have had its first beginning. Wishing therefore to give ear benignly to the same emperor in his petitions, the more that we have frequently tested his sincerity in major matters of faith, we pointedly ask and urge your university, ordering by apostolic writings to you that, carefully recalling how great difficulties and discomforts your ancestors underwent in order to imbue their early years with literary disciplines, many of you shall not hesitate to go out to a land filled with silver and gold and gems, furnished with corn, wine and oil, and abounding in all good things, in order that to the honor and glory of Him, from whom is the gift of all science, you may be of profit there to Him and others, receiving, besides temporal riches and honors, the rewards of eternal glory.

13

PROFESSORS OF THEOLOGY AT PARIS LIMITED TO EIGHT, 1207

LETTER OF INNOCENT III TO THE BISHOP OF PARIS, NOVEMBER FOURTEENTH

Chartularium universitatis Parisiensis, I, 65.

Innocent, bishop, servant of the servants of God, to the venerable brother, bishop of Paris, greeting and apostolic benediction. Just as we believe it expedient that at the city of Paris, to which there is a celebrated recourse of theologians for study of the sacred page, there should be plenty of masters to break bread for the little ones who seek it and refresh thirsting souls with the pabulum of the word of God, so also it is becoming that their numbers be limited lest perchance, because of a burdensome multitude which has nothing to recommend it, either their function be cheapened or less satisfactorily executed, since God made all things in number, measure and weight. Therefore in this matter prudently relying on the authority of those present, we firmly forbid that the number of masters of theology at Paris exceed eight, unless great necessity or utility should require this. To no man whatever, then, be it permitted to infringe this page of our prohibition or with rash boldness to act contrary to it. If, moreover, anyone shall presume to attempt this, let him know that he will incur the wrath of almighty God and of the blessed apostles Peter and Paul. Given at Sutri on November 14, in the tenth year of our pontificate.

That the foregoing limitation was none too well observed is indicated by a letter of Honorius III of November 16, 1218, in which he complains that the chancellor has refused to permit Matheus de Scotia to teach theology because of this limitation of the number of such teachers, which the pope affirms has not to date been continuously observed. *Chartularium*, I, 85.

14

THE CONDEMNATION OF 1210

DECREE OF THE BISHOPS OF SENS, PARIS, ETC., AGAINST HERETICS AND THE NATURAL PHILOSOPHY OF ARISTOTLE

Chartularium universitatis Parisiensis, I, 70.

Let the body of master Amaury be removed from the cemetery and cast into unconsecrated ground, and the same be excommunicated by all the churches of the entire province. Bernard, William of Arria the goldsmith, Stephen priest of Old Corbeil, Stephen priest of Cella, John priest of Occines, master William of Poitiers, Dudo the priest, Dominicus de Triangulo, Odo and Elinans clerks of St. Cloud—these are to be degraded and left to the secular arm. Urricus priest of Lauriac and Peter of St. Cloud, now a monk of St. Denis, Guarinus priest of Corbeil, and Stephen the clerk are to be degraded and imprisoned for life. The writings of David of Dinant are to be brought to the bishop of Paris before the Nativity and burned.

Neither the books of Aristotle on natural philosophy nor their commentaries are to be read at Paris in public or secret, and this we forbid under penalty of excommunication. He in whose possession the writings of David of Dinant are found after the Nativity shall be considered a heretic.

As for the theological books written in French we order that they be handed over to the diocesan bishops, both *Credo in deum* and *Pater noster* in French except the lives of the saints, and this before the Purification, because [then] he who shall be found with them shall be held a heretic.

Among the heresies of the aforesaid persons—we are told—were that the Father had worked without the Son and Holy Spirit before the incarnation of the Son; that the Father was incarnated in Abraham, the Son in Mary, and the Holy Spirit in us today; that whatever is, is God; that the Son had ruled until now, but that henceforth the Holy Spirit would begin to rule until the end of the world. However, it is well to repeat the caution of the recent editors of Rashdall, I (1936), 355, note 2: "Many attempts have been made to discover the exact nature and the sources of the views ascribed to Amauri and to David of Dinant, but it is still uncertain whence they derived them and how they were related to each other." Consult further G. Théry, *Autour du décret de 1210: David de Dinant*, 1925; G. C. C. Capelle, *Amaury de Bène: étude sur son panthéisme formel*, 1932.

15

RULES OF THE UNIVERSITY OF PARIS, 1215

Chartularium universitatis Parisiensis, I, 78–79.

Robert, cardinal legate, prescribes the mode of lecturing in arts and in theology, indicates what books the masters of arts should not read, formulates the discipline of the scholars and the state of the university generally.

Robert, servant of the cross of Christ by divine pity cardinal priest of the title, St. Stephen in Mons Caelius, legate of the apostolic see, to all the masters and scholars of Paris eternal greeting in the Lord. Let all know that, since we have had a special mandate from the pope to take effective measures to reform the state of the Parisian scholars for the better, wishing with the counsel of good men to provide for the tranquillity of the scholars in the future, we have decreed and ordained in this wise:

No one shall lecture in the arts at Paris before he is twenty-one years of age, and he shall have heard lectures for at least six years before he begins to lecture, and he shall promise to lecture for at least two years, unless a reasonable cause prevents, which he ought to prove publicly or before examiners. He shall not be stained by any infamy, and when he is ready to lecture, he shall be examined according to the form which is contained in the writing of the lord bishop of Paris, where is contained the peace confirmed between the chancellor and scholars by judges delegated by the pope, namely, by the bishop and dean of Troyes and by P. the bishop and J. the chancellor of Paris approved and confirmed. And they shall lecture on the books of Aristotle on dialectic old and new in the schools ordinarily and not *ad cursum*.[1] They shall also lecture on both Priscians[2] ordinarily, or at least on one. They shall not lecture on feast days[3] except on philosophers and rhetoric and the quadrivium[4] and *Barbarismus*[5] and ethics, if it please them, and the fourth book of the *Topics*. They shall not lecture on the books of Aristotle on metaphysics and natural philosophy or on summaries of them or concerning the doctrine of master David of Dinant or the heretic Amaury or Mauritius of Spain.

[1] Ordinary lectures were the regular and more important ones, given first in the morning by the older and more highly paid professors. Extraordinary lectures were delivered later in the day by lesser lights and to some extent were on supplementary or less important texts and subjects. However, the same text that had been commented on in ordinary lectures one year might be relegated to extraordinary lectures the next year, thus making way for ordinary lectures that year on some other text. According to Rashdall, I (1936), 433–34, at Paris extraordinary lectures were called cursory. The term *cursor*, however, was commonly applied to a bachelor who was giving a lecture course for practice and would not go into the subject so deeply or at such length as a full-fledged doctor. Hence a cursory treatment was more rapid and superficial. See below, Selection 74, Hours of Classes.

[2] Books 1–16 of Priscian's grammar were called *Priscianus maior*, books 17–18, *Priscianus minor*.

[3] Ordinary—and extraordinary—lectures were not given on the numerous religious holidays, but, as here indicated, some separate and special courses were put on feast days.

[4] That is, four of the seven liberal arts: arithmetic, geometry, music and astronomy. The other three, grammar, rhetoric, and logic, made up the trivium.

[5] The title of the third book of the *Ars maior* of Donatus, the fourth-century grammarian who taught St. Jerome and whose grammar was so much used in the middle ages.

In the *principia* and meetings of the masters and in the responsions or oppositions of the boys and youths there shall be no drinking. They may summon some friends or associates, but only a few. Donations of clothing or other things as has been customary, or more, we urge should be made, especially to the poor. None of the masters lecturing in arts shall have a cope except one round, black and reaching to the ankles, at least while it is new. Use of the pallium is permitted. No one shall wear with the round cope shoes that are ornamented or with elongated pointed toes. If any scholar in arts or theology dies, half of the masters of arts shall attend the funeral at one time, the other half the next time, and no one shall leave until the sepulture is finished, unless he has reasonable cause. If any master in arts or theology dies, all the masters shall keep vigils, each shall read or cause to be read the Psalter, each shall attend the church where is celebrated the watch until midnight or the greater part of the night, unless reasonable cause prevent. On the day when the master is buried, no one shall lecture or dispute.

We fully confirm to them the meadow of St. Germain in that condition in which it was adjudicated to them.

Each master shall have jurisdiction over his scholar. No one shall occupy a classroom or house without asking the consent of the tenant, provided one has a chance to ask it. No one shall receive the licentiate from the chancellor or another for money given or promise made or other condition agreed upon. Also, the masters and scholars can make both between themselves and with other persons obligations and constitutions supported by faith or penalty or oath in these cases: namely, the murder or mutilation of a scholar or atrocious injury done a scholar, if justice should not be forthcoming, arranging the prices of lodgings, costume, burial, lectures and disputations, so, however, that the university be not thereby dissolved or destroyed.

As to the status of the theologians, we decree that no one shall lecture at Paris before his thirty-fifth year and unless he has studied for eight years at least, and has heard the books faithfully and in classrooms, and has attended lectures in theology for five years before he gives lectures himself publicly. And none of these shall lecture before the third hour on days when masters lecture. No one shall be admitted at Paris to formal lectures or to preachings unless he shall be of approved life and science. No one shall be a scholar at Paris who has no definite master.

Moreover, that these decrees may be observed inviolate, we by virtue of our legatine authority have bound by the knot of excommunication all who shall contumaciously presume to go against these our statutes, unless within fifteen days after the offense they have taken care to emend their presumption before the university of masters and scholars or other persons constituted by the university. Done in the year of Grace 1215, the month of August.

16

DOMINICAN STUDIES, 1228

REGULATION CONCERNING STUDIES IN THE ORDER PUBLISHED IN THE GENERAL CHAPTER OF THE FRIAR PREACHERS UNDER MASTER JORDANUS AT PARIS, 1228

Chartularium universitatis Parisiensis, I, 112–13.

The prior of the province or kingdoms, if he shall have brothers fitted for teaching who can be trained for it in short order, shall send them to study in a place where there is a university, and let not those to whom they are sent dare to employ them otherwise or send them back to their province unless they shall have been recalled.

Since great care is to be taken concerning students, let them have some special brother without whose permission they shall not take notes or hear lectures and who shall correct those matters which require correction in their studies. And if he cannot control them, let him lay the matter before the prelate.

They shall not study in the books of the Gentiles and philosophers, although they may inspect them briefly. They shall not learn secular sciences nor even the arts which are called liberal, unless sometimes in certain cases the master of the Order or the general chapter shall wish to make a dispensation, but shall read only theological works whether they be youths or others. Moreover, we have decreed that each province shall provide for its brothers sent to the university at least three books of theology, and the brothers sent to the university shall study histories and sentences, and text and glosses especially.

In the case of those studying thus the prelate shall issue a dispensation lest they be held back or impeded from study because of the offices or otherwise. And as shall seem good to the master of studies, an appropriate place shall be set aside, in which, after disputations or vespers or at other times when they are free, they may meet in his presence to propound doubts or questions. And while one is asking or propounding, the rest shall be silent, lest they impede the speaker. And if anyone gives offense by questioning or opposing or responding indecently or confusedly or loudly or basely, he shall straightway be rebuked by the presiding officer.

Let no one receive the doctorate unless he has attended lectures in theology for at least four years.

17

A HOUSE FOR POOR SCHOLARS REFORMED, 1228

Chartularium universitatis Parisiensis, I, 116–17.

William of Auvergne, previously a canon in Paris and a master of theology in the university, author of *De universo* and other important works, was bishop of Paris from 1228 until his death in 1249. The house here reformed by him was, next to the College of Eighteen, the oldest college at Paris, but had declined scarcely forty years after its foundation. By 1247 it had come to be called "the hospital of the poor scholars of St. Nicholas of the Louvre" (*Chartularium*, I, 198), and was composed of a master or provisor, a chaplain and fifteen *boursiers* or foundationers. Presently a second chaplain was added and, in 1350, three more *boursiers*. The house was suppressed by Jean du Bellay, bishop of Paris, on January 25, 1541.

William, by divine permission bishop of Paris, to all who shall see this letter, greeting in the Lord. Your university should know that we, coming to the house of the poor scholars of St. Thomas of the Louvre, in order to correct and reform by diocesan authority those things which we might find required correction and reformation there, among other things found that certain scholars, who for a long time past had lived on the goods of that house, had reached such a point of insolence that unless they are received at night they break in and violently enter the house of the brothers. Others, as it were, sure of food, eat more than is expedient for those studying a long time; making little progress and unwilling to study, a burden to the studious, they in various ways molest the quiet and study of others. There are also other considerations which we do not wish to insert here lest we seem to aim at particular persons.

Wherefore, by the counsel of good men, by the said authority we decree that those who are there from the present feast of St. Remy shall have the accustomed distributions for a year only. At the end of a year they shall leave and make provision for themselves elsewhere, unless after eight days from leaving, because of their laudable conversation and evident progress in their studies, they shall be commended and recalled by those to whom we or our successors shall have thought good especially to delegate this. We further ordain that no scholar henceforth shall be received there for a stay of more than a year from the day of his reception, and that he who leaves the said house in the said way at the year's end shall not return, unless he be recalled according to the prescribed form by those to whom we or our successors shall have deemed good to delegate this especially. These things, moreover, for the conservation of humility and the quiet of those wishing to study and to avoid many inconveniences and burdens of the said house, which it is not expedient to mention here, having held counsel with good men, we have thought fit to decree. Done in the year of the Lord 1228, the month of June.

18

INVITATION TO TOULOUSE, 1229

A LETTER FROM THE MASTERS OF TOULOUSE TO OTHER UNIVERSITIES

Chartularium universitatis Parisiensis, I, 129–31.

After the Albigensian crusade and the suppression of heresy in Languedoc, the need was felt of a university at Toulouse. By the Treaty of Paris in April, 1229, Raymond of Toulouse agreed to pay salaries to four masters of theology, two canonists, six teachers of the liberal arts, and two grammarians. John of Garland, author of *Morale scolarium* (ed. Paetow, 1927) and *De triumphis ecclesiae* (ed. Thomas Wright, 1856), perhaps composed the announcement which follows. It was likely to attract masters and students from Paris, where lectures had first been suspended and then the university dissolved in 1229 as a result of a quarrel with the local authorities, and where the masters and scholars did not return until 1231.

To all Christ's faithful and especially to masters and scholars studying in any land who may see this letter, the university of masters and scholars of Toulouse, about to plant a new studium, wish continued good life with a blessed end. No undertaking has a stable foundation which is not firmly placed in Christ, the foundation of holy mother church. We therefore with this in mind are trying in Christ with all our might to lay the permanent foundation of a philosophic school at Toulouse, on which others may build with us whose good will is lighted to this by luminous rays of the Holy Spirit. For blessed Augustine says, "God prepares good will to be aided and aids it when prepared. He indeed causes the unwilling to will and aids the willing lest he will in vain." Therefore, most cherished, do ye will with us to prepare good will for the Lord which, when he finds prepared, he will lead on to holy works, so that where once swords cleaved a path for you, you shall fight with a sharp tongue; where war waged carnage, you shall militate with peaceful doctrine; where the forest of heretical depravity scattered thorns, the cedar of catholic faith shall be reared by you to the stars.

And lest the approach of so much labor terrify you, we have prepared the way for you, we have sustained the first hardships, we offer you the standard of security so that, with us preceding as your armbearers, you soldiers of philosophy may be able to fight the more safely with the art of Mercury, the weapons of Phoebus, the lance of Minerva. That ye may again have hope for the stability of the new university we have undertaken the load enjoined by authority of the church. For our Moses was the lord cardinal and legate in the realm of France, leader and protector and author after God and the pope of so arduous a beginning, who decreed that all studying at Toulouse, both masters and disciples, should obtain plenary indulgence of all their sins. Therefore for this cause and because of the continuity of lecturing and disputing which the masters exercise more diligently and frequently than they did at Paris, many scholars are flocking to Toulouse, seeing that flowers already have appeared in our land and the time of putation is at hand.

Therefore let no Deidamia detain our Achilles going forth to philosophic war, that he attain not this second Troy, of which our Toulousan Statius might sing once more:

> All honor there, there great names strive;
> Fearful mothers and groups of virgins
> With difficulty remain idle.
> Here he is condemned to many sterile years
> And hateful to God, if sluggishly
> He lets this new glory pass him by.[1]

So let each upright man put on the warlike mien of Achilles, lest meticulous Thersites take the laurel promised to magnanimous Ajax, so that at least, the war finished, he may admire the zeal of the militant and the zeal of the philosophizing. And that the studious may more willingly know the glory of Toulouse and its university, let them know that this is the second land of promise flowing with milk and honey, green with lush pastures, where fruit trees are leafing, where Bacchus reigns in vineyards, where Ceres rules in fields, where the temperate air was preferred by the ancient philosophers to other stations of earth. O, how incomprehensible are the greatnesses of almighty God!

> Here is peace, elsewhere Mars rages in all the world.
> But this place received Mars and death formerly.

Further, that ye may not bring hoes to sterile and uncultivated fields, the professors at Toulouse have cleared away for you the weeds of the rude populace and thorns of sharp sterility and other obstacles. For here theologians inform their disciples in pulpits and the people at the cross-roads, logicians train the tyros in the arts of Aristotle, grammarians fashion the tongues of the stammering on analogy, organists smooth the popular ears with the sweet-throated organ, decretists extol Justinian, and physicians teach Galen. Those who wish to scrutinize the bosom of nature to the inmost can hear here the books of Aristotle which were forbidden at Paris.

What then will you lack? Scholastic liberty? By no means, since tied to no one's apron strings you will enjoy your own liberty. Or do

---

[1] *Achilleid*, II, 124.

you fear the malice of the raging mob or the tyranny of an injurious prince? Fear not, since the liberality of the count of Toulouse affords us sufficient security both as to our salary and our servants coming to Toulouse and returning home. But if they suffer loss of their property through the hands of brigands in the domain of the count, he will pursue our malefactors with the forces of the capitol of Toulouse, the same as on behalf of citizens of Toulouse. To what has been said we add further that, as we hope truly, the lord legate will summon other theologians and decretists here to enlarge the university and will set a time which scholars ought to spend at Toulouse to receive the indulgence, if that prevaricator envious of the human race does not impede their stay, which God forbid, that henceforth they may magnify the place and the folk of Romanus,[2] fighting by the salubrious triumphal mystery of the cross.

As for prices, what has already been said should reassure you and the fact that there is no fear of a failure of crops. On this point you may trust both report and the nuncio and these verses:

> For a little, wine, for a little, bread is had;
> For a little, meat, for a little, fish is bought.

The courtesy of the people should not be passed over. For here is seen that courtly good humor has struck a covenant with knighthood and clergy. So if you wish to marvel at more good things than we have mentioned, leave home behind, strap your knapsack on your back, and make your motto the words of Seneca: "I shall see all lands as mine, mine as of all; I shall so live that I shall know I am known to others; for to aim high and have enlarged ideas is characteristic of a noble soul."

19

PAPAL REGULATIONS FOR THE UNIVERSITY OF PARIS BY GREGORY IX, APRIL 13, 1231

Chartularium universitatis Parisiensis, I, 136–39.

The "great dispersion" of the university of Paris in 1229, to which we referred in the introduction to the previous selection, had important results. The masters and scholars did not return until they had obtained from the

---

[2] The papal legate.

papal court a series of bulls punishing those who had injured them, requiring the king to enforce the privilege of Philip Augustus and to allow a board of two masters and two Parisians to set the rents for buildings occupied by students, and requiring the bishop of Paris and the abbot of S. Germain-des-Prés to respect the privileges of the university. The document that follows, the bull *Parens scientiarum*, was the capstone of all and has been called the *Magna Carta* of the university. It restricts the power of the chancellor of Paris in bestowing the licentiate, recognizes the right of the university to legislate and to suspend lectures, and protects the scholars in various ways.

Gregory, bishop, servant of the servants of God, to his cherished sons, the masters and scholars of Paris, greeting and apostolic benediction. Paris, parent of sciences, like another Cariath Sepher, city of letters, shines clear, great indeed but raising still greater hopes in teachers and pupils, where, as it were in wisdom's special workshop, veins of silver have their beginning and there is a proper place for forging gold, from which those prudent in mystic eloquence stamp golden earrings vermiculated with silver, fabricate necklaces adorned with precious stones, nay fit and decorate the spouse of Christ with priceless jewels. There iron is mined, whose earthy fragility is solidified by firmness, and from which is made the breastplate of faith, sword of the spirit, and other armor of Christian soldiery, potent against the powers aerial. And the ore dissolved by heat is turned to copper, because while stony hearts flame with the fervor of the Holy Spirit, they take fire and are made to herald praises of Christ in sounding preaching. Wherefore there is no doubt that he would gravely displease God and men who in the said city should strive in any way to disturb such signal grace or who should not openly oppose those disturbing it with all his might and main. Hence, since concerning dissension arisen there by instigation of the devil, greatly disturbing the university, we have diligently considered questions brought before us, by the advice of our brethren we have decided that they should be quieted by moderate provision rather than judicial sentence.

Concerning the state therefore of schools and scholars we decree that these things are to be observed: namely, that every chancellor of Paris to be named henceforth shall swear in the presence of the bishop or by his mandate in the Paris chapter, to which shall be summoned and present two masters on behalf of the university of scholars. He shall swear in good faith on his conscience, at the time and place according to the state of the city and honor and respect of the faculties, that he will not bestow the licentiate to teach theology or decretals except to the worthy nor admit the unworthy, ratification by persons and nations being abolished. But before he shall license anyone, within three months from the time of the petty license, in the presence of all masters of theology in the city and other respectable and learned men by whom the truth can be learned, he shall make diligent inquiry as to the life, knowledge, facility, and also the promise and hope of success and other points which are required in such cases, and, having made such inquiry, according to what seems proper and expedient he shall give or deny according to his conscience the license asked for. The masters, moreover, of theology and decretals, when they begin to lecture, shall publicly take oath that they will furnish faithful testimony on the aforesaid points. The chancellor shall also swear that he will in no wise reveal the advice of the masters to their hurt, maintaining in their integrity the Parisian rules, liberty and law which obtain in incepting.[1]

Concerning the medical men and artists and others the chancellor promises to examine the masters in good faith, to repel the unworthy and admit only the deserving.

But because, where there is no order, horror easily creeps in, we have conceded to you the function of making due constitutions or ordinances as to the method and hour of lectures and disputations, as to the costume to be worn, as to funerals of the dead, and also, concerning the bachelors, who should lecture and at what hour and on what subject, as to rentals of lodgings or even their prohibition, and of duly punishing rebels against those constitutions or ordinances by expulsion from your society. And if it chance that the rental of lodgings is taken from you or that—which God forbid—injury or enormous excess be inflicted on you or any of you, such as death or mutilation of a limb, unless, after due complaint has been lodged, satisfaction is given within fifteen days, it shall be permitted you to suspend lectures until condign satisfaction is given. And if any of you shall have been unjustly imprisoned, it shall be right for you, unless the injury ceases when complaint is made, to stop lectures immediately, if it shall seem expedient.

We order, moreover, that the bishop of Paris so punish the excesses

[1] Inception was the final process of becoming a master, entering the university or scholastic gild, and beginning to teach.

of delinquents that the honor of the scholars is preserved and crimes do not remain unpunished; but because of delinquents the innocent shall not suffer, nay, if probable suspicion shall arise against anyone, after honorable detention on furnishing suitable bail he shall be dismissed and exactions of the jailers cease. But if he has committed a crime which calls for imprisonment, the bishop shall retain the culprit in prison, it being utterly forbidden to the chancellor to have a prison of his own. We further prohibit that a scholar henceforth be arrested for debt, since this is forbidden by the canons and lawful sanctions. But neither the bishop nor his official nor the chancellor shall require a fine for raising an excommunication or any other censure, nor shall the chancellor demand from licentiates an oath or obedience or other pledge, nor shall he receive any emolument or promise for conceding the license, abiding by the terms of his oath named above.

Furthermore, the summer vacation shall henceforth not exceed a month, and in vacation time the bachelors may continue their lectures if they wish. Moreover, we expressly enjoin that scholars shall not go about town armed, and that the university shall not defend disturbers of the peace and of studies. And those who pretend to be scholars but do not attend classes or have any master shall by no means enjoy the privileges of scholars.

We further order that masters of arts always give one ordinary reading of Priscian and one other afterwards, and those books on nature which were prohibited in provincial council for certain cause they shall not use at Paris until these shall have been examined and purged from all suspicion of errors. Moreover, the masters and scholars of theology shall strive to exercise themselves praiseworthily in the faculty which they profess and not show themselves philosophers but endeavor to know God, nor speak in the vernacular nor confound the Hebrew popular language with the Azotic, but dispute in the schools concerning those questions only which can be settled by theological works and the treatises of the holy fathers.

Furthermore, concerning the goods of scholars who die intestate or do not commit the care of their affairs to others, we have decided to provide thus, namely, that the bishop and one of the masters whom the university shall ordain for this, receiving all the goods of the defunct and depositing them in a safe and fit place, shall set a day by which his death can have been announced in his native place and those upon whom the succession to his goods devolves can come to Paris or delegate an appropriate messenger; and if they come or send, the goods shall be restored to them with a security which has been determined. But if no one appears, then the bishop and master shall use the goods for the soul of the defunct as they shall see fit, unless it chance that the heirs for some just cause cannot come, in which case the disposition shall be deferred to a suitable time.

But since the masters and scholars who suffered injury and damage from the breaking of the oath made to them by the city of Paris have departed from the university, they seem to have pled not so much their own case as the common cause. We, with the general need and utility of the church in view, will and order that henceforth the privileges shall be shown to the masters and scholars by our dearest son in Christ, the illustrious king of France, and fines inflicted on their malefactors, so that they may lawfully study at Paris without any further delay or return of infamy or irregularity of notation. To no man then be it licit to infringe or with rash daring to contradict this page of our provision, constitution and inhibition. If anyone shall presume to attempt this, let him know that he will incur the wrath of almighty God and of the blessed apostles Peter and Paul. Given at the Lateran on the Ides of April, the fifth year of our pontificate.

20

THE BOOKS ON NATURE TO BE EXPURGATED, 1231

LETTER OF GREGORY IX, APRIL 23, 1231

Chartularium universitatis Parisiensis, I, 143–44.

In the foregoing regulations of April 13 the pope provided that the books of Aristotle on nature which had been prohibited in 1210 should not be used until examined and purged of errors. In the present letter he takes steps in that direction. Meanwhile in a letter of April 20 he had ordered the abbot of St. Victor and the prior of the Dominicans at Paris to absolve those masters and scholars who had violated that prohibition.

To masters W., archdeacon of Beauvais, Symon de Alteis of Amiens, and Stephen of Provins of Reims, canons.

Since other sciences ought to render service to the wisdom of holy writ, they are to be in so far embraced by the faithful as they are known to conform to the good pleasure of the Giver, so that anything virulent or otherwise vicious, by which the purity of the Faith might be derogated from, be quite excluded, because a comely woman found in the number of captives is not permitted to be brought into the house unless shorn of superfluous hair and trimmed of sharp nails, and in order that the Hebrews might be enriched from the despoiled Egyptians they were bade to borrow precious gold and silver vessels, not ones of rusty copper or clay.

But since, as we have learned, the books on nature which were prohibited at Paris in provincial council are said to contain both useful and useless matter, lest the useful be vitiated by the useless, we command your discretion, in which we have full faith in the Lord, firmly bidding by apostolic writings under solemn adjuration of divine judgment, that, examining the same books as is convenient subtly and prudently, you entirely exclude what you shall find there erroneous or likely to give scandal or offense to readers, so that, what are suspect being removed, the rest may be studied without delay and without offense. Given at the Lateran, April 23, in the fifth year of our pontificate.

21

AN OFFICIAL VERSION OF THE
DECRETALS ISSUED

GREGORY IX TO THE UNIVERSITY OF PARIS,
SEPTEMBER 5, 1234

Chartularium universitatis Parisiensis, I, 154.

A decretal was a pronouncement by the pope having the force of law, like an imperial constitution in the realm of civil law. The body of decretals may be compared to the *Code* of Justinian, just as the *Decretum* of Gratian, compiled in the twelfth century, may be likened to the *Digest*. *Decretum* and decretals were the chief texts lectured upon in canon law. Gregory IX herewith publishes an official collection of the decretals in five books drawn up by his chaplain, Raymond of Peñafort. At the end of the century Boniface VIII added a sixth book—*Liber sextus*—while Clement V of the early fourteenth century issued the *Clementines*. These, too, became the subject of lecture courses and commentaries by the canon lawyers. Decretals outside of these collections were called *extravagantes* (that is, wandering without) and included the decretals of John XXII and *extravagantes communes* extending down to the time of Sixtus IV (1471–1484).

The king of peace with pious miseration disposed his subordinates to be chaste, pacific and modest; but unbridled cupidity, prodigal of her gifts, envious of peace, mother of strife, matter of contention, daily generates so many new lawsuits that unless justice by its virtue repressed these attempts and explained the questions involved, the abuse of litigation would extinguish the rights of mankind, and concord, given a writ of divorce, would go forth beyond the boundaries of the world. And so the law is given to limit noxious appetite by rule of right, by which the human race is informed how to live aright, not harm another, and render to each his due. Divers constitutions and decretal letters of our predecessors are dispersed in varied volumes. Some of these canons were repetitious, others contradictory, others produced confusion by their prolixity. Yet others were scattered about outside the aforesaid volumes, and their uncertain authority made the decision of cases vary frequently. We therefore have provided, for the common utility and that of students especially, that these be collected in a single volume by our cherished son, brother Raymond, our chaplain and penitentiary, excluding the superfluous and adding our constitutions and decretal epistles, by which some matters which before were in doubt are settled. Wishing, therefore, that all use this compilation alone in cases and classrooms, we strictly prohibit that anyone presume to make any other without the special authority of the apostolic see. Given at Spoleto, September 5, in the eighth year of our pontificate.

22

BUONCOMPAGNI DA SIGNA ON THE NEW RHETORIC, 1235

Aug. Gaudenzi, *Bibliotheca iuridica medii aevi*, Bologna, 1888–1901, II, 249 *et seq.*

Buoncompagni da Signa, the somewhat bumptious author of numerous works on rhetoric, letter-writing, legal papers, and Ciceronian subjects,[1] in

[1] In addition to the two rhetorics presently to be mentioned, he wrote treatises with

1215 A.D. recited his *Rhetorica antiqua* (Old-Fashioned Rhetoric) "in the presence of all the professors of canon and civil law, and other doctors, and a numerous multitude of scholars," at Bologna, where it was forthwith "approved and crowned with laurel." [2] In 1226 the same work was read at Padua before the doctors and students, the papal legate, and the bishop and chancellor of Milan. In 1235 the *Rhetorica novissima* (Rhetoric Up-to-Date), from which the following extracts are taken, was similarly read at Bologna.

In the book which I called by my name, Good Companion (*Boncompagnus*), and in epistolary style made my chief heir, I voluntarily promised and naturally obligated myself to labor towards the discovery of an entirely new rhetoric; wherefore I began at Venice to treat of the same according to the articles of my promise. When, however, I was negligent in completing it, the venerable father Nicholas, bishop of Reggio, who is of noble stock, nobler character, courteous to all, liberal in daily intercourse, a restorer of peace, and grateful in the sight of princes, often urged me, not for his sake but that of students, that I should not leave unfinished the work I had begun. So I finished this rhetoric at Bologna, where in the presence of the venerable father Henry, bishop of Bologna, master Tancred, archdeacon and chancellor, the chapter and clergy of Bologna, and in the presence of the doctors and scholars sojourning at Bologna, it was found worthy of the glorious honor of being solemnly recited in the cathedral. But while it has thus been solemnly approved, of still greater authority

---

the following titles: *Quinque salutationum tabulae*; *Tractatus dictionum*; *Notulae aureae*; *Oliva* (concerned with privileges and confirmations); *Cedrus* (or, *notitia generalium statutorum*); *Myrrha* (instructions how to draw up wills); *Breviloquium*; *Isagoge* (or, *epistule introductorie*); *Boncompagnus* (referred to in the preface of the *Rhetorica novissima*: "In the book which I called by my name, Boncompagnus, and in epistolary style made my chief heir"); *Palma* (ed. Carlo Sutter, 1894); *Rota Veneris* (or, How to Write Love Letters) extracts were printed by E. Monaci in *Atti d. Reale Accad. dei Lincei*, Ser. IV, *Rendiconti*, V (1889), 68–77; *Liber amicitiae* (in which he distinguishes twenty-six kinds of friends) ed. Sarina Nathan, Rome, 1909; *De malo senectutis et senii*, ed. F. Novati, *Atti d. Reale Accad. dei Lincei*, Ser. V, *Rendiconti*, Classe di scienze morali, storiche, e filologiche, I (1892), 49–67.

2 ". . . recitatus, approbatus, et coronatus lauro Bononiae . . . a.d. 1215, sept. kal. apr. coram universitate professorum iuris canonici et civilis et aliorum doctorum et scholarium multitudine numerosa": quoted by G. Manacorda, *Storia della scuola in Italia*. Vol. I. *Il medio evo*. Parte ii. *Storia interna della scuola medioevale italiana nel medio evo* (Milan, 1914), pp. 260, 261, from *MS. H. 13* of Archivio Capitolane di S. Pietro.

will be its present use which will display the favor proper to the work.

But some, perchance poisoned by envy, may be swift to inveigh against me thus and say: Since from the time of Aristotle, which was about that of Moses, when Alexander of Macedon, the son of Philip, reigned, there has not been any philosopher who presumed to say that he could invent any art naturally, unaided by the examples of those who have treated of a similar art, we cannot but marvel how Boncompagnus dares assert in the presence of the learned that his genius transcends the starry heavens. Numerous hosts and brightest geniuses of inventors have preceded our age, for whom it was once less laborious to discover many things than it is for us today to rehearse a few. Also since the arts were in existence from the very foundation of the world and approved by men of greatest skill, how could he at this late date invent an entirely new rhetoric, especially since from very ancient times by Tullius Cicero, who was called the trumpet of Roman eloquence, rhetoric has been compiled from infinite precepts of rhetoricians? Also since arts are natural and what is natural cannot be imitated, how could he now invent anything, especially since there is nothing new under the sun, and the ancient philosophers and poets left nothing untried? Therefore on the ground of the reasons and authorities aforementioned we say and with assurance affirm that what he proposes is an idle dream.

Boncompagnus's Answer

Wounded within by the darts of the envious, I am forced to exclaim because I cannot keep silence: Behold, O fathers and lords, how my adversaries disparage me behind my back, not considering how rash it is to reprehend things unheard, to despise things unseen and unread, and to condemn, spurning due process of law, what they ignore. Surely no one can know of what color an animal will be before it is born, nor can anyone certify to the sex of that which is still in the womb. Yet whatever they have said and how far so ever they have raved in speaking, I, in a calm and even spirit, disregarding what is irrelevant, will answer their objections, lest by keeping silent I seem to confirm them. I say therefore that the elements which were divided from matter by too great subtlety are removed from the perception of human sense by ineffable motion, since they are simple and devoid of parts. Wherefore they may not be comprehended in any predication by anyone's artifice or genius, because their operations are invisible and incomprehensible and subject to the sole power of divine majesty. In exercises, however, which proceed from the elements by custom and nature, the spirits excite the virtues of bodies to perform their proper actions: and so singular phenomena are perpetually renovated. For when an artisan has materials at hand, he gives a new figure to the material at will. So in all invention which proceeds from nature there should be common material and private operation of the inventor. Moreover, that remark, "There is nothing new under the sun," is true in genus but not in species, since every day God creates new souls and desists not from implanting them in new bodies. And that new inventions can be made today may be proved from theology. The shaper of man is God who alone ordains and disposes all things and, after we are renewed by grace, pours new light into our mortal eyes; wherefore Paul, apostle to the Gentiles, bids the first hold his peace, if anything be revealed to another that sitteth by. However, philosophers and those crowned with natural science might adduce against me a more plausible and rational question in this wise: He who says he has invented an entirely new rhetoric must assign the principal causes and inductive matters which have led him to undertake so arduous a task. Such objectors I can commend with worthy praises, wherefore I am bound to answer their question since I have proceeded from a rational motion of nature. I say, then, that there were three chief causes for which I wearied my genius in this work.

The first was the authority of Boethius, bright with philosophy's rays, who has called the rhetoric of the ancients an empty part of learning, firmly maintaining that the rhetoric of the ancients consists in precepts alone without common utility. Wherefore I say that to divide and subdivide, define and describe, to give precepts and always issue orders is nothing else than to emit thunders and not lavish rain. Boethius also tries to prove from Aristotle that rhetoric was not handed down by the ancients. For, he says, if anyone teaches how to make different kinds of shoes, he does something useful yet does not hand down an art. What Aristotle has noted elsewhere concerning rhetorical orations is defective. For Aristotle, since he was preeminently an investigator of nature, said some things concerning rhetorical documents according to the motion of nature, but I think he knew rhetoric from the outside, not from the inside.

The second was that students in both laws could get little or no aid from the discipline of the liberal arts except from public speaking.

The third was that the rhetoric compiled by Tullius Cicero is condemned by the judgment of students, since it is never the subject of ordinary lectures, nay rather as if a fable or mechanical art is run through and taught privately.

There was also a fourth motive which not without motion of reason induced my genius to composing this rhetoric. Tullius surely was mistaken as to the origin of law when he said that it was a principle born of most honorable causes and sprung from the best reasons, and straightway gave a fabulous beginning, saying, "There was once a time when men wandered about like beasts," and then went on to say that there was a certain great and wise man who originated law; and so under a particular sign he induced confusion of time and action. Also, in the rhetoric he published there is inept construction and intricate position of dictions, so that he openly contradicts himself, especially when he directs that narration should be brief, lucid, and open. Let these testimonies suffice for you then, O unbelievers, who even till to-day have denied that an entirely new rhetoric could be invented.

Also another question might arise which would pierce my soul like a sharp sword if I did not defend myself with the shield of foresight. Since the liberal arts were comprehended under the number seven by the dogmas of the philosophers, and the order of number cannot and should not be altered, how can anyone invent an eighth art at this time? This question proceeds from the opinion of the less intelligent, wherefore I ought to remove the scales of ignorance from their eyes. For certainly this rhetoric which I have invented according to the argument of the question proposed would not be an eighth but a ninth art, since Tullius is said to have compiled two rhetorics, albeit both may be identical. I, however, have not proposed from any temerity to augment the number of liberal arts, since no one can change the natural subject of any art: but I have worked efficaciously that the rhetoric, which Boethius called an empty part of learning, should be subordinated as a small part and of little use, and that that art should remain in the number of seven crowned with the diadem of evident utility. For the law says that in new departures utility should be evident, if one is to recede from that custom which has long seemed just. But the test of utility rests in the judgment of those choosing it. For every discreet man ever desires to find something more useful, since without utility all goal for temporal actions vanishes. . . .

Narration of the Author at the End of the Work

The genius which has marched between the cliffs of cogitation and paths of laborious meditation is anxious to find desired rest. Wherefore, after treating of assemblies, I put an end to my labor, awaiting not without horrible fear the last assembly in which the third angel will sound the trumpet at whose blast heaven and earth will be moved and, the world over, those who sleep in sepulchres will hear the voice of the Son of God and come forth. Afterward, indeed, the Son of God himself will appear, terrible in the assembly of the last judgment, before whose tribunal will be congregated the company of the elect, the hosts of angels will tremble and Satan will be bound again in the pit of hell, who first introduced dissent in heaven and injurious matter of litigation. And then all conflict of opposing counsel will cease and all contentions of controversy be solved, since from the mouth of One sitting on the throne final last sentence will go forth. Finally, we implore with votive prayers the Judge supernal who is called alpha and omega, the beginning and the end, that in pronouncing the said sentence he may deign to place us, absolved from all bonds of sin, at his right hand, where with the hosts of the elect we may merit to be invited to the celestial kingdom which was prepared for the just and upright of heart from the foundation of the world.

Of the Time When the Rhetoric Was Published

This rhetoric was published at Bologna in the year of our Lord 1235, the eight of the indiction, by the hand of the orator Boncompagnus who was born in the castle called Signa Franca, seven miles distant from the florid city of Florence. For that castle is situated between four streams and two stone bridges, wherefore by reason of the descent of waters and abundance of olive trees it is endowed with indescribable charm.

23

ERRORS CONDEMNED AT PARIS, 1241

Chartularium universitatis Parisiensis, I, 170–71.

These are articles disapproved as against theological truth and disapproved by the chancellor of Paris, Eudes, and the masters teaching theology at Paris, A.D. 1240, the second Sunday after the octave of the Nativity.[1]

First, that the divine essence in itself will be seen neither by man nor by angel.

This error we condemn, and we excommunicate those asserting and defending it, by authority of William bishop [of Paris]. Moreover, we firmly believe and assert that God in his essence or substance will be seen by angels and all saints and is seen by souls in glory.

Second, that it may be the divine essence is one in Father, Son, and Holy Spirit, nevertheless with respect to form it is one in Father and Son but not one in these with the Holy Spirit, and yet this form is the same as the divine essence.

We reprove this error, for we firmly believe that there is one essence or substance in Father, Son, and Holy Spirit, and the same essence with respect to form.

Third, that the Holy Spirit, as a bond or love, does not proceed from the Son but merely from the Father.

We reprove this error, for we firmly believe that as a bond or love it proceeds from both.

Fourth, that souls in glory are not in the empyrean heaven with the angels, nor will glorified bodies be there, but in the aqueous or crystalline heaven which is above the firmament, which also is stated of the blessed Virgin.

This error we reprove, for we firmly believe that there will be the same corporal place, forsooth the empyrean heaven, for angels and sainted souls and glorified bodies.

Fifth, that the evil angel was evil in the beginning of his creation and never was anything except evil.

[1] That is, January 13, 1240–1241, the year at Paris not beginning until Easter.

This error we reprove, for we firmly believe that he was created good and afterwards by sinning became evil.

Sixth, that an angel in the same instant can be in different places and be everywhere, if he wishes.

We reprove this error, for we believe that an angel is in a defined space, so that, if he is here, he is not at the same instant there; for it is impossible that he be everywhere, for this is proper to God alone.

Seventh, that there are many eternal truths which are not God.

This error we reprove, for we firmly believe that there is only one eternal truth which is God.

Eighth, that now first and creation-passivity cannot be created.

This error we reprove, for we firmly believe that it is both created and creature.

Ninth, that he who has superior natural advantages of necessity will have more grace and glory.

This error we reprove, for we firmly believe that God, according as he has preelected and foreordained, will give unto each grace and glory.

Tenth, that the evil angel never had any standing ground, nor even Adam in the state of innocence.

This error we reprove, for we firmly believe that both had means to stand but not to progress.

24

CONDEMNATION OF THE TALMUD RENEWED, 1244

Chartularium universitatis Parisiensis, I, 173–74.

The following papal letter is connected with one of the periodic movements to destroy Jewish books on the ground that they contained blasphemies against Christianity. This time the scene of the agitation was France during the reign of St. Louis. In this connection it may be noted that one of the five men skilled in the Hebrew tongue and in the philosophy of the Jews and Arabs whom St. Louis appointed to pass upon the question was Raymond Martini, a Dominican of Catalonia, who wrote a remarkable work, *The Fist of Faith*, in which he employed a wide knowledge of Jewish and Arabic lore in the endeavor to prove the truth of Christianity against the Jews.

Innocent, bishop, servant of the servants of God, to his cherished son Louis, illustrious king of France, greeting and apostolic benediction. The impious perfidy of the Jews—from whose hearts because of the enormity of their crimes our Redeemer did not lift the veil but still permits them to remain, as is fitting, in the blindness which is characteristic of Israel—not regarding the fact that Christian piety receives them only out of pity and patiently endures dwelling together with them, commits those enormities which stupefy hearers and horrify narrators. For these ingrates to the Lord Jesus Christ, who patiently awaits their conversion out of the richness of His longsuffering, showing no shame for their fault nor respecting the honor of the Christian faith, and omitting or scorning the Mosaic law and the prophets, follow certain traditions of their seniors concerning which the Lord rebukes them in the Gospel, saying: Why do you transgress the mandate of God and irritate Him by your traditions, teaching human doctrines and mandates?

Upon this sort of traditions, which in Hebrew are called the *Talmud* —and there is a great book among them exceeding the text of the Bible in length, in which are manifest blasphemies against God and Christ and the blessed Virgin, intricate fables, erroneous abuses, and unheard-of stupidities—they nourish and teach their sons and render them utterly alien from the doctrine of the law and the prophets, fearing lest, if they knew the truth, which is in the law and the prophets, and which testifies openly that the only begotten son of God will come in the flesh, they would be converted to the faith and humbly return to their Redeemer. And not content with these things, they make Christian women nurses of their sons in contumely of the Christian faith, with whom they commit many shameful things. On which account the faithful should be afraid lest they incur divine wrath while they unworthily allow them to perpetrate acts which bring confusion upon our faith.

And although our cherished son, the chancellor of Paris, and the doctors teaching at Paris in holy writ, by the mandate of pope Gregory, our predecessor of happy memory, after reading and examining the said abusive book and certain others with all their glosses, publicly burned them in the presence of clergy and people to the confusion of the perfidy of the Jews, as we have seen stated in their letters, to whom you as catholic king and most Christian prince rendered suitable aid and favor in this, for which we commend your royal excellency with praises in the Lord and pursue with acts of grace: because nevertheless the profane abuse of the Jews themselves has not yet quieted nor has persecution yet given them understanding, we earnestly ask, admonish, and beseech your highness in the Lord Jesus Christ that against detestable and enormous excesses of this sort committed in contumely of the Creator and in injury to the Christian name, as you piously began, you laudably continue to proceed with due severity. And that you order both the aforesaid abusive books condemned by the same doctors and generally all the books with their glossses which were examined and condemned by them to be burned by fire wherever they can be found throughout your entire kingdom, strictly forbidding that Jews henceforth have Christian nurses or servants, that the sons of a free woman may not serve the sons of a handmaid, but as servants condemned by the Lord, whose death they wickedly plotted, they at least outwardly recognize themselves as servants of those whom the death of Christ made free and themselves slaves. So we may commend the zeal of your sincerity in the Lord with due praises. Given at the Lateran, May 9, in the first year of our pontificate.

On August 12, 1247, however, Innocent IV wrote Louis IX that the Jews had represented to him that they could not understand the Bible and other statutes of their law according to their faith without the *Talmud*, and that he had directed the papal legate to allow them to retain those of their books which could be tolerated without injury to the Christian faith.

The legate, however, reported to the pope that the Jews had misrepresented things to him, that their books were full of errors and, after examination, had been burned by the advice of all the masters of theology and canon law.

"And it would be no small scandal and an everlasting reproach to the apostolic see, if books so solemnly and so justly burned in the presence of the university of scholars and the clergy and people of Paris should be tolerated by apostolic mandate or should be returned to the Jewish rabbis" (*Chartularium*, I, 204).

A formal sentence to this effect was promulgated by the legate on May 15, 1248 (*Chartularium*, I, 209), and Albertus Magnus was among the signers.

25

RULES CONCERNING THE RENTAL
OF CLASSROOMS, PARIS, 1245

Chartularium universitatis Parisiensis, I, 177–78.

In the year 1244, the month of February. Let all know that the masters of the university of Paris in the church of St. Mathurin at Paris in full congregation by their common assent decreed that no master by himself or through another shall retain more than one classroom, but he may retain such for a bachelor who is about to incept or for another master, it being understood that he shall take oath to this, if required.

Also, no one except an actual teacher shall presume to retain classrooms for his use.

Also, no one shall occupy the classroom of another teacher, so long as he lectures there and pays his landlord what he should.

Also, no one shall outbid another by a higher price for classrooms which the other has rented, nor shall he receive more from another if he sublets.

Also, no one shall hold back a classroom for more than the fixed price.

Also, no master shall hold back classrooms from anyone in this way, that the lessor makes a determination [1] there, in whatsoever way a lessor whether as a layman or subletting.

Also, if any scholar has rented a house and wishes to make classrooms out of part of it, a rent shall be fixed according to the worth of the tenement compared to the total price of the house.

Also, no one shall hire a house over the head of another or others, so long as those living in the house wish to occupy it, and have done what they should according to the custom of the whole town of Paris.

Also, if a landlord has refused to give his lodgings at the fixed price, and a scholar has been willing to give the fixed price and has offered to give adequate security as to this, the said house shall be put on the black list for five years. Moreover, the scholar or scholars who take a forbidden house or stay there or will not leave as soon as they have been warned by the rector or servant sent by him, or by the proctors

---

[1] Concerning "determination" see the next selection.

similarly or their messenger, shall be deprived of the benefits of the classrooms and university.

Also, the Christmas vacation shall last from December 18 to the morrow of the day after Epiphany.[2] Moreover, these statutes are so retained in force that the university of masters can add to or subtract from or alter them as it shall see fit.

26

RULES FOR DETERMINATIONS IN ARTS, 1252

STATUTES OF THE ARTISTS OF THE ENGLISH NATION CONCERNING BACHELORS OF ARTS WHO ARE TO DETERMINE DURING LENT

Chartularium universitatis Parisiensis, I, 227–30.

This selection depicts in detail the exercise of determining or Determinations, prolonged public disputations during Lent by which the candidates for the licentiate, each in his own classroom, gave proof of their ability. For further discussion of this institution as it developed subsequently the reader may consult Rashdall, I (1936), 450–56. Incidentally the required texts in logic are listed, and explicit mention is made of the "university of artists" with its rector and common chest, and of the four Nations into which the university was divided with their proctors and statutes such as the present selection. For an earlier reference to rector and proctors see Selection 25, and for their previous history, Rashdall, I (1936), 311–14.

In the year since the Incarnation, 1251, the masters of the English nation, teaching in arts at Paris and for the good of the university and of learning taking multifold measures, and by God's grace continuing in the future without diminution, decreed by their common counsel and that of good men the form noted below for bachelors in arts determining in Lent, as is the custom. In the first place the proctor, touching the Bible, shall select two persons whom he believes qualified to choose examiners of those determining, who, touching the Bible, shall swear that without hate or love of any person or any part of their nation, they will choose three masters, whom they know to be strict and

[2] January 8.

qualified in examining faithfully, more intent on the promotion and advantage of the university, less susceptible to prayer or bribe. These three when chosen shall similarly swear on the Bible that they will faithfully examine and proceed with rigor of examination, licentiating the worthy and conducting themselves without hate of any person or group of their nation, also without envy or any rancor of mind or other sinister perturbation. Moreover, those who have insufficient standing in the examination and are unworthy to pass they shall fail, sparing no one, moved neither by prayer nor bribe nor fear nor love or any other occasion or indirect favor of persons.

The masters presenting candidates, moreover, and the bachelors themselves shall give personal security that they will make no entreaties on behalf of bachelors nor seek favor from the examiners or from the nation or from the university, either by themselves or through others, but will accept the simple statement of the examiners. By the same token, if it happens that bachelors are failed, that they will not bring contumely or complaints or threats or other evils against the examiners, either by themselves or through others, because they ought to suppose that the examiners have acted according to their consciences and good faith for the honor of the university and the nation.

Moreover, a bachelor coming up for the licentiate in arts at Paris should be twenty years old or at least in his twentieth year, and of honorable life and laudable conversation. He should not have a cope without a hood of the same cloth, nor a hood with knots. He should not wear a mitre on his head in the classrooms while he is determining. If he has the right to the tonsure, he may have the tonsure, nor may he or should he be blamed on this account. Also before he is admitted to examination he shall give personal security that he has his own classroom of a master qualified to teach in it throughout Lent, and has his own master under whom he seeks the license of determining, or a bachelor about to incept in arts at the latest before Lent, in whose classroom he will determine. Further, that he has attended lectures in arts for five years or four at least at Paris continuously or elsewhere in a university of arts. Further, that he has heard the books of Aristotle on the Old Logic, namely, the *Praedicamenta* and *Periarmeniae* at least twice in ordinary lectures and once cursorily,[1] the *Six Principles* at least once in ordinary lectures and once cursorily, the

[1] Concerning ordinary and cursory lectures see above, Selection 15, note 1.

three first books of the *Topics* and the *Divisions* once in ordinary lectures or at least cursorily, the *Topics* of Aristotle and *Elenci* twice in ordinary lectures and once at least cursorily or if not cursorily at least thrice in ordinary, the *Prior Analytics* once in ordinary lectures and once cursorily, or, if he is now attending, so that he has heard at least half before Lent and is to continue, the *Posterior Analytics* once in ordinary lectures completely. Also that he shall have heard *Priscian minor* (books 17–18) and the *Barbarismus* twice in ordinary lectures and at least once cursorily, *Priscian major* (books 1–16) once cursorily. Also he shall have heard *De anima* once or be hearing it as aforesaid. Also he shall give satisfaction that he has diligently attended the disputations of masters in a recognized university for two years and for the same length of time has answered as required concerning sophisms in class. Also he shall promise that he will respond to question for a full year from the beginning of one Lent to the beginning of the next.

If, moreover, a bachelor shall be found sufficiently qualified in knowledge according to the examiners and shall not have completed the required number of years or books or lectures, the nation reserves to itself the power to dispense with these, as shall seem expedient to it. And in such case only it shall be permissible for his master to petition the nation for him.

Also if, after the exercise of cursory lectures has been made and finally completed, he shall have transgressed in the said exercise in any way, he shall in no case be admitted to the examination for determination. Nor similarly shall a master, whether now teaching or not, who, after the said exercise has been made as stated and finally confirmed by the masters, shall have transgressed in the said exercise, be accepted as presenting a bachelor, until full satisfaction shall have been made to the rector or proctors for the university by the master or the bachelor who has transgressed.

Also the bachelor licensed to determine shall begin to determine at the latest on the next day after Brandons.[2] If he shall not have begun to determine then, he shall not be allowed to do so during Lent. And from the said Monday he shall determine continuously till the middle of Lent, unless he shall have lawful cause excusing him. And then let it be licit for no one to determine for him as substitute, unless such substitute has the license to teach in arts at Paris or has determined

[2] Brandons are the first week in Lent.

elsewhere through Lent or is licensed to determine in that present Lent, always providing that the same shall have determined continuously from the said Monday following Brandons until the middle of Lent. Also if a bachelor shall have been licensed to determine in the arts at Paris in one year and from a legitimate cause shall have failed to determine in that Lent in which he was licensed, which sometimes happens, he may afterwards determine in some subsequent Lent, regularly however and as others do, but he shall not substitute for others unless he shall have first determined during Lent in a fixed place. Also, until he shall have paid for the university a sum such and so great as he offered for personal security, and another for the nation, he shall not be given license to determine. Also if at the latest he shall not have been licensed before the last Sunday before Lent, he shall not be admitted later that year to the examination for determination.

Also, it shall be enjoined on him that all through Lent, and thereafter so long as he shall belong to the faculty of arts as student or teacher, he shall obey the mandate of rector and proctor in lawful and honorable matters. Also he shall not give drinks except on the first day he begins to determine and the last, unless this is done by the permission of the rector or the proctor of his nation, who can give him a dispensation in this regard as shall seem expedient to them, considering nevertheless the many factors about the determiners which are here involved.

Also, the examiners shall diligently collect from the bachelors the money to be paid to the university and nation and faithfully keep what is collected, and at the summons of the rector and proctors of the four nations deposit it at the day set in the common chest of the university of artists. Also the money received for the nation they shall deposit in the common chest before the Sunday after Ash Wednesday. Also none of the said examiners can by himself, without his associates deputed with him for determinations, license anyone or presume alone to examine.

Also, in addition to the aforesaid, after the candidates shall have been licensed, let them be present every Friday at the Vespers of the blessed Virgin and at mass the Saturday following, until Palm Sunday, under the penalty by which masters are bound.

But inasmuch as by this form it is not right nor will be for rich or poor, noble or ignoble, to put it off later, if they do not appear to seek license of determining in the aforesaid manner, therefore, to notify them it is provided by the masters that the present form be twice announced in classes each year, so that the first time it shall be read in the classrooms of masters between Purification and Lent, and the other time between the feast of St. Remy and All Saints or thereabouts, when there shall be a general meeting. Moreover, individual masters shall be bound on their honor to observe this ordinance. Also, however, if anyone is found acting contrary to the said ordinance, he shall be suspended from lecturing for a month.

27

AGAINST THE FRIARS

LETTER OF THE UNIVERSITY OF PARIS TO PREL-
ATES OF THE CHURCH AND SCHOLARS GEN-
ERALLY IN WHICH RELIGIOUS ORDERS,
ESPECIALLY THE FRIARS PREACHERS,
ARE ATTACKED

Chartularium universitatis Parisiensis, I, 252–58.

The Dominicans had come to Paris in 1217, the Franciscans in 1230. They not merely gave instruction, more particularly in theology, in their own convents, but sought admission to university degrees and the faculty of theology, in which effort they received papal support. At first the other masters raised little objection, but when friars who had been so admitted refused to participate in the suspension of lectures and the "great dispersion" of 1229–1231, the other masters began to look at them askance. In 1253 the two Dominican and one Franciscan professors of theology again refused to participate in a cessation of lectures, called because of injuries inflicted on scholars by the local police. When they further refused to take an oath of obedience to the university as members thereof, the university expelled and excommunicated them. In the following letter to the secular clergy and to scholars generally, the university defends its action.

In the bitter struggle which followed, the friars were temporarily victorious because of papal support, but after the death of Alexander IV in 1261 the university gradually made good its contentions. Friars were admitted to the faculty of theology but not to that of arts, and secular students could incept for the doctorate only under secular doctors. By 1318 an oath of obedience to the statutes of the university was once more imposed upon the friars.

To the reverend fathers in Christ, archbishops, bishops, abbots, deans, archdeacons, and other prelates of churches, also to chapters and to scholars generally, the university of masters and scholars studying at Paris sends greeting everlasting in the Lord. The right hand of the Most High once planted at Paris the paradise of delights, the venerable gymnasium of letters, whence the fount of wisdom rises which, distributed in four faculties of theology, jurisprudence, medicine, and rational, natural, and moral philosophy, like the four rivers of Paradise flowing through the four climes of the world, waters and irrigates the whole earth. From which how multifarious spiritual and temporal advantages Christendom experiences is clearer than light to all.

Over this venerable and wholesome gymnasium there once were masters who were men of reverend life, most illustrious in learning, religious of mind, yet all clad in secular garb, who, having become more numerous as the number of auditors increased with time as it should, in order that they could devote themselves the more freely and tranquilly to learned study, if they should be associated by a bond of special law, obtained from king and pope [1] a corporate college or university with many privileges and indulgences. Under the happy regime of these doctors the said university grew and blossomed into the most beautiful flowers and bore richest fruit of honors, because, just as they differed neither in costume nor profession, so they varied not in studies or vows, knowing that still waters run deep.

But in our recent times certain men of religion who are called Friars Preachers, living in Paris in small numbers, coming in under an appearance of piety and public utility, pursued the study of theology together with us, fervently and humbly; on which account they were kindly received by our predecessors and ourselves, embraced sincerely with the arms of charity, lodged in our own house, which we conceded to them to live in [2] and in which they dwell to this day, carefully educated with the food of learning as well as of the body; and having obtained many benefits from us and our predecessors, by entry of our scholars they simultaneously grew in science and numbers, so that today they are scattered everywhere in many colleges. But although in their first

[1] Ab utroque principe.
[2] The Hospital of Saint-Jacques, near Porte Saint-Jacques.

institution they chose to serve Christ the Lord in perfect humility, later, led by we know not what spirit against the evangelical rule of perfect humility which they professed (in which the Lord says to the perfect, "Do not wish to be called Rabbis," and a little after, "Be ye not called masters," in the first utterance forbidding the appetite for mastery, in the second interdicting too the word, Master), seeking the solemn honor of the master's degree and magisterial chairs, they nevertheless, when the greater part of the university of Paris was transferred to Angers because of an atrocious and notorious injury done us, in that paucity of scholars which remained at Paris gained their desire with the connivance of the bishop and chancellor of Paris at that time and in the absence of the masters won the master's degree and one professorial chair.

Then, when our university was reformed at Paris by apostolic provision, by means of the same chair they multiplied successive doctors for themselves against the will of the then chancellor—our predecessors who were not yet hampered by other convents of scholars of the orders dissimulating—and by themselves they erected a second professorship and for some time maintained both, acquired by such titles. But as time went on, our predecessors considered that there were six colleges of different orders, namely, Cistercians, Premonstratensians, Vallis Scholarium, Trinitarians, Friars Minor, and that other regular clergy, not having colleges among us, had come to Paris for the sake of studying theology and some of them had become professors, while others not yet properly qualified for professorial chairs aspired to them according to what they themselves said. They considered also that the canons of the church of Paris, of whom three teach in this field among us, were accustomed to increase their number as persons endowed them in accordance with the custom of their church. They considered furthermore that the state of the city and the reputation of the theological faculty, according to the apostolic statute sworn to by the chancellor of Paris and individual masters of theology, could hardly support twelve chairs because of the scarcity of scholars studying theology with us, since now in cities and other large-sized places generally the said subject is taught by the same friars and others, not without great peril. Therefore, they perceived more clearly than light that, after nine of those twelve chairs were occupied, as they were about to be, irrevocably by the said colleges, which because of the continued succession of friar teachers would never henceforth revert to secular masters, two or three at the most would be left over which could be reserved for the secular persons who flock from every region under the sun to the university of Paris. But should it happen that the said colleges double their chairs, as the Preachers had done, since from what we have said it would then follow that there would be fifteen immortal classes in theology in our university, it would inevitably result that all secular scholars, the canons of Paris alone excepted, would be excluded forever from the chairs of theology at Paris, on which account we would have, because of the regulars coming in, to leave the city of Paris, so suitable to our studies and for so long past made suitable by us at great expense, and migrate to less suitable places not without serious loss, or, alienated from the domain of theology, all turn to the secular sciences.

We, therefore, carefully observing that the eminence of sacred letters is more necessary to the secular clergy, who are frequently called to care for souls and rule churches, than to the regular clergy who are rarely promoted to such positions, noting also how a scholar is spurred to study, if he hopes that sometime he may attain a professorial chair, having held diligent deliberation, decided to decree that no convent of regular clergy in our community should be allowed to have two full professors actually teaching at the same time, not meaning by this statute to prevent the friars from multiplying their own extraordinary lecturers as they might see fit. Which statute the Friars Preachers resist with all their might.

Then after Lent, being in great anguish of heart because of death, imprisonment and other atrocities committed against our scholars by the police of Paris, in accordance with a certain ordinance of the apostolic see granted us, we made a certain mutual agreement as to following up the said injuries before God and justice, if it should happen that secular justice failed us, so far as each of us might, saving his rule or order and also without labor of his own body, not in the name of individuals but of the university. When we did this, the aforementioned masters of the Preachers who were then teaching among us would by no means agree to our said agreement, except on the condition that under testimony of our common seal we concede to their order in perpetuity two chairs in the faculty of masters of theology. This could not be conceded to them, our statute mentioned above preventing, nor was it then a question of their classes or ours but rather of removing the aforesaid injuries. Wherefore the said friars, pertinaciously resisting the said agreement, delayed it by their rebellious attitude for seven weeks, on which account our security being in jeopardy we had to abstain the longer from lecturing. Having finally effected this agreement despite their resistance, there immediately followed satisfaction of the said injuries for our future security.

But while this was still pending, lest we experience a similar rebellion in any masters in the future, we unanimously decided to decree that henceforth no master be admitted to the college of masters unless he should first have sworn to observe faithfully our statutes, licit and honorable and useful to us; further, to join in our licit and honorable and expedient agreements which have especial vigor from the tenor of our privileges, so that in the words of Augustine the part be not shameful from not harmonizing with the whole. To which statute, although we were afterwards willing in their favor to insert this clause, "provided, however, that to me who profess the rule of the Friars Preachers the said statutes according to that rule are not illicit or dishonorable or contrary to the safety of souls, or adverse to law divine or human or to public utility, nor harmful to the holy church of God," nevertheless they refused to give their assent except on the aforesaid condition of two professorships being conceded in perpetuity, and, since the condition was not accepted by us for the reason already stated, they pertinaciously resisted the same statute so far as in them lay and still do.

Now when, because of this rebellion and contumacy, in accord with the tenor of the aforesaid ordinance of the apostolic see after the lapse of fifteen days, they incurred sentence of excommunication, we on account of their excommunication for the said rebellions separating them and their adherents from our society, as is the custom, caused their separation according to our custom to be announced in all the classes. On which account the entire convent of the Friars Preachers at Paris, forgetful of its ancient humility and our beneficence, contrary to the word of the Apostle saying, "I beseech you brethren that you walk worthily of that calling in which you are called in all humbleness and gentleness," and in another place, "Forget not favors," raising their heel against our university their patron, as they themselves would not dare to deny, gravely defaming the persons of our predecessors, falsely and foully calling them persecutors of holiness and all religion, finally plotting danger against our persons, they suggested with deliberate malice to the illustrious count of Poitiers, then regent of the realm of France, with many magnates of his court assisting him and in the presence of our masters summoned for this, that we had issued statutes against God and the church universal, likewise had perpetrated conspiracies unlawful against the honor of the king and profit of the realm, which God forbid, whereas really we had done nothing whatever except what has been stated above and in which they had joined with us to the extent of their power, subject merely to their stipulated condition.

Nor yet sated with our calamities, going to the apostolic see and gravely defaming, as we have learned, our predecessors to the pope and cardinals, maintaining complete silence as to the causes of their separation, without anyone there of our side, by the elaborate falsehoods of their entreaties and their importunity they extorted from the pope certain surreptitious letters, as we have learned, to the venerable father, the bishop of Evreux, by which (although from reverence to the apostolic bull and the entreaties of the said count of Poitiers and to avoid giving scandal to many who were shocked by their insolences we were willing to readmit them to our society saving only our statutes aforesaid, at least until the pope, more fully informed, should decree otherwise) they nonetheless by means of an executor of theirs delegated at their instance by the bishop mentioned, namely a master Luke, a canon of Paris, favorable to them but entirely hostile to us—without our ever being summoned to judgment, never heard in our defense, not sufficiently warned, our exceptions not admitted nor the falsity of their pleas and many other things proposed *extra judicium* as we could before God, after a legitimate appeal interposed from these grievances and many other causes, pending nevertheless a citation by which they had had us cited to the tribunal of the supreme pontiff by a letter obtained from the apostolic see to the same judge—they procured the suspension of all masters and everyone of all faculties, all auditors even of theology, law and medicine, without any knowledge of the cause, without process of law, *de facto* since *de iure* they could not, and to the greater contumely of us and every clerk published the same in the parish churches of the city of Paris on a Sunday in the presence of all the laity and to their grave scandal.

Add to this that, to increase the peak of their presumption, when, for the sake of new scholars arriving who did not know what had happened, we caused the afore-mentioned edict of separation together with their declaration to be announced to all classes as is the custom by our public servants whom we call bedells, when the said servants came to a class of these friars and one of them began to read a copy of the edict, a multitude of the friars who were there with a great vociferation and clamor rushed at those servants, after many contumelies tore the copy of the edict from the hands of the reader, and, pushing another servant aside, struck a third so that blood flowed, and so they shamefully drove them away. Finally, when they returned to the rector of our university and revealed what had happened to them, the rector taking three masters of arts with him went to the same class. But when he tried to read another copy of the same edict, the same friars rushed at him and assailed him with many contumelies. At length when they charged that he came armed and, to find out, felt his person with their hands, the rector wishing to show his innocence turned up his cope to his neck and demonstrated in the sight of all that he was unarmed, and thus escaping their hands he returned with the business unaccomplished.

Moreover, the iniquities of the Amorites not yet completed, the friars mentioned turning wickedly to machinations of fraud, not to say falsity, extorted from their said executor by his mistake as he asserts, not without vice of falsity, a letter containing that certain of our masters and students mentioned by name to the number of forty had agreed in his presence to admit to our society and college of masters the aforesaid friars who once taught among us. Which letter indeed they displayed at secret conferences to some of us in order to induce them after the example of the aforesaid to join them and secretly withdraw from the agreement of our university, and in this way they brought about dissensions and schisms among us, until the same letter by God's aid was brought to us by one of ours and read in public, and those whose names were inscribed were aroused by such falsity and denied the fact stoutly. The said executor hearing this became red in the face and in detestation of the said letter broke his seal with an axe and sent part of the same broken seal to our rector as a sign of his own sadness and remorse. Also at the petition of certain persons named in the said letter, seized by fear, he granted them to have their letters asserting the contrary sealed with the seal of the court of Paris, since he did not yet have a seal of his own, which we keep with the prior letter aforesaid to show at the proper time and place.

The defamations and detractions, which they have not feared to make against us and especially against our predecessors in their public sermons as well as in private, we cannot explain in a few words. In all which things aforesaid not without grave damage we have experienced the truth of that vulgar proverb, "A mouse in one's wallet, a serpent in the bosom, a fire in one's lap, repay their hosts evilly," Solomon saying, "He who nourishes a serpent in his bosom will be stung by it," and also the truth of the Council of Seville where it says, "Men of diverse profession ought not to be in one and the same office," which likewise is forbidden in divine law, Moses saying, "You shall not plow with an ox and an ass together," that is, you shall not associate men of different profession in one office together. And later on, "Those cannot associate and hold together whose studies and vows differ." [3]

Lest therefore certain of the friars who are scattered through all churches, wishing perchance to justify the case of their Parisian friars to the ears of men, should succeed in obfuscating the truth of events by one-sided narration, we, taking into account the public utility of the church universal, not on our own account merely but for certain greater matters which are imminent, desiring that the said truth be known to all, have decided to give a summary of the aforesaid events, collecting briefly the terrors and oppressions and other unexpected grievances which they insolently inflict upon us—passing over for the present many things which they devise against us through the power of laymen whom they win over in wondrous ways—to your discretion, reverend fathers, in the present writing, in order that you, who are fathers by the clemency of divine providence, remembering that you once were sons, may now endure with us sons in paternal affection and, noting carefully and clearly how great perils may follow from the said insolence which they display, especially since you are given as watchmen to the house of Israel, do you ascend the watchtowers and gaze and contemplate and, if you shall deem expedient, take care to provide such means as with God you can, lest if that foundation of the church known as the university of Paris be shaken, the edifice itself in consequence unexpectedly sink in ruin. For he who begins by sap-

[3] The quotation is made indirectly through Gratian, causa 16, quaest. 7, cap. 22.

ping the foundations leaves no doubt whatever that he intends to level the entire edifice.

Given at Paris in the church of St. Julien le Pauvre and read there in the presence of the masters of all faculties, all masters being specially summoned for this purpose, in the year of the Lord 1253, on the Wednesday immediately following the Feast of the Purification of the blessed virgin Mary.

28

COURSES IN ARTS, PARIS, 1255

Chartularium universitatis Parisiensis, I, 277–79.

In the year of the Lord 1254. Let all know that we, all and each, masters of arts by our common assent, no one contradicting, because of the new and incalculable peril which threatens in our faculty—some masters hurrying to finish their lectures sooner than the length and difficulty of the texts permits, for which reason both masters in lecturing and scholars in hearing make less progress—worrying over the ruin of our faculty and wishing to provide for our status, have decreed and ordained for the common utility and the reparation of our university to the honor of God and the church universal that all and single masters of our faculty in the future shall be required to finish the texts which they shall have begun on the feast of St. Remy [1] at the times below noted, not before.

The Old Logic, namely the book of Porphyry, the *Praedicamenta*, *Periarmeniae*, *Divisions* and *Topics* of Boethius, except the fourth, on the feast of the Annunciation of the blessed Virgin [2] or the last day for lectures preceding. *Priscian minor* and *major*, *Topics* and *Elenchi*, *Prior* and *Posterior Analytics* they must finish in the said or equal time. The *Ethics* through four books in twelve weeks, if they are read with another text; if *per se*, not with another, in half that time. Three short texts, namely *Sex principia*, *Barbarismus*, Priscian on accent, if read together and nothing else with them, in six weeks. The *Physics* of Aristotle, *Metaphysics*, and *De animalibus* on the feast of St. John the Baptist; [3] *De celo et mundo*, first book of *Meteorology*

---

[1] October 1. See Selection 72 for a fourteenth-century calendar of the university of Paris.

[2] March 25.   [3] June 24.

with the fourth, on Ascension day; [4] *De anima*, if read with the books on nature, on the feast of the Ascension, if with the logical texts, on the feast of the Annunciation of the blessed Virgin; *De generatione* on the feast of the Chair of St. Peter; [5] *De causis* in seven weeks; *De sensu et sensato* in six weeks; *De sompno et vigilia* in five weeks; *De plantis* in five weeks; *De memoria et reminiscentia* in two weeks; *De differentia spiritus et animae* in two weeks; *De morte et vita* in one week. Moreover, if masters begin to read the said books at another time than the feast of St. Remy, they shall allow as much time for lecturing on them as is indicated above. Moreover, each of the said texts, if read by itself, not with another text, can be finished in half the time of lecturing assigned above. It will not be permitted anyone to finish the said texts in less time, but anyone may take more time. Moreover, if anyone reads some portion of a text, so that he does not wish, or is unable, to complete the whole of it, he shall read that portion in a corresponding amount of time.

If a bachelor shall incept before the feast of St. Denis,[6] he may end his lectures with those resuming on the feast of the blessed Remy. Those who begin after the feast of St. Denis shall finish their texts by as much later as they began later than others. Each in good faith shall according to his estimate portion out his text proportionally to the time allowed for his lectures. Further, no one shall be allowed to give more than two ordinary lectures,[7] nor to make them extraordinary, nor to give them except at the ordinary hour and in ordinary wise.

Moreover, from the feast of St. John the Baptist till the feast of St. Remy each shall arrange his lectures as shall seem most convenient for himself and his auditors. Also no one shall presume to give more than two cursory lectures on any day when lectures are held, nor more than three on a day when there are not regular lectures, nor to begin any course until he has finished the preceding course, unless he shall have been detained by serious illness over fifteen days or shall have been out of town for good reason more than fifteen days, or if the scholars do not want to hear him further. Also, no one shall be permitted to deliver any lectures on the days of the apostles and evangelists or on the three days immediately following Christmas, Easter, and Pentecost, or after the third hour on the eve

---

[4] A movable feast, forty days after Easter, usually in May.   [5] February 22.
[6] October 9.   [7] Or, give ordinary lectures more than twice.

of those three days. These things, moreover, we have decreed and ordained to be observed inviolate. Let no one, therefore, infringe this page of our ordinance or rashly go against it. But should anyone presume to attempt this, let him know that he will incur the wrath of the whole university and suspension of lectures for a year. In testimony and support of which thing we have decreed that the present letter be sealed with the seals of the four nations by their consent. Given in the year 1254 on the Friday before Palm Sunday.

29

ODOFREDUS ANNOUNCES HIS LAW LECTURES AT BOLOGNA

Savigny, *Geschichte des römischen Rechts im Mittelalter*, III, 1822, pp. 501–2, 511.

If you please, I will begin the *Old Digest* [1] on the eighth day or thereabouts after the feast of St. Michael [2] and I will finish it entire with all ordinary and extraordinary, Providence permitting, in the middle of August or thereabouts. The *Code* [3] I will always begin within about a fortnight of the feast of St. Michael and I will finish it with all ordinary and extraordinary, Providence permitting, on the first of August or thereabouts. The extraordinary lectures used not to be given by the doctors. And so all scholars including the unskilled and novices will be able to make good progress with me, for they will

---

[1] The *Old Digest*, like the Old Logic, was the portion of the text which had been longest known and of which the study was earliest revived. It comprised books 1–28 and the first two titles of book 29. The *New Digest* included the closing books of Justinian's compendium of Roman legal literature. The intervening section from book 29, titulus 3, to book 38, titulus 3, was called the *Infortiatum* and, like the other two, was usually made the subject of a distinct course of lectures.

Johannes Jacobus Canis, *De modo studendi in utroque iure*, Padua, 1476, 1485, 1488, tells us that the *Old Digest* was bound in white; the *New Digest*, in red; the *Infortiatum*, in pitch black; the first nine books of the *Code*, in green.

[2] September 29.

[3] The code of Justinian. Other books of civil law that were lectured on were *The Three Books* (*Tres libri*), a detached part of the *Code;* the *Volumen*, consisting of Justinian's *Institutes* and the *Authentica*, a Latin translation of the *Novels* of Justinian, which were new laws issued by him in Greek; and *The Book of Fiefs* (*Liber feudorum*), a manual of Lombard law.

hear their text as a whole, nor will anything be left out, as was once done in this region, indeed was the usual practice. For I shall teach the unskilled and novices but also the advanced students. For the unskilled will be able to make satisfactory progress in the position of the case and exposition of the letter; the advanced students can become more erudite in the subtleties of questions and contrarieties. I shall also read all the glosses, which was not done before my time. . . .

For it is my purpose to teach you faithfully and in a kindly manner, in which instruction the following order has customarily been observed by the ancient and modern doctors and particularly by my master, which method I shall retain. First, I shall give you the summaries of each title before I come to the text. Second, I shall put forth well and distinctly and in the best terms I can the purport of each law. Third, I shall read the text in order to correct it. Fourth, I shall briefly restate the meaning. Fifth, I shall solve conflicts, adding general matters (which are commonly called *brocardica*) and subtle and useful distinctions and questions with the solutions, so far as divine Providence shall assist me. And if any law is deserving of a review by reason of its fame or difficulty, I shall reserve it for an afternoon review.

30

PAPAL PRIVILEGE TO SALAMANCA, 1255

Chartularium universitatis Parisiensis, I, 291.

Alexander, bishop, servant of the servants of God, to his cherished sons of the university of masters and scholars at Salamanca, greeting and apostolic benediction. We think it worthy and fitting that those who till the field of study with daily lectures, in order that they may be able to behold the pearl of science, should rejoice to find us favorable and benign to their petitions, so that their studies may be pursued the more freely, as they feel themselves fortified with apostolic favor. Since therefore, as we have learned from the tenor of your petition, it sometimes happens that those who have been examined and approved at the university of Salamanca, although they are found fit to teach in any faculty, are by no means permitted to teach elsewhere unless they undergo another examination in that faculty, in order that they may not have to undergo examination as often as they happen to teach elsewhere, you have petitioned apostolic benignity to provide for your quiet in this. We therefore, moved by the supplications of our dearest son in Christ, the illustrious king of Castile and Leon, and by your own, grant by authority of these presents to you and your successors that, after any of the masters and scholars in the university of Salamanca in any faculty shall have been found qualified to teach by a legitimate preceding examination, he shall be able to teach in any university except only Paris and Bologna in the same faculty for which he has already undergone examination without further examination or contradiction of anyone. *Nulli ergo,* etc. Given at Anagni, September 22, first year [of our pontificate].

31

STUDY OF ORIENTAL LANGUAGES, 1256

Chartularium universitatis Parisiensis, I, 317-18.

To all Friars Preachers cherished in the Son of God, brother Humbert, their useless servant, greeting and joy in the Holy Spirit. The care of the regimen of your souls imposed on my frailty requires that I not merely seek with paternal solicitude to urge you on to better things with holy exhortations, but in maternal affection I mean to console you for the time being that your spirits, comforted in the Lord, may be stronger to endure all. Hence it is, dearest ones, that having every solicitude for you as to your common consolation, I have thought right to notify you of certain matters concerning the progress of the Order and salvation of souls which it was a great solace to me to learn of, in order that you may rejoice with me in the Lord. Lo, beloved, as has come to our attention by numerous letters of many in true narration, friars are now multiplied through the world by the grace of Him who called them, and they flourish marvelously before God and men, and bring forth much fruit in other important respects, while the number of so great a multitude sufficiently cared for the small matter of correcting grave excesses in our recent chapter. Moreover, who could fully express with how great favor of goodwill our order, and we who stand in holy calling, is pursued by the holy

Roman church? With how great benevolence how many prelates embrace us? With how great honor of veneration kings, princes and magnates, with how great charity almost all the religious, treat us? Finally, how great devotion the Christian people show everywhere on earth? Yet those few sons of perdition who, imitating the apostate angel, have left their home, not only with him will pay eternal penalties but also in the present age by just judgment of God with their eyes foretasting the beginnings of all pains, covered with confusion and ignominy, will close a wretched life with a more miserable exit, as is quite clear to you by various cases.

For we have written at the last chapter that brothers who have made the decision to leave their own nation and cross to barbarous nations and to sweat at learning letters and foreign tongues to spread the name of our lord Jesus Christ and his glory should make known their intention to us. O how much your charity would rejoice together with me over the holy fervor of the brothers, if you knew how many and how great from various provinces have offered themselves with most ardent desire for labors of this sort, scorning even the fear of death. Nor should one despair of improvement even in those who are seduced by varied errors, since much fruit now appears in them manifestly. Those brothers indeed have made progress and make progress who labor in divers provinces at the extirpation of wicked heresy, to such an extent that a little while ago it seemed incredible that as much could be accomplished as the Lord has already deigned to work through them in two years and less. Of the Cumani, about whom the brothers were solicitous, a great multitude has been baptized. Of the Maronites, too, tribes long schismatic and subversive are said to have offered their books for correction entirely at the will of the brothers of the province of the Holy Land, who were anxious for their rectification. Moreover, the brothers who set out for the Tartars have sent me tidings of their prosperous journey. Our brothers of great authority and men of marvelous virtues, who now among the Georgians in remotest parts of the Orient for eighteen years and more have lived a life of greatest hardship, reproach our miserable inertia by their letters filled with the ardor of charity and marvelous examples. In Spanish parts the friars who now for many years have studied Arabic among the Saracens, not only progress laudably in that language but, what is more laudable, their residence makes for salvation to the very Saracens, as is shown by many who have already received the grace of baptism. The vast nation of Prussians, recently subjugated to Christian rule, in many cases are leaving pagan rites and hastening to the grace of baptism. Who then considering these things will not hope for harvest in erring nations?

32

DOMINICANS AND EDUCATION, 1259

STATUTE CONCERNING STUDIES IN THE ORDER OF PREACHERS

Chartularium universitatis Parisiensis, I, 385–86.

At Paris license of lecturing in theology should not be sought for any brother, nor should one licensed incept, nor one lecturing leave off, except by advice of the master, if he shall be in the province of France, or by advice of the provincial prior of France, if the master of the order is not in France.

At Valenciennes in the year of the Lord 1259 by mandate of the master and those on the committee for education it was ordained by brothers Bonhomme, Florentius, Albertus Teutonicus,[1] Thomas Aquinas, Petrus de Tarantasia,[2] masters of theology at Paris, who were present at the said chapter, that lecturers should not be occupied with acts and business by which they would be taken from their lectures.

Also, that provincial priors should seek diligently for youths apt for study, who could make rapid progress, and promote them in the university.

Also, that such a search be made annually by visitors in single convents and reported to the provincial chapter.

Also, that brothers should not be sent to universities, except those of good character and likely to make progress.

Also, that, if in any province lecturers cannot be had in all convents, it shall at least be provided that brothers, and especially youths, do not remain always in those convents but be sent to places where there are lecturers.

Also that, if lecturers cannot be found qualified to lecture publicly,

---

[1] That is, Albertus Magnus.   [2] Later pope Innocent V.

at least some be provided to give private lectures or histories or a *Summa* of cases, or something else of that sort, so that the brothers may not be idle.

Also, that young brothers apt for study be spared from discourses and other occupations, so as not to withdraw them from study.

Also, that there be established in provinces which require it some school of arts or place where youth are instructed.

Also, that brothers who stay away from classes be severely punished.

Also, that the brothers at the hour of lecture shall not be occupied in celebrating masses or other things of this sort nor go to town except for real necessity.

Also, that even the priors attend classes, like the other brothers, when they conveniently can.

Also, that lecturers on vacation attend classes and especially disputations.

Also, that lecturers be not made either preachers or confessors, unless they are capable of performing offices of this sort without notable peril.

Also, that priors and visitors and the masters of the brothers take pains to inquire carefully how the brothers and especially the young are occupied with study and what progress they are making, and punish the negligent.

Also, that lecturers continue their lectures as much as possible.

Also, that the visitors each year diligently inquire of the lecturers how much they lecture in a year and how many questions they have disputed and also determined, and how many convents of their visitation lack lecturers. And that whatever they shall find about this they shall report to the provincial chapter; and also the more notable defects which they have found the provincial prior and representatives shall refer afterwards to the chapter general.

Also, that in every province each year in each provincial chapter it be ordained how to provide for the students of their province who are sent to some university.

Also, the visitors shall diligently inquire how provision is made for the students and report notable defects to the provincial chapter by which an efficacious remedy shall be applied.

Also, provision shall be made that every lecturer occupying a professorial chair shall have a bachelor who shall lecture under him.

Also, that brothers carry to class the books which are read in class, if they have them, and no others.

Also, that in every convent where there is a lecturer there be instituted some brother who shall diligently repeat, provided there is anyone qualified in the convent.

Also, that repetitions be made concerning questions and collations concerning questions once a week, where this can be conveniently observed.

33

OFFICE OF UNIVERSITY BEDELL, PARIS

Chartularium universitatis Parisiensis, I, 418.

These are the statutes which the bedells of the university of Paris obligate themselves faithfully to observe, giving personal security. They ought to attend the opening lecture of each person incepting, poor or otherwise, from beginning to end, unless it is well known that they have been sent by the person incepting or the proctor of his nation on some special errand or for some special common examination of the nation, or unless they have to attend funeral obsequies, or unless their own bodily infirmity prevents them, or unless they are detained by some other legitimate and notorious occasion, if there can be any other than those specified. If, however, they absent themselves unexcused by any of the said occasions, they ought to forfeit their portion of that purse which he gives who incepts, which portion, I say, should go to the proctor of the said bedell who forfeits it. Also, if it is enjoined upon any bedell to call a meeting either special or general, and it can be proved by three or four masters that he has not cited them, he should know that he will similarly forfeit a portion of each purse, two solidi, which portion likewise will go to the proctor of that nation. Also, if he ought to announce a course and it can be proved that he has failed to go to all classes, he should know that he will incur the same penalty and same loss in the same manner as aforesaid. Also, each bedell ought early in the morning on each day to visit the classes not only of the rector or his own proctor but also of every proctor of every nation, which if he does not do, let him know that he will incur the same loss in the same manner. Also, if he shall fail to attend the common examination of anyone of his nation or shall be proved to have betrayed the university's secrets, let him know that he shall forfeit one purse as has been said. Also, if he is absent on Friday at the vespers of his nation, he shall lose two pence and for mass two. Also, if he does not have a calendar and is deficient in announcing to individuals a Feast which is not well known, or even in not preventing disputation when he should, for each such offense he shall forfeit four pence, all which pence the proctor of the nation of the delinquent bedell should keep for the use of his nation.

34

CRITICISM OF UNIVERSITIES BY HUMBERT DE ROMANS

As paraphrased by Antonino, archbishop of Florence, 1446–1459, *Summa theologiae*, II, 5, 2, 12.

Humbert de Romans was the fifth general of the Dominican order from 1254 to 1263. His letter of 1256 to the order on the study of oriental languages is included in Selection 31. The work here cited by Antonino is his *Expositio super regulam S. P. Augustini, Maxima bibliotheca patrum*, XXV, 632–34. Strictly speaking, Humbert's criticisms were rather of the studies of members of religious orders.

Umbertus in his *Exposition of the Rule of the Blessed Augustine*, makes these criticisms of universities:

1. Seeking to know the incomprehensible, which cannot be clearly understood either by philosophical reasons or from holy scripture, as the mystery of the Trinity or sacrament of the Eucharist or predestination or knowledge of oneself and others, contrary to that verse of *Romans* XI, "O the heights of the riches of the wisdom and knowledge of God! how incomprehensible are His judgments!" [1]

2. Investigating things beyond one's capacity, although in themselves intelligible as speculative. . . .[2]

3. Learning things curious and subtle but of little use. . . .

---

[1] Verse 33.

[2] Here and in each of the following criticisms a verse of the Bible is quoted, as in the foregoing paragraph.

4. Seeking to discover new inventions and dismissing the determination of ancient goods. . . .

5. Studying under many faculties—now philosophy, now medicine, now theology, now law—and perfecting oneself in none. . . .

6. Committing nothing to memory but reading everything cursorily and, as it were, without understanding, or so confident of their memory that they note nothing in writings to the contrary. . . .

7. Not listening to others when one might, nor conferring with others, nor asking questions on doubtful points. . . .

8. Excessive concentration upon the learning of certain things, while others are neglected. . . .

9. Not setting before oneself a definite goal in one's study, such as the honor of God, the salvation of one's neighbors, one's own edification, or at least to study with temporal gain in view as an advocate or physician, whereby one may sustain oneself and one's household. . . .

10. Not putting into practice the good one has learned. . . .

35

PROVISION FOR FIVE MASTERS WHO KNOW FLEMISH, 1266

Chartularium universitatis Parisiensis, I, 460.

To all who shall see the present letters the university of masters and scholars at Paris sends greeting in the Lord. Since our cherished Nicholas, archdeacon of the church of Tournai in Flanders, gave five hundred livres Parisian to master Robert of Sorbonne, canon of Paris, provisor of the congregation of poor masters studying at Paris in the theological faculty, to invest for the support of the mentioned masters, we, wishing to reply in kind to his benevolence, have conceded that the same archdeacon, so long as he lives, may place each year in the house of the said masters five masters of good reputation and honest conversation studying in theology who have a good knowledge of the Flemish idiom, which is known to be the native language in his archdeaconry. Provision is to be made for the said masters as for the others and shall be in the future, so that the same masters trained in divine science and informed in morals from association with the good, teaching equally by word and example in the localities to which they may be called, shall bring forth fruit which does not perish. After the death of the same archdeacon we concede full power to the bishop of Tournai then in office either by himself or the archdeacon of Flanders, if he shall deem him fit therefor, similarly to place each year in the said house masters of the said Flemish idiom to the number before specified, yet so that, if the provisor of the said house signifies in good faith to the said archdeacon or bishop that one or more of the said masters is unqualified, the same provisor may eject them, and the archdeacon and bishop may substitute others for them. Also, the said masters should be presented anew the following year, no matter how qualified they may have been. Given in the year of the Lord 1266, the month of October.

36

FOUNDATION AND REGULATION OF THE COLLEGE OF THE TREASURER, 1268 AND 1280

Chartularium universitatis Parisiensis, I, 476–78, 584–85.

November, 1268

To all who shall see these, William of Sâone, treasurer of the church of Rouen, greeting in the Lord. You should know that, since I have acquired, both in the city of Rouen and outside, possessions and rents to the amount of £120 17s. 5d. of Tours, of which express mention is made in letters of the lord king, to be committed to pious uses and the good of the poor, I, of healthy body and sane mind, wishing, from the wealth given me by God and acquired, to apply some to the uses of the church universal and the advantage of the poor, especially in those things which seem directly to regard the profit of souls, of the said goods thus ordain and dispose even by donation while living, namely, that twelve students of theology, if the amount of goods and time permit, remaining together in one house at Paris or elsewhere where a university is located, shall have each three solidi of Paris per week through 45 weeks, the term beginning from the feast of St. Denis or thereabouts. Also, that twelve other poor students in liberal arts, if sometime there may be, shall have from the said rents 25 pounds of Tours for housing and for bread with the goodwill of the said theologians. I will further and ordain that all the said scholars be chosen, when the need arises, by the two archdeacons of Grand-Caux and Petit-Caux . . . and that the said scholars should be from Grand-Caux and Petit-Caux, if in those two places they find sufficient and fit persons, or if not in the two Caux, at least from the whole diocese of Rouen. And such shall be chosen, so far as the theologians are concerned, as have taught well in liberal arts, and, so far as both are concerned, as are praiseworthy and upright in morals.

I further will and ordain that, if the said theologians or any of them shall have studied theology six years or have secured some sufficient benefice, then others shall be chosen in their place . . . , unless one of them reaches such a repute for knowledge that he can give public lectures in the classroom of some master of theology, in which case let him remain, if he will, until he is able to ascend the magisterial throne. . . .

I further will and ordain that two of the said theologians, to be selected similarly, remain during the vacation period, namely for seven weeks, to guard the house and its contents.

Moreover, for the support of the said theologians I give by donation, while living, the house which I bought at Paris from William called Fructuarius near the Harp in the parish of St. Severinus. I give to the same for the use of all and each a complete theological *Corpus:* namely, Bibles with text only but complete, also all the books glossed and some in duplicate, with sufficient *Postillae* and lectures, and certain moral *Summae,* with sermons of varied compilation. Also several volumes of the *Sentences* with *Summae* and several sets of *Questions.* Also several originals and many other writings of which all the names are contained in a letter sealed with my seal.

And the said theologians shall stay together for convenience in using the library and making collations in turn and for many other reasons. And the liberal arts students, if there are any, shall likewise stay together both for convenience in study and for good behavior and in token of probity. Also, the said theologians shall swear annually to keep the statutes which I have made for them, as is contained more fully in my letters giving them in detail. . . .

August 18, 1280

To all who shall see these, William of Sâone, treasurer of Rouen, greeting in the Lord. Know that we have regulated the life of our scholars studying at Paris in this way which follows. First, we will that those who have scholarships give all their time to theology and make visible progress, having the proper books and other things essential. And if they have clerics working for them in town or if they labor for others in another subject of study, we do not wish to give them a scholarship, since our intention is to provide merely for true and pure poor students who study assiduously and to support them. We say the same of those who have acquired some sufficient benefice, on receiving which they should give way to the poverty of others. Also, if any one of them should be contentious or quarrelsome, impeding the others and disturbing their peace, we do not wish to continue his scholarship, unless he shall speedily correct himself. We say the same of those who have been of evil life or repute, and we wish that the others be required to reveal such to us or to someone by whom we may be informed, because we have no intention of providing for the perverse and unstudious and ribald and gamesters or haunters of whores and taverns, but for good and true scholars, through whom provision may be made for the church and salvation of souls.

Also, we do not want any rich student to live with them, who may provoke them to spending too much or impede their progress. If, however, our said scholars receive some quiet rich student among them, we will that they be required to pay twenty solidi Parisian for his room. Also, we do not want anyone to live with them who does not give all his time to theology. Also, we are unwilling that the books be lent about town to be copied or even studied, because thus they might be lost or mutilated or soiled, and we want the care of them entrusted to persons who can answer for them fully and who shall distribute and divide them among the rest as shall seem expedient.[1]

We also will and ordain that the senior scholar, once a week on Sunday or other feast day, shall interview the rest at some hour convenient to him and, when all have gathered in his presence, shall see and hear how they have been doing and shall correct them, if he

---

[1] Medieval standard texts or exemplars were often in loose sections (*peciae*) of eight pages each, which a student could borrow and copy or have copied one at a time. See Jean Destrez, *La Pecia dans les manuscrits universitaires du XIIIe et du XIVe siècles*, 1935. See also Selection 66 below on *Peciarii* at Bologna.

finds any excess among them. And if any one of them ought to be expelled, this should be done with the counsel of the rest, and if he shall have found anyone rebellious or not making progress, they shall expel him with severity.

And we wish that all, at least while in the house, speak Latin. And we want the others to be required to tell the truth about each equal or to accuse others, unless of their own accord these recognize and confess their fault, in which case they shall be dealt with more gently and leniently.

So far as food is concerned, they should not be divided but should receive together what the house provides, and he who has done contrary shall be expelled.

Also, we will that after they have been licensed in theology, they lecture only two years, because beyond that we are unwilling to give them anything, since our intention is merely to put them in a position to attain the degree of master of theology. Also, if any one of them binds himself to the service of any rich man or other, we do not wish to give him anything. Also, if any one of them after getting his scholarship wants to attend lectures in lucrative sciences, we do not wish to give him anything, because our intention is to aid good students and not those who are not apt to advance in theology. . . .

37

CRIMINAL CLERKS AT PARIS, 1269

PROCLAMATION OF THE OFFICIAL OF THE EPIS-
COPAL COURT OF PARIS AGAINST CLERKS AND
SCHOLARS WHO GO ABOUT PARIS ARMED BY
DAY AND NIGHT AND COMMIT CRIMES:
JANUARY 11, 1269

Chartularium universitatis Parisiensis, I, 481–82.

The official of the court of Paris to all the rectors of churches, masters and scholars residing in the city and suburb of Paris, to whom the present letters may come, greeting in the Lord. A frequent and continual complaint has gone the rounds that there are in Paris some clerks and scholars, likewise their servants, trusting in the folly of the same clerks, unmindful of their salvation, not having God before their eyes, who, under pretense of leading the scholastic life, more and more often perpetrate unlawful and criminal acts, relying on their arms: namely, that by day and night they atrociously wound or kill many persons, rape women, oppress virgins, break into inns, also repeatedly committing robberies and many other enormities hateful to God. And since they attempt these and other crimes relying on their arms, we, having in mind the decree of the supreme pontiff in which it is warned that clerks bearing arms will be excommunicated, also having in mind that our predecessors sometimes excommunicated those who went about thus, and in view of the ,fact that this is so notorious and manifest that it cannot be concealed by any evasion and that their proclamation was not revoked, wishing to meet so great evils and to provide for the peace and tranquillity of students and others who wish to live at peace, at the instance of many good men and by their advice do excommunicate in writing clerks and scholars and their servants who go about Paris by day or night armed, unless by permission of the reverend bishop of Paris or ourself. We also excommunicate in writing those who rape women, break into inns, oppress virgins, likewise all those who have banded together for this purpose. No less do we excommunicate all those who have known anything about the aforesaid, unless within seven days from the time of their information, after the proclamation issued against the aforesaid has come to their notice, they shall have revealed what they know to the said reverend bishop or ourselves and have submitted to fitting emendation. Nevertheless we specially reserve to the lord bishop or ourselves the right to absolve clerks excommunicated for the aforesaid reasons.

But inasmuch as some clerks and scholars and their servants have borne arms in Paris, coming there from their parts or returning to their parts, and likewise certain others, knowing that clerks, scholars and their servants have borne arms in Paris, fear that for the said reasons they have incurred the said penalty of excommunication, we do declare herewith that it neither is nor was our intention that those clerks, scholars and their servants should be liable to the said sentence who, coming to Paris for study and bearing arms on the way, on first entering the city bear the same to their lodgings, nor, further, those, wishing to return home or setting out on useful and honest business more than one day's journey from the city of Paris, who have borne such arms going and returning while they were outside the city. We further declare that in the clause in which it is said, "We excommunicate all those who have known anything about the aforesaid," etc., we do not understand that word, *aforesaid*, to refer to all and each of the aforesaid but to the clauses immediately preceding, namely, concerning those who rape women, break into inns, oppress virgins and those who band together for these ends. Moreover, you shall so observe the present mandate that you cannot be charged with or punished for disobedience. Given in the year 1268 A.D., the Friday following Epiphany.

38

THIRTEEN ERRORS CONDEMNED BY STEPHEN, BISHOP OF PARIS, 1270

Chartularium universitatis Parisiensis, I, 486–87.

These are the errors condemned and excommunicated with all who taught or asserted them knowingly by Stephen, bishop of Paris, in the year of the Lord 1270, the Wednesday after the feast of the blessed Nicholas in the winter.[1]

The first article is: That the intellect of all men is one and the same in number.[2]

2. That this is false or inappropriate: Man understands.

3. That the will of man wills or chooses from necessity.

4. That all things which are done here below depend upon the necessity of the celestial bodies.

5. That the world is eternal.

6. That there never was a first man.

7. That the soul, which is the form of man as a human being, is corrupted when the body is corrupted.

8. That the soul separated after death does not suffer from corporal fire.

9. That free will is a passive power, not active; and that it is moved necessarily by appetite.

---

[1] December 10, St. Nicholas day being December 6.

[2] The allusion is to the doctrine of the unity of the intellect taught by Averroes.

10. That God does not know things in particular.

11. That God does not know other things than Himself.

12. That human actions are not ruled by divine Providence.

13. That God cannot give immortality or incorruptibility to a corruptible or mortal thing.

39

VARIOUS RULES OF THE MEDICAL FACULTY, PARIS, 1270–1274

Chartularium universitatis Parisiensis, I, 516–18.

Let it be known that bachelors in the faculty of medicine wishing to open a course for the first time are held on oath to all the following requirements. They shall give security that they will observe the ordinances, statutes, honors and customs of the faculty which shall be indicated to them by the dean or someone acting in the dean's place or by the whole faculty. Also they shall assure the dean or his *locum tenens* or before the whole faculty that they have attended lectures in medicine for three years and are in their fourth year of which they have attended for five months. And if for each of the said years the bachelor has not spent nine months in the study of medicine, nevertheless the license for giving a lecture course shall be granted him provided he has diligently studied in the said science at Paris for thirty-two months, that is, hearing ordinary lectures and not counting in time of vacations. Also, they shall swear that they responded twice concerning a question in the classes of two masters, understanding thereby a formal disputation and not at a lecture, or at least once in a general disputation. Also, they shall swear that the text on which they are to lecture cursorily they have heard ordinarily. Also they shall give the four purses which are sought from a bachelor who wishes to offer a new course before all oaths are taken. Also to the bedell one purse at least. Also, they shall pledge that on each Sabbath day they will attend mass, just as masters do, so long as they are lecturing, this in penalty of twopence.

This is the form of licenciating bachelors in medicine. First the master in charge of the bachelor should testify to the chancellor in the presence of masters summoned for this purpose as to the fitness of the bachelor to be licensed. The duration of his attendance he ought to prove by two witnesses at least, and the length of time that he should have attended lectures is five years and a half, if he taught or was a licentiate in arts, or six if he was not. The form as to texts heard is that he should have heard twice in ordinary lectures the art of medicine [1] and once cursorily except the *Urines* of Theophilus, which it is enough to have heard once ordinarily or cursorily; the *Viaticum* [2] twice in ordinary lectures, the other books of Isaac once in ordinary, twice cursorily, except the *Particular Diets* which it is sufficient to have heard cursorily or ordinarily; the *Antidotarium Nicholai* [3] once. The *Verses* of Egidius [4] are not on the form. Also he should have read one book of theory and another of practice. And to this he should swear; if, moreover, anyone is convicted of perjury or lying, he can be refused the licentiate.

Let it be known that bachelors in medicine who wish to incept are held on oath to the following requirements. For they shall give faith that they will keep the ordinance as to the mass made by the masters teaching in the faculty of medicine and will ever observe the same while they are teachers. Also, they shall give faith that they have heard no bachelor in the faculty of medicine for the sake of examination except in their own classes or in the classes of others in which masters are gathered because some bachelor is incepting. Also, before all oaths four purses shall be sought from them, and before they incept they must give the servant at least twenty solidi Parisian. Also they must swear that they will observe the customs and statutes of the faculty.

No master should give cursory lectures in the morning. No one should lecture on a general feast day, neither master nor bachelor. Also, no one should lecture cursorily from All Saints to Lent on a day for disputations. Also, they should not dispute on the eve of a solemn feast. Also, according as masters incept, so it is ordered. Also, no one should engage in disputation on the first day of lectures.

[1] As to the works comprised by this phrase see Haskins, *Studies in Medieval Science*, 1924, p. 369, n. 63.

[2] Translated into Latin by Constantinus Africanus in the eleventh century.

[3] A standard text by an author as yet unidentified.

[4] That is, Gilles de Corbeil, who wrote a work on urines in verse.

40

MEDICAL RESTRICTIONS UPON JEWS, SURGEONS AND PHARMACISTS, PARIS, 1271

Chartularium universitatis Parisiensis, I, 488–90.

In the same year, namely 1271, when master J. de Racheroles was dean of the medical faculty, the masters of the said faculty ordained and made a statute against those practising in or about Paris of the following tenor.

In the name of God, Amen. Since some not yet advanced in the art of medicine and quite ignorant of the causes of medical procedure by shameful and brazen usurpation assume to themselves at Paris the office of practice, administering, without consulting skilled persons, to all comers and rashly any medicines whatever even violent ones, ignoring utterly what should be used as a base, what as a bridle, what as a spur in such medicines, which out of their own heads they wretchedly administer to simple men and so by their treatments, made not according to art but rather by chance and fortune, have criminally handed over many to the suffering of death, which is at the peril of their souls, and especially since they indubitably incur in this the sentence of excommunication launched by authority of the Official in Paris, as manifestly appears from the letter of the said Official, which also is no small peril to all residents of Paris and further tends to the disgrace and grave infamy of all skilled in medicine: therefore, we doctors teaching in the medical faculty at Paris at the devout and pious supplications of many, namely, the religious, clergy, scholars, likewise many citizens of Paris, wishing to check so many errors, perils and scandals, confirm a statute of ours made long since, supported by the said letters of the Official and also by royal ones, strengthened and confirmed too in the name of the faculty by our oaths, in this wise, prohibiting namely under the penalty contained in the said letters of the Official of Paris and of the king, likewise under every penalty allowed us by both laws, secular and ecclesiastical, that no Jew or Jewess presume to operate surgically or medicinally on any person of catholic faith.

Also, since certain manual operators make or possess some confections but totally ignore their cause and reason, nay do not even know how to administer them and the relation which medicines have to disease, especially in all particular respects, since those matters are reserved exclusively to the industry of the skilled physician, yet these manual artisans thrusting their sickle into alien crops participate, as we are assured by dependable testimony, in certain cases rashly and to public scandal, in this likewise incurring sentence of perjuries and excommunication: therefore we strictly prohibit that any male or female surgeon, apothecary or herbalist, by their oaths presume to exceed the limits or bounds of their craft secretly or publicly or in any way whatsoever, so that the surgeon engage only in manual practice and as pertains to it, the apothecary or herbalist only in mixing drugs which are to be administered only by masters in medicine or by their license. And lest any mistake be made, we ordain that the apothecary or herbalist by our dean or seal certify the decree of the faculty in these matters and other questions if any come up, excluding however from the said statute those who do not practice at Paris or in the vicinity nor even rent a house, who shall be believed on their oath. Also none of the aforesaid shall visit any sick person to administer to him any alterative medicine or laxative or anything else that pertains to a physician, nor advise it to be administered or procure it, except through a master in medicine as above specified. And this we enjoin on them on their oath and under the aforesaid penalty in the way above stated, also under privation of our prescriptions of every kind. Under the same penalties we also command that none of them presume to administer any of the said medicines to healthy men without the presence of a master, except those which are wont to be sold commonly, of which sort are sugar of rose, *dragia communis*, rose water and the like, excluding them from every way and method of treatment in which medical skill is called for.

And since there are some who simultaneously seek knowledge and the mode of knowing, which is very inconvenient, since their error, not small even in the beginning, is very great in the end, therefore under the said penalties and specially under privation of any promotion held or to be held in the faculty of medicine we strictly forbid scholars each and all, that any one of them to a well or sick person administer any drug comforting, alterative or even laxative without the presence of some master in medicine, or even visit, except once, unless there is with him some master to direct him and show the way to work. And if anyone shall know of anyone operating contrary to the said statute, he shall secretly reveal it on oath to our dean or at least to some master who is teaching, and he to whom the information is given shall shield the informer.

41

ORTHODOXY ENFORCED AT PARIS, 1272

STATUTE OF THE FACULTY OF ARTS AGAINST ARTISTS TREATING THEOLOGICAL QUESTIONS AND THAT NO ONE SHALL DARE TO DETERMINE AGAINST THE FAITH QUESTIONS WHICH TOUCH THE FAITH AS WELL AS PHILOSOPHY

Chartularium universitatis Parisiensis, I, 499–500.

To each and all of the sons of holy mother church who now and in the future shall see the present page, the masters of logical science or professors of natural science at Paris, each and all, who hold and observe the statute and ordinance of the venerable father Symon by divine permission cardinal priest of the title of St. Cecilia, legate of the apostolic see, made after separate deliberation of the nations, and who adhere expressly and entirely to the opinion of the seven judges appointed by the same legate in the same statute, greeting in the Saviour of all. All should know that we masters, each and all, from the preceding abundant and considered advice and deliberation of good men concerning this, wishing with all our power to avoid present and future dangers which by occasion of this sort might in the future befall our faculty, by common consent, no one of us contradicting, on the Friday preceding the Sunday on which is sung *Rejoice Jerusalem*, the masters one and all being convoked for this purpose in the church of Ste. Geneviève at Paris, decree and ordain that no master or bachelor of our faculty should presume to determine or even to dispute any purely theological question, as concerning the Trinity and incarnation and similar matters, since this would be transgressing the limits assigned him, for the Philosopher says that it is utterly improper for a non-geometer to dispute with a geometer.

But if anyone shall have so presumed, unless within three days after he has been warned or required by us he shall have been willing to revoke publicly his presumption in the classes or public disputation where he first disputed the said question, henceforth he shall be forever deprived of our society. We decree further and ordain that, if anyone shall have disputed at Paris any question which seems to touch both faith and philosophy, if he shall have determined it contrary to the faith, henceforth he shall forever be deprived of our society as a heretic, unless he shall have been at pains humbly and devoutly to revoke his error and his heresy, within three days after our warning, in full congregation or elsewhere where it shall seem to us expedient. Adding further that, if any master or bachelor of our faculty reads or disputes any difficult passages or any questions which seem to undermine the faith, he shall refute the arguments or text so far as they are against the faith or concede that they are absolutely false and entirely erroneous, and he shall not presume to dispute or lecture further upon this sort of difficulties, either in the text or in authorities, but shall pass over them entirely as erroneous. But if anyone shall be rebellious in this, he shall be punished by a penalty which in the judgment of our faculty suits his fault and is due. Moreover, in order that all these may be inviolably observed, we masters, one and all, have sworn on our personal security in the hand of the rector of our faculty and we all have spontaneously agreed to be so bound. In memory of which we have caused this same statute to be inscribed and so ordered in the register of our faculty in the same words. Moreover, every rector henceforth to be created in the faculty shall swear that he will cause all the bachelors about to incept in our faculty to bind themselves to this same thing, swearing on their personal security in his hand. Given at Paris the year of the Lord 1271, the first day of April.[1]

The following passage from the *Perscrutationes physicales* or commentary on the eight books of the *Physics* of Aristotle by Ludovicus Coronel, composed between 1506 and 1511,[2] shows that, while the above statute was

[1] As Easter fell at that time after the first of April, the year is 1272 according to our reckoning.

[2] In the edition of Lyons, 1530, which I have used, three other forms of the title are given: *Perscrutationes physices*, *Physica Coronel*, and *Physice perscrutationes egregii interpretis magistri Ludovici Coronel Hispani Segoviensis diligenter castigate*. Prostant Lugduni in edibus Jacobi Giunti in vico Mercuriali, 1530. The passage to be quoted occurs at fols. xcii verso, col. 2–xciii recto, col. 1.

still enforced in the days of Buridan in the middle of the fourteenth century, it had become obsolete before the close of the fifteenth century.

After stating that God could supernaturally produce a vacuum, Coronel cites Buridan's commentary on the *Physics*, book IV, question 8.

For he says that many of our masters blamed him for sometimes mingling certain theological matters with physical questions, of which sort is whether this or that which is beyond the power of nature lies within divine power, since to discuss this does not pertain to artists. But he replying humbly said that he would prefer not to be restricted to this. But all the masters, he says, when they incept in arts, swear that they will dispute no purely theological question such as concerning the Trinity and incarnation, and they further swear that, if they chance to dispute or determine a question which touches faith and philosophy, they will determine it in favor of the faith. And they will overthrow the reasons to the contrary as they shall seem to them able to be overthrown. Moreover, it is clear, he says, that if any question touches the faith it is this one whether there can be a vacuum; therefore, if he is going to debate it, he must state what he thinks should be said about it according to theology or perjure himself.

These remarks of Buridan have astonished me, first, that our masters blamed him, for from the declaration of this term, *vacuum*, to conclude that it cannot be produced naturally but can happen supernaturally seems in no way blameworthy. In the second place, Buridan's method of reply, granting that our masters were justified in blaming him, was not satisfactory, for Buridan was not forbidden absolutely to treat of theology, and they did not blame him for this, that where he had treated something concerning the faith he had determined it in favor of the faith, because he was bound to do so apart from his oath. Thirdly, that oath does not seem reasonable when it compels a man to overthrow arguments, for there might be some loyal teacher for whom some argument worked out contrary to the determination of the church, and how would he overthrow it? But to this it seems it should be said that, if the instructor does not know how to overthrow such an argument, he ought not to formulate it in public to his students. But if he should do otherwise, he would remain perjured if he had taken the oath, and will sin although no oath has preceded. Therefore, let Parisian teachers of artists who touch on theological problems look out for themselves. In the fourth place, I, inadequate and unworthy as I am, do not recall that when I was promoted to the degree in arts I took, or knew of any of my fellows taking, such an oath, but, alas, that laudable custom of the university along with others had become obsolete. In the fifth place, where two catholic masters and teachers disagreed about any matter in natural or moral philosophy touching the faith in any way, one of them would not be immune from perjury, which seems to be awkward. For example, if one held that the infinite is possible and the other the opposite; and one that matter can exist without form and the other the opposite; one that, given two things neither of which is God nor either part of the other, God could annihilate one of them and leave the other, and the other, without excepting respective entities, should be unwilling with the Subtle Doctor to concede this. And whether there was an oath or not, I would strive where occasion offered to proceed conformably to the intention of the person who ordered that oath to be taken. I therefore assert that God can render any place vacant of content. . . .

42

EARLY STATUTES OF THE SORBONNE

Chartularium universitatis Parisiensis, I, 505–14.

In the first part, where the first personal pronoun is used, Robert de Sorbonne (1201–1274), the founder of the college about 1257, appears to be speaking and the statutes seem therefore to date before 1274. At first merely a college for students of theology, the Sorbonne in the sixteenth and seventeenth centuries came to be a designation for the faculty of theology, while since the nineteenth century the name has been applied to the entire university. The following regulations furnish a detailed picture of how such an institution was run, except that it should be kept in mind that the fellows were theological students and so older and maturer than the average residents in colleges at Paris.

I wish that the custom which was instituted from the beginning in this house by the counsel of good men may be kept, and if anyone ever has transgressed it, that henceforth he shall not presume to do so.

No one therefore shall eat meat in the house on Advent, nor on Monday or Tuesday of Lent, nor from Ascension day to Pentecost.

Also, I will that the community be not charged for meals taken in rooms. If there cannot be equality, it is better that the fellow eating in his room be charged than the entire community.

Also, no one shall eat in his room except for cause. If anyone has a guest, he shall eat in hall. If, moreover, it shall not seem expedient to the fellow to bring that guest to hall, let him eat in his room and he shall have the usual portion for himself, not for the guest. If, moreover, he wants more for himself or his guest, he should pay for it himself. But if in the judgment of the fellow who introduces him the guest be a person of consequence or one through whom the house might be aided or the fellow promoted, then the said fellow may invite one or two others to entertain the guest and do him honor. These shall similarly have the portions due them from the community but always without loss to the community.

Also, no one resident in town shall eat in the house except in hall, and if he eats in a private room for cause, he shall scrupulously give his excuse before the bearer of the roll.

Also, if three or less were bled, they may have one associate who has not been bled. If they number more than three and less than eight, they may have two who have not been bled. If eight or more have been bled, then they may have three who have not been bled and who shall have their portions. If, however, more were not bled than as has been said, they shall have nothing from the common table.

Also, those who have been bled may eat in a private room for three days if they will, for as is said in the thirty-third chapter of *Genesis*, "On the third day the pain of a wound is worse." [1]

Also, when fellows eat in private rooms, the fragments are collected lest they be lost and are returned to the dispenser who puts them in the common repository for poor clerks.

Also, the fellows should be warned by the bearer of the roll that those eating in private rooms conduct themselves quietly and abstain from too much noise, lest those passing through the court and street be scandalized and lest the fellows in rooms adjoining be hindered in their studies.

Also, those eating in private rooms shall provide themselves with what they need in season as best they can, so that the service of the community may be disturbed as little as possible. But if there are any infringers of this statute who are accustomed to eat in private rooms

---

[1] I do not find the passage cited.

without cause, they shall be warned by the bearer of the roll to desist, which if they will not do, he shall report it to the master. If, moreover, other reasons arise for which anyone can eat in a private room, it shall be left to the discretion of the roll-bearer and proctors until otherwise ordered.

Also, the rule does not apply to the sick. If anyone eats in a private room because of sickness, he may have a fellow with him, if he wishes, to entertain and wait on him, who also shall have his due portion. What shall be the portion of a fellow, shall be left to the discretion of the dispenser. If a fellow shall come late to lunch, if he comes from classes or a sermon or business of the community, he shall have his full portion, but if from his own affairs, he shall have bread only.

Also, if a fellow eats in pension five days or less, he shall be a guest; but if he eats in town, he shall pay no less than if he had eaten in the house.

Also, whenever a fellow eats in town, whether he informs the household or not, he shall pay the whole pension and extras, and this in order that fellows may be discouraged from frequent eating in town.

Also, all shall wear closed outer garments, nor shall they have trimmings of vair or grise or of red or green silk on the outer garment or hood.

Also, no one shall have loud shoes or clothing by which scandal might be generated in any way.

Also, no one shall be received in the house unless he shall be willing to leave off such and to observe the aforesaid rules.

Also, no one shall be received in the house unless he pledges faith that, if he happens to receive books from the common store, he will treat them carefully as if his own and on no condition remove or lend them out of the house, and return them in good condition whenever required or whenever he leaves town.

Also, let every fellow have his own mark on his clothes and one only and different from the others. And let all the marks be written on a schedule and over each mark the name of whose it is. And let that schedule be given to the servant so that he may learn to recognize the mark of each one. And the servant shall not receive clothes from any fellow unless he sees the mark. And then the servant can return his clothes to each fellow.

Also, no outsider shall be placed on pension without permission of the master, nor shall he eat or sleep in the house as a guest more than three or four days without his permission.

Also, it is ordained that those who have lived in the house at the expense of the house until they could provide for themselves shall within a short time prepare and dispose themselves to progress in public sermons through the parishes, in disputations and lectures in the schools; otherwise they shall be totally deprived of the benefits of the house. And it may be they were able to do this by virtue of privilege: nevertheless I give them warning in all charity. Moreover, concerning those who are newly received or about to be admitted it is ordained that unless they have made progress in sermons, disputations and lectures as aforesaid within seven years from the time of their admission, they shall similarly be deprived. And if it should by chance happen that someone from fear of losing his pension should try to undertake to lecture on some text incautiously, unprepared, incompetent or unworthy, that he shall not be permitted to do so because of the scandal to others, unless by the judgment and testimony of the more advanced students in the house he be deemed competent and fitted to lecture.

Also, I wish, counsel, and decree that on fast days from All Saints to Lent those on pension in the house shall not eat except at Vespers and after all the day's lectures are over.

Also, for peace and utility we propound that no secular person living in town—scribe, corrector or anyone else—unless for great cause eat, sleep in a room, or remain with the fellows when they eat, or have frequent conversation in the gardens or hall or other parts of the house, lest the secrets of the house and the remarks of the fellows be spread abroad.

Also, no outsider shall come to accountings or the special meetings of the fellows, and he whose guest he is shall see to this.

Also, no fellow shall bring in outsiders frequently to drink at commons, and if he does, he shall pay according to the estimate of the dispenser.

Also, no fellow shall have a key to the kitchen.

Also, no fellow shall presume to sleep outside the house in town, and if he did so for reason, he shall take pains to submit his excuse to the bearer of the roll.

Also, no fellow in the presence of outsiders shall propose in hall anything pertaining to the society except the word of God, which no one shall presume to impede but all shall hear in silence him who proposes it.

Also, no women of any sort shall. eat in the private rooms. If anyone violates this rule, he shall pay the assessed penalty, namely, sixpence.

Also, no fellow shall send any dish outside the house, except by the consent of the person who has charge of them.

Also, if anyone has spoken opprobrious words or shameful to a fellow, provided it is established by two fellows of the house, he shall pay a purse which ought to belong to the society.

Also, if one of the fellows shall have insulted, jostled or severely beaten one of the servants, he shall pay a sextarium of wine to the fellows, and this wine ought to be *vin superieur* to boot.

Also, no one shall presume to take a dish or tray either at lunch or dinner except as it is passed to him by the provost and his helpers or the servants. Moreover, he who has done otherwise shall be penalized two quarts of wine. And therefore each provost should be diligent in serving the fellows well.

Also, at the deliberations of the fellows each shall peacefully remain silent until he has been called upon by the prior, and after he has had his say, he shall listen to the others calmly.

Also, no one shall form the habit of talking too loudly at table. Whoever after he has been warned about this by the prior shall have offended by speaking too loudly, provided this is established afterwards by testimony of several fellows to the prior, shall be held to the usual house penalty, namely, two quarts of wine.

The penalty for transgression of statutes which do not fall under an oath is twopence, if the offenders are not reported by someone, or if they were, the penalty becomes sixpence in the case of fines. I understand not reported to mean that, if before the matter has come to the attention of the prior, the offender accuses himself to the prior or has told the clerk to write down twopence against him for such an offense, for it is not enough to say to the fellows, "I accuse myself."

In all these and other good customs let the roll-bearer of the house be careful; but if he shall be remiss, he shall be held to the penalty assessed in the house which transgressors incur.

Part II

For the peace and utility of the community we ordain thus as to electing petty proctors and concerning those things which pertain to the exercise of their office. First, that each fellow in entering the office of proctor be required to swear according to the form of oath which fellows usually take on their admission, namely, that he will exercise the office well and faithfully and diligently.

Also, that before they leave office they ought to choose and nominate proctors to succeed themselves a fortnight before the times hitherto observed. The times are these: feast of St. Bartholomew, Christmas, and Easter. Those named are required to answer to the society the same day, if they were named at dinner; if in the afternoon, next day at dinner under penalty of twelve pence so far as answering is concerned, if they have received notice of their election which ought to be given them by the electors. Moreover, if they have accepted at that time, they may straightway receive accounts, if they wish, and their predecessors shall be prepared to render accounts. But if they wish, they may wait till the limit, unless they or one of them wishes or intends to leave the house.

Concerning those leaving we ordain as follows, that if any one of those elected wishes to leave the house within the fortnight mentioned, if he shall have accepted office he shall receive account before he leaves and his co-elect shall be required to receive the account with him and to exercise the functions pertaining to the office. Nor after they have accepted the office can they refuse it except because of a complete withdrawal from the house, without prospect of return within the term of the proctorship, or on account of grave infirmity or a lectureship, so that it cannot be fulfilled by themselves or by a suitable substitute. Because if one should allege complete withdrawal and then return within the term of the proctorship, he would be held to pay the same penalty as if he had not accepted the office. If, moreover, those chosen and nominated shall have refused the office, they shall pay the specified penalty, namely, ten solidi within a day after their nomination, which, if they fail to pay, for each day of delinquency each shall be charged sixpence and the proctors-electors shall keep choosing others until new proctors are had, in order that the utility of the society may not be retarded.

Moreover, this arrangement shall be observed in those who have held office before, that those shall be first chosen who are farthest removed from the time of office-holding, unless by the society or a majority thereof they be deemed unfit. If, moreover, of those older ones two held office before or paid the fine at the same time, it shall be at the discretion of the electors to choose this or that. Those, moreover, who were not proctors before, if they performed minor offices, namely, reading in hall, provostship, and office in chapel, can be elected indifferently at the electors' will and discretion.

To these functions, moreover, are held generally all petty proctors, forsooth to correct servants and to conduct themselves as follows: that they at any time with the persons here named, namely, the weekly reader, provost, clerk of the chapel and priest, without further deliberation of the other fellows can, or the majority of the said persons can, expel servants with or without salary on their conscience for the good of the fellows. And the proctors shall be held to provide other fit servants.

Also, all petty proctors generally shall be required at the beginning of their proctorship to receive and record a complete number of vessels and furniture from the preceding proctors and servants and to hand on to their successors a similar inventory. But if any are broken or lost, they ought first to repair these in order that the number of vessels may always remain certain and complete.

Besides, all vessels which are brought to table they should return clear, pure and whole at the end of their proctorship.

Also, they should attend to cleaning the chapel, hall, and court and cutting the grass at due seasons, and about all matters appertaining thereto.

Also, they should provide sufficiently concerning napkins and towels that the napkins be washed fresh and clean at least twice a week and the towels thrice.

Once a month they should propose what need to be provided for the fellows and, after deliberation by the greater and better part of the fellows who have remained in congregation, they should proceed in accordance with their deliberation. If no deliberation could be held, they should nevertheless provide for the needs of the society as shall seem to them expedient.

Also, they shall provide enough wine so that at least two hogsheads full are left at the close of their proctorship.

Also, the wines bought shall not be appraised by themselves but together with three or four fellows summoned for this and so precisely appraised according to the market where they are bought that equality shall be observed so far as possible.

Also, they shall call their rolls during octave in the accustomed manner and, when the time is up, they shall name the deficient for fines unless they wish to pay for them with their own money. But if they wish to pay for them, they should expunge them from the roll before the time expires. If they do not, they or the others shall be held to fines. The accustomed fine in the house is this, sixpence for absence for one day and a penny for each succeeding day of absence.

Also, they may use the money of the society for the personal utility of no one that results in damage or grievance to the society. Nay more, at the close of their proctorship they shall refund it all in cold cash or exchange, which if they do not do, they shall be charged ten solidi a day. But if they do not pay both fine and principal, for each day's delinquency each shall be penalized sixpence. If, moreover, they contumaciously delay in the said payments for a fortnight, then they shall be deprived of the fare of the society, the service of the domestics, and everything else in our power, without holding any further deliberation.

Moreover, if in some makings of change something has been lost and in others gained, the gain shall not be taken to distribute, unless first the loss has been restored.

Also, if any bad investment has been made in any debts through some unexpected cause and in some exchanges something has been made which ought to be distributed, let that bad debt he reckoned in the distribution and made up from the gain which was taken from the money of the society, and this in order that the fellows to whom the distribution ought to be made shall be more concerned about the recovery of the debt and that the money which is designated for the use of the society may always remain intact.

Along with these general requirements for all petty proctors are some special ones for certain of them, namely those who were elected at Easter: to provide concerning servants at the feast of St. John or concerning the preceding if they were fit, and to receive pledges anew, and to inquire into, to reduce to writing, and to leave to their successors the names of their sureties, the streets in which they dwell, and their standing. If they bring in new ones, they are required to do the same. And before they are hired outright and in full, they are tested for eight or fifteen days as is customary and those approved by the whole society or at least a majority are kept. Moreover, in accordance with the custom of Paris their sureties go surety for them with this added or specified that, if the servants for whom they swear contract debts which were credited to them from reverence for the house and society without the consent or knowledge of the fellows, if the servants should leave the house without paying, the sureties will be held for those debts. Moreover, those servants who are engaged shall take oath according to the form given them.

Also, the said proctors should provide wood for the hall and kitchen for a year, unless by vote of the fellows the time shall be extended after the feast of St. Batholomew.

Also, to provide for all needs of the society which fall within the time of their proctorship.

Moreover, those of the feast of St. Bartholomew [1] are required to provide wood unless it has been provided by others and for the making of verjuice unless their predecessors have attended to it, and especially to do what should be done in vintages of *salinato, rapeto* and other wines as far as the money will go.

Those, moreover, of Christmas are required to make provision for Lent of peas, beans, spices and other things as the time requires.

Also, the same are required to make in the accustomed way a collection for common expenses, namely, wood for the hall, the service of domestics, sheets, towels and other things of the sort, having summoned four or five discreet fellows a little after Christmas, in order that the collection may be fully attended to before Brandons at least. Moreover, the fellows residing for the year personally in the house or the absent who have those answering for them in the house shall alone contribute to the collection. If, however, others who were absent through the year wish for some reason to contribute to the col-

---

[1] The proctors would seem to have elected thrice a year, at Easter, on St. Bartholomew's (August 24), and at Christmas.

lection and if they have property in the house, they may contribute in this way, that the amount be beyond the sum to be placed in the collection, so that always without debts the money assigned to the society in the accounts of the proctors remain an integral whole, both in annual income and cold cash, lest by lack of cash money and reason of debts the utility of the society be retarded. Those not paying the collection shall be held at the stated term to the customary fine which we estimate at twelve pence for delinquency of one day, and one penny for each subsequent day of default.

In what we have said about fines for those not paying the rolls and collections and all other dues, in which particular fellows are bound to the society, we intend to bind both absent and present by the same law, so that they may be careful before they leave to inquire what obligations they have and to pay them, or at least leave other fellows in their place to answer for them and give satisfaction as carefully as they would for themselves.

Part III

These are the duties of the janitor. First he is required to reply courteously to every comer, and, if such a person asks for some fellow of the house, he is required to seek him and call him, unless the caller be some scholar for whom some fellow of the house has specially told him that he may have free access to his room.

When, moreover, the janitor goes to find some fellow in his room or elsewhere, he shall close the door after him. If the caller is a man of note, he shall allow him to wait in the court. If not, he shall remain between the two gates.

Also, the janitor is required to keep clean the entire court within and without and all the street so far as our house extends, and the walks and steps and all the rooms of the fellows and also the common passage to the private rooms, to provide water for the lavatory and keep the lavatory clean inside and out.

Also, he shall serve no one eating or drinking in a private room, unless after curfew when the gate is locked with a key, which key he is to carry with him.

Also, under no circumstances shall he go to town for anyone. But if for some urgent need of his own he has to go to town, he is required to have someone of the house to guard the gate, which if he does not do and the gate is found unguarded, he shall forfeit sixpence from his salary as penalty.

Also, he shall under no circumstances linger in the kitchen nor shall he do anything there.

Also, after curfew he must close the great gate and at the sign of St. James always open it and always keep the keys with him. If anyone of the house has to leave before the hour, he must rise and close the gate after him. If, moreover, any persons are accustomed to enter after the aforesaid hour or anyone to go out before, he is required by his oath to report this to the prior. Similarly, if he sees any faults in the domestics, or any of the goods of the house carried outside by anyone, he is required to reveal this. Also, if he sees any outsider carrying anything out of the house under his garment, he shall not permit him to leave, unless someone from the house accompanies him to the gate.

Also, at lunch he shall have the portion of a fellow without wine; at dinner however he shall have bread and soup as much as is deemed enough for him once, and a half trayful of the fragments remaining after the fellows are served and the domestics have their share. Also each day he shall have a pint of wine.

Moreover, he ought always to eat these at the gate while the fellows are at table. Moreover, he should reserve nothing in his room but return the fragments for the common benefit of clerics. If he shall have transgressed these provisions, let the prior himself correct him. If, by the testimony of the fellows or the majority of them he is found incorrigible, the prior may freely expel him.

His salary is twelve solidi.

43

PARIS ASKS FOR THE BONES AND UNFINISHED WORKS OF AQUINAS, 1274

Chartularium universitatis Parisiensis, I, 504–5.

To the venerable fathers in Christ, the master and provincials of the order of Friars Preachers and all the friars congregated in chapter general at Lyons, the rector of the university of Paris and proctors and other masters teaching at Paris in arts send greeting in Him who disposes all things well and wisely provides for the entire universe. We tearfully lament with voice choked with sobs the universal loss of the entire church and also the manifest desolation of the university of Paris, and in these days we choose not unworthily to mourn in common. Alas! who can bestow on us the gift of repeating the lamentation of Jeremiah which, causing in the minds of each beyond the wonted mode unheard-of ecstasy and adducing unthinkable stupor, finally pierces our inmost viscera and like some lethal poison penetrates to the heart? We confess what we can hardy express, for love draws back but grief and vehement anguish compel us to say that from common report and certain rumor of many we know that the venerable brother Thomas Aquinas has been called from this world. Who could think that divine Providence would have permitted the morning star preeminent in the world, beacon light of the age, nay, to speak more truly, the major luminary that presided over the day, to have withdrawn its rays? Surely, we are not unreasonable to hold that the sun has recalled its beam and suffered dark and unlooked for eclipse, when a light of such splendor to the entire church is subtracted. And although we are not ignorant that the Maker of nature conceded him for a time to the whole world as a special privilege, yet if we wished to follow the authority of ancient philosophers, it would seem that nature had sent him simply to elucidate its secrets.

And why do we now vainly dwell on such words? Him whom from your general chapter celebrated at Florence we could not, alas, obtain, although we requested urgently, yet not existing ungrateful, having devout affection for the memory of so great a clerk, so great a father, so great a doctor, whom alive we could not have again, now that he is dead we humbly ask his bones of you as the greatest gift, since it is quite unbecoming and unworthy that another nation or place than the city of Paris, most noble of all universities, which first educated, nourished and cherished him and afterwards received from him nutriment and unspeakable stimulation, should have his bones and be his sepulchre. For if the church deservedly honors the bones and relics of the saints, to us not without cause it seems decent and holy that the body of so great a doctor be held in perpetual honor, so that the lasting memorial of his sepulchre may preserve without end in the hearts of our successors him whose fame his writings perpetuate among us.

But hoping that you will oblige us effectually in this devout petition,

we humbly beg that also certain writings in the field of philosophy begun by him at Paris, which on his departure he left unfinished and we
believe completed where he was transferred, your goodwill will cause
soon to be sent to us, and particularly the commentary on Simplicius,
on *De celo et mundo,* on the *Timaeus* of Plato, and the book on aque-
ducts and erecting engines, about sending which to us he made mention
with special promise. If he composèd any similarly pertaining to logic,
as we humbly asked him to do when he left us, may your goodwill
deign to communicate them to our college. And just as your discretion
is well aware, in this wicked age we are exposed to many perils, we
fraternally entreat with devout prayers that in this your chapter you
support us with special affection and the suffrage of your prayers.
This letter moreover we have willed to be sealed with the seals of
the rector and proctors. Given at Paris in the year of the Lord 1274,
the Wednesday before the discovery of the Holy Cross.

44

REGULATION OF BOOKSELLERS, PARIS, 1275

Chartularium universitatis Parisiensis, I, 532–34.

The university of masters and students at Paris as a perpetual reminder. Since that field is known to bring forth rich fruit, for which
the care of the farmer *colonus* provides painstakingly in all respects,
lest we, laboring in the field of the Lord to bring forth fruit a hundred-
fold in virtues and science, the Lord disposing, should be molested or
impeded, especially by those who by a bad custom hang about the
university of Paris for the sake of gain, which they make in mercenary
works and assistance, we ordain by decree and decree by ordinance that
the stationers who vulgarly are called booksellers (*librarii*), shall each
year or every second year or whenever they shall be required by the
university, give personal oath that, in receiving books to sell, storing,
showing, and selling the same and in their other functions in connection with the university, they will conduct themselves faithfully and
legitimately.

Also, since some of the aforesaid booksellers, given to insatiable cupidity, are in a way ungrateful and burdensome to the university itself, when they put obstacles in the way of procuring books whose use is essential to the students and by buying too cheaply and selling too dearly and thinking up other frauds make the same books too costly, although as those who hold an office of trust they ought to act openly and in good faith in this matter, which they would better observe if they would not simultaneously act as buyer and seller, we have decreed that the same booksellers swear, as has been stated above, that within a month from the day on which they receive books to sell they will neither make nor pretend any contract concerning those books to keep them for themselves, nor will they suppress or conceal them in order later to buy or retain them, but in good faith, immediately they have received the books or other things, they will offer them for sale at an opportune place and time. And if they shall be asked by the sellers, they shall estimate and state in good faith at how much they really believe the books offered for sale can be sold at a just and legitimate price, and they shall also put the price of the book and the name of the seller somewhere on the book so that it can be seen by one looking at it. They shall also swear that, when they sell the books, they will not assign or transfer them entirely to the purchasers nor receive the price for them until they have communicated to the seller or his representative what price he is going to receive, and that concerning the price offered for the book they will tell the pure and simple truth without fraud and deceit, nor otherwise in any way shall they attempt anything about their office by cupidity or fraud, whence any detriment could come to the university or the students.

Also, while the laborer is worthy of his hire, which too he licitly seeks by civil law (*Proxenetica*), since nevertheless the standard which should be maintained in such matters is frequently exceeded by the booksellers, we have decreed that the stationers swear that they will not demand for books sold beyond four pence in the pound and a smaller quantity *pro rata* as their commission, and these they shall demand not from the seller but the purchaser.

Also, since many damages come from corrupt and faulty exemplars,[1] we have decreed that the said booksellers swear that they will apply care and pains with all diligence and toil to have true and correct exemplars,

[1] An exemplar was supposed to be a standard critical text from which further copies could be safely made. See above, Selection 36, note 1, and below, Selection 66.

and that for exemplars they shall not demand from anyone anything beyond the just and moderate rent or gain or beyond that which shall have been assessed by the university or its deputies.

Also, we have decreed that, if perchance the said booksellers shall be unwilling to swear to the aforesaid or any of the aforesaid, or after having sworn shall have committed fraud in connection with them, or shall not have diligently observed them all and each, not only shall they be utterly ousted from the grace and favor of the university but also henceforth they shall not have the liberty of exercising the office which they exercised before on behalf of the university. So that no master or scholar shall presume to have any business or contract whatever with the said booksellers, after it has been established that the said booksellers have committed a violation of the aforesaid rules or any one of them. But if any master or scholar shall presume to contravene this, he shall be deprived of the society of the masters and scholars until he shall have been reinstated by the university itself. Acted on after deliberation and decreed are these in the general congregation at Paris in the convent of the Friars Preachers and sealed with the seal of the university on December 8, 1275 A.D.

45

LIMITATION ON PRIVATE TEACHING, PARIS, 1276

Chartularium universitatis Parisiensis, I, 538–39.

The university of masters and scholars at Paris as a perpetual reminder. Our true Samaritan coming into the world restored sorely wounded human nature to health, pouring wine and oil into the wounds. But because a relapse is suffered, medicine should be applied which will be useful for health according to the quality of the disease, now putting on soothing remedies, now more active ones salubriously. On which account holy church has decreed diverse penance according to the nature of the faults, punishing transgressors and trying to prevent future dangers. By her mastery she teaches us what we should do in similar circumstances. Hence it is that we, noting that secret conventicles for teaching are forbidden by canon law and hostile to wisdom, whose professors we are, which lights men's minds and detests darkness, wishing for the sake of the common good to check the presumption of certain malignant persons, by common consent decree and likewise ordain that no master or bachelor, of whatever faculty he be, shall henceforth agree to lecture in private places on texts because of the many dangers which may result therefrom, but in common places where all can gather and give a faithful report of what is taught there, excepting only grammatical and logical texts in which there can be no presumption. Moreover, these things we decree and ordain to be observed inviolably according to the tenor of the privileges granted by the apostolic see to the masters and scholars of Paris. Moreover, if anyone shall presume to act against this statute or ordinance, let him know that he will incur deprivation of the society of masters and scholars. Done and ordained at St. Bernard in Cardineto [1] in general congregation, in the year of the Lord 1276, on the Wednesday before the nativity of the blessed Mary, retaining the power of adding, subtracting, changing and revoking when it shall seem good to us.

46

OATHS OF THOSE INCEPTING IN ARTS, ABOUT 1280

Chartularium universitatis Parisiensis, I, 586–87.

These are the articles which bachelors about to incept in arts are required to swear to, when they come before the rector pledging faith in person. First, it should be said to them: You are to deliver ordinary lectures in the round cope or in the pallium. You will dispute at the hour set and you will discuss your questions for forty days continuously after you have incepted. You are to carry on for fifteen (forty?) days in the said costume. You shall not have shoes with pointed toes or ornaments or openings, nor are you to wear a surcoat slashed on the sides, nor shall you have a mitre on your head so long as you lecture or dispute in the round cope. You will attend the meetings, obey the commands of the rector and proctor in things lawful and honorable.

[1] The Collège des Bernardins or du Chardonnet, founded in 1246 by Stephen Lexington, abbot of Clairvaux, for members of the Cistercian Order.

You shall not permit dances to go on before your house nor anything unseemly to occur at your opening lecture under penalty of degradation from being a master. You shall not reveal the secrets of the university. You are to be present at the burial of students on feast days when you know of them; on other days, when you shall be asked, you shall in the aforesaid costume read or cause to be read the Psalter at the death of a master of the faculty. You will observe and defend the accustomed freedom of examination of Ste. Geneviève. You will promise to incept under the master under whom you were licentiated, or with his consent under another, so that you have adequately sought his consent or would gladly have done so if you could, and so that you intend no guile or fraud towards your master under whom you gained the licentiate with respect to your inception. Also, you will observe the order or ordinance as to the method of giving ordinary lectures and of disputing. Also, you will stand with the secular masters and defend their status, statutes, and privileges all your lifetime, to whatever position you may come. Also, you will admit to examination no member of any religious order whatever, namely for the licentiate or degree, nor will you attend his inception or determination. Also, so long as you shall teach in arts, you will dispute no purely theological question, for example, concerning the Trinity and incarnation. And if you chance to discuss any question which has to do with the faith and philosophy, you will settle it in favor of the faith and answer the arguments contrary to the faith as it shall seem to you they should be answered.[1]

Also, you shall swear without any fraud that you have fulfilled the requirements in arts at Paris according to the custom hitherto observed, or in some university where there are at least twelve teachers. Also, that you will observe the ordinance recently passed as to the method of announcing general meetings to the dean of the canon law faculty and the dean of the medical faculty. Also, you shall swear that, if you shall have known that a nation is going to rise against a nation or a province against a province or a person against a person, you will reveal it to the nation against which there is to be made an insurrection of a person or province. Also, you shall swear that you will not incept while you see another bachelor incepting, but you will wait until he has given his lecture and finished his discussion before you begin. Also,

---

[1] This is in accordance with the statute of 1272 translated above, Selection 41.

that you will observe the ordinance of the masters as to bachelors examined on the island by masters not of the faculty. Also, you shall swear to, and to the best of your ability, obtain freedom of the university from debt. Also, you shall swear that you will incept in your own cope, not one borrowed or hired, if you put two solidi or more in the purse. Also, you shall swear that you are not less than twenty-one years of age. Also, you shall swear that you have heard lectures for six years in arts. Also, you shall swear that you will lecture for two years continuously unless a reasonable excuse shall occur. Also, you shall swear to defend the particular liberties of the faculty and the honorable customs of the faculty and the privileges of the whole university, to whatever position you may come.

47

THE UNIVERSITY DEFENDS AN INJURED MEMBER, 1281

DECREE OF THE UNIVERSITY OF PARIS THAT, BY REASON OF INJURY DONE TO MASTER HUGH THE PHYSICIAN, THE MASTERS SHALL NOT RESUME LECTURES UNLESS THE PRIVILEGE OF PHILIP AUGUSTUS IS OBSERVED AND DAMAGES ARE PAID THE WOUNDED PHYSICIAN

Chartularium universitatis Parisiensis, I, 589–90.

The year of the Incarnation, 1281, the Thursday after the summer feast of St. Martin, the masters of all faculties gathered in Paris at St. Julien le Pauvre in the name of the university and for the university both of masters and scholars, in resuming lectures unanimously agreed upon the form that follows, namely, that the lord king be seen personally on behalf of the university and that it be said to him:

Lord king, at your prayers and from reverence for you the masters are willing to resume their lectures, but under the firm hope that the privilege of famous memory of Philip, once king of France, renewed by your father and likewise by you, shall be observed unimpaired in perpetuity: also in the firm hope that, if the injured physician is not given sufficient damages, he shall be given what is just: also with the hope, as before, that faithful inquisition be made by those who know the truth regarding the article which you say has been proposed to you for the first time, and that according to the finding there be completion of justice.

The aforesaid masters also agreed for themselves and for their bachelors, who had met with them before, that, if justice was not done in these matters by the octave of the nativity of the blessed Mary,[1] they will be in the same state of cessation in which they were before the time of the said conventions, the same masters willing for themselves and their said bachelors that, if any rebels against the said conventions are found, in the name of the university they shall now be deprived, and having been deprived shall then be denounced from membership in the entire university. In testimony and record whereof we have ordered the seal of the university to be appended.

48

ASSESSMENT OF HOUSES IN PARIS,
1282–1283

Chartularium universitatis Parisiensis, I, 597–600.

This document gives us some idea of the scene and topography of the university and Latin quarter in the thirteenth century, for which consult further the Plan of Late Medieval Paris South of the Seine. Of 87 or 88 buildings listed, a dozen or perhaps 14 were in Grande rue de St. Jacques, 9 in Rue de la Montagne Ste. Geneviève, 6 in the short Rue Pierre Sarrasin; 3 each in two other short streets, Rue du Plâtre and Rue Pavée; 2 or 3 in Rue de la Serpente; 2 each in Place Maubert, Clos St. Benoît, Rue St. Cosme, Rue St. Victor, Rue de la Bucherie, Rue de Bièvre, Vicus Potatorii, Guellandia (Rue Coupe Gueule), and the tiny Rue des Prêtres St. Séverin. Apparently three were in Rue St. Hilaire and two in Rue du Mont St. Hilaire, but the distribution between the two is a little uncertain. Perhaps there were two, surely one, in Rue St. Étienne des Grès. Other streets of the Latin quarter with one each were Rue d'Arras, Passage des Jacobins, Rue du Chaudron, Rue de Sorbonne, Rue des Amandiers, Rue du Four, Rue Chartiere, Rue des Poirées, Rue de la Huchette, Rue des Noyers and Rue Erambour de Brie. Rue St. Germain lay outside the walls from the Porte

---

[1] September 15.

St. Germain to St. Germain des Prés. Rue St. Christophe was in la Cité, as was another house. Rue Neuve I cannot identify. For eleven of the buildings no street is named. It will be noted that it was already customary for prelates as well as nobles from other parts of the realm to have Hôtels in Paris, while many of the other householders were not native Parisians.

In the year of the Lord 1281, masters in theology Adam de Gouly and Peter de Vylarcheaus first acted as assessors on the Thursday preceding the feast of St. Peter in cathedra.[1]

The house of Clement, priest of Issy, in Place Maubert before the house *ad nassam,* six pounds.

The new house of the Sorbonists in the cloister of St. Benedict next to the still newer one, we assess at twenty pounds Parisian, the same as last year.

The house of master William de Charleis in Rue St. Cosme [2] before the house with the deer, four and a half pounds.

The house belonging to the church of Blois in the middle of the street leading from Porte d'Infer [3] to St. Jacques,[4] thirteen pounds.

Wednesday.

Classrooms to the great Breton [5] in Rue d'Arras,[6] 110 sous.

House of Droco de Cachant before St. Mathurin in Grande rue.[7]

House belonging to l'Hôtel Dieu near the vacant lot in Rue Pierre Sarrasin, seven pounds.

House of William de Seint Cuir in Rue de la Serpente, in front of the house of master Henri de Verdilly, with a yard and cellar, without stables; 18 pounds Parisian.

House of Jean de Boigeval in Rue St. Germain, 50 sous.

Thursday.

House of Richard le Fenier in Rue du Plâtre, 4 pounds, 10 sous Parisian.

---

[1] February 20, 1281.

[2] The southern extension of Rue de la Harpe (now Boulevard St. Michel), sometimes called more fully "vicus SS. Cosme et Damiani."

[3] At the end of the street mentioned in note 2; also called Porte Gibard ou St. Michel.

[4] The Dominican convent, previously occupied by the Hospital of St. Jacques. The street referred to seems to be the Passage des Jacobins.

[5] Can Abelard be meant?

[6] It ran parallel to the famous Street of Straw and was more or less identical with the present Rue de l'Hôtel Colbert.

[7] That is, Rue St. Jacques, then called both Grande rue and Grande rue de St. Jacques.

House of Peter of Auvergne in Rue St. Victor opposite Rue Alexandre Langlois,[8] eight pounds.

House of the heirs of William de Poncello in Rue Pavée,[9] next to the house of Stephen de Moret; six pounds, five sous.

House of master Hugh de Hermen in Rue Pavée with stables; eight pounds for the house and ten sous for the stables.

House of master Ivo, dean of Clicon, before the house of the counts of Bar, 16 pounds.

House of Thomas the potter in Grande rue towards St. Jacques next the house of the bishop of Lincoln, 8 pounds, 15 sous.

House of Louis Chanscon next to the house of the archpriest of St. Séverin on the long alley,[10] eight pounds.

House of the Two Sheep, six pounds, five sous.

House of William called Giffard, above the house of the Marmosets: four pounds, five sous for the entire year.

House of Theobald Brito before St. Hilaire,[11] eight and a half pounds.

Classrooms of Thomas the Fleming between three gates with columns, eleven sous.

House that used to belong to Bernard, priest of St. Nicolas,[12] in Rue St. Victor before the Serpent, four pounds Parisian.

House of master Ivo, canon of St. Melo de Pontisara, in Rue Ste. Geneviève,[13] ten and a half pounds Parisian.

House of Jean, called of St. Martin, on Mount Ste. Geneviève under the gallows.

House of Nicholas, called Le Mascon, at the Garnet in Rue St. Hilaire,[14] seven pounds Parisian.

House of Nicholas, the image-maker, in Rue Ste. Geneviève, 60 sous Parisian.

[8] In the region occupied since 1794 by the Ecole Polytechnique.

[9] Probably the one near Place Maubert, although there was another opening off Rue St. André.

[10] This perhaps refers to Rue des Prêtres St. Séverin which runs across the west façade of the church, while Rue St. Séverin runs along its north side.

[11] If "before" means opposite the west façade, this would put it in Rue du Chaudron; otherwise it might have been in Rue des Sept Voies or Carrefour St. Hilaire.

[12] Near the corner of Rue des Bernardins and Rue St. Victor, now passed by the Boulevard St. Germain.

[13] Apparently Rue de la Montagne Ste. Geneviève is meant.

[14] Probably Vicus inferior Sancti Hilarii (called, from the fourteenth century on, Rue des Carmes) is meant rather than Rue du Mont St. Hilaire (now Rue de Lanneau).

House of Pierre Morel in Grande rue, eight pounds Parisian.

House of Stephen Point Larne (l'asne?) and his mother, 110 sous Parisian.

House of Biche le Lombard in Rue St. Christophe, six pounds.

House of Master Peter of Villa Blovana, six pounds Parisian.

House of William of Seint Cuyr in Rue de la Serpente, garden, nine pounds Parisian.[15]

House of William le Mareschal in Rue des Noyers, with a yard, without a cellar, next the houses of Huguelinus, common sergeant in decretals, 65 sous.

House of John Berbette in Rue Ste. Geneviève, with garden, cellar, yard; 100 sous Parisian.

Small house of St. Stephen.[16]

In the year of the Lord 1282 the assessors were masters in theology, friar Hugh de Billonio of the Order of Preachers, friar Allotus of the Minorites, and four masters in arts and the burghers, Jean Quidornoie the Elder, Nicholas of Auxerre.

House of the nephew of the bishop of Cahors, in Rue de la Bucherie, on the long alley, 108 sous.

House of Adam of Arras, with five rooms, in Guellandia,[17] 100 sous Parisian.

House belonging to l'Hôtel Dieu in Grande rue at the longest grade, on which hangs a key as a sign, six and a half pounds.

House of Stephen of Limoges, cleric, in Rue du Plâtre, 115 sous.

New house of Michael Fresnel in Grande rue, for this year only, eight pounds.

House of William de Roseto in Grande rue, with garden, next to Hugh le Convert, with six rooms, nine and a half pounds.

Schoolhouse of the Sorbonne in Rue de Sorbonne, the first, in which clerics live, from the direction of St. Cosme, ten pounds Parisian.

House that belonged to Matthieu Rufi, now deceased, in Grande rue, with five rooms, 110 sous.

House of Theobald the tailor in Grande rue, four pounds Parisian.

House of master Gui de Gravia before the house of Robert de Torota, at the corner, nine and a half pounds.

[15] Possibly the same property as that owned by him in the same street and listed above.

[16] Perhaps in Rue St. Etienne des Grès, where the church was located.

[17] Rue Coupe Gueule, running parallel between Rue de Sorbonne and Rue des Maçons.

House of Theobald Brito, Rue des Amandiers, with four rooms and a cellar and a big kitchen,[18] seven pounds.

House of master Gui de Gravia, above St. Hilaire opposite Rue du Chaudron, with five rooms, kitchen, garden, cellar, stables; twelve pounds.

The smaller house of Matthew the Lombard in Rue du Four, with five rooms and one over the kitchen without a storeroom, 110 sous.

The house which is called Guibert de Vouta's, in Rue Chartiere, four pounds, ten sous.

House of Agnes de Gravia in Rue Coupe Gueule, called at Li plate pierre, with four rooms, a yard, stables and large storeroom; six pounds, fourteen sous.

House of Henry the Lombard in Rue Pierre Sarrasin, which is next to the house in which Henry the Lombard lives, which has four rooms, four pounds, sixteen sous.

House of Ivo Brito, once canon of Reims, in Rue Pierre Sarrasin, with five rooms and a cellar, seven pounds.

House of master Jean le Savoner, in Rue Pierre Sarrasin, which has three principal rooms and a cellar, next the house with two gutters, 100 sous Parisian.

House of Adam de Stupis, in Vicus Potatorii, belonging to the count of Mâcon; 7 pounds, 10 sous.

House of Geoffrey Mason (or, the mason), in Vicus Potatorii, belonging to the count of Mâcon, which is beyond the house in which Geoffrey himself lives, which has five rooms; 65 sous Parisian.

House of Pierre de Cloître, at the horn in Rue de Bièvre; 6 pounds, 5 sous.

House of William de Bacia, 100 sous Parisian, in Rue de la Porrée.

House of master William of Ghent in Rue de Bièvre; 4 pounds and 10 sous Parisian.

House of master Remy in Rue Ste. Geneviève, with two rooms and a good cellar and a small kitchen, ten pounds Parisian.

House of Noel Mason (or, the mason), Rue St. Hilaire, with three rooms and kitchen; 3 pounds, 10 sous Parisian.

House of Jean Pie d'Oie, Rue de l'église St. Hilaire, with four rooms and a kitchen; 76 sous Parisian.

House of the canon of St. Etienne, before the house of master Jean

[18] Presumably in a separate building.

Roman, in the long alley off Rue grande St. Jacques, with six rooms, cellar and yard; nine pounds Parisian.

House of Nicolas le Jeune, Rue de la Bucherie; 8 pounds and 15 sous Parisian.

House of the almoner of St. Germain des Prés; 60 pounds, 12 sous, on the meadow.

House of the almoner of St. Germain des Prés, on the flats above the little bridge (Petit-Pons); 8 pounds, 15 sous Parisian.

House in Rue Neuve of Jean de Douais, 10 pounds Parisian.

House of master Gandulfus, in la Cité, 100 sous.

House of Robert le Seeleur, Rue Erambour de Brie; 8 pounds, 10 sous.

Upper house of Alain le Jeune in Grande rue; 6 pounds, 10 sous.

House of Roger des Prés in Grande rue, seven pounds Parisian.

House of Michael the Fleming, that is the lower one, Rue St. Hilaire; 60 and 15 sous.

Lower house of Lambert de Barro, opposite the house of master Jean de Grand Pont in Rue Ste. Geneviève, 15 pounds.

House of master Bertaud of St. Denis in Rue du Plâtre, twelve and a half pounds.

House of the clerics of Notre Dame in Rue de la Huchette, with front rooms near the gate; 13 pounds Parisian and 5 sous.

House of the Sorbonists on the long alley before the Palace of the Thermae, 24 pounds.[19]

Upper house of the Sorbonists in Grande rue, which is called of the Marmosets, 8 pounds.

House of master Walter de Chandelis, in Rue St. Etienne des Grés, with stables; 14 pounds, 5 sous.

[19] Probably the Vicus ad Thermas, later Rue des Mathurins, is meant, or perhaps a cul-de-sac between the Thermae and the Mathurins. The Rue de Sorbonne can hardly be meant, since it is mentioned as such earlier in the document.

49

PRICES OF BOOKS AT PARIS: EXEMPLAR AND PECIA, 1286

Chartularium universitatis Parisiensis, I, 644–49.

The text has here been reduced to a somewhat more abbreviated and tabular form than in the *Chartularium*, with use of Arabic in place of Roman numerals. Concerning the *pecia* or section of an *exemplar* (standard text) which could be borrowed, copied and returned separately, consult Jean Destrez, *La Pecia dans les manuscripts universitaires du XIIIe et du XIVe siècle*, 1935. See also our later selections under the years 1317–1347 and 1396.

Title of the Book	Number of peciae	Price [1]	
		s.	d.
Originalia (*Moralia*) of Gregory on Job	100	8	
Homilies of Gregory	28		18
Objections of master Andrea against the Jews concerning our Emanuel	16		16
Isidore, On the Supreme Good, and the Contemplations of Richard of St. Victor	24		12
Hugh of St. Victor on the sacraments	40	3	
Ralph of St. Victor on Leviticus	43	3	
Originalia of St. Bernard, namely, the books on consideration, the twelve steps of humility, the steps of pride, homilies of praises of the Virgin mother; the book of the same sent to the archbishop of Sens on monastic discipline; the epistle sent to the brothers of Mons Dei	17	2	
St. Bernard on loving God and on meditation, on grace and free will, on precept and dispensation	14		12
Floreber (i.e., *Flores Bernardi*, Flowers of Bernard)	40		20
Originalia of Anselm on truth, free will, the fall of the devil, why God man, virginal conception, pro-			

[1] The abbreviation *s.* is for solidi, sous, or shillings; *d.* for denarii or pence. It will be seen that the average price was about a penny or half-penny per pecia.

Title of the Book	*Number of peciae*	*Price*	
		s.	*d.*
cession of the holy spirit, predestination, grace and free will, *Monologium*	40	2	
Incarnation of the Word, Similitudes and Dissimilitudes	12		6
De proprietatibus rerum, On the Properties of Things (Bartholomaeus Anglicus)	102	4	
On the sacraments	Not stated	2	
De naturis rerum, On the Natures of Things (Alexander Neckam)	41		18
On the Origin of the Sciences (Robert Kilwardby)	18		9
On the Principles of Nature of master John of Siccavilla	14		7
Commentary of Alexander on the Meteorology and the Physiognomy of Aristotle	19		9
Commentary of Simplicius on the *Predicamenta*	34		18
Commentary on the *Peryarmenia*	18		9
Commentary of Themistius on *De anima*	10		6
Summa of Raymond (of Peñafort) with the Apparatus		3	
Summa of master Lombard (Sentences of Peter Lombard)		3	
Concordances of Vaulisant	108	6	
Historia scolastica (of Peter Comestor)		3	

These are Exemplaria in Theology

Originalia of St. Augustine, first the Enchiridion	6		4
De trinitate of Augustine	48	3	
Confessions of Augustine	21		14
De doctrina Christiana and *De disciplina Christiana*	15		8
Of the Conflict of Vices, Augustine	2		2
Retractions of Augustine	6		6
Super Genesim ad litteram of Augustine, Ecclesiastical Dogmas (Gennadius), On Faith to Peter (Fulgentius)	36		18
Augustine on free will, against Faustus, and on the divination of demons	38		18

Title of the Book	*Number of peciae*	Price	
		s.	*d.*
On the Harmony of the Gospels; Questions of the Old and New Testament; also Augustine on the Academics or against; and on the Blessed Life; on the Order; Soliloquies; on the Immortality of the Soul; Customs of the Church; Morals of the Manicheans; Quantity of the Soul	24	2	
Augustine on conjugal good, on holy virginity, and the profession of holy widowhood, and against five heresies, and to Orosius	10		12
On the Use of Belief, the Grace of the New Testament, the Nature of the Good	8		6
Augustine, Five Replies to the Pelagians	6		3
Augustine on nuptials and concupiscence; and on adulterous marriage	8		7
Homilies of Augustine, On Penitence	9		6
Epistles of Augustine	42	2	
Text of books		2	
Dionysius with commentaries		6	

These are writings of brother Thomas Aquinas

On the first book of the Sentences	37	2	
On the second	47	2	
On the third	50	2	
On the fourth	81	4	
Matthew glossed by brother Thomas Aquinas	57	3	
Mark	20		16
Luke	40	2	
Summa theologiae of brother Thomas Aquinas, Book I	56	3	
First part of the second book	60	3	
Second part of the second book	82	4	
Questions on Truth of brother Thomas	66	3	
Questions on the Power of God	28		14
On spiritual creatures	5		3
Questions on the Soul and Virtues	24		12
Questions on Evil	28		14

Title of the Book	Number of peciae	Price	
		s.	d.
Questions *de quolibet* (what you will)	14		7
Summa contra Gentiles of brother Thomas	57	3	
On Perfection of Condition	7		4
Postille on the Gospel of John	41		20

These are writings of brother Peter de Tarantasia

On the first book of the Sentences	33		18
On the second	35		19
On the third	36		20
On the fourth	48		27
Postille on the Pauline Epistles	70	3	6
Postille on Luke	32		18

Literal commentary of Robert Kilwardby on the Sentences	44		22
Postille of brother William of Altona on Matthew	27		16
Postille of the same on Isaiah	26		16
Postille of brother William of Melton on the Psalter	96	4	
Postille of the same on the twelve prophets	61	4	6
Postille of the same on Mark	51	3	
On Ecclesiasticus	58	3	6
Postille of the same on Job	51	3	6

These are writings of brother Bonaventura of the Order of Friars Minor, namely:

Postille on Luke	73	3	
Postille of the same on Ecclesiastes	12		6
Postille on the Song of Songs	13		8
Postille on the book of Proverbs	37		20
Postille on the Song of Songs	15		8
Postille on the book of Wisdom	10		6
Postille on the Apocalypse	23		15
Postille on the canonical epistles	15		8
On the Sentences for the first book		2	
For the second		4	

Title of the Book	Number of peciae	Price	
		s.	d.
For the third		2	
For the fourth		2	
For the text of the Bible		5	
For the five books of Moses glossed		5	
For all the historical books		5	
For Job		2	
For the Psalter glossed		4	
For the books of Solomon		2	
For sixteen prophets		5	
For the Gospels with the old gloss		4	
For the Pauline Epistles		4	
For the Acts of the Apostles, canonical epistles and Apocalypse		2	
Sermons of brother William of Lyons for Sundays on the Epistles	65	2	6
His Sermons on the Saints	69	2	6
Sermons of brother Thomas Brito for Sundays on both Epistles and Gospels, namely, opening "Abiciamus"	61	2	
His Sermons opening, "Precinxisti," namely, the Communion of the Saints	47		20
Sermons opening, "Abiciamus" of (William of) Mailly, for Sundays	49		20
His Sermons for Feast days, namely from the feast of St. Andrew the Apostle to Annunciation	17		8
Sermons of brother Peter of St. Benedict, opening, "Desideratus," for Sundays	24		12
His Sermons for Feast days, opening, "Suspendium"	21		8
Communion of the Saints, opening, "Nimis honorati sunt"	20		8
Sermons of Alleabatensis for Sundays			
Sermons for Sundays and Feast days opening, "Legifer"	35		18

Title of the Book	*Number of peciae*	*Price*	
		s.	*d.*
Provincial Sermons of Tussia which open, "Sapientia sanctorum"	32		15
New Legends of all the Saints	90	3	
Sunday Sermons of Biardus	51		18
His Sermons for Feast Days	18		6
Distinctions of Mauritius	84	3	

This is the assessment of Exemplaria

For the text of the Decretals	4	
For the Apparatus of the Decretals	5	
For the text of the *Decretum*	5	
For the Apparatus of the *Decretum*	6	
For the Summa of Geoffrey	2	
For the Summa of Hugh	8	
For the Summa of master Peter de Salinis	5	
For the Apparatus of Innocent	10	
For the Cases of Bartholomew	2	6
For the Cases of Bernard	2	6
For the Summa of Raymond with the Apparatus	4	
For the books of Ranfredus in canon and civil law	5	
For the Repertory (of William Durant)	2	
For the *Copiosa* (of Henry Hostiensis)	10	
For the Apparatus of Hostiensis	30	
For his *Margarita*		12
For the text of the Old Digest	6	
For the Apparatus	5	
For the text of the New Digest	4	
For the Apparatus	4	
For the text of the *Infortiatum*	4	
For the Apparatus	4	
For the text of the small *Volumen*	4	
For the Apparatus	4	
For the text of the Code	5	
For the Apparatus	5	

50

MASTERS TO KEEP A RECORD OF THEIR SCHOLARS, PARIS, 1289

Chartularium universitatis Parisiensis, II, 35–36.

To all who shall see the present letters the rector of the university of Paris and the masters, one and all, of the faculty of arts send greeting in the Son of the glorious Virgin. Noticing that because of the multitude of scholars of our faculty we do not know the names of many and cannot discern who are good and legitimate or factitious, and some pretend to be scholars of our faculty in order to enjoy the privileges and liberties of the same and of the university and be defended, who as putrid members should be separated from such a body or association (for both on account of such the faculty is often defamed and belittled by many, and the masters of the said faculty are in various ways impeded from study and contemplation, and good scholars because of the association and influence of such persons withdraw from the university so that they are unable to acquire the precious pearl of science): we, wishing to apply a wholesome remedy for this, decree and also ordain that the masters of the said faculty, one and all, and also those who are about to incept in the said faculty, shall be required by oath, all fraud aside, to write down the names of their own scholars, that they may have knowledge of the good ones and be able to give lawful testimony about them in place and time and on any necessary occasion, so that only those attending the university and conducting themselves towards masters as is customary and statutory with respect to both ordinary and cursory lectures and making due compensation for the same, if they are so required by their own masters, and if the masters shall be content with them, shall enjoy the privileges and liberties of the faculty and university and may be promoted to particular functions in the said faculty. But fictitious scholars and hangers-on of the university shall not be written down with the good, but as useless shall be removed from the bosom and association of the faculty, so that without dispensation from the faculty they may not be promoted to any standing in the faculty nor enjoy the privileges and liberties of the university but shall be held for non-scholars by each of the masters by their oaths. Moreover, we will and ordain that every rector upon his institution shall be bound by oath that he will cause the present ordinance to be circulated annually through the classes of the masters by a sworn servitor. Nevertheless, we wish that, these things notwithstanding, all statutes and privileges of the university be inviolably observed in all and by all. And that these may have firm validity, the seals of the four nations are affixed to the present schedule. Given in the year of the Lord 1289, at St. Julien le Pauvre, the Friday following the feast of St. Denis.

51

A SCHOLAR DIVORCED, PARIS, 1290

Chartularium universitatis Parisiensis, II, 39.

To all who may see the present letters the Official of Paris sends greeting in the Lord. We make known that in our presence John, called Florie, a cleric and scholar of Paris, asserted on his oath in law before us with personal security from the same cleric, that a divorce was made between him on one side and his wife Simonia on the other by the venerable man and discreet Official of the court of Rouen, as he said. And the same cleric promised by the said oath that, if the said divorce should be revoked in any way so that there should be a reconciliation between them, thereupon the said John would be deprived of the function of teaching at Paris in the faculty of arts. What we have heard, this we bear witness to. In testimony of which thing at the request of the cleric himself we have seen fit to append the seal of the (ecclesiastical) court of Paris to the present letters. Given in the year of the Lord 1290, the Monday after *Jubilate*.

52

SALE OF PARCHMENT AT PARIS, 1291

Chartularium universitatis Parisiensis, II, 48–51.

Parchment was precious to masters and students as writing material and for the multiplication of books, as indicated in Selection 49. The university found it advisable to regulate its sale and the dealers in it. Paper was already being manufactured in Italy, first at Fabriano about 1269–1276, then at Bologna in 1293, at Cividale, and a little later at Padua, Genoa, and Treviso. The university of Paris, however, accepted dealers in paper only in 1415. The mills of Fabriano were the most successful in improving the technique of paper-making during the later thirteenth and fourteenth centuries. The long-accepted legend of a paper made of cotton by the Arabs has been destroyed by microscopic examination by botanists, showing that the extant specimens are made of rags of linen or hemp. It was new processes, rather, which distinguished the paper of Fabriano from that of the Arabic world and of Jativa in Spain, where paper was first manufactured in Europe. There the paste had been beaten with wooden pestles, glued with starch, and contained long fibres. At Fabriano the paste was better masticated by metal mallets run by water power, was glued with gelatin, had short fibres, and was marked with filigranes. It was this improved paper which ultimately came to replace parchment.

To all the faithful of Christ who shall see the present page the university of masters and scholars studying at Paris send greeting in the Son of the glorious Virgin. Since at our request and for our common advantage, the religious men, the minister and brethren of the house of St. Mathurin at Paris of the Order of the Holy Trinity and Captives, have conceded to us a place in the court of their house for the receiving and sale of parchment of their sheer grace and so long as they please, until we shall provide us with another suitable place, know ye all that we make no claim to the said place of right, usage, dominion or perpetuity. In testimony of which thing we have conceded to the said religious the present letter patent fortified by the muniment of our seal. Given the year of the Lord 1291, the month of June.

When first any foreign merchant having parchment to expose for sale has entered the city of Paris, he shall be required to bring or have brought the said parchment to the accustomed place, namely to St. Mathurin and, this done, to go or send someone to the rector of the university of Paris in order that the rector may send one of his assistants to inventory the said parchment and, this done, to have it inspected and valued by four sworn parchment-dealers of the same university. And the same rector shall be required to post or have posted notices and bills on behalf of the said university stating that, if any scholar or other needs parchment, he shall seek the said place of Mathurins to buy parchment, if it seems good to him. And the said evaluation made, the said merchant of the same parchment shall be required to occupy or have occupied the said place where the parchment is on view and there for twenty-four hours to await scholars, practitioners and others desiring to buy parchment. And during the duration of the said time of twenty-four hours the parchment-dealers of this city of Paris or any one of them may not and should not buy, nor should the said foreign merchant expose his parchment or any part thereof for sale to them under penalty of the fine accustomed to be levied in this case. When the said twenty-four hours are elapsed the said merchant can sell and expose for sale, and the same parchment-dealers of this city of Paris may buy, if they see fit.

To all who shall see and hear the present letters the university of masters and scholars at Paris sends greeting in Him who is the true salvation of all. It is written in canon law: "It is fruit divine to have often dispensed justice." For the supreme good in life is to cherish justice and deal out to each one his deserts, whether he is to be rewarded with a prize or afflicted with penalty or punishment. Since therefore between us on the one hand and the parchment-dealers of Paris on the other there has long since been dissension over this, namely, that the same parchment-dealers committed many frauds and many acts of ill will in buying and selling parchment to the prejudice and injury of university and state, therefore at that time we made them swear that they would commit no frauds in buying and selling, rather would buy faithfully and sell faithfully. But that which they promised by oath they have not legally observed, as recent investigation has shown. Rather adding fraud to fraud, evil to evil, to the peril of their own souls, and damage and loss of many persons, they have repeatedly acted contrary to their own oath. And since it is written that humility little aids the humble, if contempt does not harm the contumacious, and that crimes should be punished wherever they are detected, nay 'tis certain that he will not scruple at underhand conspiracy who fails to check manifest crime: therefore we, desiring to check their so many and great deceits as best we can, with the profit of the university in mind, have drawn up certain articles which, first put into Romance or French, we have made them swear to publicly.

The first article is that the said parchment-dealers make no conspiracies to the prejudice and injury of the masters and scholars and of the parchment-dealers to each other.

That in buying they observe good faith and legality towards one another.

That they sell lawfully without fraud to the said masters and scholars, nor shall they hide good parchment, if they have it with them.

That they shall not go to merchants outside the fairs to buy parchment by themselves or through others, and that they shall not buy parchment in pelts for future years at their pleasure, and that they buy nothing by candlelight in secret.

That they make no agreement with foreign merchants at the time of the fairs or any other time, arranging or assessing with them as to the price to be charged.

That they do not buy parchment except at St. Mathurins or in the public place of the fairs.

That if the parchment-dealers at Paris buy parchment in the presence of a master or scholar who needs parchment, that the said master or scholar shall have part of that parchment for the price at which it was bought. However, the master or scholar shall be required to give the said parchment-dealer sixpence in the pound for his service and labor. Moreover, we mean by present that he should be there before the parchment is divided.

That single merchants present share in the purchase. Moreover, we mean by present as said above.

That on the first day of the fairs of Lendit [1] or St. Lazare they do not buy parchment before the merchants of the king, of the bishop of Paris, and masters and scholars have bought, unless foreign merchants on the said day have bought before the said time.

We order that scholars may not buy except for themselves and their associates and may not resell to others unless they should have to leave (i.e. leave the university).

At the time of the fairs the bedells of the university shall be sent to the fairs and diligently inquire if scholars or parchment-dealers are committing fraud in selling or buying there.

We ordain that the parchment-dealers agree that during the term of every rector careful investigation about these matters be made by

[1] Held at St. Denis the second Wednesday in June.

those deputed or to be deputed by the university, and that these things each and all be published each year in sermons and in classes, that masters and scholars who know anything of the aforesaid may reveal it to the rector. Given in the year of the Lord 1291, the Tuesday after the feast of All Saints.

53

PLAINT OF THE UNIVERSITY OF PARIS,
1292–1316

Chartularium universitatis Parisiensis, II, 182–83.

It is not stated just when or by whom this memorandum was drawn up, or to whom it was addressed, or from what university action it resulted.

Articles or defects of the university. The university suffers injury in this, that privileges granted it by the apostolic see are ill observed, in that we have no conserver of certain privileges. For, although the university has the privilege that a licentiate of Paris in any faculty may incept and lecture at Paris or elsewhere, yet this is not carried out in some regions such as England and Montpellier, and in some other universities, where a master or licentiate of Paris is not admitted to a master's functions, no matter how great may be his reputation.

Also, that little or no provision is made in these days for masters and scholars, albeit deserving.

Also, that students, of whatever kingdom or province they are, cannot enjoy their property freely.

Also, that scholars are molested to pay taxes on their houses. The university asks that a letter, granted long since as to this, be handed over and preserved in the archives.

Also, it asks letters of the king by virtue of which those who for the time being are chaplains of the university may freely receive their fruits or rents at the times assigned.

Also, the university asks that judges, secular as well as ecclesiastical, be forced to observe the privileges of the university and, without delay and hindrance to students, to administer justice as often as they may be required.

Also, the university begs the lord king that he deign to make pro-

vision for the dean of St. Marcel near Paris as a venerable man who
has long served the university laudably and honorably, and likewise
for others specially nominated to him by the university.

Note that those who seize the property of scholars at present cannot be compelled to make restitution, as is clear in the case of a scholar
to whom 123 pounds are owed by a burgher of Lille; also in the case
of master William of Louvain, a bachelor of theology, whose goods
were taken by Reginald Canet, royal collector near St. Quentin *in
claustro Foviensi,* to the value of 120 pounds Parisian. Further make
note of a master in medicine who was beaten at St. Antoine. Also,
concerning another who, contrary to the privileges, was detained in the
prison of the bishop of Troyes.

54

FLEMISH STUDENTS AT PARIS AND ORLÉANS NOT TO BE MOLESTED DURING THE WAR, 1297

Chartularium universitatis Parisiensis, II, 75.

Philip, by the grace of God king of the Franks, to all our justiciars and
ministers to whom the present letters may come, greeting. Although
to all who are intent on the pursuit of good arts we gladly display
that favoring attitude by which they may be preserved from molesta-
tion which would withdraw them from praiseworthy works, yet to
those who engage in scholastic disciplines we the more gladly show
the opportune favor which they seem to deserve by their merits that,
the more bent upon wisdom, in which our soul continually delights,
they may conform to our grace. Wherefore lest on the pretext of the
rebellion of Guy, once count of Flanders, or any other of our adversaries, masters and scholars studying at Paris and Orléans or their
servants, wherever they may have been born, should be molested, we
wish them to remain under our protection in the universities of Paris
and Orléans, ordering you and each of you that you defend from injuries and violence the said masters and scholars and their servants
who may wish to be laudably engaged in the same universities, permitting their messengers, bringing their money and other necessities to

them at Paris and Orléans with letters patent which they may send to Flanders or may be sent from there to them at Paris and Orléans, provided they are free from all suspicion, to pass going and returning in the customary way. Given at Paris the 25th day of February in the year of the Lord 1296.

55

RAYMOND LULL URGES THE STUDY OF ORIENTAL LANGUAGES, 1298–1299

Chartularium universitatis Parisiensis, II, 83–84.

Raymond Lull (c. 1235–1315), prominent in the history of Spanish literature, of Latin learning, and of the history of religion, here engages in propaganda which was to result in the decree of the Council of Vienne in 1312 (see Selection 60.) A good deal had already been done, however, to promote the study of oriental languages for missionary purposes. Innocent IV in 1248 had ordered ten boys skilled in Arabic and other oriental languages to be trained in theology at Paris in order to go out as missionaries to convert the East (*Chartularium*, I, 212). The provincial chapter at Toledo in 1250 named eight Dominicans to study Arabic. In 1276 Lull persuaded the king of Aragon to establish a college in Majorca for the study of Arabic. In 1281 Fra Joan de Periguentos founded a college for the study of Arabic at Valencia, while Raymond Martini became professor at the *studium hebraicum* of Barcelona. See also above, Selection 31, 1256 A.D.

Faithful to God is he and burning with supreme charity who in the knowledge and enjoyment of supreme wisdom and love directing the ignorant, illuminating the blind, leading back the dead to the way of life, fears not perils of his own adversity and bodily death for the testament of God. Who shall tell his glory and great splendor? Who shall number the generations of infidels who today know not God? Who shall estimate how many from the blindness of error slip into the shadows of hell? Alas! the devout Christian people of the faithful justly laments so great evils. O fount of science supernal, that at Paris hast intoxicated wtih marvelous doctrine so many professors of so great authority, extend thy torrents to the lands of the infidels, and irrigate the totally arid hearts of the erring with dew celestial, and drive away darkness, open to them the rays of light eternal. Ah, when shall all nations walk in thy light and every man walking in the splendor of thy sun see the salvation of God? With desire have I, Raymond Lull, desired this which is supremely desirable for all faithful Christians and obtainable by those whose intellects the supreme wisdom has divinely illuminated. Happy is that university which bears so many defenders of the faith, and happy that city whose soldiers armed with the wisdom and devotion of Christ can subdue barbarous nations to the supreme king. When shall all the earth adore Thee, God, hymn and bless Thy name, and every tribe and tongue serve Thee?

Consider this, reverend fathers and sirs, with intellects and wills whose object is the highest truth and highest goodness. Since just as God is intelligible and lovable because supremely true and supremely good, so He is everywhere and much, because immense, and present at all times, because eternal. O how happy were the apostles and martyrs, since their sound has gone forth into all the earth and their words to the ends of the world preaching Jesus Christ! O how precious their death in the sight of the Lord, who recalled many from death unto life! O would that there were now many repairers of their ways, since it would be indeed glorious and necessary for the whole Christian people. Because as I know, since I speak from experience, there are many philosophers of the Arabs who strive to pervert Christians to the perfidy of Mahomet and the sons of unbelievers pester us saying, Where is their God? And further, the Jews and Saracens to the best of their ability try to bring the Tartars into their sects. And if it happens, which God forbid, that the Tartars become Jews or Saracens or constitute a sect by themselves, it is to be feared that this will result in incomparable detriment to all Christendom, just as happened from the sect of Mahomet at whose foundation the Saracens invaded us and about a third part of Christendom was lost. Innumerable is that generation of Tartars, in a short time indeed it has subjugated many kingdoms and principalities by warlike hand.

You, reverend fathers and masters, see peril threaten the entire church of God, and unless your wisdom and devotion, by which all Christendom is sustained, opposes the shield of salvation to the perfidy of the Saracens, and if it neglects to restrain the impetuous torrent of Tartars—I will not say more—but think what may happen! And strange it is that there are more adversaries of God than defenders,

and more men vituperate than praise Him; and God was made man
for men and died that they might live; and many, too, have now declined from the unity of the church, like the Greeks and many other
schismatics. Consider how great evil is returned for good to God and
how great opprobrium by those who were created to praise God, and
how great persecution threatens us faithful, and what question we
must answer to God at the last judgment, when He requires from us
the death of those who should have enjoyed life eternal from our
preaching and example.

Here the prick of conscience stings me and compels me to come
to you, whose high discretion and wisdom it behooves to act in such
a matter, so pious, so meritorious, in a service so grateful to God and
useful to the entire world, namely, that here at Paris, where the
fountain of divine wisdom rises, where the light of truth shines on
Christian peoples, there should be founded study of Arabic, Tartar and
Greek, that we, having learned the languages of the adversaries of
God and ourselves, by preaching to and teaching them may overcome
their errors in the sword of truth and render the people acceptable
unto God and convert enemies into friends. If this be done and it
please God that it so be, Christendom will receive the greatest exaltation and extension. And of this so inestimable thing you will be the
foundation, and thou, university of Paris, will by no means be least
among thy doctors, for from thee will come light to all peoples, and
thou wilt offer testimony to the truth, and masters and disciples will
flock to thee, and all shall hear all sciences from thee. What of good
will the Greeks and Arabs have in their volumes that will not be
known to thee, when thou shalt understand their tongues without an
interpreter? Who will estimate how great praise, how great honor to
God, how great compassion of charity towards poor sinners, and how
great good would result in and from this place? And this can easily
be done, if you direct your prayers to the illustrious king of France,
that he, who is noblest among the kings of earth, see fit to bestow his
well-merited alms on this noblest of all undertakings, namely, to
found and endow the said study or studies. And he will listen to you,
I believe, after he has understood the importance of this undertaking.

56

ARNALD OF VILLANOVA APPEALS FROM THE FACULTY OF THEOLOGY OF PARIS, 1300

Chartularium universitatis Parisiensis, II, 87–90.

Arnald of Villanova, famous as a medical writer and for his personal relations with several kings and popes, has left the following account of his difficulties with the faculty of theology at Paris in 1299–1300, where he had come with a message from Jayme II of Aragon to Philip the Fair. It will be noted that it was not his writings in astrology or alchemy which got Arnald into trouble but his tendency, although a layman, to dabble in theology and urge clerical reform, and in this case more particularly a work in which he had predicted the coming of antichris .[1]

In the name of the Lord, Amen. In the year from His nativity 1300, indiction 13, in the presence of me, a notary, and the witnesses signed below, the prudent and discreet man, master Arnald called of Villanova, a resident of Montpellier, has protested to the apostolic see, provoked and appealed and done the other things written below, and to the appeal made by him as contained in another public instrument written by the hand of me, the notary below named, he has adhered and renewed it now and has wished and ordered a copy of the same to be made by hand of a notary to whomsoever under this form of words.

It may be I am a worm and not a man and an opprobrium to men, yet I have a conscience and inner monitor, nor can I expunge or reject its murmur by which I am often blamed. And so with God and my conscience as witnesses I notify you, reverend college of theologians at Paris that recently, namely on the day and hour at which you dragged me before the presence of the reverend father, the bishop of

---

[1] Concerning the life and works of Arnald of Villanova one may consult further the article on him in the *Histoire littéraire de la France*, vol. 28, various articles by P. Diepgen in the *Archiv für Geschichte der Medizin*, III (1910), etc., and his volume, *Arnald von Villanova als Politiker und Laien-theologe*, 1909, Heft 9 of *Abhandl. z. Mittle. u. Neuer. Gesch.*, and chapter 68 in vol. II and chapter 4 in vol. III of my *History of Magic and Experimental Science*.

Paris, fear and trembling came over me and covered me stupefied by the gloom of terror as I compared things past to those which were then in actual process. For recalling that, albeit I had come quickly, gladly and reverently at each summons of the lord chancellor, as he himself stated in the chapel of St. Denis de Passu, nevertheless you, sirs, I know not with what motive or words, because of purely scholastic acts, called in the Official of Paris who thence treacherously summoned, craftily retained, and rudely and impiously imprisoned me in a house pernicious to me from my bodily suffering and calamities. And again I recalled that, when in the said chapel you irregularly received me in your grace to private converse, I conceded to you that I had written the articles which you had read to me not in the sense they sounded as extracted by you from my work but in the sense which they made in their proper context. And because you, sirs, said that they were rashly written, I conceded that out of reverence for you I would be prepared to temper them according to your judgment, and you were to take time to deliberate concerning the suitable method of amending them. But when finally a day was fixed to notify me of the form of amendment thought out and ordained by you, it appeared to me that in the ordinance dictated and written by you on a certain form it was expressly stated, "qualify and revoke," although these are acts different in kind corresponding to diverse objects, one for rash and the other for erroneous utterances. Also, I saw that you had brought the aforesaid bishop for the publication of the promised qualification, although I had been prepared to temper anything rashly said in a reasonable manner. I considered that, albeit I instantly sought reasons in writings by which the said articles seemed to be impugned somehow, that I might inform and settle my conscience and not take action while it was fluctuating and murmuring, you would not grant me this, although it is incumbent upon you to confirm and preserve the consciences of men from fall or ruin.

Again, there being present and assisting me Almaric, viscount of Narbonne, and Guillaume Nogaret, a knight of the king of France, and Alphinus of Narnia, a cleric of the same king, and master Gerard de Novavilla, cantor of Tyarnus, and master C. de Poilaco, canon of Vivarais, and Simon de Marcay, knight of the king, I heard from the reverend father, the archbishop of Narbonne, and from the discreet man, the archdeacon of Algya, who passed back and forth between you and me and reported proposals on both sides, treating for concord and offering on my behalf that I was prepared straightway to go to the supreme pontiff and stand in his judgment, that you, sirs, ordered me to be arrested and imprisoned by the aforesaid bishop, if I would not yield to your will. I learned further from these same men that that one of the masters who bore the standard of humility, namely the cord of the angel of God and signet of God the Savior, that is, of the blessed Francis, was more keenly intent on sinking me than the others, which I afterwards learned no less by experience, when, at a signal from him and certain others, moving their heads in ridicule, they said carelessly and calumniously, "You sit in the watch tower, you are a prophet." Carelessly indeed, because they did not remember that the spirit bloweth where it listeth and the Lord does not cast out little ones but supplies them with wisdom. Calumniously, moreover, because it is not contained in my work that I sat or sit on a watch tower but that the watchmen of the church of Christ ought to reply in kind to the questions of their adversaries.

Since with all the aforesaid therefore I knew by probable conjecture that permanent imprisonment was prepared for me, before you doctors and masters of the college of theologians of Paris and all present I, master Arnald called of Villanova, resident of Montpellier, by the present writing protest and protesting say or pronounce that whatever I said recently before the lord bishop, reading the form of your ordinance which the lord chancellor placed in my hands insisting that I read it without any delay, I did not say nor did I pronounce reading or otherwise except struck by fear of the pernicious house in which I feared to be imprisoned because of the aforesaid. And therefore, since the process instituted by you and the aforesaid lord bishop is *ipso jure* invalid, null and void, since it lacked foundation and I did not swear to observe it, I accordingly do now commit my work on the coming of antichrist to the examination and judgment of the apostolic see and myself to its protection, prepared with the aid of Christ to answer there to the arguments of whoever wish to impugn the said work. And whoever wish to attack or proceed against it openly or publicly, of whatever rank or dignity or station they may be, I now summon to the presence and audience of the supreme pontiff, where streams of science abound, and I assign to them as term the fourth week after next Easter.

Moreover, besides this I beg all you masters of the aforesaid college with humble supplication that in like matters your modesty or maturity henceforth be so known to men that what requires a year of deliberation and sifting in the din of public disputation and the scrutiny of studious determination, you do not try to smother in one month by a swift attack, especially where probable scandal of neighbors is involved, saying in imitation of Christ, suffer and cherish the little ones and not persecute them, since it is detestable to God and men to be stirred by appetite and rabid motion against a stranger who is not a Parisian by origin or residence or school attendance or commission of a crime, who is not infamous, is common to all God's servants, and is the solemn nuncio on urgent business of a serene prince to the most serene—and this without notifying and totally disregarding the majesty of royal excellence.

Moreover, on behalf of the king of France, who owes it to him who sent me as ambassador to himself to return me safe and sound with all my possessions, not despoiled or robbed by anyone of his kingdom, I require of you, lord chancellor, that you restore to me my writing which I committed to your faith and freely conceded as an exemplar, that you make to me full amends for its violent retention made against my will from the day on which by my associate, master Raymond of Poitiers, I asked you to restore it to me.

Moreover, similarly as ambassador I require you, the whole college, to make full amends to me for having dragged me, not harmful to you nor blasphemous to God nor a foe to the faith, without any reason into the presence of the bishop and compelled me to read a form dictated and ordered by you.

And you, master Geoffrey of Chartres, I require on behalf of the king and apostolic see to redact in public form all the aforesaid and what was read and the replies which those sirs may make to the above requests, in order that it may be clear in judgment who is the rasher, he who is said to write rashly or he who acts rashly, and that the innocent may exclaim before the angels of God, "May the proud be confounded because they worked iniquity against me: but I will labor in thy mandates. Let those turn to me who fear Thee, Lord, and who know thy testimonies." [1]

And since recently within the time prescribed by law for making

[1] Psalm 118, 79.

appeal I could not obtain the presence of the lord bishop, therefore as a precaution I have appealed in writing from the will of a superior to the apostolic see, from a wicked and unjust judge, against the process of the bishop and his accessories in his hall. And I adhere to that appeal, and I renew it now, and I wish a copy to be made for whomsoever by hand of the notary, and also one of the present protest.

Done at Paris in the manor of the lord said bishop of Paris on October 12, in the presence of the venerable men the archdeacon of Paris, chancellor of the church of Paris and master Peter of Auvergne, masters of theology, hearing what was done for the other masters in the theological faculty, Ralph de Roseto, penitentiary of Paris, and the Official of Paris, canons in the said church of Paris called on behalf of the bishop, and the following witnesses, the reverend father, the archbishop of Narbonne, the most noble count of Arras, the noble lord Almaric, viscount of Narbonne, the venerable masters Nicholaus de Cathan, archdeacon in the church of Reims, professor of laws, master Thierry, treasurer of the count of Arras, and many others summoned for the purpose in the same year, indiction, place and day.

The venerable chancellor of Paris having been requested, as said above, to restore to the said master Arnald his writing or opuscule which he had entrusted to his faith and freely conceded as an exemplar, as he said, the said chancellor replied that he had passed it on to other masters in the said faculty and that he would speak to them about it.

Done in the presence of those above mentioned. And I, Geoffrey, called Ligator, of Chartres, by authority of the holy Roman church public notary, was present at the above and wrote them down and as requested published them and signed them with my mark as duly requisite.

57

THE FACULTY OF THEOLOGY AND THE PROCESS OF THE TEMPLARS, 1308

Chartularium universitatis Parisiensis, II, 125–27.

On October 13, 1307, all Knights Templars in France were arrested, their property sequestered, and their persons given over to Inquisitors to question under torture as to charges of heresy, blasphemy, idolatry, and gross immorality made against them. The pope took action against the order in a bull of November 22, 1307. Philip the Fair was reluctant to surrender direction of proceedings in France to the pope and put the questions referred to in the following document to the faculty of theology at Paris. Ultimately he gave over nominal jurisdiction to the ecclesiastical authorities but kept actual control. Many Templars had confessed under torture and later protested their innocence in vain. But the opinion came to prevail that the charges against them had been largely trumped up, and that the king coveted their riches. When, however, the pope dissolved the order at the Council of Vienne in 1312, its property was assigned to another crusading order, the Knights Hospitalers. The French crown, however, turned over only a remnant left after Philip's death.

To the most serene and Christian prince Philip, by grace of God most illustrious king of the Franks, his humble and devoted chaplains, the masters in theology at Paris, albeit unworthy, those teaching as well as those not giving instruction, with all subjection promptly and willingly ever offer grateful and devoted service to royal majesty. The most Christian kings of the most illustrious realm of the Franks are known to have shone from the start of their kingdom not so much by magnitude of power as moral excellence and piety of Christian religion. Hence it is, most excellent lord, that you, imitating the praiseworthy morals of your sainted predecessors, flaming with zeal for the faith, yet desiring to defend even the faith with due rule of reason and without usurpation of the right of another power, although you might command us as your clients, yet of your great condescension have preferred to ask our opinion in friendly fashion by your letters, how namely you might proceed without infringement of another jurisdiction against certain subversors of the faith itself, thereon proposing certain articles, to which the importance of the affair and the absence of some of our chief members has forced us to reply tardily, on which account may the accustomed benevolence of royal piety pardon us the offense of so great delay. Moreover, having held careful and mature and frequent deliberation over the said articles, we have decided to reply thus, that, to avoid prolixity and taking too much of your majesty's time, we may state precisely the conclusions which we, persuaded by rational motives, believe to be true. Therefore to the aforesaid articles let us reply in the way which follows:

To the first, in which it is asked whether a secular prince may arrest, examine or punish heretics, we say that it seems to us that the authority of a secular judge does not extend to opening any prosecution in the matter of heresy against anyone not abandoned by the church, unless the church requests or has requested it, except when evident and notorious peril threatens, in which case under sure hope of ratification the secular power may arrest them with the intention of turning them over to the church so soon as opportunity shall offer. Nor does it seem to us that from any authority of the Old or New Testament it can be expressly held that the secular prince ought to interfere otherwise in the said crime. Moreover, as to this question whether, if princes seemed to have jurisdiction in a case of the said crime from the Old Testament, the same would be restricted in any way by the New Testament, we say that if restriction means the revocation of any statute or right which has virtue solely from the institution of the old law, every such is so restricted in the time of the new law, so indeed that all the virtue it has from the sole institution of the old law is revoked in the time of the New Testament.

To the second main question, which asks whether the Templars, because they are soldiers, are to be regarded as not religious and as not exempt, we say that it seems to us that soldiery ordained for the defense of the faith does not impede the state of religion and that such soldiers professing a vow of religion instituted by the church should be regarded as religious and exempt. If, moreover, any have not made such profession but have only bound themselves to that heresy, they are not religious nor to be so regarded. If, however, it is doubtful whether they have so professed, it belongs to the church which instituted their order to settle the matter. For by reason of the crime all that touches the crime pertains to the church in every person until, as has been said, he has been abandoned by the church.

To the third, when it is asked whether the order should be condemned because of the suspicion arising out of the confessions already made, we say that, since, from confessions now made, strong suspicion exists against all of the order that they are heretics or accomplices—that is, for not accusing or notifying the church, since a strong presumption exists that they were by no means ignorant that the said heresy flourished in the order, especially when masters of the whole order, and other persons of importance who had received many in the order, and many others have confessed to a crime of this sort—this should suffice to condemn the order to the odium of particular persons or to inquiring against the entire order thus publicly sullied by so great a crime.

To the fourth, when it is asked what should be done about those who have not confessed or been convicted, if there were any such, we say that since there is a strong presumption against all members of the order, as was said, although such are not to be condemned as heretics, since they have neither confessed nor been convicted, nevertheless because there is much to fear concerning them because of the said suspicion, it seems to us that such wholesome provision should be made for them that the danger of infecting others be guarded against.

To the fifth, when it is asked concerning the thirty or forty remaining, the answer is clear from what has been said in the third and fourth articles.

To the sixth and seventh, when it is asked what should be done with the possessions of the Templars, we say that since the goods of the Temple were not given to the Templars outright and as owners but rather as servants for defense of the faith and support of the Holy Land—and this was the final intention of those giving those goods, and those which are for an end, have reason and necessity from the end, since the aforesaid end remains while they are found wanting—the said goods should be faithfully ordained and preserved for the said end. As to guardianship it seems to us it should be so ordered as is most expedient for the said end.

These therefore, most serene lord, as best we could, we have concluded and written in unison, heartily wishing to follow the orders of the king and also the truth. We hope that they may be acceptable to his majesty, because we are prepared to expend much diligent study on those matters which shall please so great highness. And may so great injury to the faith, of which you are the chief fist and defender, which is so scandalous and horrible to all Christian people, be speedily punished according to your holy desire. Your royal majesty which we firmly believe is fruitful not only to the temporal rule of the republic but also to the spiritual advantage of the church, may the Most High long preserve, and may your benign eminence deign to hold in favor us, your devoted and humble chaplains. In testimony, moreover, of all the aforesaid we have decreed that our seals be affixed to the present document. Given on the feast of the Annunciation of the blessed Virgin, the year of the Lord 1307 (old style).

THE CONFESSION OF THE GRAND MASTER
OF THE TEMPLE

Ibid., II, 129–30.

These are the rubrics made of the confession and testimony of the Grand Master of the Order of the Temple, made in the presence of brother William of Paris of the Order of Preachers, inquisitor of heretical depravity in the kingdom of France, and many other trustworthy persons, namely, master Yvo de Cordellis, rector of the university of Paris, and master Stephen, chancellor of Paris, and six masters in theology, the abbot of St. Germain, the Official of Paris, the prior of the Preachers, in which is contained:

Brother Jacobus de Molay, master of the entire order of the knights of the Temple, for himself and brothers Gerard de Gauche, Guido Dalphinus, Geoffrey de Charnay, and Walter de Lienticuria, knights of the said Order there present, confessed, proposed and asserted that for a long time since those who were received into the said order denied the Lord Jesus Christ and spit in contempt of Him upon the cross which was showed with the effigy of Jesus Christ at the reception of each one. And at the said reception they had so far committed other enormities, for opportunity of committing which the abuse of receiving secretly the brothers of the said order had been introduced under the pretense of good by the author of crimes. Which offenses indeed the author of light had brought into the light through the assistance of the most Christian prince, lord Philip, king of France.

The same master, writing to each and all of the brothers of the said order within the kingdom of France tells how they compelled new brothers on being received to deny Jesus Christ and spit on the cross, and how many other enormities they added to these, which were long concealed and continued, as each of them knows from his own reception. Wherefore he exhorts the said brothers in the Lord, enjoining in virtue of holy obedience that, notwithstanding promises or oaths to keep secrets of this sort, they reveal the pure truth in these and other matters touching the catholic faith of which they may know, and with sincere mind confess to the aforesaid inquisitor or his commissaries or ordinaries whatever they know about themselves or others in these matters. And he has sanctioned the sending of these writings to the houses of the said order in the kingdom of France in a form approved by him and sealed with his seal. Also he himself has confessed that at his reception he thrice denied Jesus, twice spit on the cross and once on the ground. Afterwards, moreover, the same master sought to obtain absolution, pardon, grace and mercy of holy mother church through those standing there for himself and brothers penitent and confessed, offering himself and the said brothers penitent for the aforesaid and humbly confessing to receive penance and fulfill and accept the mandates of the church.

58

A STUDENT'S COLOPHON TO HIS REPORT OF A COURSE OF LECTURES, 1308

Auguste Pelzer, "Barthélemy de Bruges," *Revue néoscolastique de philosophie*, XXXVI (1934), 472, from University of Leipzig MS 1426.

In the year of the Lord 1308, at the time when pope Clement was residing at Poitiers, on Friday, the vigil of St. Peter, the 29th of June. Here end the Questions on the book of Physics of Aristotle reported at Paris in the street of Straw under the venerable man and assiduous devotee of philosophy, master Bartholomew of Bruges, by Francis of Città di Castello.

Moreover, if any fault be found in these questions, let no one dare impute it to so great a man, unless he himself shall first have made better ones, and such are not to be hoped for in these times. And so I know that whatever defect there may be should rationally be imputed to me, for although I gave the best attention I could, yet I was not capable of complete understanding of so great a work and author.

Nevertheless I give thanks to the Creator because, just as I planned to report the lectures from the start, so I completed the task omitting nothing, although many a time I hesitated from excess of labor.

These Questions number 140 in all and begin thus: "Quemadmodum nostrorum corporum habitus spectat ad celum, sic et animus," and end thus, "perscrutationis quod dictum est."

59

PIERRE DUBOIS' SCHEME OF EDUCATION, 1309

De recuperatione terrae sanctae, ed. C. V. Langlois, Paris, 1891, pp. 49–53, 58–72.

Pierre Dubois, who calls himself an advocate of cases of the kings of France and England at Coutances in Normandy, addressed his treatise *On the Recovery of the Holy Land* first to Edward I of England, then, after adding chapters 111–142 favorable to the universal dominion and exaltation of the French crown, to Philip IV the Fair of France. We are not here concerned with this side of it or with its anti-clerical, anti-papal and secularizing tendencies, but with the plan which its author outlines for educating certain specially selected young people to fit them to hold the Holy Land and to convert the Orient. His plan discloses certain analogies with the camps, schools and courses for hurriedly educating prospective army and navy officers which were organized in this country in 1917–1918, to say nothing of still further analogies with Waves, Wacs and the program of training in international administration in connection with the present war. But, although cramming and attempted short-cuts play a prominent part in it, it is a much more deliberate and far-sighted program, involving a prolonged and thorough training from infancy to maturity. No doubt this program for the most part remained on paper and, except for the provision for the study of oriental languages made in 1312 by the Council of Vienne,[1] was not realized or put into effect, for there is only one manuscript of *The Re-*

[1] See our next selection.

covery of the Holy Land extant. Probably, too, it was in many respects impractical, and it certainly seems somewhat fantastic and overdrawn. Nevertheless it is obviously an attempt to modify for a special purpose and to improve upon the ordinary curriculum of grammar and secondary school and of university. It therefore reflects for us fairly faithfully, if we allow for a little distortion, the actual educational program with which Dubois was acquainted.

In each province, according to the resources of the localities available for this purpose and the size of the population, instead of the priories of the Templars or Hospitalers there located, there should be established what would be more opportune for this purpose—two or more schools for boys and about the same number for girls, who should be chosen to be instructed there at the age of four or five years. And let them be selected by some wise philosopher who would recognize the natural disposition likely to make progress in philosophical studies. To these should be added nobles of either sex, if and in so far as they shall be found; afterwards others who shall be taught continuously according to the program below outlined, which may be altered, perfected and added to by more prudent persons. These children are to be taken on the understanding that they shall never henceforth be returned to their parents, unless they refund all expenses incurred on their account. The others shall be sent from school to school and finally to the Holy Land and to other regions, as the holy Roman church may decide by persons deputed to this purpose. These students and their teachers shall live on the goods of the said priories and the funds provided for the Holy Land, or as the trustees of the foundation, selected by the archbishop with the advice of skilled suffragans, may see fit to arrange.

All these children shall be instructed first in the Latin language to the extent that they know it sufficiently, or at first little by little; and after that they shall be instructed more fully, some of them in Greek, others in Arabic, and so with other literary idioms, especially of the catholics in the far east, so that in the end the Roman church and likewise catholic princes may through them, instructed in speaking and writing in all languages, communicate with all men, drawing them to the catholic faith and the unity of its single head. Now when the youth are instructed in grammar, in which the younger are occupied, if some are instructed in logic, so much the better. Of whom let some be rapidly instructed in the articles of faith and sacraments the Old and New Testaments; so that instructed, as soon as they are prepared, they may be sent to the said land to take charge of souls and may be promoted to the priesthood, and provision be made for the churches and people. Let others be trained in medicine, others in surgery both human and veterinary, by whom the whole army and populace of both sexes may be helped.

Girls should be instructed in medicine and surgery with other subjects prerequisite to these. These girls, thus trained and knowing how to write, namely the noble and other more prudent ones, suited in body and form, will be adopted as daughters and granddaughters of the greater chiefs of those regions, the Holy Land and others near it, so that they may conveniently be given as wives to the greater princes, clergy and other wealthy Orientals; being so adorned by the aforesaid foundation that they will be taken for the daughters of princes; which expenses, after they are married to all the magnates, they will promise to repay during their lifetimes, if they can, to the aforesaid foundation, and if not then, at least when they die, in order that the fund may thus be increased without measure. It would be a fine thing if the married eastern prelates and clergy who are quite unwilling to join the Romans and other westerners in renouncing the privilege of matrimony, should have such wives, by whom, lettered, articled, and believing in the sacraments in Roman style, it is likely that their children and husbands would be drawn to so hold, believe, and sacrifice by far stronger reasons and occasions than those which induced Solomon, the supreme sage, to idolatry by the counsel of women. These from affection for their land of birth would procure many girls from the foundation established for schools of this sort to marry their sons and other great men of the country; they also would have chaplains celebrating and chanting by the Roman ritual, and gradually would draw the inhabitants of those places to the Roman ritual, especially the women whom they helped by their practice of medicine and surgery, especially in their secret infirmities and needs. It could hardly help but be the case that they, nobler and richer than other matrons and everywhere having knowledge of medicine and surgery and experimental science, would attract matrons who required their counsels, who admired their prudence and proficiency, and who loved them on these accounts—would attract these strongly to communicating with them, delighting and agreeing in the same articles of faith and sacraments.

Also any future pope, at such time as such persons could be instructed in the idioms of oriental catholics, would keep near his court such elegantly lettered persons through whom he could write to the prelates and other magnates of those regions. Greek scholars could easily be procured for this purpose. Moreover, when in the more remote schools many were well founded in Latin and Greek, those who seemed to get on better than the others and were more teachable should be selected to study, hear lectures, and afterwards teach, some in civil and canon law, others in astronomy and in other mathematical and natural sciences, others in theology, others in medicine. Of these sciences there would be fervent schools, separated from one another to prevent their hampering one another by jealousy or other causes, for as the Philosopher says in his *Rhetoric*, "Philosophers are naturally invidious." Then, if the pope for arduous causes should send a legate to the land of the Greeks—and I mean the same for other idioms and lands—he would send with him at the same time two or more of those most skilled in each science, who would overcome the experts of that land in disputations, giving counsel, holding conferences, and every way, so that naught could resist the wisdom of the Roman church. And by those employing reason the wisdom of the Romans would be praised and feared in eastern parts, just as the queen of the east commended the wisdom of Solomon.

By provision of schools of this sort and transmission of instructors of both sexes to oriental parts we westerners would get trade in precious commodities abounding in those regions, lacking to us and very dear here, and we would import them cheaply once the world were made catholic. . . .

Let boys be chosen not more than four or five or six years old at most with heads well formed and disposed for learning, never to return to their parents without permission of the foundation. Of these a hundred or more should be instructed in one place well suited for this, first in reading the Psalter, later in the third part of the day in singing and things pertaining thereto, in other parts of the day successively in Donatus, composed in the Roman style, in accidents, declensions, and in turn in other matters of grammar. When the boy comes to hear the book of Cato and other minute authors, let him have four long lessons a day or as much as his ability can stand, over which he shall not go to sleep. Let him first hear the teacher read, then another pupil repeat, after whom he shall immediately repeat as many times what he seems to know. Let declensions and rules of voices be first told him, afterwards let him quickly repeat as he is asked for each. Let the rules be told him in winter; only in the evening shall he do Latin composition. But when they have begun to make a little headway, they are always to speak Latin, accustoming themselves to this at all times and in every place. After several elementary authors they shall hear the Bible in childish fashion three or four times a day; of its historians and poets only shall they do Latin composition in order, because they write but rudely. When they first begin to construe on solemn days, let them construe the *Gradale*, afterwards the *Breviary*, not the *Missal* except the Biblical portion; when they've finished construing the *Breviary*, let them construe the *Golden Legend of the Saints* [2] and stories extracted from the poets briefly and in prose. Besides these let them make compositions from histories that will be of future use to them, not from the usual superfluous tales; or, what is more appropriate, let them Latinize; then they will lose nothing in idle time as has hitherto been the case; all that they do will be of enduring worth to them. When they have heard the entire Bible, let them repeat it daily for at last one *sexternum*, and the same with the histories of the saints, and they shall do the verses of poets but only plain ones for a short time.

At length when they are about ready to study logic, in the three months of summer they shall hear all poetry, namely, on the first day Cato, the second Theodulus, the three following Tobias,[3] and so on with the others; on each day they shall hear six lessons with two teachers, which they could almost all see by themselves, having acquired the stories and the figures of common words. In such writings, where simply the arrangement and conception of what is figured is sought, any youth as soon as he has begun to make any progress can see

---

[2] The standard thirteenth-century collection by James of Voragine.

[3] Similarly, at Troyes in the early fifteenth century the authors read were Cato, Theodulus, Facetus, Carmen de contemptu mundi, Tobias of Matthew of Vendôme, Aesop's Fables, the Parables of Alanus, and Horace. A. F. Leach was of the opinion that such reading was more suitable for a Christian society than the Caesar, Cicero, and Vergil of the humanists and classical scholars.

and read as if it were a romance. At every season of the year and by day and night, deducting sufficient time for sleep, continuously laboring at these tasks, those well disposed towards learning by their tenth or at least their eleventh year, others at least by their twelfth year, God granting, could have gone over all the grammatical sciences. Among which let the boys, as their teachers may deem expedient, hear the *Doctrinale* as far as it is concerned with declensions of nouns and conjugations of verbs, and finally the *Graecismus* so that they briefly comprehend its literal sense,[4] not yet insisting on other solemnities.

When they have got this far, the boys will change their locality and in another school begin to be taught in logic, and at the same time in Greek, Arabic, or any other language which those in charge think fit, in the study of which new language they shall first be taught word forms and order as far as matters of grammar. In logic let them hear treatises and *summulae* composed to explain these; it ought to be arranged that someone wise in this art should extract briefly and plainly for them the art obscurely handed down by the Philosopher in each logical treatise, and succinctly so that after the treatises they may hear that brief art, not requiring exposition of writings, two or three times in a short time after they have once heard the books solemnly. This much ought to be accomplished by their fourteenth year.

Then let them begin to hear natural science, on account of the prolixity and profundity of which it is desirable that the *Naturalia* of brother Albert, containing fully the whole thought of the Philosopher with many additions and digressions should be abbreviated as far as may be, and so plainly that readers can understand this extract sufficiently without the writings themselves. The youth will hear this extract entire in the first year at the rate of four lessons a day without questions; this they will hear a second time with questions; afterwards they will hear the books once as they are read in the schools. Also it would be well for them to have Natural Questions extracted

---

[4] The *Doctrinale* of Alexander de Villa Dei, written in 1199 for the nephews of the bishop of Dol whom he was tutoring, in 2,645 leonine hexameters, is strong on syntax where Priscian was weak. Some 250 manuscripts are extant and nearly 300 editions are known.

The *Graecismus* of Eberhard of Bethune, written in hexameters in 1212, was so called because it contains chapters on Greek words and Latin synonyms and Greek etymology, although Eberhard knew little Greek.

from the writings of brother Thomas, Siger,[5] and other doctors, all arranged in one collection, for instance, concerning first matter, form, composition, generation, corruption, each of the senses, their objects, each faculty of the soul, their operations and natures, concerning the elements of nature and their operations, concerning the heavenly bodies, their natures, influences and movements; in this holding to such order that things could easily be found and because of their orderly arrangement be more easily understood. But such an arrangement would be very difficult, though very advantageous from the pedagogical standpoint, since in this way things would be learned easily in a short time, retained when acquired, and readily recalled to mind.

When they have done this, they would hear the moral sciences, monostica, ethics, rhetoric and politics, similarly extracted and abbreviated. I have seen the *Ethics* in ten books abbreviated by Hermann the German. After this preliminary survey, they would hear the books solemnly with questions, as in the case of the *Naturalia*, in order, with a few arguments written in each science, since a multitude of arguments rather induces confusion of intellect and rational judgment than science.

Having accomplished this in one year, let them hear the Bible twice a day biblically and the book of *Summae* in the morning with questions, omitting those on nature. Those who are to be preachers will so hear for two or three years, but if some do this, it will be enough for others to hear it once for a year or even less time. After that certain ones would hear the laws for two years and they could perfectly hear the five volumes of the *Corpus Iuris*, and afterwards the *Decretum* and Decretals, the *Decretum* twice a day and the Decretals once. Those who were to live as clergy in the church of God could omit the laws but not the Decretals and *Decretum*; those who were to live secularly could omit the *Naturalia* and spend the more time on morals, and civil and canon law. Those who want to hear medicine could do so after *Naturalia*, although it would be better not to ignore the Bible and *Summae*, since in these are touched the principles which are the foundations of all the sciences, conformant to that saying of the Philosopher, "Moreover all the sciences are connected." And it is indeed a great thing to

---

[5] Thomas of Cantimpré (rather than Aquinas) and Siger de Brabant seem meant.

know the principles of all sciences or at least not to be ignorant of them.

Those who are ruder in learning, after they know a little logic and more natural science, when that is possible, let them hear the surgery of men and horses; and with this, if possible, medicine, at least those who are more capable, so that they can apprehend the art of surgery more readily by the aid of the medical art. Let those physicians and surgeons have wives similarly instructed, with whose assistance they can relieve the sick more fully.

Some may oppose our foregoing argument thus, "What advantage will it be to those who cannot carry so many volumes with them to hear the laws for two years?" I answer, If they do not have books when they ought to use them, it will profit them little; yet on account of the canon law it will do them some good and they will not totally be ignorant of it; if, however, they carry their books with them, it will profit them far more. We ought to suppose that there will be some auditors who will bring books with them, and others who don't bring any will acquire them, and because of their good foundation in the sciences they will make progress even by studying the books by themselves after they have left the schools.

Moreover it would be a good thing for those scholars who are shortly to govern and judge great states and peoples to have the laws in a single volume, plain, brief, and clear, written just once without repetition of like points, containing perfect opinions so that they could be read and understood without glosses and commentaries, with all the laws on one subject comprehended under one title so that persons, who were well-educated otherwise, could understand them without a teacher. It would be advantageous to have the *Decretum* and Decretals similarly abbreviated, so that scholars pressed for time from laws confused and prolix could carry away with them and retain in brief form the general and special law of each subject, combining which with experience they would rule themselves and others civilly by these general and special powers to which they would gradually become accustomed, and, aided by experience, and acquiring books, they would grow more perfect in them. These abbreviations and extracts would be portable books of poor scholars, and even those occupied with other sciences as philosophy and theology would not carry their usual and necessary study to perusal of great volumes, because the brevity of human life and the occupations of spiritual and secular business rarely permit men to study and know perfectly the civil and canon law, so prolix, together with philosophy and theology. Yet those continuing right docilely in the prescribed mode of study could by thirty become skilled enough in philosophy, civil law, canon and divine law, and expert in how to preach. For the Old and New Testament with the Legends of the Saints learned in childhood, repeated solemnly with the book of *Summae*, as is prescribed, for one year after the attainment of philosophy, sufficiently disposes them from boyhood on to understand, deliver, and commit to memory sermons for single feast days, so that the way to preach would become a sort of second nature to them, according to what the Philosopher says, that Plato taught boys to grow used to works of virtue, so that in the process of time these might become natural to them, and that they might be as ready towards these as towards natural impulses. For as he says there, "Custom is a second nature;" that is, it alters nature.

That it is thus expedient that prelates who rule the church should be learned in philosophy, theology, and both laws, and in the use and experience of sciences of this sort is sufficiently taught by experience, that supreme mistress of life, as many sacred canons acclaim, having regard to the defects of those prelates who learn only civil law without canon and divine, though it may be very thoroughly, and also of those who study only canon law, like some monks and regular canons. . . .

Moreover, in mathematical sciences on account of their many utilities, especially touched upon in the little book *Super utilitatibus* made by brother Roger Bacon of the order of Minorites, it will be advisable to instruct some disciples of this foundation, as they shall appear to show intelligence, skill, and speed therein, but rather dwelling on those matters which may be of service in taking and keeping the Holy Land. It is especially desirable that every catholic should know written figures, the situation and places of the elements, their magnitude and shapes; the thickness of the celestial orbs, their magnitude; the velocity, motion, and influences of sun, moon, and other stars; and how small the earth is compared to them, and how great with respect to man; so that admiration of these may swell the praise of their Creator, and that, repelling the lust for things worldly, man may not grow proud because of all these inferior things, which are as nothing in the universe that contains them all, and should be regarded as nothing.

In each study of this foundation it will be advisable to retain some who would be feeble for crossing the sea, who, that it may be done more perfectly, themselves educated beyond the prescribed amount, may teach others and finally be made heads of studies. It will be advisable to seek many Greek, Arabic, and Chaldean [6] doctors, and so in the case of other idioms, as they are thought more helpful, to instruct our better students in their literary languages, and others, who may be somewhat less learned in literary matters, to be linguistic interpreters in speech with uneducated persons. I think that, just as among us Latins, we see under each literary idiom diverse native vernaculars contained, of which it would be enough to learn the more common, as French is among Latins, in the case of those who are not thought able to learn several.

It will be advisable that scholars of this foundation, namely the more robust, be instructed in the military art; and others, who as time goes on are found stupid at their books, in mechanical arts, especially those of service in war, as smiths and carpenters. . . .

It will also be advisable that some of them be instructed according to the contents of the aforesaid book, *De utilitatibus mathematicarum*, in making various instruments such as burning glasses and other instruments useful for war, as this may be feasible by the perspective of mathematics and the natural sciences, by which arts many things might be made which are unknown in these western regions. . . .

It is certain, as anyone can see, that in two scarcely, and in as many as three arts never, is anyone found skilled; how then could anyone be found skilled in all the arts which are infinite in number among us? If not in the arts, then not in their determination, causes, and diversity. Whence it follows that their perfect doctrine cannot be set forth by one author, of which the reason seems to be that the Author of nature, wishing to take away any occasion of pride and also of lusting after the things of the world, and further to give color, cause, and occasion to everyone to tolerate with himself possessors of property and workers in the arts with no more selfishness and envy than is due, made all things of human interest infinite in number, namely languages both

[6] That is, Aramaic.

literary and vernacular, places, regions; also he so multiplied the arts that neither one man nor a hundred, nor a thousand, nor a hundred thousand, nor a hundred thousand thousand could suffice unto themselves to live well, and in order to attain well-being, as is customary, the men of one province would not suffice unto themselves, nor of one kingdom, nor of three, nor of ten. Which is in so far true that it appears that all the men of this world need to help one another to produce well-being, whence it follows that without selfishness or envy of each other's natural prosperity men ought to be mutually tolerant after the example of those gregarious animals which tolerate one another. So the Saviour of all souls expressed his will more in his acts than in his words. . . .

It will be advisable that all the girls of the foundation like the males be instructed in Latin grammar, afterwards in logic, and in one other language, later in the rudiments of natural science, finally in surgery and medicine. These subjects, except grammar and surgery, are intended for those who are found docile and disposed towards these things above the rest; and let these too be instructed only in those parts of each science bearing on medicine and surgery, in a manner as far as possible more perceptible to the senses and plainer and easier because of the weakness of the sex, and because they run through their ages more quickly than men, attain more rapidly to such perfection as is possible for them, which is a sign of the weakness of their natural virtue. We see the like, as the Philosopher says, speaking of this in the book on animals, in trees and other plants, "Those which last less long grow more quickly." Of these girls those more prudent, who seem too weak to cross the sea, may stay permanently with us to train others, by whose aid the others will be kept more securely and instructed more fully both in theory and practice of surgery as well as medicine, and in those matters pertaining to the apothecary's art.

But it will be expedient that those girls whom it is intended to marry with those who do not hold the articles of our faith as the Roman church holds, teaches, and observes, be taught to carry with them briefly and plainly written all the articles so that they may understand them sufficiently. And the same knowledge would likewise not harm, rather be advantageous, to other disciples of the said foundation who have not had fuller theological training. Besides, to educate the girls in medicine and surgery it will be advisable that two girls more highly trained than the others in medicine and surgery and their experiences remain to teach the others both theory and practice, so that the girls when they leave school may have skill in practice with the sciences. In school more readily than later they could learn and get much experience without which such sciences are of little use, as the Philosopher testifies, saying: "In human activities we see that those having experience without art do better than those having a notion of the science without experience."

Similarly it would be a good thing to train the male auditors of sciences of this sort in experience of them while they were in school, and to hold there an apothecary shop and make compound medicines, so that they might learn to know the herbs and other medicines, the unguents and other customary concoctions, so that when they left school they would know enough and might practice.

In divine science especially should its students exercise themselves in its practice, preaching to the scholars of this foundation, repeating the sermons of their elders, and still more frequently making brief collations. . . .

60

STATUTE OF THE COUNCIL OF VIENNE,
1312

Chartularium universitatis Parisiensis, II, 154–155.

Clement, bishop, servant of the servants of God. In perpetual memory of the matter. Among our cares. . . . And so, imitating the example of Him whose place on earth we unworthily fill who wished the apostles to go throughout the world preaching the Gospel trained in every language, we desire holy church to abound in catholics acquainted with the languages which the infidels chiefly use, who may come to know the infidels themselves, and be able to instruct them in sacred institutions, and add them to the company of worshipers of Christ by knowledge of the Christian faith and reception of baptism. Therefore, that linguistic ability of this sort may be obtained by efficacy of instruction, with the approval of this holy council we have provided for establishing courses in the languages to be mentioned, wherever the Roman curia happens to reside, also in the universities of Paris, Oxford, Bologna, and Salamanca, decreeing that in each of these places catholics having sufficient knowledge of the Hebrew, Greek, Arabic and Aramaic languages, namely two trained in each tongue, shall offer courses there and, translating books faithfully from those languages into Latin, teach others those languages carefully and transfer their ability to these by painstaking instruction, so that, sufficiently instructed and trained in these languages, they may produce the hoped for fruit with God's aid and spread the faith salubriously to infidel nations. For whom we wish provision made: for those lecturing at the Roman curia by the apostolic see, in the university of Paris by the king of France, at Oxford by that of England, Scotland, Ireland and Wales, in Bologna by Italy's and in Salamanca by Spain's prelates, monasteries, chapters, convents, colleges, exempt or not, and rectors of churches in competent stipends and expenses, imposing the burden of contribution according to the ability of each to pay regardless of any privileges and exemptions to the contrary, by which however we do not wish prejudice to be generated so far as other matters are concerned.

In execution of this statute we find later in the *Chartularium* a letter of February 24, 1319, from John XXII to the bishop of Paris bidding him provide adequately for the teacher of Hebrew and Aramaic at Paris, and another of July 25, 1326, inquiring as to the teachers in Hebrew, Greek, Arabic, and Aramaic at Paris.

61

ACADEMIC DRESS REGULATED, TOULOUSE, 1314

STATUTES OF THE UNIVERSITY AND FACULTIES OF CIVIL AND CANON LAW

Fournier, *Les statuts et privilèges* . . . , I (1890), 493–94.

Since superfluity of clothing in clerics is reproved by the holy fathers and holy canons and humility commended, since too because of the superfluity of clothing which clerics and scholars residing at the university of Toulouse have hitherto been wont to make, not only expense to the clerics and scholars themselves but many injuries have come to the entire university, from this forsooth that many, abhorring the said superfluity of clothing and not unjustly fearing the immoderate cost of the same, have refused to attend the said university and have gone to others which were not so expensive, while many who came to the said university have withdrawn from the university because of the cult and cost of the same clothing. Some too residing in the said university, spending or rather consuming upon the said clothes not only the money by which they could and should attend and remain in the said university but, what is more serious, their books with which and in which they intended to study and make progress, often have withdrawn from the said university before the end of the texts, with their money gone and substance wasted and not only their own books but sometimes those of others pawned, sold, entirely gone and lost for the aforesaid cloth and garments, and cannot without shame and confusion remain in the said university with the others who remain and make progress. Therefore we, Bertrand de Turre, prior of Rabastens, doctor of decretals and rector of the university of Toulouse, together with the other doctors, lords and masters teaching in the aforesaid university, whose names are included below, with the advice and assent of the counselors and the will of the whole university aforementioned, desiring to obviate the foregoing as far as may be and provide a healthful remedy, have decided to set an affixed price for the said cloths and garments, in order that by a fixed price and tariff this reprehensible superfluity of clothing may be checked and an approved mediocrity in respect to costume be maintained in the said university.

Moreover, the said price was fixed, set and assessed so forsooth that the yard of cloth from which doctors, masters, licentiates, bachelors, and scholars make their garments to wear in classes and through the town shall by no means exceed the price of twenty solidi or at most 25 solidi of petty solidi of Tours, and that the yard of cloth contain eight palms in length according to the custom of Toulouse. And if elsewhere it runs more or less, let the buyer who is going to make a garment of that cloth estimate the amount according to the above measure and let his conscience be his guide. And that the said cloth have a breadth of five palms and a half, and if the said cloth is narrower, allowance may be made *pro rata* for the cloth and assessed price, so that, having made allowance for cloth and price according to the breadth and narrowness and length of the same cloth, the garment made or to be made from the said cloth shall under no circumstances become dearer because of the allowance nor any fraud be committed in this connection.

It was further ordained that all masters, licentiates, bachelors, and scholars wear their garments of the said price everywhere through the city or in the city and in the buildings of the city outside their lodgings or those of others. But within the said lodgings or outside around them for a distance of twenty houses in any direction they may wear any garments, provided they do not go farther than twenty houses. But from this ordinance are excepted masters in theology and whoever lectures on the *Decretum* in the said university. To these, out of respect for the science and course, it is permitted to make or wear garments of any price.

But this which has been decreed as to cloth and clothing above is to be understood of the garments made to wear in classes and about town, namely, the closed overtunic, the upper tunic, excepting open overtunics, togas, hoods and tunics, which anyone may wear anywhere outside of academic functions, on a day when he eats outside his own lodgings, except vests without sleeves or with sleeves which don't show and mittens, shoes and berets.

Moreover, if anyone wishes to go on horseback through town or outside town for exercise or other purpose, then going and returning or in getting ready he may put on and wear what garment he pleases.

Furthermore it is ordained that those who receive cloth or garments from others, as from bishops or prelates or others not studying in the said university, who are accustomed to give or send many garments by reason of dignity, rank, nobility or power, may wear these wherever they are outside academic functions. But at academic functions, as in classes and at the university mass and wherever the university goes as a university or meets, there they shall wear and be required to wear garments of the cloth and price stated, unless perchance they come to the university or to the place where the university will meet with the lord from whom they received the aforesaid garments.

As to garments already made, moreover, it was decreed and ordained that those who have their cloth and garments which they have already made or have or have bought, or those who in ignorance of this statute buy or make their clothes before they come to the said university, may wear and use these everywhere, provided however they have not committed fraud in the foregoing.

As to new doctors and masters, moreover, it was ordained that, if anyone is admitted to the doctorate or mastership, he may make his garments or even those of others as he shall see fit out of any cloth at any price. And if the garment or cloth of the said garments is above the said price, he and those who receive them from him may wear them on the day on which he receives the insignia of the doctorate and for a month immediately following. But afterwards, when the month has elapsed, he shall make and wear garments at the said price, as is ordered above in the case of other doctors.

As to the canons, moreover, of St. Etienne and St. Saturnin and the monks of the Daurade and St. Pierre des Cuisines it was ordained that within the precincts of the said churches, monasteries, priories or places or thirty houses beyond, even if the university be there, they may wear their habit or what garments they wish, whether they study in the said places or monasteries or in town or wherever they are or go with their convent or college or chapter of churches, monasteries or priories aforesaid. They may do the same in churches or places belonging to their monasteries or churches. The canons of St. Etienne may do the same in the church of St. Jacques and in the episcopal residence, or if any of them go to preach or on other ecclesiastical business to the churches or chapels of the Nazarene, St. Bartholomew, St. Romain, or other chapels of their parish, or if they go to the said places or outside the city for exercise or whenever they go on horseback through town or outside. The same may be observed if any of the aforesaid go through town or elsewhere on ecclesiastical business of the same churches or monasteries or by reason of dignities or benefices of the same or even of the said places and priories.

Moreover, as to the cloth which some have made, in their lodgings or others, or which is made in the houses of their parents, those who have said cloth made or those who receive said cloth from their parents may wear it in classes and through town provided according to a fair estimate they do not exceed the stated price and do not do this or have it done from a fraudulent motive.

Moreover, if by chance any member of the university without fraud has lost his garment, or if it has been torn or damaged or notably soiled, in this case he may wear another so long as he cannot wear the aforesaid, provided he does not offend the above ordinance.

Moreover, since the coinage or money of Tours now current may be altered with time and from its alteration doubts arise, therefore for the future, to remove all possible doubt, it is ordained and declared that, if the said current coinage or money of Tours should be changed, the yard of cloth may be bought at the value which denarii of Tours had at the time of the statute and as much money then current may be given for the yard of cloth as shall then be worth, forsooth at the time of purchase, twenty solidi or 25 of the coinage of St. Louis common among money-changers, all fraud utterly removed, so that nothing may be done contrary to the intent of those statutes which are above ordained for the common utility of the said university. . . .

62

LETTER FROM A PHYSICIAN OF VALENCIA TO HIS TWO SONS STUDYING AT TOULOUSE, 1315

British Museum, MS. Sloane 3124, fols. 74r–77r. Introduction and Latin text printed in *Speculum,* VI (1931), 110–114; translation reprinted from *Annals of Medical History,* III (1931), 17–20.

The following very human document in the shape of a letter from a physician of Valencia in the Spanish peninsula to his two sons, studying at Toulouse, throws light upon such homely, daily matters as food, clothing and costume, both for summer and winter, day and night. It gives illuminating details as to personal hygiene, and suggests the error of the view that, because the medieval universities did not build stadiums, indulge in intercollegiate athletics, or institute departments of physical education, therefore the medieval student took little or no exercise. It illustrates both student and family life, our fourteenth-century father being even more solicitous that his boys keep out of draughts and wear sufficiently warm clothing than a modern mother would be. It is naturally of much medical interest for its particular prescriptions of drugs and medicines as well as its counsels of hygiene and preventive medicine. By its insistence upon personal cleanliness and its advice to select lodgings removed from all foul smells of ditches or latrines, and insistence on the importance of breathing pure air, it confirms my contention that the Middle Ages have been unjustly represented as normally unsanitary.[1]

Rather surprising is our physician's statement that about six hours of sleep a day is enough, especially in the case of two growing boys, and also centuries before development of artificial lighting beyond the candle stage had made staying up late at night a temptation. But if the fourteenth century youth at Toulouse had no cinemas or "great white way" to seduce him from early retiring, study at night appears to have been at least as common then as now. It is true that the sons may have been at taverns or on the streets when the father thought of them as occupied with evening studies. However, he does not object to their "enjoying themselves with their friends."

The letter also seems of some linguistic importance, since a number of words of an unusual sort, difficult to translate exactly, or to find in existing medieval Latin dictionaries, are used for herbs, drugs, contemporary articles of clothing, and other things in common use. Thus we find *libellus* employed in the sense of a small stove, oven, or heater. Moral and religious counsel are not given to the extent that many would expect from such a medieval letter, but a tactful word on the subject is inserted under the heading, "Of accidents of the soul". But perhaps the chief service of our treatise is to make us feel that we are dealing with actual persons, to take us back with vivid verisimilitude into the fourteenth century, and to drive home the conviction that the men of that period were not very different beings from those of today. Prescriptions have changed more than physicians, and curricula have altered more than students, while the danger of coughs and colds remain about the same.

The letter occurs in a fifteenth-century membrane manuscript of the British Museum, MS Sloane 3124, fol. 74r–77r (old numbering, fols. 82r–85r). The manuscript once was at Montpellier, where it formed a part of the library of Franciscus Ranchinus. It contains somewhat more than three hundred and fifty leaves, and its contents are largely medical. Our letter, as it is found in this manuscript, is evidently a copy and not the original, being in the same handwriting as medical treatises of other authors which precede and follow it. Indeed, a work of Arnald of Villanova begins on the same page on which our letter leaves off. Our treatise is dated 1315, and while there is evidence that the copyist at first wrote, or started to write, 1415, the earlier date seems the more acceptable. Toulouse was threatened with war in 1415, and most of the works which compose the present manu-

---

[1] "Sanitation, Baths, and Street-cleaning in the Middle Ages and Renaissance." SPECULUM, III (1928), 192–203.

script are of thirteenth- and fourteenth-century authorship or translation.[2]

While our physician is said to address his two sons, his advice—at least in the copy of it which has reached us—seems to be addressed to one recipient for whom the second person singular is employed. This may be because it has come to be thought of as meant for an indefinite general reader or member of a student body. In connection with our physician's name, Peter Fagarola, as it appears to be spelled in the Sloane manuscript, it may be noted that a Bernard Figarola was *médecin de chambre* at the court of Aragon about 1387, while about 1389 Pedro Figuerola, master of arts and medicine, drafted statutes for a proposed school of liberal arts in Valencia.[3] Possibly they were of the same family.

There follows a Regimen composed by Peter Fagarola, master of arts and medicine, which was sent by him from the city of Valencia to the city of Toulouse to his two sons, students residing in that city of Toulouse, in the year of the Lord one thousand, three hundred, and fifteen.

Of Foods, or How to Eat

Beware of eating too much and too often especially during the night. Avoid eating raw onions in the evening except rarely, because they dull the intellect and senses generally.

Avoid all very lacteal foods such as milk and fresh cheese except very rarely. Beware of eating milk and fish, or milk and wine, at the same meal, for milk and fish or milk and wine produce leprosy.

Don't have fresh pork too often. Salt pork is all right.

Don't eat many nuts except rarely and following fish. I say the same of meat and fruit, for they are bad and difficult to digest.

Thy drink be twice or thrice or four times during a meal. Between meals drink little, for it would be better once in a while to drink too much at table than to drink away from table. Don't take wine without water, and, if it is too cold, warm it in winter. For 'tis bad to grow used to strong wine without admixture of water.

---

[2] The latest definite date of authorship appears to be September 23, 1393, for a treatise on the pestilence made by the counsel of the medical faculty of Bologna and written by Gandolphus of Padua. It occurs at fol. 51v–61v. But possibly the *Practica mag. Philipi Alanfancii Englici*, fol. 196v–220, opening, "Cura effimere ex oppillatione . . ." is a later work.

[3] Luis Comenges, "Contribution à l'étude de l'histoire de la médecine dans le royaume d'Aragon," *Janus*, VIII (1903), 523–529, 574–582: page 528; Rashdall, *The Universities of Europe in the Middle Ages*, II (1936), 107.

Remember about the well water of Toulouse. Wherefore boil it, and the same with water of the Garonne, because such waters are bad.

Also, after you have risen from table wash out your mouth with wine. This done, take one spoonful of this powdered confection:

Of meat prepared with vinegar and dried coriander similarly prepared a modicum each; of roast meat, fennel seed, flowers of white eyebright, two ounces each; of candied coriander, candied anise, scraped licorice, each one ounce and a half; of cloves, mast, cubebs, each three drams; of galingale and cardamomum each two drams; of white ginger six drams; of white loaf sugar three drams; made into a powder and put in a paste. And keep this in your room in a secret [or, *dry*] place, for it will comfort your digestion, head, vision, intellect and memory, and protect from rheum.

As to Sleep

Sufficient and natural sleep is to sleep for a fourth part of a natural day or a trifle more or less. To do otherwise is to pervert nature. Too much is a sin, wherefore shun it, unless the case is urgent and necessary.

Avoid sleeping on your back except rarely, for it has many disadvantages, but sleep on your side or stomach, and first on the right side, then on the left.

Don't sleep in winter with cold feet, but first warm them at the fire or by walking about or some other method. And in summer don't sleep with bed slippers on your feet, because they generate vapors which are very bad for the brain and memory.

Don't go straight to bed on a full stomach but an hour after the meal. Also, unless some urgent necessity prevents, walk about for a bit after a meal, at least around the square, so that the food may settle in the stomach and not evaporate in the mouth of the stomach, since the vapors will rise to the head and fill it with rheum and steal away and cut short memory.

Also, avoid lying down in a rheumatic place, such as a basement or room underground.

Of Air or One's Surroundings

Choose lodgings removed from all foul smells as of ditches or latrines and the like, since in breathing we are continually drawing in air which, if it is infected, infects us more and more forcibly than tainted food and drink do.

Likewise in winter keep your room closed from all noxious wind and have straw on the pavement lest you suffer from cold.

Furthermore, if you can have coals or chopped wood in a clay receptacle of good clay, or if you have a chimneyplace and fire in your room, it is well.

Also, be well clad and well shod, and outdoors wear pattens to keep your feet warm.

Also, don't make yourself a cap "de salsamentis," [4] as some do, for they are harmful.

And when you see other students wearing their caps, do you do likewise, and, if need be, put on one of fur.

And at night, when you study, you should wear a nightcap over the cap and about your cheeks (or throat?).

And when you go to bed at night, have a white nightcap on your head and beneath your cheeks, and another colored one over it, for at night the head should be kept warmer than during the day.

Moreover, at the time of the great rains it is well to wear outdoors over your cap a bonnet or helmet of undressed skin, that is, a covering to keep the head from getting wet. Indeed, some persons wear a bonnet over the cap in fair weather, more especially when it is cold, so that in the presence of the great they may remove the bonnet and be excused from doffing the cap.

Also, look after your stockings and don't permit your feet to become dirty.

Also, wash the head, if you are accustomed to wash it, at least once a fortnight with hot lye and in a place sheltered from draughts on the eve of a feast day towards nightfall. Then dry your hair with a brisk massage; afterwards do it up; then put on a bonnet or cap.

Also comb your hair daily, if you will morning and evening before eating or at least afterwards, if you cannot do otherwise.

Also look out that a draught does not strike you from window or crack while you study or sleep, or indeed at any time, for it strikes men without their noticing.

---

[4] Literally, of sauces or pickles or salt fish or sausages, which seems an impossible translation. Probably we have to do with a slang phrase for some current type of head-covering.

Also, in summer, in order not to have fleas or to have no more of them, sweep your room daily with a broom and not sprinkle it with water,[5] for they are generated from damp dust. But you may spray it occasionally with strong vinegar which comforts heart and brain.

If you will, walk daily somewhere morning and evening. And if the weather is cold, if you can run, run on empty stomach, or at least walk rapidly, that the natural heat may be revived. For a fire is soon extinguished unless the sticks are moved about or the bellows used. However, it is not advisable to run on a full stomach but to saunter slowly in order to settle the food in the stomach.

If you cannot go outside your lodgings, either because the weather does not permit or it is raining, climb the stairs rapidly three or four times, and have in your room a big heavy stick like a sword and wield it now with one hand, now with the other, as if in a scrimmage, until you are almost winded. This is splendid exercise to warm one up and expel noxious vapors through the pores and consume other superfluities. Jumping is a similar exercise. Singing, too, exercises the chest. And if you will do this, you will have healthy limbs, a sound intellect and memory, and you will avoid rheum. The same way with playing ball. All these were invented not for sport but for exercise. Moreover, too much labor is to be avoided as a continual practice.

Of Accidents of the Soul

Accidents of the soul have the greatest influence, such as anger, sadness, and love of women, fear, excessive anxiety: concerning all which I say nothing more than that you avoid all passions of the soul harmful to you and enjoy yourself happily with friends and good companions, and cultivate honesty and patience which bring the more delights to the soul, and especially if you love God with your whole heart.

For a Cough

If you are troubled with a cough, beware of all cold or sour things, or salt and fried. And if cold rheum is the cause of the cough, then make a bag of camamille, salt, and calamint in equal parts mixed to-

[5] It will be noted that the straw, with which the pavement was to be strewn in winter to prevent cold, is evidently removed in summer, and that there is no condition to correspond with Erasmus' experience in the sixteenth century of rooms where the rushes on the floor had been unchanged for years and were full of fleas and filth.

gether, and make a pepper poultice which should be placed on top of the head or over the commissure. And a small piece of licorice should be kept in the mouth and chewed between the teeth, or a candy should be made of licorice.

Equally good is sirup of Venus' hair, sirup of hyssop, sirup of bugloss, if they are taken with water of scabiosa, water of lily, elder water, water of betony, water of rosemary in equal parts, or wash the mouth with a tepid gargle.

Equally good are dyera yeris of Solomon, diapenidion, cold diagragant, preserved penidiarum, grains of pine,[6] and the like.

And if the cough is accompanied by hot rheum, of which the signs are extreme heat, a burning sensation in the throat, saltiness, and great thirst, in this case take cold diagragant or diapenidion without spices with sirup of violets or sirup of pepper. And let this be taken in sips and not swallowed suddenly. And this is to be done without eating anything morning and evening. Immediately afterwards take a fine linen cloth and dip it in tepid oil of roses and apply it tepid to the commissure of the head, and this do twice daily.

And in cold rheum beware of all broth and meat puddings as much as is possible and of superfluous drink. And eat only roast meats not stewed in water, and eat any thick foodstuffs such as sweetbreads, split beans with their skins removed, and the like, cooked with meat.

Also in hot rheum one should eat barley-gruel, rice, oatmeal cooked with milk of almonds and sugar, pears and apples cooked with sugar, which are also good in case of cold rheum.

And one should drink yellow wine, clear and limpid.

Also equally beneficial in this case are cold diagragant, diapenidion without spices, sugar of violets, preserved penidiarum, and the like. And let this suffice so far as rheum is concerned.

Thus it ends. Thanks to God. Amen, Amen.[7]

---

[6] Guy de Chauliac, "La grande chirurgie," ed. Nicaise, Paris, 1890, p. 653, says: "*Pin*, arbre: duquel les grains sonts chauds et humides, et son escorce froide et seiche, auec tres-grande adstriction."

[7] This final paragraph was presumably added by some later copyist.

63

WHETHER A MASTER TEACHING THE-OLOGY SHOULD BE REQUIRED TO KNOW CANON LAW?

Augustinus Triumphus of Ancona, 1243–1328, *On ecclesiastical power*, as quoted by Antonino, *Summa*, III, 5, 2, 2.

. . . Yet theology and canonical science differ in their method of consideration in five ways. First, in that matters concerning the sacraments and other divine things and the morals of the faithful are determined by theology in a subtle way and *quasi propter quid*, yet also by that method which can be assigned in theology *propter quid*, but in canon law in a gross and positive manner and only *quia*.[1] Second, in that these are determined by the theologian chiefly for the contemplation of truth, by the canonists chiefly on account of a (particular) legal case and the solution of the questions involved therein. Third, in that theologians deal chiefly with divine worship and things which concern the integrity of the faith of one God, while canonists are more concerned with the order of ministers and of ecclesiastical business pertaining to that worship. Fourth, in that by theology are determined canons how the pious shall be enriched and defended against the impious, in canon law the pious are enriched and defended against the impious. Fifth, in that matters are determined by the theologian more universally and in the forum of conscience, in which is tried the case between God and man, but by the canonist more particularly, making application to particular actions in the exterior forum of judgment where cases are tried between man and man.

And since general exhortations are of little use in the moral realm, as is said in the *Ethics*, therefore I think that it would be a far-sighted ordinance if the master qualified to teach theology should be required after lecturing on the *Sentences* to teach the book of the Decretals, in order that he might become more familiar with and experienced in those things which are necessary for counseling the salvation of souls.

Antonino then adds:

[1] *Quia* refers to the apparent, *propter quid*, to the underlying, cause. *Propter quid* implies knowledge of a thing's essence, *quia*, merely of its existence.

. . . For canonical science is a sort of practical theology. But the contemplation of God, to which theology is ordered as its end, cannot be truly and usefully acquired except through charity and virtuous works and the observance of mandates which pertain to practice. Moreover, just as theology does not spurn human sciences which are mixed with many errors, so too canon law spurns not the laws of earthly empire, which contain less error than the secular sciences. Wherefore, just as he who is to become a master in theology ought first to know human sciences that he may more clearly and subtly understand holy scripture, so much more should he know the canons of the saints, that he may better and more fruitfully consult the safety of souls.

64

RECEPTION OF THE CLEMENTINES AT THE UNIVERSITY OF TOULOUSE, DECEMBER 22, 1317

Fournier, *Les statuts et privilèges*, III (1892), 521–22.

Know all present and to come that Johannes Margoti, sergeant at arms as he said of our lord the pope, in the chapter-house of the Friars Minor at Toulouse in my presence as notary and before the witnesses listed below, presented on behalf of our lord the pope certain constitutions included under a papal bull, comprising five quinternions (of which quinternions the first begins, "Clement V in the council of Vienne . . ." and the same quinternion closes, ". . . expresso."). Whereupon the discreet men Johannes de Vernhola, doctor of laws and then rector of the university of Toulouse, Cicardus de Vauro, Benedictus de Puteo, Guido the Poitevin, Johannes de Viridi Sicco, doctors of decrees, Armandus de Narcesio, doctor of laws, and many other discreet men there assisting, for themselves and in the name of all the said university of Toulouse received joyfully the said constitutions and apostolic mandates, the said rector and doctors offering for themselves and in the name of the said university to complete and preserve the said constitutions and each and all things contained in them diligently and studiously, and to obey loyally the apostolic mandates.

And there the said Johannes Margoti required me, the notary signed below, that I make and render to him a public instrument concerning the aforesaid presentation, reception made by himself, and response of the said doctors.

Done the tenth day from the end of the month of December in the reign of Philip, king of France and Navarre, in the city of Toulouse raised to metropolitan rank but not yet provided with an archbishop, so far as is known, in the year since the Incarnation 1317.

Of which thing are witnesses Johannes Radulphi, Ademar de Textoria, bedell of the university mentioned, and Jacobus Bay banker, and Raimundus Revelli, public notary at Toulouse, who wrote this paper.

65

SPECIAL DUTIES OF THE RECTORS AT BOLOGNA

From the Statutes of the Jurists from 1317 to 1347, Rubric xi: Carlo Malagola, *Statuti delle università e dei collegi dello studio bolognese*, Bologna, 1888, pp. 13–14.

Reducing the honor of charity to due action we have decreed that the rector of one university shall accompany the rector newly elected of the other university to his house and conduct him through his university in the accustomed manner and with trumpets.[1] Also the new rectors shall be required within the first month of their incumbency to have read all the statutes. They shall also be required to visit each new podestà and captain of the commune of Bologna within ten days after they have entered upon the office of podestà or captain and recommend and present the university to them. Also the rectors are required to make all copyists, illuminators, correctors and keepers of colors and erasers of books, binders, dealers in paper, and those who make their living from the university and scholars, swear that they are subject to the rectors and university and will serve everyone faithfully. They

[1] In this selection the word university is not used in its present sense but in its medieval meaning of a gild. At the beginning of the thirteenth century the law students at Bologna had been organized in four such universities. By the fourteenth century these had combined into two universities, ultramontane and cismontane, each with its rector.

shall also be required on the first, second, or third day, on which at the opening of the university there are no lectures, to convoke the university and there have the statutes read, at least of the third book. They shall also have read in classes at the opening of the university those statutes which relate to doctors and classes and contain the manner and course of lectures. Also let them take care that in their matriculation lists they do not enter as scholars those who do not study in law or who do not take the oath, unless they abstain for good reason and one approved by the rectors. They also are required at the request of a scholar to have read in classes a statute which it is highly expedient for that scholar to have read. Nor shall the aforesaid be read except by a notary of the university or, if he is prevented, by the bedell who shall be required to read it at the command of either rector alone, even if the other forbids it. The rectors are also required by such means as shall seem to them proper to procure that the bells which are rung for the convenience of the scholars are rung in a manner, at a time, and at an interval which are acceptable, and they shall especially watch as to the ringing for review (*repetitio*) that it is done at a convenient hour and for a proper length of time. They shall also make proclamation in classes during April by the university notary that, if there is anyone who wishes to say anything or to criticize any official of the university, he shall report to the rectors and councillors of the university. Also the rectors are required after the first of November to make sure that the doctors' salaries are paid. But if these have not been paid by the first of January, they shall be required to hold a meeting of the councillors about this at least once every week and deliberate with them on ways and means of paying the salaries. But if they haven't been paid by the first of March, from then on the rectors with the councillors shall have full power of the university concerning this, and without action of the university they or the majority of them can do all that the university itself could do. But they may not suspend the university; however, the university can be assembled to do this at the request of the salaried persons. Also the rectors are required to demand within ten days the pecuniary penalties incurred by doctors, scholars or others enjoying the advantage of the university, and every person who knows of any penalty incurred and overlooked and not exacted is required to report it to the rector, otherwise he shall be condemned for the same amount by the syndics at the close of his incumbency, nor can any proposal to remit the said fines be proposed in council or to the university. Moreover, half of the fines shall go to both universities and half to both rectors, nor can the rectors remit their share. Also, the entrance fees of those who come to Bologna are common to both universities. Also, one rector is required at the request of the other to give his councillors, when he demands them, for a meeting of the university, and when one rector with the majority of the councillors of either university so orders, the bedell is required to convoke the university, even if the other rector and majority of councillors forbids it. Otherwise, except in cases stated in the statutes, he may not convoke the university unless the councillors have previously agreed to call it. . . .[2]

The rectors are also required, when the university meets for some principal business, to prevent something else being proposed incidentally when it has not been finished. Also, that no reform be proposed there which has not previously been approved by the councillors, except perhaps against the rectors themselves or one of them or unless previously something had been mentioned there which a nation or person wished to propose. Also, the rectors shall have transcribed the writings which the university is now found to have within a month after the publication of the statutes is completed, unless the multitude of writings calls for more time. Moreover, of writings which shall be had in the future transcription shall be made within a month after their receipt, and in both cases the originals shall be preserved in the university box or ark, so that they may not perish as many others have perished. Decreeing also that within a month after it has been announced to them the rectors shall be required to do all that they can to recover documents or any other possession of our university which has been lost or mishandled by its officials or others and concerns past, present, or future matters.

Also, the rectors shall investigate four times a year straight and flat whether the university chapel situated in Borgo S. Mamolo is conducted as it should be. If they do not do this, they may be corrected, the bishop or his vicar reporting and in any way convenient. And we further provide that the old rectors within ten days after surrendering their office should consign to the new rectors delegated to this the pieces of university property which are in the university box

---

[2] Some further regulations as to meetings of the universities are omitted.

at the Friars Preachers, and then an inventory of them shall be made by the notary of our university, which they ought to assign to their successors according to the terms of the inventory. The negligent shall incur a fine of twenty pounds Bolognese to go to both universities to be collected by the new rectors and syndics and, if they fail to pay up, they shall be punished by these with a proper penalty.

66

PECIARII AT BOLOGNA

Statutes of 1317–1347, Rubric xix: Malagola, *Statuti . . . dello studio bolognese*, 1888, pp. 20–21.

We have decreed that each year on a day selected by the syndics there shall be chosen by the rectors and councillors from the bosom of our university six good men, foresighted and discreet, who bear the marks of clerical orders and of whom three are ultramontane and three cismontane, to be *peciarii* to the number of six, and they shall be chosen by that form by which electors are chosen. . . . When elected, they shall have full freedom in the matter of *peciae* and jurisdiction of taking cognizance, pronouncing and executing in cases of *peciae* and corrupt texts. By reason of defects in *peciae* they may and should demand from certain copyists and correctors an oath that they will report *peciae* which they find corrupt. We will that a stationer, for each corrupt *pecia* which he gives out and for each offense, shall incur a fine of ten solidi Bolognese, and nonetheless he shall be required to reimburse the scholar [1] double. Half the penalty shall go to the university, half of the remaining half to the *peciarii*, the remainder to the denouncer.

Moreover, the same *peciarii* on feast days at some place assigned by them shall see and examine all *peciae* and quaternions of all the stationers, first requiring of all stationers an oath that they will bring all exemplars of *peciae* or *quaderni* which they rent out to the place designated by the *peciarii* and will conceal none. To this place all stationers, all fraud and deceit removed, are required to bring the exemplars which they have. And if the majority of the said Six judge any insufficiently corrected, they shall see to it that they are corrected

---

[1] Who borrowed the *pecia*.

at the expense of the stationers to whom they belong by certain correctors deputed by the Six themselves at the expense of the stationer to whom the *peciae* belong. At the request of four of whom, and of the rectors, any doctor or scholar may be required to supply his own copy, if he has a good one for this purpose. And if the doctor or scholar refuses to loan his copy, after it has been judged critical, even for use within his own house, he shall be penalized with a fine of five pounds Bolognese to go to our university. And if any copies are not assessed, the stationers shall be required to assess them. And if any stationers shall have scorned to do so, for each offense they shall incur a fine of five pounds Bolognese to be applied to the use of the university, and no scholar henceforth should receive *peciae* or quaternions from such to copy or correct under penalty of ten solidi Bolognese and perpetual privation, and that the rectors then in office at the request of the said Six, as aforesaid, by virtue of their personal oath shall be required to enforce the said penalty. And the *peciarii* should pay the correctors of the *peciae* and are required to receive the money from the stationers in the presence of the correctors and to pay it immediately to the correctors, nor shall the stationer pay the correctors.

Also the said *peciarii* at the expense of the general bedell are required to have the questions, disputed during their term by doctors and given to the bedell, published in a twofold exemplar and corrected in duplicate within twenty days after they were handed in, under penalty of forty solidi Bolognese for each question, to be inflicted on the bedell if he has not done this at their command and demanded at their request by the rectors or either of them from those writing the questions. The stationer of the questions is required at his own expense to have the questions inscribed on a quaternion given him by the notary which the notary shall give to him from the book of questions which we wish to be kept for perpetual memory in the university box. Also, the university notary is required to write out gratis all questions of required disputations in a book to be purchased by the university treasurers and given to him before the tenth of January. And the rectors should make the treasurers do this, and the notary is required to have finished it within a month after the feast of the Resurrection under pain of three pounds Bolognese for every question omitted. And then the book shall be placed by the rectors in the university strong-box within eight days. And we wish the said *peciarii* to be careful about this too. Also the said *peciarii* are required to meet at least once a week under pain of ten solidi Bolognese, and the rectors are to compel them to do so by virtue of their personal oath. And that the said Six may attend the more diligently to the aforesaid matters, we have decreed that they shall not be required during that year to attend general convocations or funerals or be compelled to take any other university office that year. And this statute the notary is required to read *seriatim* at each of the four seasons, namely, four times each year.

67

DOMINICAN LEGISLATION AGAINST ALCHEMY, 1323

ORDINANCE OF THE CHAPTER GENERAL AT BARCELONA IN MAY

Chartularium universitatis Parisiensis, II, 271.

Because books are singularly opportune for the progress of students, we will and ordain that books in chains or in the common chest for use may not be pledged, sold, loaned or otherwise alienated by the priors or their vicars or the convent. But if they do otherwise, they shall be compelled by the provincial priors to make good the value of the book or books from their own goods for the common chest.

Also, since the art called alchemy has been strictly prohibited in many general chapters under heavy penalties, and still in various parts of the order perilous scandals have arisen from this, the master of the order commands in the virtue of the Holy Spirit by the council of the definers and assent of the brothers generally, under penalty of excommunication, that no one shall study or take lessons, operate or have operated in the said art, and, if he has any writings concerning it, shall not keep them but within the space of eight days from the present notice destroy and burn them. Against those practicing it still the master of the order publicly issued sentence of excommunication in chapter in writing, and those against whom it is proved he will henceforth adjudge to imprisonment. And if any know of those practicing the art and do not report it to their prelates, they will be subject to heavy penalty for their fault. . . .

68

STUDY OF GRAMMAR AT TOULOUSE, 1328

Fournier, *Les statuts et privilèges*, I (1890), 501.

Also, since according to the usage and custom of the university of Toulouse and of the masters.both in arts and in grammar certain books are assigned for the lectures of the entire year, both ordinary and extraordinary, while the statute is only about the artists, therefore the grammarians too in winter ought to lecture in the morning, after determination of their proverb [1] with questions, on Priscian major and immediately afterwards on the *Doctrinale* and Alexander. And after dinner, after roll call of the boys by the principal bachelor and review of the lessons, the said masters in grammar shall be required in winter time at Nones to lecture on Ebrardus,[2] the Story of Alexander, and Hymns and Metrification, at the hours and times by them ordained and accustomed. And during Christmas vacation the said masters shall be required to lecture on authors and the *Computus manualis*. And in summer in place of Priscian major they shall lecture mornings on Regimen and Construction and afterwards one lecture on the *Doctrinale* concerning declensions, beginning at the beginning and continuing from the beginning of Alexander, and they shall be required to continue in addition the lecture on Ebrardus, so that the whole of Ebrardus may be finished in the time of one winter and summer.

See also Selection 124, Teaching of Grammar at Toulouse, 1426.

69

LEGISLATION OF THE FRENCH OR GALLICAN NATION, PARIS, 1328

Chartularium universitatis Parisiensis, II, 307–308.

In the year of the Lord 1327, the Saturday before Brandons, the Gallican nation met at St. Julien le Pauvre at the hour of Prime. The masters of our Gallican nation, having been summoned by the prin-

---

[1] The *Distichs* of Cato are perhaps meant.
[2] The *Graecismus* of Eberhard de Bethune.

cipal servant as is the custom, deliberating concerning the common good of our said nation and for the common good, we decided to ordain, decree and inviolably observe by ourselves and our successors those things which follow.

First, that each year five masters be elected from the five accustomed provinces of our nation who shall visit the classes of our nation with a servant to learn who hold or shall hold classes, who is teaching and who not, to the end that those actually giving instruction may be paid and others not, lest the money of the nation be wasted. Adding to this our statute or ordinance that the said five masters on oath under penalty should register the classes of those teaching and report it to the nation. It was also ordered that the servants of our nation be relied on for the names and classes of those teaching. Which servants too are to be bound by their oath to tell the truth to the said five masters as to the names and classes of those actually teaching, and the same servants shall be believed unless some master wishes to prove the contrary. And the same master shall be required on his oath and under penalty of deprivation to inform the nation or its deputies of the contrary within two days immediately after, if he can conveniently do so.

Secondly, we have ordained that one master giving instruction be elected, who shall receive from each master having a determinant or determinants 13 solidi and 4 denarii for each determinant, and each master shall be required on his oath to satisfy the receiver elected by the nation as to the said sum for each determinant before Easter. The receiver, moreover, is and will be bound by his oath to satisfy the landlords of the schools of our nation as to the money received by him according to the assessment of the schools by the first day of lectures after Quasimodo.[1] And that these things may be firmly observed by us and our successors we have decided to affix the seal of our nation to the present schedule, statute or ordinance in the year, day, place, and hour aforesaid.

To all who may inspect the present letters we all and singly, masters of the Gallican nation at Paris teaching in the faculty of arts, everlasting greeting in the Lord. You should know that in the year of the Lord 1327, the Saturday before the Sunday on which is sung *Reminiscere*, in the time of the proctorship of master Nicolaus de Villanis, our nation having been specially convoked by the common bedell, as

---

[1] The first Sunday after Easter.

is the custom, at St. Julien le Pauvre to legislate, because in the same year for certain halls situated outside the street of Straw, in which many masters lectured or were accustomed to lecture, a great part of the money of our nation had been squandered, whence the nation seemed more depressed than usual: we, therefore, caring for the common welfare of the whole nation and wishing to conserve the money intended for the common good and to obviate many frauds which might be committed in this connection, all and each without exception deemed it expedient to legislate, and decreed and ordained by way of expedient in this fashion, that henceforth no master lecturing in hall or room of any house outside the street of Straw shall receive towards the rent of that hall or room from the nation more than the value of two determinants, unless it is made clear to the nation that he lectures in such a place because of a great number of scholars, and that he has made a diligent effort to procure suitable class rooms in the said street of Straw.

70

ALVARUS PELAGIUS ON THE VICES OF MASTERS [1]

As reproduced from *De planctu ecclesiae* by Antonino, *Summa*, II, 5, 2, 10.

The first is that, although they be unlearned and insufficiently prepared, they get themselves promoted to be masters by prayers and gifts: *Extravagans* concerning masters, chapter opening, 'Quanto.' And when they are called upon to examine others, they admit inept and ignorant persons to be masters.

Second, moved by envy, they scorn to admit well-prepared subordinates to professorial chairs, and, full of arrogance, they despise others and censure their utterances unreasonably. . . .

Third, they despise simple persons who know how to avoid faults of conduct better than those of words. . . .

Fourth, they teach useless, vain, and sometimes false doctrines, a most dangerous course in doctrine of faith and morals, yet one espe-

[1] Alvarus Pelagius (Alvaro Paes) was grand penitentiary at Avignon under pope John XXII and died in 1352.

cially characteristic of doctors of theology. These are fountains without water and clouds driven by whirlwinds and darkening the landscape. . . .

Fifth, they are dumb dogs unable to bark, as Isaiah inveighs against them, 66:10. Seeing the faults of peoples and lords, they keep silent lest they displease them, when they ought to argue at least in secret—which they also sometimes omit to do because they are involved in like vices themselves. . . .

Sixth, they retain in their classes those who have been excommunicated, or do not reprove scholars who are undisciplined and practice turpitudes publicly. For they ought to impress morality along with science.

Seventh, although receiving sufficient salaries, they avariciously demand beyond their due or refuse to teach the poor unless paid for it, and want pay whether they teach on feast days or not, or fail to lecture when they should, attending to other matters, or teach less diligently.

Eighth, they try to say what is subtle, not what is useful, so that they may be seen of men and called rabbis, which is especially reprehensible in masters of theology. And in this especially offend, remarks the aforesaid Alvarus, the masters of Paris and those in England at Oxford, secular as well as regular, Dominicans as well as Franciscans, and others, of whom the arrogance of some is inexplicable. In their classes not the prophets, nor the Mosaic law, nor the wisdom of the Father, nor the Gospel of Christ, nor the doctrine of the apostles and holy doctors are heard, but Reboat, the idolatrous philosopher, and his commentator, with other teachers of the liberal arts, so that in classes in theology not holy writ but philosophy is taught. Nay more, now doctors and bachelors do not even read the text of the *Sentences* in class but hurry on to curious questions which have no apparent connection with the text.

71

ALVARUS PELAGIUS ON THE FAULTS
OF SCHOLARS

Antonino, *Summa*, III, 5, 2, 11.

1. Sometimes they wish to be above their masters, impugning their statements more with a certain wrong-headedness than with reason. . . .

2. Those wish to become masters who were not legitimate disciples. . . .

3. They attend classes but make no effort to learn anything. . . . Such are limbs of Satan rather than of Christ. . . . And these persons who go to a university but do not study cannot with clear consciences enjoy the privilege of the fruits of benefices in a university: *Extravagans* on masters, chapter 1. And if they receive such, they are held to restitution because they receive them fraudulently, as the tenor of the canon cited makes evident.

4. They frequently learn what they would better ignore . . . such things as forbidden sciences, amatory discourses, and superstitions.

5. On obscure points they depend upon their own judgment, passing over scripture and canonical science of which they are ignorant. And so they become masters of error. For they are ashamed to ask of others what they themselves don't know, which is stupid pride. . . .

6. They defraud their masters of their due salaries, although they are able to pay. Wherefore they are legally bound to make restitution, because, says Gregory XII, query 2, One serving ecclesiastical utilities ought to rejoice in ecclesiastical remuneration.

7. They have among themselves evil and disgraceful societies, associating together for ill. And while in residence they sometimes are guilty of vices, against which their masters ought to provide and take action so far as they can. . . .

8. They are disobedient to the masters and rectors of the universities and sometimes transgress the statutes which they have sworn to observe. And sometimes they contend against and resist the officials, for which they should be subjected to blows of rods, a method of coercion

admissible against clerics by masters of liberal arts and by their parents: case of attack on the archbishop.

9. On feast days they don't go to church to hear divine service and sermons and above all the full mass which all Christians are supposed to attend (*de conse. di.i. missas*), but gad about town with their fellows or attend lectures or write up their notes at home. Or, if they go to church, it is not for worship but to see the girls or swap stories.

10. They foment rows and form parties and tickets in electing the rector or securing the appointment of professors, not following the interests of the student body as a whole but their own affections, sometimes to this intent alluring with gifts and flattering attentions for their own masters, and sometimes drawing scholars away from other teachers and persuading them to come to theirs, and not for the best interest of the scholars. . . .

11. If they are clergymen with parishes, when they go off to universities, they do not leave good and sufficient vicars in their churches to care diligently for the souls of their parishioners. . . . Or they hear lectures in fields forbidden to them, such as the law.

12. The expense money which they have from their parents or churches they spend in taverns, conviviality, games and other superfluities, and so they return home empty, without knowledge, conscience, or money. Against whom may be quoted that observation of Jerome, "It is praiseworthy, not to have seen Jerusalem, but to have lived well." So, not to have studied at Paris or Bologna, but to have done so diligently merits praise.

13. They contract debts and sometimes withdraw from the university without paying them, on which account they are excommunicated and do not care, but they may not be absolved; *de reg. iur. peccatum*, libro vi.

72

FOURTEENTH CENTURY CALENDAR OF THE UNIVERSITY OF PARIS[1]

Chartularium universitatis Parisiensis, II, 709–15 (omitting the Egyptian days and length of the month and moon given for each month and the sixteenth-century additions).

In the following calendar there are indicated 71 full holidays for all faculties, 9 additional for the faculty of theology alone, 39 for "the street of Brunellus" or faculty of canon law with 5 more for *Decreta* and 2 for decretals, and 8 for the street of Straw or faculty of arts. Also on various eves of holidays there are no lectures after Tierce. There are further 22 "festive" days when apparently there were no ordinary or extraordinary lectures but only such courses as were given on and limited to feast days. Also various cessations and resumptions of ordinary lectures are noted which we will not attempt to reduce to a numerical basis, while certain days especially in the street of Straw are set aside for cursory lectures.

January

1	A	Kal.	Circumcision. No lectures in any faculty
2	B	iiii	Octave of St. Stephen
3	C	iii	Ste. Geneviève the virgin. No lectures in theology or decretals but in the other faculties
4	D	ii	
5	E	Nonas	On this day which is the eve of Epiphany there are no lectures after Tierce in the street of Straw, nor in the Nones of Notre Dame in the street of Brunellus[2]
6	F	viii	Epiphany. No lectures in any faculty
7	G	vii	On the day following Epiphany no lectures in the street of Brunellus, but in the other faculties
8	A	vi	On this day masters begin ordinary lectures again in the street of Straw

[1] The calendar is presumably later than 1325 when the feast of Romanus on Oct. 23 was accepted as a holiday by the Norman nation of the university. See *Chartularium*, II, 288.

[2] Rue du Clos Bruneau, where the law lectures were given.

9	B	v	On this day no lectures after Tierce in the street of Straw out of respect for the blessed William
10	C	iiii	William, archbishop of Bourges. No lectures in any faculty
11	D	iii	Paul, the first hermit. No lectures in any faculty. A sermon at the Augustinians on this day
12	E	ii	
13	F	Idus	Finding of St. Firminus, bishop of Amiens and martyr. No lectures in any faculty
14	G	xix	Note that on the first Tuesday after Epiphany the doctors of *decreta* begin to lecture again and should continue till the eve of Palm Sunday
15	A	xviii	
16	B	xvii	Maurus, abbot and confessor. No lectures *in decretis* but lectures on the decretals that day
17	C	xvi	St. Antony, abbot and hermit. No lectures in the street of Brunellus but there are in the other faculties
18	D	xv	Sun in Aquarius
19	E	xiv	
20	F	xiii	Fabian and Sebastian. No lectures in the street of Brunellus but in the other faculties
21	G	xii	Agnes, virgin and martyr. Festive.[3] And on the preceding day, festive
22	A	xi	Vincent, Levite and martyr. No lectures in any faculty
23	B	x	
24	C	ix	
25	D	viii	Conversion of St. Paul. No lectures in any faculty
26	E	vii	Polycarp bishop and martyr. Festive
27	F	vi	Julian, bishop and confessor, and John Chrysostom. Cursory.[4] And no lectures in the street of Brunellus, but there are in others
28	G	v	

[3] Festive seems to indicate that the day was given over to lectures for feast days, and cursory to cursory lectures. It will be observed that over a third of the days in the month were without lectures in the faculty of canon law.

[4] See preceding note.

29 A iiii
30 B iii
31 C ii

February

1 D Kal.   On this day no lectures in any faculty after Tierce because of the Feast of Purification

2 E iiii   Purification of the blessed virgin Mary. On that day a sermon at the Carmelites

3 F iii   Blasius, bishop and martyr. No lectures in the street of Brunellus but in the other faculties

4 G ii   On the morrow of St. Blasius no lectures in the street of Brunellus but on that day is recovered the morrow of the Purification

5 A Nonas   Agatha, virgin and martyr. Festive

6 B viii

7 C vii

8 D vi

9 E v

10 F iiii

11 G iii   Note that until the fifth day following there are no ordinary but cursory lectures in the street of Straw

12 A ii

13 B Idus   Note that on the day when "Esto mihi" is sung the rector should preach at the Jacobites, and after his sermon the privilege of the Freshmen is read by a bedell, and afterwards comes the main sermon

14 C xvi

15 D xv   Note that on the first day of Lent (*die carnis privii*) there are no lectures in the street of Brunellus or in the street of Straw, but lectures elsewhere. Sun in Pisces

16 E xiiii

17 F xiii   Note that on the first day of Quadragesima (Ash Wednesday) there are no lectures in any faculty. On the morning of the same day there is a ser-

mon at the Franciscans but there is no collation that day after dinner

18	G	xii	
19	A	xi	
20	B	x	
21	C	ix	
22	D	viii	Chair of St. Peter. No lectures in any faculty. Spring starts
23	E	vii	
24	F	vi	Matthew the Apostle. No lectures. On the same day is the dedication of the church of St. Denis, and there are great indulgences there that day and a vast throng of people
25	G	v	
26	A	iiii	
27	B	iii	
28	C	ii	Translation of St. Augustine. No lectures in any faculty and a sermon at the Augustinians

March

1	D	Kal.	Note that on Saturdays in Lent there are no lectures in any faculty after dinner except in the street of Brunellus. And always on these Saturdays in supplement there is a collation at the Franciscans
2	E	vi	
3	F	v	
4	G	iiii	Note that bachelors giving ordinary lectures in the street of Brunellus ought during Lent to lecture until the bell in the cathedral ceases ringing for Prime, but at all other times they should dismiss their classes immediately the bell begins to ring
5	A	iii	
6	B	ii	
7	C	Nonas	Thomas of Aquinas, Dominican. No lectures in any faculty. On the same day a sermon at the Dominicans
8	D	viii	

9	E	vii	Note that the bachelors *in decretis* who lecture at the Nones of St. Jacques before and after Quadragesima lecture at Tierce all through Lent. Those lecturing on the Bible do likewise
10	F	vi	
11	G	v	
12	A	iiii	Gregory, pope and doctor of the church. No lectures in any faculty
13	B	iii	
14	C	ii	
15	D	Idus	
16	E	xvii	
17	F	xvi	
18	G	xv	Sun in Aries
19	A	xiiii	Note 'tis the last day for ordinary lectures before the feast of the Annunciation in the street of Straw. On the same day a new rector is chosen and he goes on until the eve of St. John the Baptist
20	B	xiii	
21	C	xii	Benedict the abbot. No lectures in theology or *in decretis,* but in other faculties; cursory in the street of Straw
22	D	xi	
23	E	x	Note that on the eve of the Annunciation they do not lecture beyond Tierce in the street of Straw nor in the street of Brunellus
24	F	ix	
S25	G	viii	Annunciation Sunday. No lectures in any faculty
26	A	vii	On the morrow of Annunciation no lectures in the street of Brunellus but in all other faculties
27	B	vi	Note that on White Thursday, on Good Friday and on the eve of Easter (i.e., three days before Easter) there always is a sermon at the Franciscans after dinner but not before
28	C	v	
29	D	iiii	Note that among the Augustinians on Good Friday in the morning there is a sermon in Italian,

French, and German at one and the same hour
in three places in that house

30 E iii

31 F ii   Note that on the eve of Palm Sunday and on the
Wednesday next following during the Nones of
Notre Dame there are no lectures in the street
of Brunellus

Also note that from the fourth day before Easter to
the Thursday following the same feast there are
no lectures in any faculty.[5]

April

1 G Kal.   Note that the doctors *in decretis* do not lecture from
the eve of Palm Sunday until the Tuesday fol-
lowing Quasimodo

4 C ii   St. Ambrose, bishop and confessor and doctor of
the church. No lectures in any faculty

17 B xv   Sun in Taurus

22 G x   Revelation of the bodies of St. Denis and his companions. On the same day there are great indulgences in St. Denis

23 A ix   George the martyr. Festive. No lectures in the
street of Brunellus but lectures in other faculties

25 C vii   Mark the evangelist. Long litany. No lectures

26 D vi   Dedication of Ste. Chapelle of the palace of the
king of France. On that day and for an octave
there are great indulgences there and a great
throng of people

30 A ii   Peter the Dominican and martyr. No lectures in
any faculty except in the street of Straw where
there are cursory lectures. And on the same day
there is a sermon at the Dominicans

May

1 B Kal.   Philip and James the Apostles. No lectures

3 D v   Finding of the holy Cross. No lectures

[5] For the remainder of the calendar only those days will be noted against which
there is some annotation.

6	G	ii	John before the Latin gate. No lectures
8	B	viii	On the eve of the night of St. Nicholas there is no lecture after Tierce in the street of Straw nor in the Nones of Blessed Mary in the street of Brunellus
9	C	vii	Translation of St. Nicholas, bishop and confessor. No lectures. Beginning of summer
10	D	vi	On the morrow of the Translation no lectures in the street of Brunellus
13	G	iii	On Rogations no disputation in the street of Straw
14	A	ii	On the eve of Easter, Ascension, Pentecost and Trinity no lectures after Tierce in any faculty
15	B	Idus	On the morrow of Ascension no lectures in the street of Brunellus but lectures elsewhere
17	D	xiv	Note that from the Sunday on which is sung "Vocem jocunditatis" until the morrow of holy Trinity there are no ordinary lectures in the street of Straw but cursory
18	E	xv	Sun in Gemini
19	F	xiiii	Yvo, confessor of Britain and advocate. Not the custom to lecture anywhere
24	D	ix	Translation of St. Dominic. No lectures in theology but in other faculties
25	E	viii	Translation of St. Francis. No lectures in theology but in other faculties
28	A	v	Germain, bishop and confessor of Paris. Festive
29	B	iiii	Note that doctors *in decretis* do not lecture from the eve of Pentecost till the Tuesday after the feast of holy Trinity
31	D	ii	Note that on the Tuesday following Ascension is always celebrated the feast of the revelation of the head of king St. Louis. And on that day and for an octave there are great indulgences in the royal chapel. And that day it is not customary to lecture in the street of Brunellus but there are lectures elsewhere

June

3	G	iii	On the eve of the holy Sacrament no lectures at Nones of Notre Dame in the street of Brunellus
			On the day of the holy Sacrament no lectures in any faculty
			Note that on the morrow of the holy Sacrament there are no lectures in the street of Brunellus but are elsewhere
11	A	iii	Barnabas the Apostle. No lectures in any faculty
13	C	Idus	Anthony the Franciscan. No lectures in theology but lectures in all other faculties
17	G	xv	Sun in Cancer
19	B	xiii	Gervase and Prothasius brothers and martyrs. No lectures in the street of Brunellus but lectures elsewhere
22	E	x	Note that always on the eve of St. John the Baptist a new rector is chosen and runs to the morrow of St. Denis
23	F	ix	On the eve no lecture after Tierce in the street of Straw nor in the street of Brunellus because of the eve
24	G	viii	Nativity of St. John the Baptist. No lectures
25	A	vii	Eligius, bishop of Noyon. No lectures in the street of Straw or the street of Brunellus, but lectures in other faculties
28	D	iiii	Eve of the Apostles Peter and Paul. No lecture after Tierce in any faculty
29	E	iii	Peter and Paul. No lectures in any faculty
30	F	ii	Commemoration of St. Paul. No lectures in the street of Brunellus but in all other faculties

Note that from the eve of the holy apostles Peter and Paul there are no ordinary lectures *in decretis* by doctors nor in theology by masters until the morrow of the holy Cross, but sometimes during the said period there is extraordinary lecturing in the street of Brunellus by a doctor *in decretis*

Also note that from the eve of the Apostles there

are no ordinary lectures in the street of Straw
until the morrow of St. Louis king of France

July

4	C	iiii	Translation of St. Martin, bishop and confessor. No lectures in the street of Brunellus but lectures in other faculties
11	C	v	Translation of St. Benedict, abbot and confessor. No lectures in theology or in the street of Brunellus but in other faculties
18	C	xv	Arnulph, bishop and martyr. Sun in Leo
21	F	xii	St. Victor the martyr. Festive
22	G	xi	Mary Magdalene. No lectures in any faculty
25	C	viii	James the Apostle, Christopher and Cucufas. No lectures in any faculty
26	D	vii	Blessed Marcellus, bishop of Paris and confessor. Festive
28	F	v	Blessed Anna, mother of the virgin Mary. No lectures in the street of Brunellus but elsewhere
31	B	ii	Germain, bishop of Autun and glorious confessor. Festive

August

1	C	Kal.	Petrus ad vincula. No lectures in any faculty
3	E	iii	Finding of St. Stephen the first martyr. No lectures in any faculty
5	G	Nonas	St. Dominic. No lectures in any faculty. On the same day a sermon at the Dominicans
6	A	viii	Transfiguration. No lectures in theology but in other faculties
9	D	v	Eve of Lawrence
10	E	iiii	Lawrence, archdeacon and martyr. No lectures
11	F	iii	Corone Domini. No lectures in theology but in all other faculties
14	B	xix	Eve of the Assumption of the blessed Mary. No lecture after Tierce in the street of Straw or in the street of Brunellus

15	C	xviii	Assumption of the blessed virgin Mary. On the same day a sermon at the Carmelites
16	D	xvii	On the morrow of Assumption no lectures in the street of Brunellus but in other faculties
19	G	xiiii	Louis of Marseilles, Franciscan. No lectures in theology or *in decretis* but in all others. On the same day a sermon at the Dominicans
20	A	xiii	Bernard the abbot. No lectures in any faculty. On the same day a sermon at the Bernardines
24	E	ix	Bartholomew the Apostle. No lectures in any faculty
25	F	viii	Louis, king of France. No lectures in any faculty and a sermon at the Collège de Navarre. On that day ordinary lectures resume in the street of Straw
28	B	v	Augustine, bishop and confessor and doctor of the church. No lectures and a sermon at the Augustinians
29	C	iiii	Beheading of St. John the Baptist. No lectures in any faculty

September

1	F	Kal.	Egidius, Lupus and Firminus, confessor and bishop of Amiens. No lectures in the streets of Straw and Brunellus but lectures elsewhere
3	A	iii	Ordination of St. Gregory the pope. Festive
7	E	vii	On this day no lectures after Tierce in the street of Straw nor in the Nones of Notre Dame in the street of Brunellus
8	F	vi	Nativity of St. Mary the Virgin. No lectures
9	G	v	Morrow of the Nativity, festive. No lectures in the street of Brunellus but lectures elsewhere
14	E	xviii	Exaltation of the holy Cross. No lectures in any faculty
15	F	xvii	Morrow of the Exaltation, festive
17	A	xv	Sun in Libra
20	D	xii	Eve
21	E	xi	Matthew, Apostle and evangelist. No lectures in any faculty.

22	F	x	Mauritius and his companions. Festive. No lectures *in decretis* but lectures in decretals
25	B	vii	Firminus, bishop and martyr. Festive
27	D	v	Cosme and Damianus, martyrs. Festive. No lectures *in decretis* in the street of Brunellus but lectures in decretals
28	E	iiii	Note that from this day till the morrow of St. Denis there are no lectures in the street of Brunellus at any hour
29	F	iii	Michael the archangel. No lectures in any faculty
30	G	ii	Jerome, the presbyter and doctor of the church. No lectures in any faculty. On the same day the king is wont to show the holy cross in the palace in the morning and the Franciscans are required to say hours in the royal chapel
			Note that doctors *in decretis* do not lecture from the eve of blessed Michael to the Tuesday following All Saints

October

1	A	Kal.	Remy, archbishop and confessor. On the same day cursory lectures in the street of Straw
2	B	vi	Leodegarius, bishop and martyr. Festive
4	D	iiii	St. Francis the confessor. No lectures in any faculty and a sermon at the Franciscans
9	B	vii	Denis, Rusticus and Eleutherius, martyrs. No lectures in any faculty
10	C	vi	On the morrow of St. Denis a new rector is elected and lasts till the first O [6]
11	D	v	On that day ordinary lectures are resumed in the street of Straw
16	B	xvii	Dedication of the church of St. Michael of Mount Tumba. No lectures in the street of Brunellus but elsewhere
18	D	xv	Luke the Evangelist. No lectures in any faculty. Sun in Scorpio

---

[6] That is, the day when "O Sapientia" is sung. See December 16.

23	B	x	Romanus, archbishop of Rouen. No lectures in the street of Straw but lectures elsewhere
27	F	vi	Eve
28	G	v	Simon and Jude, Apostles. No lectures in any faculty
31	C	ii	Quintinus the martyr. Eve of All Saints. No lectures after Tierce

November

| 1 | D | Kal. | Festivity of All Saints. No lectures |
| 2 | E | iiii | Commemoration of all who died in the faith. No lectures. On the same day a sermon at the Franciscans |

Note that on All Saints' day the rector ought to speak before the main sermon, and immediately after the rector's speech is read the privilege of Freshmen by a bedell, and thereafter comes the main sermon.

| 6 | B | viii | Leonard the confessor. Festive |

Note that on the Tuesday following All Saints the doctors *in decretis* resume ordinary lectures in the street of Brunellus. And on that day there is no lecture hour in decretals

8	D	vi	Mathurin, confessor. Cursory lectures in the street of Straw
11	G	iii	Martin, bishop and confessor. No lectures in any faculty
12	A	ii	On the morrow no lectures in the street of Brunellus but in all other faculties
13	B	Idus	Bricius, bishop and confessor. Festive
17	F	xv	Sun in Sagittarius
19	A	xiii	No lectures in the street of Straw after Tierce because of the day following but lectures elsewhere
20	B	xii	St. Edmund, king of England and martyr. No lectures in any faculty
21	C	xi	On the morrow no lectures in the street of Straw but in all other faculties
22	D	x	Cecilia, virgin and martyr. Festive

23	E	ix	Clement, pope and martyr. No lectures in any faculty
24	F	viii	On this day no lectures after Tierce in the street of Straw nor in the Nones of Notre Dame in the street of Brunellus because of the feast of the blessed Katherine
25	G	vii	Katherine, virgin and martyr. No lectures anywhere
26	A	vi	On the morrow no lectures in the street of Straw or in the street of Brunellus, but everywhere else
29	D	iii	Eve
30	E	ii	Andrew the Apostle. No lectures

December

1	F	Kal.	Eligius, bishop and confessor. No lectures in the street of Straw or in the street of Brunellus, but lectures elsewhere
2	G	iiii	Octave of St. Katherine. Festive
4	B	ii	Barbara, virgin and martyr. Festive
5	C	Nonas	Eve of Nicholas. No lectures after Tierce in the street of Straw or in the Nones of Notre Dame in the street of Brunellus
6	D	viii	Nicholas, bishop and confessor. No lectures
7	E	vii	On the morrow no lectures in the street of Straw or in the street of Brunellus but lectures elsewhere
8	F	vi	Conception of the holy Virgin Mary. No lectures in any faculty
9	G	v	On the morrow no lectures in the street of Straw or in the street of Brunellus but lectures elsewhere
12	C	ii	Note that doctors *in decretis* do not lecture from first O [7] to the Tuesday following the octave of Epiphany
13	D	Idus	Lucia, virgin and martyr. Festive.
14	E	xix	Note that from the second O till the morrow of Epiphany there are no ordinary lectures in the street of Straw
16	G	xvii	"O sapientia." Here a new rector is chosen and runs

[7] The allusion is to "O Sapientia": see December 16.

			to the last day of ordinary lectures in the street of Straw before the feast of the Annunciation
20	D	xiii	St. Thomas the Apostle. No lectures
23	G	x	Note that from Christmas eve till the morrow of St. Thomas, archbishop of Canterbury and martyr, there are no lectures in any faculty
24	A	ix	Christmas eve. No lectures after Tierce in any faculty
25	B	viii	Christmas. No lectures
26	C	vii	St. Stephen, first martyr
27	D	vi	John, Apostle and evangelist
28	E	v	Holy Innocents
29	F	iiii	St. Thomas, archbishop of Canterbury and martyr
31	A	ii	On this day no lectures at Nones of Notre Dame in the street of Brunellus from reverence for the day of Circumcision

73

UNIVERSITY HOLIDAYS

STATUTES OF THE LAW SCHOOL, MONTPELLIER,
JULY 20, 1339

Fournier, *Les statuts et privilèges*, II (1891), 53, 70.

Also, because by the many vacations which are accustomed to be taken in the said school, not so much utility as waste is known to have resulted, we have decreed by the same authority that lectures shall cease on the following days only, namely, on the feasts of St. Luke, the Apostles Simon and Jude, All Saints, Commemoration of the Dead, St. Martin bishop and confessor, St. Rufus bishop and confessor, St. Katherine the virgin, St. Andrew the Apostle, the blessed Nicholas bishop, the Conception of the blessed virgin Mary, Lucia virgin and martyr, St. Thomas the Apostle; also Christmas eve inclusive to Circumcision also inclusive, Epiphany, St. Hilary bishop and confessor, St. Anthony, the blessed Fabian and Sebastian, Vincent the martyr, the Conversion of St. Paul, Purification of the blessed virgin Mary, St. Blasius, St. Eulalia, Ash Wednesday, the Chair of St. Peter, St.

Matthew the Apostle, St. Thomas Aquinas, St. Gregory the pope, St. Benedict, the Annunciation of the blessed virgin Mary, St. Ambrose the bishop; also from the Wednesday of Holy Week inclusive to the Wednesday following also inclusive, on the feasts of St. Mark the evangelist, St. Peter, of the Order of Preachers, the holy Apostles Philip and James, the Discovery of the Holy Cross, St. John before the Porta Latina, Ascension, St. Yvo confessor, Pentecost with the two days immediately following, Corpus Christi, St. Barnabas the Apostle, Nativity of St. John the Baptist, the Apostles Peter and Paul, St. Mary Magdalene, St. James, St. Peter ad Vincula, St. Dominic, St. Lawrence, Assumption of the blessed virgin Mary, the blessed Louis bishop and confessor, St. Bartholomew the Apostle, St. Augustine, the Beheading of the blessed John the Baptist, the feast of the Miracles of the blessed Mary de Tabulis, St. Egidius, the nativity of the blessed virgin Mary, the Exaltation of the holy Cross, St. Matthew the evangelist and Apostle, St. Michael the archangel, St. Jerome the presbyter, St. Francis confessor, St. Denis, St. Firminus and Sundays.

But on other days vacations and cessations of lectures shall by no means be indicated or taken for any cause or occasion, even if a whole week passes without a holiday. For the funerals of students, moreover, exercises shall be suspended only for that hour in which the body is given to ecclesiastical burial, provided however that an ordinary lecture shall not be lost on this account. Moreover when solemn commencement takes place, on that day there shall be no extraordinary lectures. On the day following, moreover, there shall be ordinary and extraordinary lectures, nor shall anyone of whatsoever condition be deferred to in cessation of the morrow.

This makes about 78 holidays without counting the additional Sundays.

The calendar accompanying the statutes (Fournier II, 44–48) lists all these holidays except Corpus Christi and in addition the feasts of the Translation of St. Nicholas, the Translation of St. Benedict, St. Margaret the virgin, St. Anne the martyr, St. Germain bishop and confessor, and the consecration of the church of St. Firminus, not to mention a fifteenth-century addition of Barbara virgin and martyr, St. Roch, and Cleofa.

This list of holidays may be compared with that given in the fourteenth-century Calendar of the university of Paris in the preceding selection.

A calendar which Fournier, II, 308–12, prints with the statutes of 1303 of the university of Avignon omits four of those listed above but notes some thirty additional saints' days and holidays. A calendar of the university of

Perpignan, 1380–1390 (Fournier, II, 655–58) omits eight but adds seven.

The medical school next year in its statutes made somewhat different regulations as to holidays, as the following excerpts will illustrate (¶XXXII–XXXV, Fournier II, 1891, 70.)

We have decreed that, if during a week there are several feasts ordained by the church, from those which are designated by name as to be observed in the Calendar inscribed below, or only one such, it or they shall be observed without the day following except the feast of blessed Luke and blessed Nicholas and blessed Katherine, which feasts alone we wish to have a morrow. But if there is no feast day in the week, Wednesday shall be a holiday.

Also, the feasts which we wish celebrated in the university are inscribed in the Calendar.

Also, these are vacations: from eight days before Christmas until Epiphany, the three days immediately preceding Quadragesima, from eight days before Easter till its octave, from the eve of Pentecost till its octave, from July first till the Assumption of the blessed Mary, from eight days before Michaelmas till eight days after.

We have decreed that after the morrow of the Apostles Peter and Paul until the feast of the Assumption of the blessed Mary, bachelors may lecture cursorily except on feast days commonly observed by the people.

74

HOURS OF CLASSES

FROM THE STATUTES OF THE LAW SCHOOL OF MONTPELLIER, JULY 20, 1339

Cartulaire de l'université de Montpellier, I, 687 *et seq*. Reprinted in Fournier, *Statuts et privilèges*, II, 50–51, section 10.

About the order of lectures, moreover, we in the first place ordain and decree that there should be in the university of Montpellier, in the faculties of canon and civil law, four hours according to the custom hitherto observed there, namely, a first morning hour, also the hour of Tierce, also the hour of Nones, also the hour of Vespers. In the first and morning hour doctors alone lecture in the manner which follows: for doctors lecturing ordinarily on the Decretals will occupy the morning hour, as aforesaid, in which they will lecture for a full year on the first, fourth and sixth books of the Decretals and also the *Clementines*, during which year one or two or more doctors shall lecture in the way stated below, keeping for the extraordinary lectures of all doctors at the hour of Vespers the entire second book and of the third up to the title "Of parishes" exclusively. Or they may read with the said second book the titles from the fifth "On accusations," "On the sentence of excommunication," and "On the significance of words," as may please those who are deputed to this below. Moreover, in the second year those giving ordinary lectures on the Decretals shall read the second, third and fifth books, in which year the extraordinary lectures at the hour of Vespers for all doctors shall be on the *Liber sextus* with the *Clementines* or fourth book. Moreover, the bachelors of canon law shall begin their lectures at Tierce or Nones, as they may see fit to choose, who may also choose what books they wish to lecture on of the Decretals, whether they give ordinary or extraordinary lectures or not, provided however that in these lectures and titles they do not conflict with those giving ordinary or extraordinary lectures at the same time. Also those giving ordinary lectures on the *Decretum* will always begin at the hour of Tierce and in two years they will cover completely the entire *Decretum* at the said hour, so that in one year they will get from the beginning of the *Decretum* to the tenth *Causa* exclusive and the tractate, "On consecration," while in the following year they will lecture on the rest, namely, from the tenth *Causa* up to the treatise, "On consecration." Moreover, those giving extraordinary lectures on the *Decretum* will always lecture at Vespers on the other part which is not assigned that year for ordinary lectures, proceeding with the same as far as they can.

75

ACADEMIC COSTUME REGULATED, PARIS, 1339

Chartularium universitatis Parisiensis, II, 486.

To all who shall inspect the present letters the masters one and all of the four nations, namely, Gallican, Picard, Norman, and English, greeting everlasting in the Lord. It is to be deemed just that those who preside over others and are entrusted with their education, especially when on duty or treating some common matter, should be distinguished by some decency of garb. Since, therefore, it is apparent to us from actual evidence that some masters do not shrink from attending congregations and disputations in their mantles, sleeveless tunics, or tabards, while bachelors or scholars presume to take their seats at disputations in other costume than the long-sleeved cope (*cappa*), from which practices grave scandal may arise against us in the future: hence it is that we, desiring to make provision on these matters, decree that henceforth masters shall come to disputations or meetings in proper dress, namely, cope, cassock long or short, trimmed with fur. And if they come in other costume, their votes in the said meetings shall go for naught.

And if they are asked to leave, in general or faculty meetings by the rector, in meetings of the nation by the proctor—and rector or proctor at the request of any master at the meeting may be required by his oath to ask them—or at disputations by the master in charge, and don't leave, they shall know that they are deprived of three ordinary lectures. Moreover, as to bachelors and scholars we have thought well to ordain that if, warned by the master in charge of the disputation, they do not leave, all scholastic activity for a year shall be forbidden them. These things were done at St. Mathurin in our special meeting for that purpose 1339 A.D. the Monday after the feast of the apostle Matthew. In testimony whereof we have decided to affix our seals with the signet of the rector.

76

HAZING OF FRESHMEN FORBIDDEN, PARIS, 1340

Chartularium universitatis Parisiensis, II, 496.

This is the ordinance made by the deputies of the university as to the punishment of those hazing Freshmen. First, that no one, of whatever faculty he be, shall take any money from a Freshman because of his class or anything else, except from roommates with whom he lives or as a voluntary gift, under penalty of deprivation of any honor now held or to be held from the university, which deprivation from now as from then the said university brings upon any offending thus.

. . .

Fourth, the said university bids the said Freshmen, under penalty of deprivation of any honor from the said university, that if anyone does any wrong to them by word or deed on account of their class, they shall straightway secretly reveal this to the proctors and deans of the faculties who in general congregation shall be required to reveal the names of the offenders by their oaths.

Fifth, the said university enjoins all those renting lodgings to students that, as soon as they know that any corporal violence or threats have been made to a Freshman because of his class, they immediately reveal this, as above directed.

Sixth, the said university enjoins all who have taken its oaths that, if they know any person or persons to have inflicted bodily violence or insult, threats and any injury upon Freshmen because of their class, they reveal this by their oaths as quickly as they can, as has been said above.

77

STATUTES OF THE FACULTY OF CANON LAW, PARIS, OCTOBER 12, 1340

Chartularium universitatis Parisiensis, II, 503–4.

No one hearing the Decretals at a morning or other hour shall be deemed a scholar in canon law or of the faculty of *Decreta* unless he shall himself have heard the *Decretum* from a doctor giving instruction in the said faculty at least two or three times a week. Also, no bachelor in the morning or other hour can review for a scholar arrested by the Official, provost or any other judge ecclesiastical or secular under pain of perjury, since such reviewing is known to pertain to a doctor giving instruction. Also at the hour when the *Decretum* is read, the Decretals may not and should not be read. Also, no one shall invite or solicit any scholar, after he has entered the classes of a doctor or bachelor, under pain of removal and perjury. Also, if any scholar is arrested who has no particular doctor from whom he hears the *Decretum*, as has been said, he shall not be considered [1] a scholar; and if any such demands privileges and help as a scholar in the faculty of *Decreta*, it shall not be given him. Also they shall wear proper and decent garb, especially the outer garments. Members of religious orders for their outer garments shall have frock or cowl or other habit befitting their order. Also the same, of whatever state or condition they may be, shall not wear pointed or openwork shoes, red hose or sandals, nor knotted hoods, or other clothing or colors of cloths prohibited by law. Also, they shall not impede the doctors or other lecturers, or bedells or other officials of the said faculty in the exercise of their scholastic duties by whistling, stamping and disturbances of any sort.

Also, at disputations, reviews, lectures on solemn decretals, set harangues and feasts of doctors they shall be required to defer to those of older grade and greater importance in seating themselves, so that henceforth the students in such cases shall leave the first and second rows of benches vacant for persons of such grades and others above mentioned, just as is the custom in the faculty of theology. Also, they shall not hear the canon law outside the street *Clausum Brunelli*, unless the faculty so arrange. Also, we wish in case of a conflict between a lecture in canon law and another subject that attendance on both be not counted. Rather we wish that he who has thus attended canon law and another subject simultaneously take oath and count his time in the one of those faculties only which he elected first. Also, considering and having in mind the great utility of bringing one's books to class, we have decreed and ordained that henceforth no one shall receive credit in canon law or be admitted to lecture on the Decretals or to the degree of bachelor, unless he regularly brings or has brought to classes his books, if he has any, especially at the morning hour or others which he attends in person, unless he shall show in college good excuse for not bringing them, which excuse shall be judged adequate by the college.

Also, observing that, where there is no foundation, there can be no superstructure, nor may one abruptly without immediate steps but gradually and maturely ascend to honors and more advanced subjects, and that grammar, logic, physics and other inferior sciences are the road to and basis of other superior sciences, we decree and ordain

---

[1] *Repetetur* evidently should be *reputetur*.

that no one should be admitted to the baccalaureate in canon law or the faculty of *Decreta* at Paris, no matter how long he may have heard the *Decretum* and Decretals as ordered by other statutes, unless he shall previously have been adequately grounded in elementary subjects, as to which he shall be required to give satisfaction before the college, both as to place of study and subjects as well as the time spent on them, by his own oath or other sufficient means.

78

OCCAMIST ERRORS REPROVED

STATUTE OF THE FACULTY OF ARTS, PARIS, DECEMBER 29, 1340

Chartularium universitatis Parisiensis, II, 505-7.

To all who may see the present writing, from all and each of the masters giving instruction at Paris in the faculty of arts, greeting in the Lord. Everyone is supposed to oppose errors to the best of his ability and to close the road to these in every way, the more since by these knowledge of the truth may be concealed. But since it has come recently to our attention that some in our faculty of arts, adhering to the pernicious cunning of certain men, not founded on firm rock, seeking to know more than is fitting, are striving to disseminate unsound views from which intolerable errors not only about philosophy but even concerning divine scripture may arise in the future, hence it is that, desiring to remedy this so pestiferous disease, we have collected their profane assumptions and errors as we could, decreeing concerning them in this wise:

Forsooth, that no masters, bachelors or scholars in the faculty of arts lecturing at Paris shall venture to say that any famous proposition of the author whose text they are lecturing on is false absolutely or is false literally, if they believe that the author had the right idea in propounding it. But they shall either concede it or distinguish the true meaning from the false sense, because statements of the Bible might with equal reason be denied in their literal wording, which is perilous. And since an utterance has no virtue except by the employment and common usage of authors and others, therefore the force of an utterance is such as authors commonly employ it and as the matter demands, since utterances are to be received according to the subject matter.

Also, that no one should assert absolutely or by virtue of wording that any proposition is false which would be false according to one's personal interpretation of its terms, because this error leads to the previous error, for authors often use other interpretations.

Also, that no one should say that no proposition is to be distinguished, since this leads to the aforesaid errors, because if the disciple takes the proposition in one sense and the doctor understands it in another, the disciple will be misled until the proposition is distinguished. Similarly if an opponent takes one meaning and the respondent understands another sense, the disputation will be in name only, if a distinction is not made.

Also, that no one should say that no proposition is to be allowed unless it is literally true, because to say this leads to the aforesaid errors, since the Bible and authors do not always employ words in their literal sense. Therefore, more attention should be given to the subject matter in affirming or denying statements than to the literal meaning. For a disputation based on literal meaning and receiving no proposition except in its literal sense is nothing but a sophistical disputation. Dialectical and doctrinal disputations which aim at investigation of truth have slight regard for names.

Also, that no one should say that there is no knowledge of things which are not signs, that is, which are not terms or expressions, since in the sciences we use terms for things which we cannot carry to disputations. Therefore, we have knowledge of things, albeit by means of terms or expressions.

Also, that no one should assert without distinction or explanation that Socrates and Plato, or God and creature are nothing, since those words at first sight sound bad, and since such a proposition has a false sense, namely, if the negation implicit in this word, Nothing, is understood to fall not only on *ens* singly but on *entia* plurally.

If moreover anyone shall have presumed to violate the above articles or any of them, him from our society now and for the future we expel and reject and wish to be considered expelled and rejected, saving in all respects what we have decreed elsewhere as to the doctrine of William called Ockham, which we wish firmly maintained in every way. Given at Paris under the seals of the four nations, namely French, Picards, Normans and English, together with the signet of the rector of the university of Paris, A.D. 1340, the Friday after Christmas.

79

ATTEMPT TO IMPROVE THE CLUNIAC SCHOLARS AT PARIS, APRIL 25, 1344

Chartularium universitatis Parisiensis, II, 549–50.

Since to have been a student at Paris and not to have studied is far from praiseworthy, and in the house of the scholars of Cluny at Paris for twenty years past no one has been made a doctor of theology and few, bachelors, which works to the discredit of the said scholars and opprobrium and downfall of the order, which is in dire need of educated men, therefore, that henceforth some fruit result from the said scholars, the definitors define decreeing that, if henceforth there shall be any scholar in the said house who has accepted the pension of a scholar at Paris in the same house, studying for seven years in logic and philosophy, and, when the seven years are elapsed, is not capable of lecturing on logic according to the report of the prior and the subprior of the said scholars, he shall be deprived of his pension *ipso iure.* And if, after the said seven years, he shall study for another seven in the faculty of theology or shall accept the pension of a scholar for the same seven years, and, when the said seven years are elapsed, shall not begin effectually his courses in the same faculty of theology, he also shall be deprived of the pension of scholars *ipso iure.* Moreover, those scholars who now have a pension in the said house who have held the pension for twelve years, if within the present year they shall not begin to lecture effectually in that science for which they have enjoyed the said pension for the twelve years now elapsed, when the present year is over, shall be deprived *ipso facto* of their pension and, when deprived, return to their convent and be forced to do so by ecclesiastical censure by the subprior of the said scholars. And when in the future it shall happen that any persons or person, as has been said, shall be deprived of his or their pension, the prior of the scholars, with the advice of his associates, shall nominate in his place another suitable and docile person well founded in grammar, and this nominee the chief prior of Cluny by ecclesiastical censure and other remedies shall cause to be received at Paris in the house of the said scholars.

80

DISPUTATIONS IN THE COLLÈGE DE SORBONNE, 1344 A.D.

Chartularium universitatis Parisiensis, II, i, 554–56.

In the year of the Lord 1344, the 14th day of November, master Petrus de Crozo, master of theology, bishop elect and confirmed of Senlis, overseer of the college of Sorbonne at Paris, considering that there would be much future fruit, if the fellows of the said house were occupied in honest exercises of disputations and collations, having convoked all the fellows in the hall of the Sorbonne, no one dissenting, appointed as is customary four fellows, one from each nation, to consider how the said disputations could be made more useful to the said fellows and more honorable to the house. These deputies, profiting by the sound advice of many, ordained as follows:

First, that to regulate the disputations . . . there be chosen one of the fellows to be called master of the students who shall have the following duties.

First, that in summer, when the prior shall hold his disputations and they cease from their disputations, he shall provide questions for the whole year, listing the titles on a roll in the chapel, so that he shall diligently select important and useful theological questions according to the text of the *Sentences,* one from one distinction, another from another, thus running through the entire book without interpolation of distinctions, and so that the questions of one year shall not be identical with those of the preceding or following.

Second, that if the master of students shall see that the disputants are not of the same mind, he shall bring them to unity of understanding, and if they seem to contend for vanity rather than truth, he shall impose silence. If anyone does not obey him after the third warning, expressed in these words, "I impose silence upon you," he shall pay two quarts of wine of the house at the end of that disputation to those who were present to the end, and the master of students shall enforce this.

Third, if it chance that he who should respond is absent for any reason, the said master of students shall be held to take his place himself, as the prior is accustomed to do at collations, or to provide another suitable substitute.

Fourth, if the person elected master of students is unwilling to accept the election and does not give a sufficient excuse to the four persons appointed by the prior, he shall be required to pay one purse.

Fifth, the said master of students shall be required to assign a question to the opponent and respondent at least a fortnight before each disputation. If he doesn't and on this account there is a break in the disputations, the master of students shall be fined two quarts of wine of the house. The lord prior shall enforce all such penalties against the said master.

They further decreed that every Saturday after the singing of *Salve regina* or other antiphone in its season, as is customary in the house, in the afternoon, except the time aforesaid, there shall be honest and useful disputation in chapel or other fitting place of the house, so that the opponent in general argument and rebuttal, in order that others may have an opportunity, shall not give more than eight reasons, and each of the others only three, nor shall anyone make bifurcated arguments, divisive or copulative or leading to *impossibilia,* accumulating many arguments in one. The respondent may draw only three conclusions, each of which he may confirm by one authority and one reason, if he can, or by one authority alone or one reason alone, without corollaries.

They further willed that immediately after the principal opponent the master of students argue, then the prior of the house, then the masters in theology, if they wish to argue, then the bachelors, then the cursors in the order that they attained their degrees, so that he who shall have finished the *Sentences* first shall argue first, and he who has read two courses before him who has given one course, and he who has first finished his course or courses before him who did so last. Then other fellows shall argue but those who have been longer in the house. And if outsiders chance to attend these disputations, if they are persons of good repute, which should be left to the judgment of the master of students, and are not so numerous as to impede the fellows of the house from their own exercise, if they wish to argue, they shall be allowed to do so according to their degrees; or, if anyone has no degree, provided he is a noble or cleric or enjoys other prerogative, the master of students shall place him in the arguing as it seems fit to him.

Moreover, in this statute we do not intend to prejudice other statutes and customs of the house, in which it is warned explicitly or by implication that equality is to be observed in all respects between fellows of the house, since in the house all are as fellows and students, not as greater and lesser masters and scholars and the like.

Further they decreed that these disputations should so proceed that on the first Saturday after the nativity of the blessed virgin Mary he who has last entered the house should respond first to him who immediately preceded him in responding, and so ever proceeding up to those longest in the house; and he who was first on the first Saturday on the Saturday following shall be the opponent.

And to this we wish all fellows to be bound from their entrance to the house for six years, unless they were masters of theology, and they should be required to swear this to the lord overseer when they enter the house. Moreover, if any one of the fellows, prevented by reason of weight, is absent from opposing or responding, he shall procure a substitute, but must appear himself on the next Saturday immediately after that when he should have opposed or responded, so that no one may absent himself from these exercises. Nay rather he shall respond or oppose once a year, if possible, in his own person. And as often as anyone is absent and does not perform these exercises in his turn in the way set forth, so often shall he be required to pay two quarts of the wine of the house as stated above.

Further they willed that, if on Saturday or Sunday there be a great feast or other notable event on account of which it is not possible to dispute on that day, the disputation be set forward or back a day or two, as may seem good to the master of students and the majority of the fellows, or if necessary and for urgent reason may be deferred to the next Saturday.

Further they willed that no one be held to these exercises unless he had made his first collation in the house, nor at that time assigned him for collation, nor at a time when anyone was lecturing.

They further willed that the fellows of the house who are not bound by this statute, such as those who have been more than six years in the house, if they wish to respond or oppose gratis, shall be admitted in order of seniority, or otherwise, if it shall seem good to the majority of the fellows. And this should be understood always of the majority of fellows who were present at the disputation at which this is proposed by the master of students.

Further they willed that each person shall make the first response and opposition after entering the house by himself, nor may this be done by any substitute. The master of students is required to attend the disputations from start to finish, unless reason of necessity intervene, under pain each time of paying two quarts of wine in the way aforesaid or providing another suitable master in his place.

They further willed that the master of students for each disputation as a return for his labor receive eight sous Parisian on the house.

Done in the time of the priorship of master Geoffrey Brito, at his insistence, with the consent of all the fellows then resident in the house less than six years, the same fellows being ready to assume all the said obligations provided newcomers to the house henceforth incur similar obligations. All which the said overseer ordained that fellows henceforth to be received in the house should swear before their entrance with the other oaths, and he made master John of Cologne, when he received the others, swear in the presence of all the fellows.

81

COMMENDATION OF THE CLERK: AN EDUCATIONAL TREATISE

Vatican Palatine Latin MS 1252, fols. 99r–109v.

The following treatise or part of a longer work [1] occupies the closing pages of a large fifteenth-century paper manuscript in the Palatine collection of the Vatican library.[2] It seems to have no connection with the preceding

---

[1] At fol. 102r at the close of his first chapter the author refers to our text as "this third economic book of mine." Also his expressed intention of telling how clergy "should be trained and perfected in ecclesiastical functions" is not carried out in our present manuscript, which ends abruptly.

[2] Vatic. Palat. lat. 1252, 15th century, paper, 291 x 198 mm., fols. 99r–109r. There is a photographic copy at Columbia University.

contents of the volume, which consist of medical extracts [3] and recipes, a brief discussion of rational entities,[4] and astrological [5] and miscellaneous matter. The anonymous author of our treatise appears to have written it at some time between the death of William of Ockham in 1347 [6] and the foundation in 1365 of the university of Vienna by the dukes of Austria and its approval by pope Urban V.[7] He was apparently a German clergyman who had attended the university of Paris and who was much given to sermonizing, biblical citation, metaphorical illustration and to derivations of words which are often of the type made famous by the *Etymologies* of Isidore of Seville. He also manifests a frequent interest in natural phenomena, especially animals, and quotes from the poets and classics as well as from scholastic authors. The incipit of our treatise happens to be the same as that of the *De bestiis et aliis rebus* or *Columba deargentata* variously ascribed to Hugh of St. Victor and Hugo de Folieto,[8] because both works open by quoting that verse of the Psalm which in the *Vulgate* begins, "Si dormiatis inter medios cleros." [9] The complete extant Latin text of our treatise is reproduced in an appendix at the close of this volume. The fourteenth chapter, which is the last in the manuscript, is very brief and apparently breaks off incomplete, while perhaps yet other chapters followed in the original. Or possibly the author never finished his work. As it stands, however, it presents a very vivid picture of educational ideals and practice in the fourteenth century.

If ye sleep amid the clerics, ye shall be as the wings of a dove covered with silver and its tail feathers with yellow gold.[10] In these words, if one regards their deeper meaning, the spirit of the Lord by the mouth of the prophet as through a golden trumpet sounds the blessing of the happy clerk. Since, although we here consider clerics in the

---

[3] The manuscript opens with the fourth chapter of some medical work; fols. 36v–47r appear to continue a medical treatise.

[4] Following two or three blank pages, fol. 49r opens: "Entia rationalia non volunt . . ."

[5] Fols. 88r–89v: "Spera Saturni . . ./ . . . Explicit de planetis et elementis."

[6] On fol. 99r he criticizes adversely the philosophy of Ockham and his followers.

[7] In chapter 3, fol. 103r, he speaks of Vienna as still a school without privileges from the pope or princes.

[8] Concerning it see Lynn Thorndike, *A History of Magic and Experimental Science*, II, 15–18.

[9] In Hetzenauer, *Biblia sacra vulgatae editionis*, 1922, p. 520, it is Psalm 67(68), verse 14, as against 68, 13 of the King James version which I have usually cited in the footnotes.

[10] Psalm 68:13.

scholastic sense, these words are fitting for their praise. While if we have the service of the church militant in mind, they are most evidently suitable to clerical renown. For what is sleeping amid the clergy except their resting in the midst of all the extremes of human activity? For all human virtue consists in observing the mean between two evils, as I have elucidated when monastic life allowed. And those who do not abstain from vices, although they may know all scriptures, are not moderate clerics but extreme, for they are not virtuous but rather vicious. And of the extremes indeed there are two kinds: the deficient clerk and the excessive clerk. For the clerk who falls short of the happy medium is he who shuns the labor of study but glories much in show of knowledge. This attitude is called feline. For a cat likes fish but shuns the river. And in the rites of the church militant there are some who wish to scale the heavens but do not lay aside worldly delights. Moreover, the clerk who exceeds the mean is he who oversharpens his talent and seeks to fly higher than his strength allows. To whom the Apostle says, We ought not to know more than is seemly but soberly and in convenient measure.[10a] So too there are some who go to excess in the works of the church militant, wishing to equal the desire of their minds by exercises of the body. Since the spirit is indeed willing but the flesh is weak.

Or it can certainly be said that he is a clerk deficient in the scholastic life who denies the natures of many things, as did brother William of Ockham the Englishman and his followers, who assert that relations as well as *situs, habitus,* where and when, exist outside the soul as things indistinct from absolute things. And they affirm that quantity is the same as substance. The movements too in which the actions and passions of things are fixed they say are things indistinct from permanent things. Those moreover in scholastic life exceed the mean who invent certain conceptibles outside the soul which they themselves deny to be things but represent as intrinsic modes of things or surely formalities of things. And these men place a plurality of such formalities in God contrary to the fact that the supreme absolute is found in Him. And deficient clerks indeed might be called nausigraphs because they simulate nausea at writing on things or the ascription of a distinct nature. For nausigraph is called from *nausea* and *grahos* [11] which is writing.

[10a] Cf. Romans 12, 3.   [11] *Graphos* is perhaps meant.

The exceeders are called pleographs from *pleos* which is excess as writing too much, whence too pleonasm is called superfluous addition of wording, as in speaking I said everything. (fol. 99v)

But clerics properly speaking are those who do not depart from the mean of virtue nor decline from the center of truth to empty circumferences. For it is a saner practice to keep in the middle. These are the happiest of men, to whom alone it is appropriate to rule the world of men. They are like gods housed in human bodies, in whose schools the spirit of the Lord resides, and God is exalted in their hearts, since they are the divine mean from participation in God's grace, in which mean the God of gods judges them to be gods, that is, the masters of wisdom. As the prophet says, "God stood in the congregation of the gods; in the midst he judged the gods." [12] And again, "I said, Ye are gods and all sons of the Most High." [13] For although God sees all things, yet with richer grace doth He discern the happy clerk in the midst of all virtues. I call clerk him who has mortified all his desires in this world and who has received God as his lot and inheritance, or who is on the Lord's side. For just as Papias [13a] says, *Cleros* is the same as lot or inheritance, whence clerics are called because the Lord is their lot and inheritance. Therefore those who desire the goods of this world more than God or love them more than God are in truth no clerics, because the Lord is not their inheritance nor a part thereof. For every true cleric has the force of the spirit of God and by that spirit like the prophet of old he speaks with burning lips saying, "Lord, thou art the portion of my inheritance and of my cup; thou restoreth my inheritance to me." [14] Finally, of the same happy man, as sharer in the fatherland, God is the entire inheritance and, as a traveler in this life, is as a portion of his inheritance, since no one here fully enjoys the divine goodness as in the fatherland but, as it were, partially, since in less amount.

Cleric also can be named from *cleos* which is the glory and dew of dews, as it were, the dew of human glory. Or because the glory of mankind is roscid and fruitful, the cleric is blessed. For just as the dew of heaven impregnates the soil and brings forth flowers and grass and vegetation in general, so beyond doubt the happy clerk paints and

---

[12] Psalm 82: 1.　　　　　　　　　[13] Psalm 82: 6.

[13a] Papias was a Latin grammarian of the eleventh century. His *Vocabularium* was first printed at Milan in 1476.

[14] Psalm 16: 5.

adorns mankind with virtues and wisdom and crowns with celestial glory and the honor of divine sweetness, which sweetness of the goodness of God, moreover, the clerk dispenses by divine favor to other men. Or cleric is called from *cleus* which is a high mountain and dew of dews, as it were, the mount of God, lofty and dewy. For the cleric is called a high mount from the peak of his lofty speculation and divine contemplation, and dewy mount with regard to his fertility in holy doctrine and richness in good works. Or cleric is named from *cleus* which is ascent and dew of dew, as it were, a bedewed ascent, that is a fruitful ascent to God. For these are the light of the world and lamps and torches by which the church of God is illuminated as by serenest rays. Lo! cleric is ascent and mount cemented by the firmness of fortitude and perseverance. As it is written, "He who shall have persevered even unto the end, shall be safe." [15] Mount rich in the fruit of happy works, so that to it is said, Of the fruit of thy works shall the earth be content. For this mount is that of which the prophet saith, "Mount in which God is pleased to dwell, for in it shall the Lord dwell to the end." [16]

I call on you, O laity, saying, Why do you not sleep? Why do you not rest amid the clergy? Don't you see what they have within? But you gnaw at their externals, not at what lies within, and so you judge the shell, not the kernel. You do not sleep among them but you turn yourself against them with external vexations and sickening suspicion, as we indeed look askance at massive mountains. (fol. 100r) Why, like beasts of the reed, do you temporal soldiers lacerate them, you, I say, whose movements are from the reed which is stirred by the wind of vainglory? I call you reeds of vain appearance which have nothing inside except the air of inflation and inane pride. Woe to you, unhappy wild beasts, exercising inhuman ferocity against the patrimony of Christ which is divided among you as spoil and rapine. But no less sin has, against the cows of the people, the congregation of bulls, who call themselves domestics of the church of God and advocates of ecclesiastical persons but scatter the milk-giving sheep, such as are the fruits and obventions of the churches, like lascivious bulls and continually despoil to their own use the church of God so that they exclude ecclesiastical men who are approved for their purity and divine discourse. Lord my God, chide the beasts of the reed, rebuke the mad bulls, scatter the

[15] Mark 13:13.   [16] Psalm 132:13–14.

gentry which war against thy church. For they sleep not amid thy clerks but disturb them with wicked movements, not knowing that they are nourishers and pastors of thy immaculate spouse, thy blessed dove. Dove, I say, of simplicity, turtle-dove of beauty, whose voice is first heard on our earth through thy only begotten Son, the word evangelizing us, the word of the Father, the word of truth, the word of peace and eternal felicity. On earth, I say, which from the chaste closes of the blessed Virgin he put on, in the earth of our humanity.

The wings of that dove are covered over with the silver of the fecundity of divine eloquence with which flies most sweetly the church service among the souls of Christ's faithful. Those are the wings with which fly those evangelizing the word of God. Wings how high flying which bring divine things to men, transcend the skies, and reach the prince of heaven! He who desires to hear the sweet song of the church whose head is Christ, let him listen to the Song of Solomon and assuredly, if he tastes well their sweetness, he will say with the prophet, "How sweet to my taste are thy words above honey in my mouth." [17] O truly blessed and delightful dove of Christ, for even its tail feathers are yellow gold. The back is a bony spine running down the entire body of an animal having ribs attached to it as support for the entire body. Moreover, this spine goes in knots and joints from top to bottom. What else therefore is the back of the church sustaining it than the catholic faith? For it is an articulated faith and knotty with joints and knots which are placed in the Christian symbol. And to this adhere ribs, that is appendages to scripture and certain additions which the church of God added, which surely concern the integrity of the faith and sustain the substance of the church of Christ. The posteriors of the back are the final and ultimate supports without which faith would be dead and without the marrow of vivacity, such as charity in the wisdom of God and wisdom in charity, charitable works and operative charity. For without these faith in the divine is that of a dead soul having no comeliness in the eyes of God. And witness to me in this is the chosen vessel, that I lie not. "If I speak," says he, "with the tongues of men and of angels, but have not charity, I am become as sounding brass and a tinkling cymbal." [18] These indeed are the last supports of faith into which all goods of faith are ultimately resolved, although

[17] Psalm 119:103. [18] First Corinthians 13:1.

they are first in foundation and vigor and magnitude, because the greatest of these is charity, yet last in resolution. We see the like of this (fol. 100v) in the principal parts of a material house, for what are the first principles of the house by way of putting it together as foundations are the last when it is taken apart. Moreover, these posteriors of the orthodox faith are most beautiful and covered as it were with yellow gold. For just as gold is above all metals in splendor and nobility and by its nature comforts the heart of man, so in truth charity comforts all and every work of piety.

Who, therefore, sleeps outside the clergy of God sleeps outside the church of Christ, not indeed in the sleep of quiet and safety but in the sleep of death, not temporal death but eternal death. And so infidels sleep outside the priests of Christ and sleep by cessation of good works, so that they work nothing aright in faith. There are others, however, within the church and among the clergy from whom they receive the sacraments of the church. But they do not sleep amid the clergy, that is, they do not rest themselves in quiet or felicity, nor can it be said of each of them, If he sleeps, he will be safe, but rather they sleep as if suffering lethargy or other disease by which they sleep like those who have tasted seed of jusquiam or whom the snake *ypnapis* has bitten. For the snake *ypnapis*,[19] as Solinus says, is of the genus asp, which also Jerome and the *Gesta Romanorum* call asp, who kills those whom it bites by sleep, because its poison induces sleep which can in no way be averted. They have eaten seed of jusquiam who within the church of Christ have received the name of Christians, but there is not in them any spark of charity, nay they freeze with the chill of envy and the frost of hate, so that they neither love their neighbor nor the Lord their creator. For so the frigidity of jusquiam, that is, of earthly vanity, has congealed them to the hardness of stone. For this herb is by its nature most frigid according to the statements of scientists, and with it the serpent *ypnapis* has bitten them and has intoxicated their souls. The serpent, I say, of malice, the devil, foe of our human progeny, so that they sleep incessantly in the sleep that closes calm reason inclined to every good, although they are awake sensually like beasts and brute animals. These are they whom sloth permits to perform no

[19] *Hypnale* in Solinus, *Polyhistor*, Leipzig, 1777, cap. 27, section 31, p. 173. *Hypnalis* in Isidore, *Etymologies*, XII, 2; Rabanus Maurus, *De universo*, VIII, 3.

godly work but they stagnate as it were in all things with Byrrian in-
dolence. To whom, if it is said with the morning star, Arise Byrria,[20]
Byrria arise! they do not arise but scratch their arms and stretch their
feet at length, turning their heads this way and that. For they prefer
to wallow in their beds rather than watch to the praise of God.

There are also other men who do not so much cease from good
works as vex the church of Christ and the pastors of the churches with
continuous care, although they have the name of Christians. And these
within the church are on the watch day and night not so much outside
the church as against the church, that they may disinherit their sacro-
sanct mother of her dowry and drive her out, bringing themselves to
confusion and eternal punishment. Which tyrannies, alas, have grown
so in our times in some parts of Germany, that not only the patrimony
of Christ is plundered by base tyrants but even ecclesiastical liberty
is reduced to utter servitude. They sleep not amid the blessed clergy
nor cherish the dove of the living God, under whose judgment they
are, but rather plot against the same like a certain kind of snake whose
nature it is to lie in wait for doves. (fol. 101r) We read in books on
nature that in the east there is a certain tree which in the Greek language is called of Paradise, while in Latin it is called as it were *Circa
dexteram*.[21] Of that tree the fruit is indeed sweet, in which doves take
rare delight and are protected by its shade and branches from the
snakes that lie in wait for them. Since snakes of this sort by nature
abhor these so much that they fear to come within the shadow of that
tree. Wherefore while the doves sit on this tree, the snakes lie in wait
at a distance and diligently watch whether any of them leaves the
tree and falls into their power. Moreover, the snakes in hunting the
doves display such cunning that if the shadow is on the right side they

[20] Birria is the name of a slave who appears in the *Andros* of Terence. The name
also occurs in the third book of the *Architrenius* of the twelfth century poet, Johannes
de Altavilla: *Rolls Series*, vol. 59, part i, p. 278,

> Nudus in annoso tunicae squalore ministrat
> Geta dapes, dum vile meri libamen in urbe
> Birria venatur, pretio vestitus eodem.

But in these earlier contexts the name denotes an unscrupulous and disreputable rather
than lazy person. A *Liber Birriae* occurs in a MS. described in the *Sitzungsberichte*
of the Vienna academy, 33 (1860), 158. It is preceded in the MS. by the twelfth century *De planctu naturae* of Alanus, but among the contents following it are three pest
tracts of 1370 or thereabouts.

[21] I do not find this appellation for a tree in the glossary of Hermann Fischer's
Mittelalterliche Pflanzenkunde, 1929.

lie in wait on the left and vice versa, or if it falls in front, they lurk behind and vice versa.

So the most happy dove of Christ, the holy church of God, has no other help except the blessed tree and wood of the holy cross whose fruit is most sweet, its flowers more redolent than all spices, its leaves most broad to cool those who are overheated. On which account the same dove on the day of Christ's passion hymns special praises inwardly thus sweetly singing, Cross, faithful among all, one noble tree, no forest ever bore such in frond, flower, twig. For the fruit of this both admirable and venerable tree is Christ. Than whom there is no fruit sweeter or more wholesome or, as I would say, more laudable in heaven or on earth. Whom he who eateth shall live forever. Its flowers, encircling and adorning this fruit on all sides, are the friends of Christ, for example, the martyrs in the red color of their passion, virgins in the white of their purity, confessors in the violet hue of their contrition, and doctors evangelical in the deep-blue or gold of their venerable information. And its fronds, finally, or leaves are the delights of divine goodness, namely, mercy, piety, largesse or charity, and generally the riches of the wisdom of God, by which the church of Christ is defended from foes who plot against it and will be defended forever. For if sometimes it suffers ills almost to the point of ruin, yet there is no lasting detriment from these to the church. O wicked dragons whose leader is the devil, whither tend your plots? I think that nowhere except to your own destruction. You cannot bear the dove, a simple and harmless bird, although you bear with ungrateful hoopoes and noxious crows.

This bird is in truth without gall. According to Bede [22] it feeds on pure grain, it harms no one, does not live by killing, gladly rests above the waters that it may quench its thirst and spy the reflection of the approaching hawk in the water. And it has a sigh for song. Look, I pray, and regard diligently these properties of the dove and you will see how they become the church of Christ, since the church has not the gall of bitterness and fraud. For it wishes to aid all and harm none after the ensample of its Beloved who is Christ the only-begotten of God. It feeds on pure grain because it lives on tithes and other donations which are turned to pious uses. These forsooth are pure food because they should be performed without contracts of iniquity. It lives not

[22] I have not succeeded in finding the passage in Bede.

on what is killed, that is on lucre by which mortal spot is incurred. Above the waters of wisdom, science, fortitude, counsel, intellect and other gifts of the Holy Spirit it gladly rests, scripture saying of it, "I saw something beautiful like a dove descending (fol. 101v) upon the streams of waters." Which waters indeed Christ promised that he would give to his disciples and to all believing on Him, wherefore He said to the woman of Samaria, "Whoso drinketh the water which I give, there shall be in him a fount of water springing up into eternal life." [23] These waters the church drinks to satisfy its thirst of love for God according to the measure of divine fruition in this life, which however is slight and as it were equivocally called compared to that fruition which is in heaven. It also drinks those waters to restrict the thirst after carnal desires, since where the spirit of the Lord is snares of the flesh are absent. Also in these waters the dove of Christ fortifies itself against the wiles of the hawk which hunts it, that is, the devil and the vain desires and empty promises of the flesh and the world. The church militant has a sigh for a song, since, although its spouse who is everywhere is present, yet it misses Him as if absent in comparison to those delights with which it will embrace him in heaven. And because of this absence of the Beloved it languishes from love for him, wherefore referring to this meaning of its sighing it says in the Song, "Tell my beloved that I languish from love." [24]

From what has gone before it is therefore clear that those sleeping amid the clerics sleep the sleep of safety under the wings of the dove and arms of the spouse, the spouse, I say, of God, most beautiful of all women, whose clerics are the rulers and dispensers of her riches. These clerics, pastors and prelates of peoples, possess the silver of divine plenty, drink the nectar of celestial eloquence, and have as well gold that is the light of the church, which they happily distribute to particular persons as these are capable of receiving it. But how masters and disciples in scholastic houses employ silver and gold will appear in this treatise, since the liberal sciences which are ordered towards eloquence as their goal may properly be compared to silver. Such are grammar, rhetoric and logic, and they are called the trivium. While other sciences which have as their object knowledge of truth, such as arithmetic, music, geometry and astronomy, and others included under these, are reasonably compared to gold. Wherefore scholastic discipline

[23] John 4: 14.   [24] Song of Solomon 5: 8.

which bears and nourishes prelates of the church until the years of their maturity is deservedly called the dove, marvelously winged with silver pinions so far as the sciences of the trivium are concerned, and surely with its tail feathers of yellow gold so far as the quadrivium is concerned.

If therefore you, O my sons, sons I say of seven summers ready for apprenticeship to letters, rest amid the clerics, that is, venerable and virtuous scholastic doctors, and are nourished by them, you will be enlisted under the wings of the blessed dove, you will be nourished under the arms of all virtues, beneath the cloak of scholastic philosophy which is beloved wisdom, mistress of all the good, whose marvelous delights are firm and pure. Moreover, scholastic discipline is, as it were, the nurse of the church militant and can be called the offspring of the dove, since it educates and nourishes the young in the church to become pastors of God.

But if you sleep amid the sophists you will bear a jackdaw as a sign of your vanity. For the jackdaw is a bird which repeats frequent cries, as it were, all of one sort. So lovers of error (*errophyli*) absorb nothing else of virtue and goodness except what they inanely cackle all day long. For *errophylus* is derived from *error* and *phylos* (fol. 102r) which means love, as it were a lover of errors. And all those are such who in their utterances prefer to proffer oddities to truth, as if unusual conclusions, although untrue, would prove the greatness of their genius. But the backbone of the truly scholastic dove is the holding of first principles naturally arrived at, through which all possible conclusions are ultimately established. Such are these categoric enunciations: *Ens* is *ens, aliquid* is *aliquid, res* is *res*. Also these conditional statements: if *ens* is *aliquid* and vice versa; if something is, it is *ens;* if a thing exists, it is something. And similarly these distinctions: every concept is either *ens* or not *ens*, in the case of anything it is or is not, but in no case both. The ribs, moreover, of this dove may be called the first principles of particular sciences, because each science rejoices in its own first principles. But its tail feathers are the light of the Holy Spirit and the virtue of the active intellect. For as these shine into the rational soul, in the direction of the passive intellect, there are received in it the first conceivables, and in their virtue the speculative intellect is led on to posteriors as in the light of human knowledge. Wherefore on this point that illustrious man of Lincoln (Robert

Grosseteste) remarks in First *Posteriors*,[25] "Not merely does the doctor teach by speaking outwardly to the ear, not merely does reading a book teach, but that true doctor who illumines the mind within and demonstrates truth."

Wherefore let us now see more particularly concerning school houses, since according to the order promised at the start, this third economic book of mine will deal with the regimen of divine houses. And reason requires that in these we first search how prelates who preside over God's houses and generally over ecclesiastical personnel are nourished in scholastic discipline, and presently we ought to subjoin how they are sufficiently nourished in schools, and afterwards how they should be trained and perfected in ecclesiastical functions.

CHAPTER 2. DESCRIBING THE SCHOOL HOUSE

The school house is the association of a human teacher and those who learn from him in a building devoted to letters. I say association to distinguish it from the house of a single man, since association is characteristic of several men. So a hermit who dwells under a solitary roof does not constitute a school house. And I say human in distinction from brute animals which, it may be, herd together in a common building, yet are not personalities, because a person is a rational being individual in essence, and thus the society of bees is excluded, because they lack reason. I say further teacher and pupils in distinction from other household association such as that of husband and wife, lord and servant, and so on. And I say in a building to mark the material house, which is called a school, in which scholastic discipline is exercised. For this house built of stones and wood is not the association of teacher and pupils but rather the workshop in which this association performs its operations. I say further, devoted to letters, in distinction from persons associated together without a purpose or, if with one, not literary but of some other occupation. And for this reason those are not properly school houses where either the doctor is not zealous in instructing (fol. 102v) or the pupils in learning. For school is derived from *scolon* which means zeal, and this both master and dis-

---

[25] Grosseteste's commentary on the *Posterior Analytics* has not yet been printed: for the MSS see Ludwig Baur, *Die philosophischen Werke des Robert Grosseteste*, 1912, Band IX of *Beiträge zur Geschichte der Philosophie des Mittelalters*, pp. 16*–19*, and S. Harrison Thomson, *The Writings of Robert Grosseteste*, 1940, pp. 84–85.

ciple should have, the one in instructing and the other in absorbing. Nor is a place properly called a school house where they are occupied with other matters than the knowledge of letters, for example, training in military agility, whose proper place is a gymnasium, although because of a certain resemblance between these occupations one term is interchanged for the other. Moreover, if anyone has been paying close attention, he will realize that I have used the plural above not without reason and spoken of those who learn from him, since the tuition of one person by one person does not properly constitute a school. For we had in mind that association of persons which involves a certain formality and distinct gradation of the pupils, as will appear below. And furthermore I spoke of the human teacher in distinction from the spirit of God and the active intellect, through which some learn sciences new to them, secretly discovering them, as it were, by themselves. And also by this the elements of the scriptures are renewed by which we are instructed and taught as if by a dead or painted man. Moreover, a dead man is not a man except equivocally, and so neither is the holy spirit a man nor the active intellect a man, but these two are rather principles of human composition.

CHAPTER 3. DIFFERENT KINDS OF SCHOOL HOUSES

There are four kinds of school houses, because there are schools of artists, medicine, jurists and theologians. For so they are distinguished by our venerable mother, the university of Paris, which assigns distinct places as auditoriums to these four faculties and dispenses distinct costumes to their representatives. For the artists cultivate the liberal arts near the river Seine in the street of Straw, at whose ends straw is sold. And they go forth in black round copes [26] of noble brunet or of fine perse lined with fur, frequenting the chairs of ordinary lectures at daybreak. Moreover, they are called artists from the seven liberal arts and others comprehended under these, whose exercise is only for those of subtle genius, since gross and rude natures cannot attain the fine points of these arts. Their costume befits lords of liberal philosophy,

---

[26] As to the nature of the academic *cappa* see Rashdall (1895), II, ii, 639–40. The *Medieval Latin Word-List from British and Irish Sources*, 1934, seems deficient in giving only the meanings, "cap. hood," and "part of a whip."

because it is the nature of black to collect the sight. For they must collect their powers of internal vision who seek to inspect intelligently such subtle volumes on nature and to speculate profoundly both as to the different principles and the varied derivatives of the whole machine of the universe. The round cut of their copes denotes the gyration of the created orb, which they seem to enclose by the capacity of their brain, measuring the qualities of the stars, the varied movement of the winds, the natures too of animals and plants, the virtues of minerals, and the origination of every meteorological phenomenon. Whence too the tassel of the beret with which the philosopher crowns his head is a sign of the capacity of his brain and the breadth of his mind. Moreover, the flower in his bonnet signifies decorum of morals and treasures of companions of liberal sciences. Since he is not a perfect philosopher whom every human virtue does not adorn with good morals. The gold on the fingers with which masters of art were adorned of old signifies wisdom of mind, and the gem set in the gold connotes the excellence of the sage to common men, because the sage is naturally lord of the rude populace. Time past once bestowed on the lords of philosophy round scarfs, likewise (fol. 103r) in front a *patula* also lined with fur, which were made of scarlet flaming with the best red color. And the roundness of the scarf had the same significance as the spherical cope. But this flaming fervor suggested that they above all other men were fervent to increase human knowledge of the world's marvels. For true philosophers care nothing for external utility, but all their labor is to this end, that they may learn the truth as to origins and things originated. And because of unity as to this goal the latitude of all liberal sciences is called one faculty of artists.

Next the medical men dwelling in the houses of their habitations elucidate their aphorisms venerably to their auditors. And these rejoice in ordinary copes of brunet somewhat brighter than the artists and more nearly red like the color of thick rouge. And in the closeness of this color to true brunet is figured the connection between these faculties, since he is a poor physician who knows no logic or who has no recourse to natural philosophy. Rouge too, since it is black declining towards red, signifies the disturbance of disease combined with the fixing of hope on the physician. For unless one was sick, one would not want a physician, nor would the patient seek medical advice, if he did not hope to be aided thereby.

After these the erudite among the jurists flourish, for whom at Paris the street Chnobernelli [27] is set aside, which also is called the street of asses.[28] These rejoice in scholastic copes of scarlet and of a fiery red, since the red color signifies an inflamed mind. For these are afire concerning the tranquility of mankind and involve themselves in innumerable questions to settle matters of lawsuits and to repress the countless efforts of litigators. Or this color, like that of the inside of the *patula*, is bestowed on them because they are solicitous concerning public affairs and human morals.

The highest chairs of all the schools are happily scattered through monastic cloisters and the Sorbonne and other blessed colleges to lecture on books of theology and expound the marvels of divine Scripture. The reverend masters of theological profundity are clad in copes of their Order, if they are regular clergy, or in any simple garb or humble color, if they are secular clergy, to denote the humble and innocent preaching of this science. And as the medical men are derived from physical scientists, so the canonists spring from the theologians, because the sacred canons are often the conclusions of divine utterances, as is clear to one who carefully studies the decrees of the fathers.

Another division may be made between schools, as when it is said that some schools are authentic, others illegitimate (*leninoma*). An authentic school is one whose studies are laudably founded on apostolic privileges and imperial liberties, as in the case of the schools of Paris, Bologna, Padua and Oxford. An illegitimate school is one of slight reputation lacking privileges from princes of the world, such as in Germany are the schools of Erfurt, Vienna, and so on. And the difference between them is indeed great, since in the authentic schools knights are dubbed and lords of sciences crowned, so that they enjoy both special costumes and liberties and are revered with marked reverence no less by princes lay and clerical than by the people, and such are laudably entitled masters and lords of the sciences. But in the illegitimate schools although masters are nourished actually, they lack a privileged title, whence it follows that the name of master is equivocal in many respects. For one man is a master in title and reality, another

[27] The reference seems to be to the schools "in clauso Brunelli," concerning which see *Chartularium univ. Paris*, I, 266–67, and the documents there cited.

[28] In *The Mirror of Asses* of the twelfth century poet, Nigellus, Brunellus visits Salerno and Paris and says of the latter, "What madness possessed me to visit these parts and the schools of Paris?" *Rolls Series*, 59, i, 65.

in reality but not in title, (fol. 103v) a third in title but not in reality, a fourth neither in title nor reality but in name only. The master in title and reality is most properly called master, since he has the holdings of the sciences and with this enjoys a title acquired by outstanding merit and privileged by the liberties of princes. For title is derived from titan, which is the sun, because, as the sun adorns the corporeal orb with its light, so the true title laudably adorns the one to whom it is applied. But a master is so called as thrice great, set above others in mental capacity, reasoning power and moral conduct, of which if he lacks one he is not a good master. How moreover a true master obtains his title will be made clear below. The master in reality but not in title is he who has the treasure of science and the heritage of virtue but does not have a privileged title. And he is like a noble, strong and praiseworthy in arms, who has not yet been knighted. But the master in title and not in reality is he who by prayers or price simonaically receives a title he does not deserve, lacking the knowledge for so high a title. He is like a timid man who never has been or will go to war but accepts the title of knight so that he may appear in silk at church and adorn his fingers with gold. Moreover, he is master neither in reality nor in title who neither is acquainted with the sciences nor has acquired the title in privileged schools but on some occasion has taken the name of master, perhaps as notary to a lord or pleader in the law courts.

CHAPTER 4. PERSONS AND ASSOCIATION OF PERSONS IN THE HOUSE

In the illegitimate school house of the artists there are at least four kinds of persons necessary, to wit, master, disciple, pedagogue and monitor. The master is the paterfamilias and lord of the school house whom the particular persons associated in the same house are bound reverently to obey. But the disciple is the son and heir of the master, to whom the father venerably dispenses the treasure of his mind or at least tries to. The pedagogue is the guide of the schoolboy and his vice-master in the house. Moreover, we call him the monitor who notes the faults of the scholars and reports their offenses to the master. Between the said four persons there are three associations, to wit, of master with disciples as of father with heirs, of master with assistant masters and monitor as of lord with servants, and the association of these servants with the sons of the venerable master. For in this divine house we do not have the association of man and wife as in the domestic house; nevertheless there is no master without mistress, nor poet without muse. For the lawful mate of the philosopher is that leading lady of all delights in this life, Philosophy herself, who the Lord ordering is mistress of all virtues. Since taking the name of philosophy literally, it extends to all wisdom possessed by the human species whether acquired from man or God. For philosophy is, so to speak, loved wisdom, wherefore the artist is a philosopher, the medical man too is a sort of natural philosopher, who starts from the branches of things of nature leaving their roots to the natural scientist. The jurist is a philosopher from a sort of moral philosophy, since juridical erudition is subordinated to moral science, as Johannes Monachi comments on the sixth of the Decretals. The theologian is a philosopher from divine philosophy. But since the artists deal with all the interests of the aforesaid philosophers, for example, about the generation of man and his nature and parts, as is clear in the books of Aristotle on the generation of animals—and in this (fol. 104r) coincide with students of medicine —and also deal with human morals and the rule of households and cities bidding men live virtuously, as is evident to one perusing the ethical and economic and political books of illustrious Aristotle—and in this coincide with the jurists—and similarly dispute concerning God and the number and natures of the intelligences, as is clear in the books of metaphysics—and in this coincide with the theologians—therefore the artist is called the true philosopher by the very name and *par excellence*.

Returning therefore to what we were saying, we assert that the true wife of each philosopher is his philosophy from which he begets books like himself according to the forms and cast of his mind, and that his disciples are in a fashion his sons. His household consists of the assistant masters and custodians of the schools, who, according to the master's command, instruct the scholars and keep them from things illicit. And assistants are more opportune in unlicensed schools of artists than in others, because their hordes are younger and more heterogeneous and so require more tutors in acquiring both morals and knowledge. In authentic schools of artists, however, only three persons are needed except for the janitors who keep the keys to the schools and the *predones* or bedells who announce the lectures of the masters and disputations to the community. For in the authentic school there is master, bachelor and disciples. Moreover, what the master or disciple is has been stated before, but the bachelor is an arch-scholar who gives cursory lectures in the place of the master and who goes about the classes of the doctors arguing and responding, but has not yet received the laureate of doctoral knighthood, yet is close to the degree of master. And he is called bachelor from *baca* which is a gem and *lar*, house, as it were a gem in the school house. Or he is called bachelor from *bachalus* which is father Liber and *lar*, fire, as it were the burning fire of a free father, i.e. master, which fire illuminates indeed the school house of the master. Or he is called bachelor not by *a* but by *v* from *baculus* which is the support of a vine or a man, since the bachelor in a way sustains the master. Or by *a* he is called a bachelor from *baca* which is the fruit of the laurel and *lar laris* which is *casa* or house, as if the fruit of the laurel in the school house. For, as Isidore says,[29] the laurel is a tree so called from the word for praise (*laus*), since with it once in token of praise the heads of soldiers and victors were crowned, whence among the ancients it was called *laudea*. And natural philosophers assert that this tree cannot be struck by lightning. It never sheds its leaves, and they are very fragrant and comfort by their aroma and are very efficacious medicinally, whence this tree appropriately signifies the doctor who is not harmed by the bolt of worldly adversity nor burned by the heat of lust like other men but in every state of variable fortune is green with the leaves of good morals and redolent with the pleasing aroma of virtue. Now the ripened fruit is the *baca*, that is, the archscholar who is called bachelor and will soon be fit for mastership.

In some universities, however, such as Bologna, in place of the bachelor there is a reviewer (*repetitor*), especially in the law faculty which flourishes there. And he after the lecture of the doctor repeats the same lecture to the others who wish to hear it. At Paris bachelors enjoy a certain angelic garb which is called the wrinkled cope because this costume is full of wrinkles or pleats from shoulders to heels, signifying not without reason the plenitude of involved speculations in which the bachelor abounds. This garment also has two wings reaching to the ankles to signify the flight of speculation both by means of the senses and the light of reason. For no one is an ingenious speculator

---

[29] *Etymologiae,* 17, 7: Migne PL 82, 609.

in this life without the force of the material powers of the soul and the clarity of the rational soul. Or these two wings might signify the capacity of the possible intellect and the activity of the active intellect, because with these two wings the speculator flies to the peak of the speculative intellect, which peak the philosophers call the adept intellect, as appears by Averroes, third *De anima*.[30] Therefore these are the persons required in the school house and between whom there are quasi-angelic associations as will appear presently.

CHAPTER 5. REQUIREMENTS OF THE MASTER IN ARTS

We ought to begin with the discipline of masters in arts as from the venerable mother, without whose essential preliminary regime no one by human effort is raised to the chairs of other faculties. Wherefore anyone who derides the faculty of arts either is a clodhopper, because he knows no letters, or hates the womb in which he was formed, curses the breasts which he sucked, denies his daily bread, refuses the air which he otherwise breathes, and shamefully blasphemes as to be shunned that which is necessary to him. We say therefore that a master in arts occupying a chair in authentic schools and especially in Paris, where this faculty of old possessed singular prerogatives, should combine in himself eight praiseworthy traits: of which the first is that he instruct himself by study, the second that he continue his lectures fruitfully, the third that he proceed systematically, the fourth that he love the truth rather than strive for singularity, the fifth that he shall not snarl at the catholic faith, the sixth that he live a moral life, the seventh that he provide for the necessities of life, and the eighth that he shun influenced promotions as simony.

The reason for the first requirement is that he who lectures without preparation does not speak as well as if he had prepared, wherefore doctors who refuse to study in order to seem more ingenious rather take away their scholars' talents than bestow any on them.

The reason for the second is that a lecturer who does not continue thins out his auditorium and renders the minds of his hearers ungrateful. Wherefore let the doctor postpone his leisure or outside occupations, otherwise he will empty his classroom rather than make it fecund.

[30] In the Venice, 1560, edition of the works of Aristotle with the commentaries of Averroes, vol. VII, fol. 121v.

Nor does he fruitfully continue, although he does not interrupt his lectures who tries to recover what has been spent, striving to turn the sea back into the Danube. But no more does he continue fertilely who does not cover the texts in the allotted time, so that they may be completed in due season in accordance with the university statutes.

The reason for the third requirement is because there is an order in the books of any science according to the order of the things comprised in it. Moreover, the best arrangement is to begin with the easier points and those better known to us and so proceed to those which are more difficult and occult. Wherefore that teaching is not best arranged which proceeds from things which are first in the order of nature to those which follow them, as Plato did, but rather the Aristotelian method is to be followed going from posteriors according to nature to priors.

The reason for the fourth requirement is that he who tries to be singular in everything strives rather to be *sui generis* than to be judged accurate. And so working against the minds of all he is detested by all rather than praised. For no one has sufficient ability to solve all questions, but it is the part of the true speculator to borrow many ideas from others and discover some by himself.

The reason for the fifth requirement is that he who snarls at the catholic faith dishonors God his Creator, prefers his own fancies to divine miracles, reveals arcana of God which he completely ignores, and indeed makes stupid assertions and casts prudence to the winds. Perhaps you will tell me that divine miracles do not concern you when you are discussing natural questions. And what do I say? You certainly are discussing miracles of God when you revolve his creatures in your mind. Has not the prince of this machine of the universe (fol. 105r) established everything with marvelous wisdom? And if He founded particular things for us in an accustomed course, by his omnipotence he can work marvels with any of them beyond its nature.

The reason for the sixth requirement is that the philosopher who lacks good morals is not a lawful philosopher but rather a counterfeit. For the law of philosophy is to live virtuously, act purely, and reason truly in particular matters. Wherefore a speculator living in iniquity or working impurity or not knowing the truth is entitled *errophilus* rather than philosopher, for he repudiates philosophy disgracefully and wickedly.

The reason for the seventh requirement is because it is shameful to lower the reverence of so high a name to become in torn tabard a laughing stock in public squares, or for such honorable intellect to beg its bread. It is more laudable for the arch-scholar in the lowest grade to suffer the woes of Codrus than disgracefully to beg in the van of so great a militia.[30a]

The eighth requirement is based on this reason, that a master promoting an unworthy scholar to the summit of mastership, corrupted by prayer or price, dishonors the loftiness of such a name, bridles an ass instead of a bear, crowns an ape in place of a man, and honors a clodhopper as a knight. He is an unhappy and ungrateful soldier of wisdom who from favor advances a fool to solemn mastership as if a wise man. Since he detracts from his own honor who gives his honor to aliens, and those are alien from the honor of an honest man who are unworthy of that honor. For just as timidity does not deserve to receive knighthood, but everyone who is truly knighted is of proven bravery, so ignorance wins no venerable mastership, while for laudable experience of the sciences any arch-scholar is made a revered master.

CHAPTER 6. SHOWING THAT THE TRUE PHILOSOPHER IS LIKE A SWAN

The requirements already stated make the true philosopher comparable to a swan according to the assertions of the ancients, since it is read in the stories of the lives of the philosophers [31] that, when one morning Socrates was about to begin lecturing in his school, and his disciples as is the custom wanted news, he disclosed a dream which he had had during the night. It is said that he had seen Plato, who had not yet begun his education, in the form of a swan, since Socrates in a dream saw a swan standing in his bosom and from his bosom fly above the gate of the Academy and there extend its neck beyond the skies. While Socrates was still relating this dream, lo! Plato's father brought his son to the school and entrusted him to Socrates, concerning whom Socrates straightway prophesied, as it were, with prophetic lips saying, Behold the swan which will penetrate the arcana of the heavens!

[30a] According to legend, Codrus, king of Athens, sacrificed himself in order to defeat the enemy.

[31] In *Gualteri Burlaei liber de vita et moribus philosophorum*, ed. Hermann Knust, 1886, pp. 214–216, the story is told more briefly than by our author.

Evidently Socrates uttered a true prophecy concerning Plato, because, as blessed Augustine recites in his book of Confessions, Plato set forth the whole gospel concerning the incarnate word of God in almost the very same words as John the evangelist writes when he says, "In the beginning was the word," etc., as far as this place, "There was a man sent from God." But whether this same first part of the Gospel sings the generation of God the Son from God the Father most appropriately, so it is. And except Plato no philosopher, no matter who or how great or of what sort, ever touched these celestial secrets. Well therefore did Plato appear in Socrates' dream as the swan which took the intellect of the human soul, to wit, the speculative, beyond the skies and carried it to divine generation. (fol. 105v)

For the swan is a bird with white feathers but black feet. With one foot it swims and with the other steers itself as with a sail. As the philosophers say, it eats little for the size of its body, has its strength in its wings, sounds with a sweet voice, swims in pure waters, has a long neck. So too the perfect philosopher and candid lover of true wisdom is white with candor of character and purity of virtue. He sings sweetly, since he teaches studiously, continues fruitfully, and pronounces truly what is to be known about the universe. He has strength in the wings with which he flies in speculation, to wit, the possible intellect and the active intellect. He has black feet with which he navigates safely amid the waves of human frailty, namely, patience and humility. With one of which feet, to wit, patience, he cleaves the waves and overcomes the inroads of adversity, but with the other foot, namely humility, he steers himself as with a sail amid the blasts and detractions of the proud. Moreover, these feet are black because despised among the vulgar crowd. For common men possess little patience and humility. The philosopher eats little, that is, is content with a few necessaries of life. For he does not seek to be a ruler of land and sea but to have someone to cook his herbs for him, which is little enough compared to his magnitude, since the loftiness of his sciences requires by natural law that he be the master of all foolish and common people. Also the true philosopher wishes to swim in pure waters, that is, to view the waters of wisdom and science with purity and abstinence from the snares of the world. He has a long neck because he has the power of reason raised to the heights of speculation.

CHAPTER 7. CONCERNING THE PRINCIPAL OF A BOYS' SCHOOL

Now let us see how a master of arts in schools which are not authentic but unlicensed should conduct himself with regard to the scholars and arch-scholars. And first concerning schools where often not a master in arts presides but a teacher of boys is named without title, who however sometimes is really a master although he lacks the title, sometimes indeed in our days is neither a master in fact nor in title but a vainglorious leader. The true teacher of boys ought to consider carefully the different individualities of his pupils, for they come at seven, as the age of infancy is most often reckoned, to receive the first rudiments. In such novices four things are to be considered, to wit, the state of the weather, a normal body, the physical constitution, and the mental capacity. I say that the state of the weather must be noted, because tender limbs are easily struck with cold or penetrated by heat. Wherefore it is advisable to start young children in school about the middle of springtime, and to be on the safe side it is well to have two classrooms for boys in the same building, one to wit adapted to resist the summer heat and with its windows facing north, which may receive the throng of scholars in summer with the air somewhat cooled off, the other carefully enclosed, which in winter time can be heated with burning coals according to the custom of the region, and this method is observed in many northern regions. Others build their schools on a slope with a subterranean depression well-walled with planks of fir-wood or of pine, which in summertime resists the heat and as winter grows severe shuts out the cold. Also different clothing should be worn, so that in winter for example the boys should be clad in heavy clothing and lighter in summer.

Also from the time a boy begins his schooling the soundness of his members should be watched with respect to continuous as well as discrete quantity and also the disposition of parts of the body. Moreover, I say continuous quantity so that none of his organs may exceed or fall short of its appropriate size (fol. 106r) and that neither hand nor foot nor head may be bent or crooked. And I say discrete quantity lest forsooth any one of them be substantially lacking, as when boys are found without arms or feet, or lest the number be superfluous, as the sexual parts are in hermaphrodites, or as in the case of monsters with two heads and one trunk, or those with too many fingers or toes and the like. I say also the disposition of parts of the body, because hunchbacks and those with clubfeet or one eye or infected with major diseases such as epileptics, lepers and the like, are not to be endowed with the nobility of letters, since those with noticeable physical defects neither adorn professorial chairs nor become the divine priesthood, in order to avoid scandal. But neither are they advantageously admitted in schools, because the boys wantonly laugh at them and disturb their peace of mind. Besides, those who have contagious diseases may infect the other scholars.

Moreover, the physical constitution is to be noted in schoolboys, since there is not one measure of scholastic discipline for all constitutions, just as there is not the same portion of food and drink for all. For those of sanguine temperament are gentle and pacific amid the turmoils of their associations and with capacity for learning, who seem to pick things up quickly as if it were play and without any great effort. But wantonness often seduces these. The choleric are somewhat less capable but retain more tenaciously and firmly. These as if in a fury disturb the others by various movements, for they jump about like young goats and are seldom found in the same place, wherefore they are deluded by inconstancy, unless God has given them the love of discipline. The phlegmatic indeed are sluggish and sleepy and of slower receptivity and ready forgetfulness because of the abundant humidity in them, wherefore they should be stirred up with some frequency, so that their brains may be warmed up. Those who are melancholy with stony hardness acquire with the greatest labor but retain with indelible memory, and their obtuseness is overcome by diligent study. The first therefore should be aided with due correction to repress their wantonness. The second lot should be threatened by the monitors and custodians so that their restlessness may be quieted. The third and fourth groups are to be fortified by reviews, which help them by frequent repetition of the lessons, for they aid themselves who help others, and he who teaches another instructs himself.

But the mental capacity of boys in the process of learning is quickly ascertained. For in the same kind of composition some are found bright, others brighter, and others brightest of all. So also some are dull, others duller, and others so dull that their mind is despaired of. And this variety comes from the latitude of degrees of the elements which no scientist or even physician can precisely measure, various aspects of the stars contributing to these differences and their quasi innumerable influences on the conception, formation and birth of children, which somehow spread occult affections in human bodies by which human talents are rendered more or less gross or subtle, since, as the art of physiognomy bears witness, the mind follows the body in its dispositions. Therefore let the teacher of boys so direct them that he corrects the timid by words, masters the frivolous with rods, and bestows upon each according to his exigencies the gifts of letters. Nor should the scholars be always kept intent upon their books and writing tablets, but they should be given an occasional recess and set at suitable games, so that their spirits may be raised and their blood stirred by the pleasure of play. For thus the boys' minds which before were fatigued (fol. 106v) by the tedium of classes are refined and refreshed.

CHAPTER 8. ON GRADUAL ADVANCEMENT IN THE ORDER OF THE SCIENCES

Now descending to particulars let us say that when the seven year olds have first begun to study grammar and have learned the letters of the alphabet and how to write them correctly together in syllables and to put the syllables together into words, it is opportune that they note the meaning etymologically, that is both the significations of the words and the properties of the parts, which the perspicacity of the moderns calls modes of signifying, dwelling upon them for some time, and when they have got the gist of these, let them work at dyasynthetical constructions of speech. Nor is it a bad plan to teach these together, since either profits by the accompaniment of the other. Meanwhile moreover texts of a moral character and of poetical deduction should be combined, in which is acquired both fruit of virtues and fertility of good morals, while traces of rhetorical polish are found in the same. This course of study develops from the first year in school at seven until the end of the scholar's fourteenth year. For then the light of reason begins to gleam in him, and then is the time to propound the involutions of dialectic to the brighter and better pupils together with examples of fine rhetoric, likewise occasionally mixing in something from the easier introductory works of the other sciences. For it is customary in the education of schoolboys to combine the practice of music with the milk of grammar, and also the art of the algorism which serves practical arithmetic. Similarly treatises on the celestial spheres introductory to astronomy concur with dialectical and rhetorical dissertations. Next from the twenty-first year the scholastic angels generally attack more solid subjects such as embracing natural science in its latitude, hearing metaphysics, and speculating over Euclid's propositions until the end of the third seven year period of education. And thus in his twenty-eighth year the arch-scholar is fitted for the chair of the master. But these three seven year periods of schooling might be reduced to five year periods in the case of very bright pupils. Nevertheless it is difficult for any human mind thoroughly to master so many, so great, and such subjects in these spaces of years. And he to whom is given from above so great mental capacity will do well to set for himself far ampler measures. But for him who turns to the sacred page or who seeks canon law it is enough to have the trivium in order to comprehend the eloquence of divine scriptures. And such an one when he has heard the secular arts should also attend the classes in theology and frequent the chairs of the jurists until he has acquired a sufficient hold on these subjects. But the more proficient he is in the arts, the more praiseworthy he will be as a theologian, because it is for the theologian alone to dispute concerning anything and to know the universe, so that he may be able to declare the more clearly the invisibles of God through those things which are visible. For the sacred Scriptures make mention of all the things of the universe. The medical man should have knowledge at least of the trivium and natural science and astronomy. Perhaps a little of the last will do, but if he knew it thoroughly, he would be a more circumspect practitioner.

CHAPTER 9. SOLVING SOME DOUBTS AS TO WHAT HAS BEEN SAID

The question arises from what has been said whether it is permissible for a Christian clergyman to study secular arts. And it seems not. For it is read concerning Saint Jerome that when he read Cicero he was chastised by an angel because he a Christian was absorbed in the figments of the pagans.[32] Besides reason convinces us that a Christian

[32] Our author owes this, like a number of his other references, to the *Decretum* of Gratian, Pars prima, Dist. xxxvii, Migne, *Patrologia Latina*, vol. 187, col. 203, which

should not sweat over the books of the Gentiles, because their arguments are contrary to the catholic faith. For Aristotle has reasoned in the eighth book of the *Physics* and the first book of *De celo et mundo* that the world is eternal and that there was no first man and will be no last. But that is expressly contrary to what is believed concerning creation, as is clear in the *Book of Genesis* of Moses. Again Averroes, Third *De anima*,[33] proves that there is an individual rational soul in all men, which is apportioned to each of them like one sailor to many boats. And this indeed manifestly denies eternal life in the paradise of delights and unceasing punishment for those who are condemned to the pains of Tartarus by the just judgment of God. Wherefore it follows that it is not right that Christian boys be educated in these vanities, because what we are accustomed to the more readily affects and governs our minds. With this too agrees what some write concerning the prodigal son, comparing him who ate the husks for the pigs and was fain to fill his belly with these to those who pore over the books of the Gentiles and fill their minds with the same. So too Origen by the insects and frogs [34] with which the Egyptians were afflicted understands the idle garrulity and sophistical arguments of the dialecticians. Jerome moreover writing to Damasus of the prodigal son says: "We see priests of God, laying aside Gospels and prophets, read comedies, sing the amatory words of bucolic verse, clasp Virgil in their hands, and make a criminal pleasure of what for boys is a hard requirement." [35] And again, "Does not he seem to us enmeshed in vanity of sense and obscurity of mind who is twisted night and day in the art of dialectic, or who as an investigator of nature lifts his eyes across the skies and beyond the depth of earth and the abyss is plunged into empty space, who gets excited over iambics, who distinguishes and stores away in his studious heart such an underbrush of metres?" So from these statements it would seem to some, that the works of Gentile philosophers should not be read by us, nor should we linger over the verses of the poets.

---

cites Rabanus, *De pressuris ecclesiasticis* for the story. But the real author of *De pressuris ecclesiasticis* appears to have been Otto, bishop of Vercelli (945): see d'Achery, *Spicilegium*, Paris, 1723, I, 423.

[33] Ed. of 1560, VII, fol. 101.   [34] Migne, *Patrologia Graeca*, XII, 322.

[35] Epistola 21: Migne, *Patrologia Latina*, XXII, 386.

CHAPTER 10. ARGUING TO THE CONTRARY

Nonetheless it is argued to the contrary: since in the books of secular science on nature it is doubtful to no one that useful things are found, why should we be prohibited from reading what is useful? For there are truths in them which are gifts of God. Whence Isidore in his book on the supreme good says: "Philosophers state much in the world as to measurement of the course of the seasons and the stars and the discussion of the elements, and yet they derived this only from God."[36] And if in their utterances they sometimes make mistakes, we may read these in order to avoid them. Wherefore Ambrose on Luke: "We read some things lest they be neglected, others lest we be ignorant, but others not to hold them but to repudiate them." We are exhorted to the same end by what Bede writes on the *Book of Kings* saying: "He disturbs and weakens the wit of readers who thinks they should be forbidden to read secular works of any sort."[37] In which if aught useful is found, it is lawful for them to make it theirs. Otherwise Moses and Daniel would not have been allowed to be trained in the wisdom and letters of the Egyptians and Chaldeans, whose superstitions and pleasures they at the same time abhorred. Nor would the master of the Gentiles himself, forsooth Paul, have included some verses of the poets in his writings or speeches, if they ought not to be read. To the same conclusion leads what Gratian asserts in the *Decretum* saying: It is read that the Lord bade the children of Israel to despoil the Egyptians of their gold and silver, thus pointing (fol. 107v) the moral that whether we find the gold of wisdom or the silver of eloquence in the poets, we should turn it to the use of salubrious erudition. In Leviticus too we are ordered to offer first-fruits of honey, that is, the sweetness of human eloquence to the Lord. The magi also offered three gifts to the Lord, by which some would understand three parts of philosophy.[38] These are the words of Gratian. And he understands by the three parts of philosophy the philosophy of speech which consists of the trivium, and real philosophy which concerns the quadrivium and other sciences comprehended under the quadrivium, as I have deduced above. Then the third part of

---

[36] *De summo bono*, I, xvii, 2.
[37] Both passages from Ambrose and Bede quoted by Gratian, *Decretum*, I, 37.
[38] *Idem.*

philosophy is moral philosophy, which in general is called ethics, having three principal divisions as set forth above. Corroborative too of our thesis is this which Jerome writes on the Epistle to Titus. If anyone, he says, knows the art of grammar or dialectic, so that he is able to speak correctly and to distinguish between truth and false, we do not blame him.[39] Geometry moreover and arithmetic and music have truth in their science. But it is not the science of piety. The science of piety is to know how to read the scriptures, to understand the prophets, to believe in the gospel, not to ignore the apostles. But the learning of the grammarians can profit life, provided it is utilized for higher ends. And so it is with all the other sciences of the Gentiles and the Chaldeans which are called liberal.

CHAPTER 11. SOLVING THE SAID QUESTION

Moreover in order to solve the said question we must carefully weigh the ends for the sake of which we labor in these and other sciences. For some men study just to know and so delight in this, that they contribute nothing further in the way of happiness or utility to themselves or others. And those who thus read secular studies are detestable, because they do not fructify to life eternal. To whom Isidore says in his book on the supreme good: "The philosophers of the Gentiles, not seeking God as they ought, fell upon prevaricating angels, and the devil became their mediator to death, as Christ is ours to life." [40] And again: "Therefore are prohibited to Christians the figments . . . of idle stories, because they excite the mind to lustful thoughts." [41] And later he says: "Some are more pleased to ponder the sayings of the Gentiles because of their sounding and ornate speech than holy scripture for its lowly eloquence.[42] But what profits it to progress in worldly doctrines and stagnate in things divine, to follow blind figments and shun celestial mysteries? Such books are to be avoided and discarded for love of holy scriptures." To finish what he has to say:

Some study worldly sciences primarily in order to know, and their goal is vainglory. To whom Isidore says: "Love of human or mundane science does nothing else than to extol a man with praises. For the

---

[39] These last words, "non improbamus," occur in the *Decretum*, I, 37, but not in the text of Jerome as printed in Migne, *Patrologia Latina*, XXVI, 593 A.

[40] *De summo bono*, I, xvii, 1.   [41] *Ibid.*, III, xiii, 1.   [42] *Ibid.*, III, xiii, 2.

greater are his studies of literature, the more his soul is inflated with arrogance and swells with pride." [43] Lo! they admit almost nothing of divine truth, nay they deride it with the teeth of canine snarling, and what they know to be true, because it is not their invention, their pride will not admit. To whom again Isidore says: [44] "The philosophers of the world indeed knew God, but because the humility of Christ displeased them, they left the true way for a byway." And so dimming the glory of God they inclined toward a lie and leaving the right way fell into tortuous error.

There are also a third set studying the sciences to make money and their master is avarice. Who, if they possessed worldly goods to begin with, would rarely thumb or study the volumes of the scriptures. So moreover the liberal arts in our times are not loved (fol. 108r) except as they lead on to the possession of other sciences. For the mere artist, unless he is equipped with other sciences, is almost found among us as a beggar. Noticing which, the poet says:

> Art thirsts, the Decretals are fat,
> The law itself is proud, Moses plays the pontiff,
> Medicine sneaks in the chamber door.

A fourth group study for edification to comprehend matters of faith and understand those things which lead to human happiness. And so it is licit for us to read mundane sciences, as is proved by the reasons and authorities cited in opposition to the question above. For the subtlety of all sciences has left its traces in divine eloquence, wherefore Cassiodorus in his exposition of the Psalter says: All splendor of rhetorical eloquence, every mode of poetical locution, each varied refinement of pronunciation takes its exordium from the divine scriptures. And with this agrees what Ambrose says on the Epistle to the Colossians. Every reason, he says, of supernal science or of terrestrial creature is in Him who is their head and author, so that one who knows Him need search no farther. [45] Because this is perfect virtue and wisdom, and whatever is sought elsewhere is found here in perfection.

A fifth group study the sciences not merely to be edified but that they may edify others, and their master is charity and love of their

---

[43] *Ibid.*, III, xiii, 9.   [44] *Ibid.*, I, xvii, 4.

[45] Migne, *Patrologia Latina*, XVII, 451; Gratian, *Decretum*, I, 37.

neighbor. To these it is indeed permitted to know the sciences of the Gentiles, in order that they may be able to decry their evil sayings and convert what they find useful in them to the use of sacred erudition as happy men. Wherefore Jerome on the Epistle to Titus says: How anyone exposes himself to ridicule who tries to write against the *mathematici* without knowledge of *mathesis* and to dispute against the philosophers without knowing their systems! Therefore let them learn the doctrine of the Chaldeans in the same spirit in which Moses learned all the wisdom of the Egyptians.[46] And again he says: If sometimes we are forced to recall secular letters and discuss some of those matters which we once abandoned, it is not of our free will but so to speak of the gravest necessity in order that we may prove that those things which were predicted by the holy prophets many centuries ago are contained in the literature alike of the Greeks, Latins and other Gentiles. From this may be seen to what intent the fathers of divine scriptures forbade the liberal arts of Gentile masters and to what extent they commended the same. Since one should not cling to those arts so fondly as to desert the delights of the Faith.

CHAPTER 12. HOW SCHOOL TEACHERS ERR IN THE TRIVIUM

It is enjoined by the synod of pope Eugenius [47] that all care and diligence be taken to set up masters and doctors who will teach assiduously literary studies and the principles of the liberal arts, because, as the same holy synod affirms, in these are especially manifested and declared the divine mandates. But in our times in many parts of Germany little attention is paid to this, since provision for school teachers is by no means made as it should be, nor do the bishops attend to their promotions as they ought. On which account enlightened men are forced to leave this calling and go into other occupations. And certain wretches come forward who were never any good as pupils and profess to teach what they completely ignore. And, which I say regretfully, such men, seductors rather than doctors, are preferred to noble intellects.

Grammar they harass with undeserved derision, affirming that

[46] The passage occurs rather in Jerome's commentary on the book of Daniel, cap. 1, Migne, *Patrologia Latina*, XXV, 519, and is so cited in the *Decretum*, I, 37.

[47] Roman council of 826, canon 33: *Monumenta Germaniae historica*, Legum sectio III, Concilia, II, ii; Gratian, *Decretum*, Pars prima, Dist. 37, cap. 12.

no construction of the parts of speech is transitive in the way that Appollonius the Greek, Priscian too the Latin, and before him Donatus the Roman construed some words as transitive, others as intransitive. For they assert that nothing transits unless it has feet. (fol. 108v) Wherefore according to them water does not move in streams nor winds fly, since they lack wings. Nor can it be said that one of the parts of speech rules another according to the proportions of the modes of signifying, since the human intellect rules and directs all parts of speech. For the properties of the parts of speech are nothing, they say. In fine they work so much fraud on the boys, that they neither know how to speak grammatically nor do they understand what they are saying but, like crows cawing and grackles screeching, they barbarize their words and shamefully solecize their speech. Yet because they ignore their own ignorance, they strut magisterially with heads erect, and although they know almost nothing, they dispute fully about everything.

Rhetorical eloquence they so debase by their blindness that they recognize neither flowers of words nor colors of sentences, but insist that flowers grow in meadows and that painters compose varied colors and beautifully shade them in imitation of nature. How they interpret the sweet speech of sacred scripture is seen from their total lack of system. Nor is there any doubt that they give rise to many heresies. For the holy scripture more than once calls the womb of the Virgin a rod and the Son conceived thence a flower. And if those words are false as applied to speech, it follows that rhetoric in its most beautiful species of transumption has no verbal virtue, and so the whole purpose of rhetoric seems to vanish.

Logic moreover they assert that they know when they have impressed upon a blindness impervious to grander visions a dozen so-called *insolubilia* or a poor half-dozen *obligationes*. They deny any consequences both as agreeable by reason of matter, because they are totally ignorant of the natures of things, and also as convenient by reason of form, since they have by no means reached the scope of logic. What is more, their error has grown so great that even an aged greybeard does not shrink from sweating over such elementary matters. And to this contributes the facility of error and the cautious conservatism of true philosophy. For it is easier to err in particulars than to attain the bounds of truth. Wherefore a master of error is turned out every day but one who philosophizes in thirty years.

CHAPTER 13. HOW SOME MASTERS OF ARTS EXTOL TOO HIGHLY THE PHILOSOPHY OF THE GENTILES

Some are so attached to both the natural and moral philosophy of the Gentiles that they call all sciences optional except the philosophy of the Gentiles, saying that the others are not essential except as a matter of human custom. This is an error, since theology is necessary for the salvation of mankind above all human sciences, which propounds the marvels of God and disputes concerning human morals with eternal happiness in view. So too the science of the sacred canons is essential for living well in the orthodox faith as the most blessed of all the moral sciences. Also they say that there is no question disputable by reason which a philosopher trained in the doctrines of the Gentiles may not dispute and settle, because reasons are derived from things, moreover human philosophy has to consider all things according to their diverse parts. They are wrong, because the principles of theology, which is divinely inspired in the holiest men, are unknown to philosophers who philosophize humanly. And consequently only a theologian who is versed in the same and assumes them as true can dispute and settle theological questions. It may be that the Gentile philosopher considers all things from another angle yet not in all real modes or ways possible for God, for human philosophers deny the miracles of God, which flow supernaturally from the plenitude of divine goodness. (fol. 109r)

They assert further that what is possible or impossible absolutely, that is in all modes, is possible or impossible according to philosophy. An incorrect statement, since the impossible for human philosophy, which is acquired by the light of nature, is possible for divine philosophy, which comes to us by divine inspiration and illuminates us by miracles of God. For how could a human philosopher tell that God is incarnated, or that the accidents of the bread without the subject (substance?) are in the sacrament of the altar? Nor do I learn from the philosophy of the Gentiles that the divine mind is of greater capacity without comparison than any human genius. Cannot then God by his genius accomplish things innumerable which entirely escape human comprehension? I am unwilling therefore to say that nothing is possible with God except what you can comprehend by human reason. Wherefore Isidore in the book on the supreme good says: [48] "The sacred books are written in simple language so that they may lead men to the faith not by verbal wisdom but by spiritual manifestation." For if they had been put forth by the cunning of dialectical skill or the eloquence of the art of rhetoric, the faith of Christ would be thought to consist not in the virtue of God but in arguments of human eloquence, and so we would in no wise believe that we were moved to faith by divine inspiration but rather induced by power of words. Furthermore some adherents of human philosophy affirm that philosophers are the world's only wise men. It is an error, since, as Isidore says in the same work: [49] All secular doctrine resounding with frothy words and exalting itself on the swell of eloquence is deflated by simple and humble Christian doctrine, as it is written, God made the wisdom of this world stupid in name to the fastidious and loquacious. Therefore they are far wiser who rely on divine miracles than those intent on human wisdoms. Yet these reach such a point of pertinacity that they say there is no more excellent state than to study philosophy. It is an error, since no one is more excellent than he who is more friendly to God, no one moreover is more friendly to God than he who is found more fecund in God, more obedient to God, and more filled with God's grace. Wherefore we know that those are greater and gladder in their studies who have learned something by revelation of the Holy Spirit than those who are imbued with human doctrines, whence Isidore in the same book in the chapter on the Holy Spirit says: I certainly believe that he feels great joy who learns something by revelation from the spirit of God. [50]

CHAPTER 14. OF THE ERRORS OF CERTAIN ARTISTS, WHOSE FIRST PART CONCERNS ERRORS ABOUT GOD

Moreover that you may recognize the species of the chief errors for which idle philosophers are detested, you should know that all the

---

[48] De summo bono, III, xiii, 5.   [49] De summo bono, III, xiii, 6.
[50] Ibid., III, xiii, 7.

articles listed below were refuted as inimical to the catholic faith by the mature counsel and keen consensus of the masters of theology at Paris. The first is that God is not three but one, because Trinity is not consonant with the Absolute. For where plurality exists in nature, there is addition and composite, for example, in a heap of stones. It is the error which the abbot Joachim incurred and it is condemned as to the supreme Trinity and catholic faith in the first of the Decretals. Nor is the example valid, since many stones are not of one undivided substance as are the three divine Persons. For no one by human disputation can engulf this holy and individual Trinity in its lofty divine simplicity or cross such depths with human feet. But as the Truth full of grace has told us, we should believe absolutely in those things which have become clear by divine miracles, for which no one can assign a natural explanation.

82

ROYAL ORDINANCE AGAINST THE ILLICIT PRACTICE OF MEDICINE AT PARIS, DECEMBER, 1352

Chartularium universitatis Parisiensis, III, 16–17.

John by the grace of God king of the Franks. We make known to all present and future that having heard the humble petition of the dean and masters of the faculty of medicine of the university of Paris, asserting that many persons of both sexes, women and old wives, monks, rustics, some apothecaries and numerous herbalists, besides students not yet trained in the faculty of medicine or coming from foreign parts to the town of Paris to practice, ignorant of the science of medicine and unacquainted with human constitutions, the time and method of administering and the virtues of medicines, particularly laxatives in which lurks peril of death if they happen to be administered unduly, also altering medicines quite contrary to reason and the medical art, administer, prescribe and advise the administering of strongly laxative clysters and other things unlawful for them in the city, town and suburbs of Paris, calling into consultation no physicians whatever, which results in scandal of our people, grave danger to souls and bodies, and derision, prejudice and injury of the said petitioners, the science of medicine, and those expert in it. From which undue administrations also result clandestine homicides and abortions on every hand and sometimes publicly. Wherefore the said petitioners, unable further to tolerate the said practices with clear concience or to wink at them, humbly beseech us that we deign to provide a suitable and lasting remedy for this.

We, therefore, wishing to prevent such damnable interference, presumption and fatuous rashness of unskilled operators and to provide wholesome, suitable remedies for the public utility of our subjects, ordain and decree by our royal authority and plenitude of power by the present ordinance to hold good in perpetuity that no one, of whatever sex or condition, in the said city, town and suburbs of Paris shall henceforth make, or advise the making, or dare to administer any medicine alterative, laxative, sirup, electuary, laxative pills, clysters of any sort—for fear of death from flux or aggravation of bad symptoms in which it is not likely that they know how to apply a remedy—opiate or anything else, or offer medical advice or otherwise exercise the office of a physician in any way, since the administration of the aforesaid belongs to experts and those learned in operating certainly on the human body and not to others, unless he is a master or licentiate in the said science of medicine at Paris or some other university, or unless that medicine was ordered by the advice and direction of some master or other person approved by the said faculty to practice.

And, decreeing that these practices are not permitted to them, we forbid them to them, all and each, by the present ordinance, giving power to our prévôt of Paris, present and future, or his *locum tenens*, in the present mandates that he cause to be enforced and inviolably obeyed our present ordinance and statute and all and every thing by us above ordered, and that he correct and punish those acting or attempting to act contrary thereto by administering any of the aforesaid drugs or visiting or counseling others in any way, according to the quality of the fault, disobedience and crime committed, by pecuniary and other civil penalties, as right and reason shall dictate. And that it may remain firm and stable for the future, we have thought well to affix our seal to the present writing, saving our right in other respects and all third parties. Given at Paris 1352 A.D. in December by the king.

83

METHOD OF LECTURING IN THE LIBERAL ARTS PRESCRIBED, PARIS, DECEMBER 10, 1355

Chartularium universitatis Parisiensis, III, 39–40.

In the name of the Lord, amen. Two methods of lecturing on books in the liberal arts having been tried, the former masters of philosophy uttering their words rapidly so that the mind of the hearer can take them in but the hand cannot keep up with them, the latter speaking slowly until their listeners can catch up with them with the pen; having compared these by diligent examination, the former method is found the better. Wherefore, the consensus of opinion warns us that we imitate it in our lectures. We, therefore, all and each, masters of the faculty of arts, teaching and not teaching, convoked for this specially by the venerable man, master Albert of Bohemia, then rector of the university, at St. Julien le Pauvre, have decreed in this wise, that all lecturers, whether masters or scholars of the same faculty, whenever and wherever they chance to lecture on any text ordinarily or cursorily in the same faculty, or to dispute any question concerning it, or anything else by way of exposition, shall observe the former method of lecturing to the best of their ability, so speaking forsooth as if no one was taking notes before them, in the way that sermons and recommendations are made in the university and which the lectures in other faculties follow. Moreover, transgressors of this statute, if the lecturers are masters or scholars, we now deprive henceforth for a year from lecturing, honors, offices and other advantages of our faculty. Which if anyone violates, for the first relapse we double the penalty, for the second we quadruple it, and so on. Moreover, listeners who oppose the execution of this our statute by clamor, hissing, noise, throwing stones by themselves or by their servants and accomplices, or in any other way, we deprive of and cut off from our society for a year, and for each relapse we increase the penalty double and quadruple as above.

We further ordain for the stricter observance of this statute that each rector at his creation shall swear and make his successor swear to proceed to the punishment of such transgressors.

Those incepting and determining shall similarly swear to observe the statute, otherwise they shall not be admitted to the degree of bachelor and of master. Moreover, we do not mean by this statute to exclude dictation of any determination, notable treatise, or exposition which youths sometimes write in the street of Straw on feast days, provided nevertheless that it is not done at the time of the university sermon. Nor shall anyone venture to give dictation of this sort outside the classrooms of the said faculty, otherwise he will incur the same penalty to which we have subjected auditors. Neither by this do we mean to derogate from the ancient statutes as to the method of lecturing, but these shall remain in force.

In testimony of which we have thought fit to append to the present statute the seal of the rector together with the seals of the four nations, namely, the Gallican, of Picardy, Normandy, and England and their consent together with the mark and subscription of the undersigned notary. Given and enacted in the congregation of our faculty, non-teachers as well as teachers, specially convoked for this at St. Julien-le-Pauvre in Paris, 1355 A.D., the tenth day of the month of December, ninth indiction, the third year of the pontificate of our most holy father in Christ and lord, Innocent by divine providence the sixth, pope, there being present for this the discreet men, Jacobus de Pavillione, John Candellus, Peter Guerardus, Conrad Almannus, serving the university of Paris in the said faculty of arts and many other witnesses called together specially for this.

And I, Simon called Quinimo, a clerk of the diocese of Tulle, public notary by apostolic and imperial authority, etc.

84

OATHS AND STATUTES CUSTOMARY IN THE LOWER SCHOOLS OF GRAMMAR OF THE TOWN, CITY, UNIVERSITY, SUBURBS AND BANLIEUE OF PARIS, c. 1357

Chartularium universitatis Parisiensis, III, 51–52.

Each master or mistress is held to these points by oath.

1. That he will exercise faithfully the office of teaching boys, diligently instructing them in letters, good morals and good examples.

2. That they show honor and reverence to the cantor and observe his regulations faithfully to the best of their ability, to whatever state they may come.

3. That in matters pertaining to the regulation of classes they will show obedience to the same cantor.

4. That no master shall keep boys allocated to another without his permission but rather be content with what he has.

5. No one shall remove by his own or other agency boys who have a contract with another.

6. No one shall defame another by detraction but he may report him to the cantor.

7. No one shall farm his classes out or have a partner but he may have a submonitor.

8. No one shall keep a submonitor who was with another master except in the three intermediate grades.

9. No proctor of any court shall teach school.

10. The same for any chaplain.

11. No submonitor shall hold a school near his master except in the three intermediate grades.

12. No master shall keep a woman of ill fame.

13. Each shall maintain peace with his fellows, and discord that arises as to schools shall be settled by the cantor under penalty of deprivation of one's school.

14. No one shall hail another before anyone except the cantor for a case concerning the schools under the aforesaid penalty.

15. No one shall take a school from another source in any parish, supposing that another person than the cantor actually offers it to him.

16. Everyone should attend vespers on the eve of St. Nicholas, on the day itself mass and at vespers the vigils for the dead, and on the morrow mass.

17. Every master or mistress shall keep within his alloted bounds, not exceeding in number or sex of pupils or even in quality of books.

18. Everyone shall turn in his permit at the end of the year, namely, on the nativity of St. John or when school is dismissed.

19. The cantor means to assign no one classes except until the nativity of St. John and unless he takes oath and has a permit.

20. If anyone has too many pupils, the cantor will keep the fees above the number allowed.

21. No one shall leave town except on a holiday unless by permission of the cantor and unless he leaves a satisfactory submonitor and that with the cantor's permission.

22. All masters and mistresses should attend the funerals of masters and mistresses.

23. A woman should teach only girls.

24. No one shall teach books of grammar unless he is a good and sufficient grammarian.

25. If anyone knows of anyone teaching boys without a license, he shall report it.

26. They shall swear that they have given or promised nothing to obtain classes and that in the future they will give or promise nothing.

27. Similarly to procure schools for any master they will take nothing from anyone or make any agreement.

28. Also, if you happen to hire a vice-master, you will present him to the cantor within eight days and before you have made any arrangement with the vice-master; and if the cantor is away, you will similarly present him to the proctor, in which case you will go to him whom the proctor shall name to you, and you shall not receive the vice-master except at the pleasure of the cantor.

29. Also, you shall not take a vice-master except by consent of the cantor or in his absence of his proctor or one deputed by him.

A later document in the *Chartularium* gives the names of forty-one men and twenty-one women teaching grammar schools in Paris who appeared before the cantor on May 6, 1380, and testified that they had already taken the required oaths to the above articles. Of the men named, who included both clerics and laymen, seven had the degree of master of arts, while two were bachelors of canon law.

85

CLOSING THE STREET OF STRAW AT NIGHT, MAY, 1358

Chartularium universitatis Parisiensis, III, 53–54.

Charles, firstborn of the king of France, regent of the realm, duke of Normandy and dauphin of Vienne. We make known to men now and to come, that, although to our beloved sons, the masters and scholars studying at Paris in the faculty of arts, from the first foundation of the university or almost so, a certain street beyond the Petit-Pont known in French as la rue du Feurre [1] was assigned to the same masters for lecturing and to their scholars for listening and learning, and in the same street in times past the said masters lectured in peace and the scholars listened without disturbance or notable interruption, now, however, with increasing malice of men and the enemy of science sowing tares amid the wheat, in the said street at night filth and refuse are brought and left there, which corrupt and infest the hearts and bodies of those dwelling there. But what is more horrible and detestable to be found among students and philosophers, at night the entrances to the schools are most vilely and dishonestly broken in by panders and foulest men who have neither God nor science before their eyes, nay, as is to be expected of such, who desire rather to impede the flower and pearl of science, and common whores and impure women are brought into the schools and often pass the night there most vilely and dishonorably, and make and leave disgusting filth on the chairs of the said masters as well as through the classrooms and places where the scholars sit and should sit. In the morning the masters coming there to lecture, the scholars to learn, finding such a disgraceful and stinking mess, flee and withdraw from such a fetid, horrible and impure place—and what wonder, since it behooves philosophers to be pure and honest and to

[1] More commonly spelled, Rue du Fouare (Vicus straminis).

inhabit pure, decent and seemly places—and so, which is lamentable and injurious, the said masters and scholars are defrauded of their school, lecture, and auditorium, and also of their main objective, namely, the pearl of science.

As a result of these continued and lasting obstacles, disturbances and annoyances, the same petitioners say that they cannot inhabit the said street longer, unless we of our special grace provide them an opportune remedy. And since in the said street there are two extremities or exits which could be closed to remove the said impediments and nuisances by making gates there which would be closed at night and opened by day, as is done in many other places of the town of Paris, the same masters and scholars most humbly petition us that we deign of our special grace and certain science to grant permission for this closure and making gates, especially since they have long had this privilege of closure from the landlord. We, therefore, who from the depths of our heart desire the tranquillity, good name and quiet of our dear and devoted daughter the university of Paris, of which the said faculty of arts is a noble fourth part and a noble fourth member, also desire the continuation of the said university with all our heart, noting further that the said faculty, which is called the faculty of the seven liberal arts, is the foundation, origin and source of all other sciences, without which no other science can be had perfectly, commodiously and completely, in order that henceforth the oftmentioned masters and scholars may more freely, attentively and securely study in lecturing and listening, do concede to them of our special grace, certain science and our plenitude of power and will that, for their security and that of the entire street, they may and it is permitted them to make gates or closures at the said extremities or exits of the said street, which can and should be closed at night and opened all day by good, lawful and sure guards by the same petitioners deputed there, giving notice to the prévôt of Paris, present and future, and also committing to mandates after the tenor of the present, also to all our justiciars of our realm or their *loca tenentes* present and future and to each of them, so far as may pertain to him or them, that they make and permit and allow the said masters and scholars of the said faculty of arts to enjoy and use peaceably and without any impediment, of our present special grace. Notwithstanding any letters obtained or to be obtained to the contrary, which do not make full and express mention word by word of this grace by us made and conceded to the same masters and scholars. Saving our right in other matters and in all any third party. And that this remain firm, lasting and stable for the future, we have caused our seal to be affixed to the present papers. Given at Compiègne, A.D. 1358, in the month of May by the lord regent.

86

SERVITES STUDYING AT PARIS, 1363

ORDINANCE OF THE CHAPTER GENERAL OF THE SERVANTS OF THE BLESSED MARY, CELEBRATED UNDER THE PRIOR GENERAL, NICHOLAS OF VENICE, AT FLORENCE, APRIL 28, 1363

Chartularium universitatis Parisiensis, III, 103–4.

No one shall be sent to Paris to study who previously has not interpreted all logic and philosophy for at least three years in Italian parts.

To each student going to Paris shall be assigned by his province one hundred gold florins: eight for the journey there, eight for the return, and the rest for food and clothing, in the hands of the chamberlain at Paris.

Every student returned after three years at Paris shall be required to interpret logic and philosophy and theology for another three years, to pray, preach and dispute as often and wherever required by the general, nor may they occupy that time in other functions.

Every brother licensed in sacred theology shall have from the treasury of the Order for the expenses of his master's degree one hundred gold florins, and wherever he lectures he shall have from the provincial ten florins for lecturing and five for clothing, and provision shall be made for the brother who acts as his servant.

87

STATUTES FOR ALL FACULTIES OF THE UNIVERSITY OF PARIS

ISSUED BY TWO CARDINALS WITH THE ADVICE OF THE CHANCELLOR AND CERTAIN MASTERS AT AVIGNON, JUNE 5, 1366

Chartularium universitatis Parisiensis, III, 143–46.[1]

First, concerning the faculty of theology we decree by the said authority that all incepting and from the moment they begin to lecture on the *Sentences,* even cursors in the said university, shall parade through town in costume befitting their state, degree, and the honor of the said faculty, visiting in particular classes, churches and sermons.

Also, that no one be admitted to lecture on the *Sentences* in vacations.

Also, that students may be promoted to honors in the said faculty not by leaps and bounds but according to merit, we have decreed that cursors in theology conduct their courses in order, commenting on the text and noting important glosses according to the ancient method approved in the said university.

Also, that no cursor of the Bible presume to cover more than one chapter of the book which he is reading in a single lecture except those giving ordinary biblical lectures.

Also, that no one be admitted to giving courses in theology unless he has reached his twenty-fifth year.

Also, that every cursor in theology in the time between his first course and the *Sentences* be required to respond in theology at least once, unless he shall have been lawfully excused by will of the chancellor and said faculty.

Also, that scholars who are just beginning to study theology for the first four years shall bring or have brought to classes of the Bible teacher the Bible, in which they shall hear lectures on the Bible diligently.

Also, that scholars just beginning to hear the *Sentences* shall for the first four years bring or have brought to classes of the bachelor from

[1] Two opening and a number of closing paragraphs are here omitted.

whom they hear the *Sentences* copies of the same in order that they may follow the text attentively.

Also, that lecturers on the *Sentences* shall perform their collations and *principia* honorably without any proud or offensive or scandalous words, abstaining from any injury and preserving to each the honor due him.

Also, that lecturers on the *Sentences* do not treat logical or philosophical matters and questions, except so far as the text of the *Sentences* requires or the solutions of arguments demand, but they shall raise and treat theological questions, speculative or moral, bearing on the Distinctions of the *Sentences*.

Also, that lecturers on the *Sentences* read the text of the same in order and expound it for the utility of their hearers.

Also, that no one lecturing on the *Sentences* shall read his question or *principium* from a manuscript. However, by this we do not forbid a bachelor to carry to the lecturer's desk some memorandum from which he can, if need be, recall to memory difficult points touching his question or arguments and authorities bearing on the question and its exposition.

Also, we decree that no master or bachelor who lectures on the *Sentences* shall communicate his lectures directly or indirectly to the booksellers until his lectures have been examined by the chancellor and masters of the said faculty.

Also, that no one can become a licentiate in theology or incept to lecture on the *Sentences* or any course in theology under any master absent from Paris, unless that master is recognized as giving instruction by the faculty, nor shall the bedell of the absent master receive anything in any way from those incepting.

Also, we ordain that those bachelors who have lectured on the *Sentences*, if they wish to obtain the master's degree, shall be required to remain in the university for the time accustomed to elapse between the lecturing and master's degree, in order that their science, character and life may be tested more certainly.

Moreover, concerning the reformation of the faculty of *Decreta* we decree by the aforesaid authority that no dispensation be granted anyone as to the books and lectures which according to the ordinance of the apostolic see and statutes of the faculty should have been heard and read before admission to the licentiate.

Moreover, concerning the faculty of medicine we decree that the medical students hear their books, complete their lectures, frequent disputations, as is contained in the statutes of the faculty of medicine, all dispensation to the contrary being forbidden.

Moreover, concerning the faculty of arts, which is as it were the foundation of the others, we decree that those determining and about to receive the licentiate be required to wear their copes or cassocks to classes when they go to hear their lectures and at sermons, especially from the feast of All Saints till the end of great Ordinary,[2] that the faculty may be honored in them and their degree recognized.

Also, that the said scholars hearing their lectures in the said faculty sit on the ground before their masters, not on seats or benches raised above the ground, as was the custom when the studies of the faculty were more flourishing, so that occasion of pride may be removed from the young.

Also, we decree by the said authority that scholars, before they are admitted to determining in arts, be properly trained in grammar and have heard the *Doctrinale* and *Graecismus*, provided the said books are read in the schools or other places where they have learned grammar.

Also, that they have heard the entire *Ars vetus*, the book of *Topics* or at least four books of it, and the *Elenchi, Prior* and *Posterior Analytics* completely; also *De anima* in whole or part.

Also, that no one be admitted to determining in arts unless he has studied at Paris for two years at least, all dispensation being prohibited.

Also, that no one be admitted to the licentiate in the said faculty either in the examination of the Blessed Mary or in that of Sainte Geneviève,[3] unless in addition to the aforesaid books he has heard at Paris or in another university the *Physics, Generation and Corruption, Celo et mundo, Parva naturalia,* namely the books *De sensu et sensato, De sompno et vigilia, De memoria et reminiscentia, De longitudine et brevitate vitae,* the *Metaphysics* or that he will hear it and that he has heard other mathematical works.

Also, that no one henceforth shall be admitted to the degree of mas-

---

[2] "The period from 1 October till Easter was styled the 'grand ordinary,' the period from Easter till the end of June constituting the 'little ordinary' ": Rashdall I (1936), 489.

[3] The licentiate could be obtained either from the chancellor of Notre Dame or the chancellor of Ste. Geneviève.

ter in arts unless he has heard the said books, also the moral works, especially most of the *Ethics,* and the *Meteorology,* at least the three first books, all dispensation being prohibited.

Also, that no one be admitted to the licentiate in any examination of the said faculty, unless he has attended disputations of masters of the same faculty for a year or the greater part of a year at the time of great Ordinary and unless he has responded in two disputations in the presence of masters, concerning which he shall be required to inform the chancellor in whose examination he seeks to obtain the licentiate by notes from the disputing masters.

Also, that in the tests of the examination of Sainte Geneviève there be present four masters of the four nations with the chancellor or vice-chancellor, who have sworn in the presence of the faculty that they will examine faithfully, admitting the deserving and rejecting the unworthy, just as there are four masters sworn and chosen by the chancellor of blessed Mary as examiners.

Also, we decree that the chancellor of Ste. Geneviève shall be a canon of that monastery, a master of arts, if such there be there, and should swear before the faculty that he will give the license according to the merits of persons and the deposition of the masters who examine. But if no such master is canon in the monastery, that the existing chancellor, who always should be from the said monastery, shall be required to choose a master in theology who shall swear in his hands and in the presence of the faculty to bestow the licenses in the way above said.

Also, that bachelors in arts may read cursorily such books as they wish pertaining to the same faculty, as they did of old, notwithstanding a statute of the same faculty made to the contrary, by which it is forbidden that any bachelor lecture on a text cursorily at that hour at which any master lectures on that book cursorily. . . .

88

WHEN MORNING LECTURES ARE TO BEGIN, PARIS, MAY 18, 1367

Chartularium universitatis Parisiensis, III, 160–61.

To all who shall inspect the present letters the rector of the university of Paris, also all and each of the masters of the faculty of arts, greeting in the omnipotent Maker of all things. Right reason attests that as new diseases arise with variation of times, we should carefully seek out new remedies to meet them before the diseases have advanced too far, lest the disease because of its long continuation and increase become incurable. Since therefore some of our masters teaching in our faculty are beginning to enter their classes to lecture too late in the morning, and are accustomed to enter them around Prime of St. Jacques or when the bell of the Carmelites sounds for second mass (by which time according to old custom they should have finished their lectures for the greater part), whence to the masters themselves prejudice is generated because they cannot attend their lectures in theology and to the scholars injury because they spend the best part of the day in sleep, and to our faculty great discredit and complaint (because the laudable practice of our predecessors is abandoned and a less good one substituted for it); hence it is that we masters, one and all, by our oath at the meeting of our faculty held at St. Mathurin gathered for legislation, May 18, 1367 A.D., at the hour of Prime and summoned by the venerable and discreet man, master John de Dunghen, of the Picard nation, then rector of the university of Paris, desiring to retain the praiseworthy ancient customs of our faculty and to guard against new diseases by useful preservations, as our oath binds us and each one of us, by unanimous consent of the nations, namely, Gallican, Picard, Norman, and Anglican, and of individual masters of the same, decree and likewise ordain and deem forever to be observed:

That henceforth all masters teaching at Paris in the faculty of arts enter their classes as our predecessors were wont to do, namely, at the striking of the bell or *clinketi* [1] of the Carmelites by which they give the signal for the first mass to be celebrated by them, by what-

---

[1] Probably for *cliquetum*, ringing of the morning bell.

ever name it is called. And they shall begin to give their lectures according to the ancient custom mentioned, at the same time as bachelors *in decretis* or masters in medicine lecturing in the morning are accustomed to open their lectures, fraud and craft in the said statute being entirely excluded. And we wish that henceforth each teaching master shall be bound by force of the statute sworn to by him to enter his classes in the manner stated. In testimony and perpetual vigor of which thing we have ordered affixed to the present letters the seal of the rector together with the seals of the four nations. Given and done in the meeting of our faculty, teachers and non-teachers, specially summoned for this purpose at the year, month, day and hour above specified.

89

TRAVELING EXPENSES FOR STUDENTS IN GRAMMAR, 1369

Fournier, *Les statuts et privilèges,* II (1891), 295–96.

On the same day, since by order of our lord the pope certain students in grammar in St. Germain of the diocese of Mende were sent to the university of Montpellier, and there came thirty-one scholars and their teacher, master Johannes Bonafos, to Avignon to the treasurer's, each to be examined as to his industry and sufficiency, twenty-one were selected to be sent to the university of Montpellier and ten rejected, of which ten some were sent back to school at St. Germain and some rejected entirely. To all whom for God there was given, to pay their expenses coming from St. Germain to Avignon, and going from Avignon to Montpellier or St. Germain as the case might be, for each scholar and master four *grossi,* amounting in all to fourteen florins and so entrusted to their master, the said master Johannes Bonafos.

90

FOUNDATION OF TWO FOURTEEN-YEAR SCHOLARSHIPS, 1371

FOUNDATION OF TWO BENEFICES FOR ERECTION OF AN ALTAR IN THE PARISH CHURCH OF ALSFELD, MADE BY SIBOLD ROTZMAUL, PRIEST OF HOENBERGH, TOGETHER WITH NUMEROUS ARTICLES PRESCRIBED BY HENRY, LANDGRAVE OF HESSE, AND HIS FUTURE SUCCESSOR, HERMANN, WHICH THE TWO BENEFICIARIES OF THE ALTAR SHOULD OBSERVE AND CONDUCT THEMSELVES IN ACCORDANCE WITH, AS WELL IN THE EXERCISE OF DIVINE WORSHIP AS IN THE PROGRESS OF STUDIES. THE YEAR 1371

Valentinus Ferdinandus Gudenus, *Codex diplomaticus exhibens anecdota Moguntiaca*, 1743–1768, III (1751), 499, 501–4.

After paragraphs granting Sibold the right to endow the foundation and regulating the same, come the following paragraphs having reference to the holders of the scholarships.

First they shall perform the following masses each year, forsooth at Christmas, Easter, Pentecost, the Assumption, on the feasts of the aforesaid patron saints (i.e., St. John the Evangelist and the blessed Anna, mother of the glorious virgin Mary), on All Saints, on the anniversary of the dedication of the aforesaid altar, and last for all the faithful departed. And to more they shall not be obligated, but each of them shall provide four masses for the time before his promotion. But after they shall have received holy orders they shall officiate at the said altar so often as the blessed Lord shall give them grace. Furthermore, the masses are not to be celebrated except at such an hour as will not inconvenience or injure the parish priest of that place, accepting nothing which would be injurious to him and his church but rather showing him, as their superior, the honor and reverence due him. Moreover, any offerings made at the altar they shall turn over entire to the parish priest, retaining nothing whatever for their own use.

Likewise the aforesaid beneficiaries shall not share in the distribu-

tions made in the choir of the church on the anniversaries of the faithful departed now or in the future, unless out of devotion they shall
have willed to attend vigils in the choir and to celebrate masses for the
dead. Also, the said beneficiaries after they have taken holy orders
and have begun to reside in person ought to occupy their places in
person at Vespers, Matins, in the processions of masses, in the masses
of the chief feasts, in the Dedication of the Temple, at the feast of
the aforenamed patron saints, unless prevented by a legitimate cause.
And in actions and observances of this sort they shall be bound in strict
obedience to the parish priest.

Furthermore, each of the beneficiaries now incumbent shall spend
two seven-year periods at a privileged university, first training his intellect in the liberal arts or laws according to the career he has in view,
afterwards in sacred theology or canon law perfecting it happily.[1]
When these years are accomplished, they shall be promoted to holy
orders. However, this same is not forbidden them during their time
of study. And they shall officiate humbly and devoutly at the altar
by aid and grace of the Holy Spirit, unless from legitimate causes the
contrary shall be permitted them by the venerable father and lord in
Christ, the lord archbishop of the holy see of Mainz.

Also, the said beneficiaries, if they both shall be well grounded in
grammar, which is necessary in order to go on to more advanced subjects, shall enter a privileged university, applying all diligence. And
the fruits of the altar shall be supplied them by the procurator of the
said altar. But if only one of them shall be qualified to enter a privileged university, his share of the revenues shall be presented to him
by the procurator. But if both or one of them want to take private lessons to acquire training in the rudiments of grammar, so much of the
income shall be supplied them or him as the character and circum-
stance of the place requires and demands.

Also, during all the time that these beneficiaries or either of them
are not ready from lack of education to take private lessons to learn
the rudiments of grammar, or rather from definite malice refuse to
prepare themselves for and enter a privileged university, they shall
have no right or power whatever to claim revenue and pension from
the said altar. But the procurator shall apply such revenues and pen-

---

[1] That is to say, the liberal arts are prerequisite to theology, and civil law to canon
law.

sions to the utility of both benefices, augmenting the principal for the support of the benefices. And this he shall do so long as it shall be necessary in order that the beneficiaries by this penalty may be forced to the study of the arts and sciences. But if both or one of them shall fall sick . . . and shall be penitent, the necessities shall be supplied them or him during the period of illness. Also, throughout their lives the beneficiaries shall associate together so far as possible and join in mutual charity.

Furthermore, the patron or patroness, whoever he or she shall be, should enforce the above-written conditions with diligence and moderation. When he has clear evidence of infamy of the beneficiaries or of either of them while attending a privileged university, or living disgracefully and immorally outside a university, and they refuse to attend a university of true faculties, then the said patron may either lovingly warn them to desist from their vanities and vices and to be rather a lover or lovers of moral and intellectual virtues. If upon being thus warned they shall not repent, nay rather the more obstinately persist, then the patron shall ask the ordinary judge, forsooth the local judges of the holy see of Mainz or the Official at Amelberg to warn the beneficiaries of the said altar in writing that within a certain time, month or months, they cease their vices and immoralities and subject themselves to the study of the virtues and sciences. But if they shall spurn all and each or any one of those things contained in the admonition of the lords judges and as contained in the present letter, turning away from salubrious penitence, and this shall be sufficiently proved against them or him before the said judges, then the beneficiaries or beneficiary should be deprived of that position *ipso facto*, and the patron should have a free hand to confer and bestow the benefice of the altar on others.

Moreover, if the beneficiaries or either of them being at a university will not attend classes and pursue their studies with diligence but rather seek leisure and rest, or if they have absolutely neglected to spend the aforesaid time, forsooth fourteen years, usefully in study, then they shall be deprived of the benefice according to the form set forth immediately above.

Furthermore, the patron ought to appoint a discreet, God-fearing man, priest or layman, as he shall judge best and as often as shall be opportune, who shall faithfully oversee the altar and beneficiaries, faithfully collecting the rents and pensions and wisely disposing of them according to the patron's instructions. And each year the patron should hear his account of receipts and expenditures with two friends of his suited to this. If he shall have kept the accounts legally and justly, the patron shall ask him for God's sake to continue in the office. If he shall be found incompetent, let the patron substitute another of good repute, God's grace aiding.

Moreover, every patron or patroness of the said altar—a first patroness being excluded for legitimate reasons—within the first year in which the right of patronage shall have devolved on him or her, unless prevented by reasonable cause, shall present himself to the parish priest of the said church or to the master of the citizens, if the priest has no domicile there, swearing that he will be faithful and diligent to the best of his power, that the rents and pensions of the altar may be conserved and increased and duly distributed to beneficiaries by the procurator during his time, and that he will zealously execute justice, taking counsel of the Wise Men in advance, if the beneficiaries or either of them shall have presumed to violate the present articles, for which they ought to be deprived according to the above form before the said lord judges in ordinary.

Furthermore, the beneficiaries shall not have vicars, to whom access to the altar is committed by the lord provost of St. Stephen or his Official at Amelberg.

91

A CHURCH USED FOR MEDICAL
LECTURES, 1380

THE BISHOP OF PAVIA GRANTS THE USE OF THE
CHURCH OF ST. BENEDICT FOR LECTURES
IN MEDICINE

Codice diplomatico dell' università di Pavia, I (1905), 65: Document 121, dated 1380, 13 October, Pavia.

Francis, etc. To our dear savants in Christ, masters John of Sartirana and Silanus de Nigris, doctors of medicine now lecturing in our happy university of Pavia, greeting in the Lord, everlasting. Benignly inclining to your supplications on this point, of giving lectures on medicine in the church of St. Benedict near the house of the Friars Preachers within the city of Pavia and carrying on in the same all doctoral examinations and scholastic activities, in such a manner, however, that should the same church be granted to any priest as incumbent, it be not disturbed by lectures and other activity of the sort during the times set for the celebration of masses and other divine offices, as you have voluntarily agreed in writing, we grant that such academic exercises be held during our pleasure, in witness whereof we have caused these presents to be registered and impressed with our seal. Given at Pavia, etc., 13 October 1380.

92

HOURS OF CLASSES

Fournier, *Les statuts et privilèges*, II (1891), 679, 532.

I. FROM THE STATUTES OF THE UNIVERSITY OF PERPIGNAN, 1380–1390, LVII, 6

Also, we have decreed that the medical professors shall not be bound by the hours of the jurists, since the medical men have six hours a day for lectures, namely, three magisterial and three for bachelors. The first magisterial is at dawn, the second magisterial at the hour of Prime. The first hour of the bachelors is at Tierce; the second hour of the bachelors is from Tierce till midday; the third of the bachelors at Nones immediately after dinner. But the third magisterial is the hour of Vespers.

II. FROM THE STATUTES OF THE UNIVERSITY OF AVIGNON AS REFORMED IN 1503, SECTION 59

. . . We have likewise decreed and ordained that the said bell of the university from All Saints to Lent be rung for the doctoral hour before the striking of Prime. And he (the bedell) shall pull the rope three times at the beginning, and in the middle of the mass which is celebrated give one pull and when the mass is over another, ringing the said bell. And the hour shall last an hour and a half without interruption, and from Lent to the next feast of All Saints after the striking of Prime. And all through Lent the duration shall be an hour and a half, and thenceforth one hour. Moreover, the hour of Tierce shall last for the space of an hour and a quarter. Nones shall begin to be sounded in the first hour after noon, and he shall ring three times, and the duration shall be for the space of one hour. And for the hour of Vespers he shall ring thrice, and it shall last for the space of an hour and a quarter, to be understood exclusive of the bell.

93

FEASTS OF THE NATIONS AND OF THE THREE KINGS, ORLÉANS

FROM THE STATUTE OF THE GERMAN NATION, OCTOBER, 4, 1382

Fournier, *Les statuts et privilèges,* I (1890), 147–48.

Finally it should be known that there are seven nations in this dear university which by certain superstitious celebrations, vulgarly known as feasts of the nations, by multifarious harmonies of odes and muses and public games and spectacles for amusement, whence sometimes arise quarrels and many evils, suspending lectures for two days while the harvest of study is at hand, the fruitful quiet of winter nights, call others away from study and disturb their repose.

But our most splendid nation and likewise those of Lorraine and Scotland, not because they cannot but because they will not, impelled by the highest motives, renounce such wantonness with a certain simplicity, improve themselves, and do not offend others. Nevertheless, if it shall please you, O our esteemed successors, know that it is by no means forbidden you to obtain from the doctors who have charge of holiday celebrations, when we are not in session, that you be allowed to dedicate the day of holy Epiphany with that following to such rites in honor of the Three Kings, the same period which once our forebears consecrated to the same solemnities, as palpable traces still remain at Paris in the province of the lords of our nation there.

For this day in the midst of the festivities of other nations is clearly situated at a most convenient time for rejoicings. Then everyone no matter how studious is accustomed to make glad holiday. Then every foreign nation indulges in unusual jollification and bearing images of the kings in memory of the true child King and the three most blessed kings bursts forth in hymn and song; hearts throb with joy at the sound of the chorister's voice; no tongue is silent from praises; through all the world men sing to instrumental accompaniment, renewing the annual festivities. How much more, therefore, our venerable nation which from the outstanding relics of those kings housed in the most splendid metropolis of Germany, namely, holy Cologne, is known the world over with grace, honor, name and fame! Shall not she, adorned with these lofty pledges in her localities, revere this day with peculiar exultation, as by it she enjoys an ampler dignity? For there does not exist beneath the starry firmament any region which is endowed with such glorious relics as ours. . . .

94

TEACHING APPOINTMENT CONDITIONAL ON RECEIVING THE DOCTORATE

U. Dallari, *I rotuli dei lettori legisti e artisti dello studio bolognese dal 1384 al 1799*, 4 vols., 1888–1924, I, 5, 13, 27, etc.

Master Jacobus de Farneto of the Roman patrimony is appointed to teach grammar for the year 1384–1385 at Bologna in the quarter of the Sterian gate at a stipend of fifty pounds Bolognese, and he must take his doctor's degree or at least the licentiate before next Christmas, otherwise he is to receive no salary.

James appears to have fulfilled the injunction, or the threat remained unexecuted, since he is found in the service of the university as a teacher of grammar until 1396. But at the last date at which the amount of his salary is mentioned, in 1388–1389, it was still only fifty pounds Bolognese.

Other examples of the same stipulation in other subjects occur at later dates. In 1439–1440 Charles of Mantua was appointed to lecture in surgery, "so that within the year he takes his doctor's degree." In 1448–1449 Andreas de Mapheis of Verona was named to teach logic in the afternoon on the same condition. In both these cases the name of neither appointee appears again in the salary lists.

95

ONLY CHRISTIANS ADMITTED, PERPIGNAN, c. 1389

Fournier, *Les statuts et privilèges*, II (1891), 679–80.

Also let a statute be made anew that no one of an alien sect, such as a
Jew or Saracen, or anyone else of whatever alien sect he may be, be
given instruction by any doctor, master, licentiate, bachelor, scholar,
publicly or privately in grammar, logic, philosophy, medicine or law,
or other science. And let a good penalty be included as shall have
seemed best, so that it may be the better observed.

96

THE TRANSIT OF LEARNING TO GERMAN UNIVERSITIES

HENRY OF HESSE TO DUKE ROBERT OF BAVARIA, 1391

Otto Hartwig, *Henricus de Langenstein dictus de Hassia*, 1857,
p. 62, quoting MS Wolfenbüttel 76.

For why is it that the universities of France are breaking up, that the
sun of wisdom is eclipsed there? Learning withdraws to light another
people. Are there not now four lamps of learning lighted among the
Germans, that is, four *studia generalia* shining in concert with rays of
glorious truth.[1] Surely now the mouth is closed of those saying ma-
liciously: "There is no splendor of truth among the Germans but only
the headlong fury of brute force." Let now that Italian Boethius be
silent, let him no longer say, "We have seen a few marked by German
fury."

Why has blindness fallen on the part of Israel? That the multitude

[1] The four universities meant are probably Prague, founded in 1348, Vienna in
1365, Heidelberg in 1385, and Cologne in 1388. Erfurt was authorized in 1379 but
really started in 1392. Henry of Hesse himself had gone from the university of Paris
to that of Vienna.

of the Gentiles may be enlightened. And what should be the outcome of this unless that the rulers of the Germans employ learned men and through them stabilize a changing world, calming the schismatic whirlwind of this time.[2] Now let strenuous princes and potentates, kindled with zeal for God, rejoice that they have been preserved to the present moment, when they can bring aid to Christ and his spouse holy church and win such great glory with God and the world that their memory shall be blessed from generation unto generation throughout eternity!

97

RECANTATION OF BLASIUS OF PARMA, 1396

Codice diplomatico dell' università di Pavia, I (1905), 334: Document 532, dated 1396, 16 October.

Blasius of Parma or Biagio Pelacani received the doctorate at the university of Pavia in 1374, after which he taught there and at Bologna and Padua until 1411, dying in 1416. He composed commentaries on Aristotle and in the fields of logic, mathematics, physics and astronomy—also astrological predictions.[1] In a theological writing he discussed the theme of predestination. But just what the utterances referred to in the following document were, we are not informed. At least his difficulties were only temporary, for on the very day of his recantation he presented a candidate for the doctorate and on the next day examined Hugh of Siena, who was to make such a name for himself in the history of fifteenth-century medicine and philosophy.

On the 16th of October the lord bishop asked master Blasius of Parma, who had been brought before him, if he was dissatisfied with those remarks which he had made against the catholic faith and holy mother church. And he said he was. Also the bishop asked him if for the rest he intended to hold to the catholic faith and its articles and the decisions of the church. He said that he did, asking pardon for his transgressions. This accomplished, the lord bishop reinstated him

---

[2] Referring to the great schism which lasted from 1378 to 1417.
[1] For further details and bibliography consult my *History of Magic and Experimental Science*, III, 65–79.

in his professorship and salary and accustomed dignities, etc., ordering me as notary to draw up papers to that effect. Done at the episcopal palace. Witnesses: master Roger of Sicily, rector of the medical students, lord master Marsilius of Sancta Sophia of Padua, lord master Francischus de Strazapatis of Pavia, doctors in arts and medicine.

98

RENTING OF PECIAE, MONTPELLIER, 1396

STATUTE OF THE FACULTY OF LAW

Fournier, *Statuts et privilèges*, II (1891), 161–2.

. . . We have decreed that *peciae* [1] be kept in the way stated below, that no *pecia* be handed out under penalty of surety pledged except in the way below stated, namely, that for a *pecia* in which there are eight pages and more, one *alba* shall be paid per week; for one in which there were less than eight pages, three *pataci* shall be paid per week. And a *pecia* shall never be given out except with a pledge of gold or silver worth double the price of the said *pecia*. And another *pecia* shall never be given out, unless the first has been returned. And if a *pecia* is lost, one gold shield [2] shall be paid for each one thus lost. And the keeper of the *peciae* shall have for his labor a *patacus* for every *alba*, and *denarius* for three *pataci*. And the poor shall pay nothing, but for each *pecia* they shall repeat seven psalms for the soul of the defunct [3] and shall give the custodian a penny for his labor. Also, if the poor do not have a pledge of gold or silver, they shall give an equivalent security.

[1] The *pecia*, as explained before, was a section of an *exemplar* or standard text which could be borrowed, copied and returned separately. Thus many persons might copy the same work simultaneously.

[2] The *scutum*, ecu, or shield was a coin like the *alba*, *patacus*, and *denarius*.

[3] The *peciae* had belonged to the recently deceased university bedell, master Raymond of Sanctum Veranum, as whose executors the faculty act.

99

STUDENTS FORBIDDEN TO CATCH THE BURGHERS' PIGEONS

Eduard Winkelmann, *Urkundenbuch der Universität Heidelberg*, 1886, I, 63–64, No. 42, November 24, 1396.

The Rector of the University

To all the members and scholars of our university, we command, under most strict order, that no one of you by artifice or any other method, directly or indirectly, by himself or through another, shall catch or cause to be caught, the doves of the citizens within the wall of Heidelberg, under double penalty and their restitution. That is, he shall pay the value of the doves or dove, to be restored to those to whom they belong, and a like amount to the university. Given under the seal of our rectorate on the eve of the feast of the virgin Katherine, which we have caused to be read and published by the bedell in the classrooms of those giving ordinary and extraordinary lectures, in order that no one may allege ignorance.

100

STATUTE AGAINST OATHS AND BLAS-PHEMY, HEIDELBERG, 1398

Eduard Winkelmann, *Urkundenbuch der Universität Heidelberg*, 1886, I, 65, No. 45, August 1, 1398.

At a meeting of the doctors and masters it was agreed harmoniously and enacted by oath, among other matters, to make penal statute against persons of the university swearing beyond measure, as follows: Since it has often been brought to our notice by persons worthy of faith that some members of our university not only do not fear to blaspheme by the name of our Saviour Jesus Christ, of the glorious virgin Mary and of the saints, taking them in vain and repeating them without reason in oaths, but also by the parts of the very body of the Lord and so by the humanity of God and in other far-fetched ways which we grieve to record, setting a pernicious example to simple persons, to the great shame and scandal of the clergy of our university, and since wilful oaths and blasphemies of this sort are quite contrary to the divine precept and to the institutions of both laws, canon and civil, and likewise by moral standards are undoubtedly forbidden, therefore we, Nicholas de Cuba, the rector, and the doctors and masters aforesaid, having held mature deliberation and counsel concerning this, to restrain the aforesaid insolences for the honor of our Lord Jesus Christ, the glorious virgin Mary, his mother, and the saints, have decided to order and enact, and do order and enact, and furthermore under obligation of obedience in so far as we can prescribe, that henceforth no person of our university, of whatever grade, status, or condition, shall presume to swear, or rather blaspheme, by the forbidden sacred members, namely of Christ, blessed Mary or the saints, that is, by the head, hair, viscera, blood and the like, or in any other farfetched or unaccustomed or enormous manner, under penalty of two pounds of wax to be paid irremissibly each time he shall have so sworn to excess, of which one pound shall be applied by this our orders to the church of the Holy Spirit, the other to the chapel of the university, for lights. But if, which God forbid, any person shall be found continuing oaths, or rather blasphemies of this sort, he shall be punished more severely, according to our pleasure and according to the quality of his excess. Given and enacted in the congregation held in our chapel, in the year of the Lord 1398, on the very day of blessed Peter *ad vincula*, etc.

101

MAGIC ARTS CONDEMNED, PARIS, 1398

CONCLUSION OF THE FACULTY OF THEOLOGY ON A MATTER OF THE FAITH RECENTLY RAISED AND JUST NOW SETTLED: SEPTEMBER 19, 1398

Chartularium universitatis Parisiensis, IV, 32–35.

Considering the feat or principal operation and its makeup in itself and all its accompanying circumstances, namely, the great circle conscribed with divers unknown names and marked with various characters, the little wooden wheel raised on four wooden feet and a stake in the midst of the same great circle and the bottle placed upon the said wheel, above which bottle on a little paper scroll were written certain names, whose meaning is unknown to us, forsooth Garsepin, Oroth, Carmesine, Visoc, with the sign of the cross and certain characters interposed between the said names, and also thrones, earthen pots, a fire kindled, suffumigations, lights, swords and many other characters and figures and divers names and unknown words and also the naming or writing of four kings on four small paper wheels, forsooth, king Galtinus of the north, king Baltinus of the east, king Saltinus of the south, king Ultinus of the west, with certain characters written in red interposed between the names of the said kings; considering also the time and the suspect place and the behavior of those who were present at the said work and participated in it and the things they did after oaths had been taken by them many times as to making a legal division of the treasures to be found, also repeated after the declaration of the said work by the principal actor of that artifice, as appears from their confessions, from which it is learned that in a certain room in which were the said instruments, superstitious in themselves, with lights lit and suffumigations about the bottle and circles, in which were the said inscriptions and said characters, the said co-workers, stripped to the waist in their smallclothes, holding swords by their hilts each one before a throne, sometimes fixing the points in the earth and sometimes circling about with the said swords near the thrones and circles and bottle, raising the points of the swords to the sky, and sometimes placing their hands together with the hand of the protagonist over the bottle, which he called holy and in which, as they said, should come the spirit who would reveal and make known hidden treasures; in view of all the aforesaid and their accompaniments our deliberate conclusion is as follows, that not only those who use such figments and sorceries to find hidden treasure or learn and know things secret and occult, but also all professed Christians in possession of reason who voluntarily operate and employ such things in such manner are to be held superstitious in the Christian religion, are to be deemed idolaters, are to be deemed invokers of demons and strongly suspect in the faith.

To all devotees of the orthodox faith the chancellor of Paris and the faculty of theology in the dear university of Paris, our mother, with full honor of divine worship, to have hope in the Lord and not look upon vanities and false insanities. From olden darkness a foul flood of errors newly emerging has warned us to recall, that often catholic truth which escapes others is quite clear to those studious in sacred writ, since certainly every art has this property of being clear to those trained in it, so that thence comes that maxim, "Believe the man who is skilled in his art." Hence that line of Horace, which Jerome quotes writing to Paulinus, "Physicians utter what is medical, smiths handle tools." [1] To this in the case of sacred writ is added something special which neither experience nor sense can give as in the other arts, nor can readily be apprehended by eyes wrapped in the mist of sin. For their malice has blinded them,[2] says indeed the Apostle, so that from avarice many have erred from the faith.[3] Moreover it is not irrationally named by the same the service of idols.[4] Others from ingratitude, who, "although they have known God, have not glorified Him as God," [5] have fallen, as he too relates, into all impiety of idolatry. Furthermore, unbridled pleasure led Solomon to idols; Dido, to magic arts. Others have been turned astray by proud curiosity and the dire desire to investigate the occult. Others, finally, wretched timidity, hanging breathless on the morrow, has driven into most superstitious and impious observances, as is noted in Lucan [6] of the son of Pompey the Great and in the historians of many more. Thus it happens that the sinner withdrawing from God falls into vanities and false insanities [7] and turns unto him who is the father of falsehood, finally imprudently and openly apostasizing. Thus Saul, abandoned by the Lord, consulted the witch whom he had previously opposed; [8] thus Ochozias spurning the God of Israel sent to consult the god Acharon; [9] thus in fine it needs be that all those, who in faith or works are without the true God, should be deluded by a false god.

Perceiving, therefore, that the nefarious, pestiferous and monstrous abomination of false insanities with its heresies has developed more than usual in our times, lest perchance the monster of such horrid impiety and pernicious contagion avail to infect our most Christian realm, which once was free and by God's protection shall be free from monsters, desirous of checking every attempt, mindful besides of our profession and burning with zeal for the faith, we have decreed to brand with the cautery of damnation a few articles bearing on this

---

[1] Horace, Epist., II, i, 115.   [2] Liber sapientiae, pars prior, II, 21.
[3] First Timothy 6: 10. [4] Galatians 5: 20. [5] Romans 2: 21.
[6] Lucan, VI, 419 et seq. [7] Psalm 39: 5. [8] First Kings 27: 7.
[9] Fourth Kings 1: 2.

matter, lest henceforth they deceive unawares, recalling among innumerable others that saying of the most sapient doctor Augustine concerning superstitious observances, that those who believe in these or go to their houses or introduce them into their own homes or question them, should know that they have belied their Christian faith and baptism and become pagans and apostates, that is backsliders, and enemies of God, and have incurred the wrath of God gravely for eternity, unless, corrected by ecclesiastical penance, they are reconciled to God. Such his words. Not that it is our intention in any way to derogate from lawful and true traditions, sciences and arts, for it will keep us busy to extirpate and uproot, in so far as we may, the insane and sacrilegious errors of the foolish and fatal rites that harm, contaminate, infect the orthodox faith and Christian religion, and to restore its due honor to sincere truth.

Moreover, the first article is that by magic arts and sorceries and nefarious invocations to seek the intimacy and friendship and aid of demons is not idolatry. An error.

Second article, that to give or offer or promise to demons such-and-such a thing in order that they may fulfill a man's desire, or in their honor to kiss or carry something, is not idolatry. Error.

Third article, that to enter on a pact with demons, tacit or express, is not idolatry or a species of idolatry and apostasy. Error.

Fourth article, that to try by magic arts to include, coerce and bind demons in stones, rings, mirrors, images, consecrated in their name or rather execrated, or to wish to make these alive, is not idolatry. Error.

Fifth article, that it is licit to use for a good end magic arts or other superstitions forbidden by God and the church. Error.

Sixth article, that it is licit or even permitted to repel sorcery by sorcery. Error.

Seventh article, that anyone may give anyone a dispensation in any such case, so that he may employ such rites licitly. An error.

Eighth article, that magic arts and like superstitions and their observance are prohibited by the church irrationally. Error.

Ninth article, that God is induced by magic arts and sorcery to compel demons to obey invocations. An error.

Tenth article, that incensings and suffumigations, which are performed in the exercise of such arts and sorceries, are to the honor of God and please Him. An error and blasphemy.

Eleventh article, that to use such things in such wise is not to sacrifice or immolate to demons and consequently not damnable idolatry. An error.

Twelfth article, that holy words and certain devout prayers and fasts and ablutions and bodily continence in boys and others, and the celebrating mass and other works of a good sort, which are performed in carrying on such arts, excuse these from evil and do not rather accuse them. An error.

Thirteenth article, that the holy prophets and others made their prophecies by such arts and performed miracles and expelled demons. An error and blasphemy.

Fourteenth article, that God himself directly or through good angels revealed such sorceries to holy men. An error and blasphemy.

Fifteenth article, that it is possible by such arts to force the free will of a man to the will or desire of another. An error.

Sixteenth article, that on this account the said arts are good and from God and that it is licit to observe them, because sometimes or often it happens through them, as those employing them seek or predict, or because good sometimes comes from them. An error.

Seventeenth article, that demons are really forced and coerced by such arts and do not pretend to be compelled in order to seduce men. An error.

Eighteenth article, that by such arts and impious rites, by sortilege, by incantations, by invocation of demons, by certain glances and other sorcery, no effect ever follows by aid of demons. An error.

Nineteenth article, that good angels are shut up in stones, and that they consecrate images or vestments, or do other things which are comprised in those arts. An error and blasphemy

Twentieth article, that the blood of a hoopoe or kid or other animal, or virgin parchment or lionskin and the like have efficacy to compel and repel demons by the aid of arts of this sort. An error.

Twenty-first article, that images of copper or lead or gold or white or red wax or other material baptized, exorcized and consecrated, or rather execrated, according to the said arts and on certain days, have marvelous virtues which are recited in the books of such arts. An error in faith, in natural philosophy, and in true astrology.

Twenty-second article, that to use such and believe in them is not idolatry and infidelity. An error.

Twenty-third article, that some demons are good, some benign, some omniscient, some neither saved nor damned. An error.

Twenty-fourth article, that suffumigations which are performed in operations of this sort are converted into spirits, or that they are due to them. An error.

Twenty-fifth article, that one demon is king of the east and by his especial merit, another of the west, another of the north, another of the south. An error.

Twenty-sixth article, that the intelligence which moves the heaven influences the rational soul just as the body of the heaven influences the human body. An error.

Twenty-seventh article, that our intellectual cogitations and inner volitions are caused immediately by the sky, and that by a magic tradition such can be known, and that thereby it is licit to pass certain judgment as to them. An error.

Twenty-eighth article, that by certain magic arts we can reach the vision of the divine essence or of the holy spirits. An error.

Done are these and, after mature and frequent examination between us and our deputies, concluded in our general congregation at Paris at St. Mathurin in the morning specially set aside for this, September 19, 1398. In testimony of which thing we have decreed to append the seal of the said faculty to the present letters.

102

SALUTATI ON DISPUTATIONS

Leonardi Aretini ad Petrum Paulum Istrum Dialogus, in Theodor Klette, *Beiträge zur Geschichte und Litteratur der italienischen Gelehrtenrenaissance*, II (1889), 43–47, 52–53.

In this selection from the dialogue of Leonardo Bruni (1369–1444) to Vergerio, Colluccio Salutati (1330–1406), chancellor of the republic of Florence, is represented as urging the revival of the practice of disputation upon the young humanists of that city.

It can scarcely be told, young men, how much your gathering and presence delights me. For you are those whom I embrace under certain peculiar good will and love, either because of your characters or of your studies and what you have in common with me, or also because I see that I am esteemed by you. But in one thing you seem remiss to me, and that a very important matter. For while in other things which have to do with your studies I see in you such care and alertness as ought to be in those who wish to be called fruitful and diligent men, in this one respect, nevertheless, I see you fall short, nor sufficiently take into account what is to your advantage, since you neglect the custom and practice of disputing, than which I can think of nothing that would be found more useful to your studies. For what is there, by the immortal gods, that is of more avail in learning and discussing subtle matters than disputation, in which man's eyes view from all directions the subject placed in the midst, as it were, so that there is nothing in it that can be camouflaged or hidden or that escapes the gaze of all? What is there that more refreshes and restores the mind, tired and exhausted and almost loathing these studies from long sittings and close reading, than discussions carried on in assembly and company, where you are strongly incited to reading or learning either by glory, if you have overcome the others, or by shame if you have been defeated? What is there that sharpens the ingenuity more, what is there that renders it more clever and cunning than disputation, since in it it is necessary that at a moment's notice one apply oneself to a matter and then reflect, digress, gather together, draw conclusions, so that it is easy to understand that one stirred by this exercise is made quick to discern other matters? Nay more, how it polishes our speech, how it trains us in extemporaneous utterance, no one can say. For you can see this in many persons, who, although they profess that they know literature and read books, nevertheless, because they have abstained from this exercise, are not able to talk Latin except with their books.

Therefore I, who am eager for your welfare and who desire to see you as flourishing in your studies as possible, am not unjustly angry at you, because you neglect this custom of disputation from which so many advantages flow. For it is absurd to talk with oneself between walls and in solitude and to agitate many matters, but before men's eyes and in a company to remain dumb as if you knew nothing, and to pursue with great labor those things which have only one advantage to them, but to be unwilling to engage in disputation from which come so many advantages with extreme pleasure. For just as he is thought not to be much of a farmer who, when he might cultivate an entire estate, merely plows some sterile pastures but leaves the most fertile or richest part of the estate uncultivated, so he is to be reprehended who, when he might fulfill all the functions of studies, although he applies himself most accurately to other trivial points, yet spurns and neglects the exercise of disputing from which so many rich fruits are collected.

Indeed, I remember when I was a boy once at Bologna and studied grammar there, I was accustomed every day either by irritating my fellows or by questioning my masters to leave no time free from disputation. Nor what I did in my boyhood did I afterward abandon with increasing years, but at all times of my life nothing was more agreeable to me, nothing that I sought so much, as to lay before learned men, if only the opportunity was given, both what I had read and what I had been thinking about and what I had doubted about, and to ask their judgment in those matters.

I know you all hold in memory—and you the more, Niccolò, who because of the close relationship which you had with him especially frequented his house—Lodovico the theologian, a man of keen ability and remarkable eloquence, who died several years ago. I often visited him when he was alive in order to lay before him the sort of things I was just mentioning to you. And if, as is sometimes the case, I had not thought up at home what I would want to talk about with him, I would think it over on the way there. For he lived across the Arno, as you know. I made that river a sort of sign and mark to myself so that, at the time of crossing it on the way to his house, I should reach the middle point of the argument which I proposed to discuss with him. And, indeed, when I came to him, I protracted the conversation for many hours and yet I always departed from him unwillingly. For my mind could never be sated with that man's excellence. Ye immortal gods, what power of utterance he had, what copiousness, what a memory! For he was master not only of those matters which pertained to religion but also of those which we call pagan. He always had Cicero, Virgil, Seneca and other ancients on his very lips, nor did he merely repeat their views and opinions, but often their very words, so they seemed not taken from another, but his own. Never was I able to suggest anything to him that seemed new to him: everything had already come under his consideration and knowledge. But I heard much from him, learned much, and by the authority of that man I confirmed many things of which I was doubtful.

But someone will say, why do you talk so much about yourself? Are you the only disputant? By no means. For I could mention many who did the same thing but I have preferred to speak of myself so that I might assure you from my own knowledge how great utility there is in disputation. For I, who have so lived to this day that I have spent all my time and all my efforts in zeal for learning, seem to myself to have gained so great fruits from these debates or conversations which I call disputations, that I attribute a great part of what I have learned to this single source. Wherefore I beseech you that to your praiseworthy and distinguished labors you add this one exercise which hitherto has been lacking in you, so that, deriving advantages from all directions, you may more easily attain the goal you desire.

In reply to Salutati, Niccolò Niccoli says among other things:

But what of dialectic, which is the one art especially necessary for disputation? Does it still reign and flourish and has it suffered no calamity from this war of ignorance? Far from it. For even the barbarism which dwells across the ocean has made an onslaught upon it. And nations, ye gods, whose very names I dread, Ferabrich, Buser, Occam, Suisset, and others of the same sort, who seem to me to have derived their names from the cohort of Rhadamanthus. What is there, Colluccio, to stop jesting, what is there, I ask, in dialectic that has not been disturbed by British sophisms? What is there that has not been separated from that old and true method of disputation and dragged down to trivial nonsense?

103

A CONTEST FOR THE BEST
LECTURE HALLS

LETTER OF BONIFACE OF GENOA, RECTOR OF THE ARTISTS AT PAVIA, TO THE DUCHESS OF MILAN AND THE COUNT OF PAVIA, APRIL 26, 1403

Codice diplomatico dell' università di Pavia, II (1913), 28-30.

Your excellencies, our most illustrious duchess and count. Because scandals, so far as may be, are to be entirely avoided, and injustice done to no one, from which chiefly such scandals would arise, therefore I signify to your serenities that master Luchino Bellocchio, doctor of arts and medicine, has been to me complaining of grave injustice done to him and asserting that by your serenities, at the instance of Bertolomeus de Dinis, the rector of the jurists was ordered to provide for the said Bertolomeus de Dinis halls proper and sufficient for his lecture. From which there arose a contention between master Luchino on the one hand and the said Bertolomeus on the other, because Bertolomeus asserted that the rooms in which master Luchino lectured belonged to him, since they were formerly used by the decretists and not the physicians, although at the beginning of the present academic year they were assigned to master Luchino.

Finally, the matter was referred to the illustrious doctor of both laws, Benedictus de Plombino, who, after hearing both sides, although Luchino was in the right, wishing to induce concord between them, with consent of the parties and before the rector of the jurists, who joined in the agreement, did pronounce and decide that the said master Luchino ought to lecture in the aforesaid rooms and keep them until other sufficient rooms were constructed in the house of a certain Giliolus, a spice dealer, and when these were ready, then master Luchino should in turn offer the other halls to Bertolomeus, but in the meantime Luchino should retain them, and so both parties then present agreed.

But then the said rector, at the suggestion of Bertolomeus who perhaps misrepresented matters to him, wrote to your excellencies that, for several reasons mentioned in the letter, forsooth that the said Bertolomeus might not be forced to cease lecturing for lack of halls because other new ones could not be constructed for reasons expressed in the said letter, and from this scandal might be caused among his hearers; and also because certain rooms adjacent to the said halls, which he had been thinking of assigning to Bertolomeus since the opening of the academic year, were not dignified enough for Bertolomeus because of the prelates and other venerable persons in his class, it seemed good to him that the halls in which master Luchino lectured should be assigned to Bertolomeus, and that the other halls nearby be assigned to Luchino, etc., as is set forth more at length in those letters, whence your dominations were moved by the reasons given in the letters to write to the rector of the jurists letters to the effect that you are content that, according to his suggestion, he assign the rooms of the aforesaid Luchino to Bertolomeus and provide others for Luchino as he had written, etc., as is set forth at greater length in those letters given at Milan, April 21, 1403. In execution of which letters the rector of the jurists intimated to master Luchino that he should resign his rooms to Bertolomeus, and likewise on the other hand he intimated to master Martin de Viqueria that he should give up the other classrooms near by to master Luchino. This master Martin also complains of an injustice, since he has lectured in these rooms from the first of the year until now, and that to be expelled now seems to him absurd and unjust. Wherefore, both master Luchino and master Martin, complaining bitterly, have requested me to seek a fitting remedy, first because it is an injustice to them, secondly because they are not subject to that rector.

Wherefore, I intimate to your said serenities that I wish to be informed of the reasons written to you by the aforesaid rector of the jurists, by occasion of which your serenities were moved to write the letters mentioned, and moreover it seems to me absurd and wrong that master Luchino, who is a most excellent doctor of long standing in medicine and who has now lectured for twelve straight years at Pavia and Piacenza, should be put second to Bertolomeus, who is a new doctor and has never lectured except since the beginning of the term. And with this especially in mind, that the same master Luchino has more and more honorable scholars enrolled under him in his subject, albeit that sometimes, from friendship and to honor the said Bertolomeus, some scholars, but only rarely, attend his classes, although the said rector, perchance trusting in the words of Bertolomeus himself or of others who spoke at the prompting of Bertolomeus and did not tell the truth, has written as above stated. Note besides that from the beginning of term the rector of the jurists with his whole college of doctors wished to have the choice of all the better and more honorable halls to the loss and detriment of the entire college of physicians. And so they took all the best and more honorable halls, and all the others, among which that in dispute is one, they unanimously surrendered to the college of physicians as ones which they did not want. Nay more, they would not grant to the supreme monarch of medicine, master Marsiglio,[1] one of the honorable halls but only the least honorable of four; nay, they wholly excluded him and the other

[1] Of the famous family of physicians, Sancta Sophia.

physicians from the more honorable halls. And note above all that a judgment had already been rendered as to those rooms by the aforesaid Benedictus de Plombino, and if it is claimed by Bertolomeus that new halls cannot be constructed, he ought to take the damage from this himself and not another, since the judgment said that meanwhile, until new halls were provided, Luchino should keep his. And truly, if Bertolomeus is to have the rooms, the greatest scandal would follow, with contention and division between the faculties of law and medicine, which is utterly unseemly and absurd and a great shame and injury to both faculties. Therefore, I beg that you deign to order the reverend father in Christ, the bishop of Pavia, chancellor of your university of Pavia, that, setting aside all other letters, he administer justice to the parties in accordance with the judgment described above, for otherwise the greatest scandals would arise, which it is believed would not be agreeable to you. Or do you otherwise provide in the aforesaid matters as to your benign dominations it seems should be provided. Given at Pavia the 26th day of April by the faithful and humble servitor of the same serenities, Boniface of Genoa, rector of the artists and physicians of your university of Pavia.

To the most serene princes and illustrious lords, the duchess of Milan, countess of Pavia and Anghiera, and lady of Bologna, Pisa, Siena, and Perugia, and to the count of Pavia, lord of Verona, etc.

104

AN ASSISTANT MASTER FOR THE COLLÈGE DE NAVARRE, PARIS, 1404

Launoy, *Regii Navarrae gymnasii Parisiensis historia*, 1667, I, 103-4.

It was ordained by the superiors of the college at the request and advice of the masters and other zealous persons especially concerned for the welfare of the college of artists, that a vice-doctor be instituted to instruct the scholars particularly in the elements of logic in the said college of artists. And the best arrangement for the present seemed to be that upon his entry to the aforesaid office two fellowships (*bursae*) be conferred on the person judged suitable. And he shall swear to exercise his office faithfully, diligently instructing all the scholars without distinction, and especially in the elements of logic, commonly staying with them in the morning from after the lecture on the *Sentences* until dinner. And after dinner he shall hold a quiz section on new points or reviews or otherwise, as the master shall direct. And he shall lecture in the street or in the morning lecture room or in the new schools.

Also, he shall hear disputations and readings in the afternoon with the master, and likewise sometimes by himself, if the master is otherwise occupied. Moreover, he shall note how the scholars dispute between the bell "Pro mappis" and the last bell. And after dinner he shall hear that which the master shall order to be done over.

Further he shall go to church with the scholars and to the fields when they are allowed to go there. For he shall look after the scholars on Sundays and holidays, in order that because of his presence they may behave the more seemly.

105

STUDENT FEES AT BOLOGNA, 1405

Carlo Malagola, *Statuti dell' università e dei collegii dello studio bolognese*, 1888, rubrics 36, 38, 39, pp. 248–50, 252, 253.

The next half-dozen selections (105–110) are all taken from the statutes of the university of arts and medicine of 1405. "The earliest complete collection of statutes" for Bologna "dates only from 1432": Rashdall, I (1936), 173; see p. 88 for bibliography. Our earlier selections (63–64) were from the incomplete statutes of 1317–1347. While the statement of Rashdall that for the university of Bologna "the materials are singularly scanty compared with those which we possess for the history of Paris," is quite true, the aforesaid bibliography fails to note that in 1924 a fourth volume was added to U. Dallari, *I rotuli dei lettori legisti e artisti dello studio bolognese dal 1384 al 1799*, 1888–1891, including six rolls between 1370 and 1384 as well as others after 1384 not in the previous volumes. It may also be well to inform the reader that the *Chartularium studii Bononiensis*, 1909–1936, 10 vols. and still in process, is a collection of supplementary rather than basic material, as in the case of the *Chartularium universitatis Parisiensis*, Malagola having already published the statutes, Dallari the faculty rolls, and so on, before 1909.

Since nothing is so agreeable to natural equity as to keep pacts, since the Praetor says, I will enforce agreements, therefore they saw fit to decree that, if any scholar in the future rents by himself or another a room or rooms or the house or lodging of any doctor or reviewer (*repetitor*), and it comes about that he does not wish to inhabit the place rented, nevertheless he must pay the full pension, and in that case he may transfer all his rights to another or others equally suitable to exercise them, provided the occupancy by that person or persons does not inconvenience the others living together in the said lodgings or room of the said reviewer or doctor.

Moreover, with regard to the payment of the salary and fee of each doctor and reviewer in logic and the other arts who has sworn to obey in lawful and honorable matters and keep the statutes of the university, the procedure should be as follows, namely, that every scholar can try out the teaching of any doctor and reviewer for the space of fifteen days beginning from the feast of St. Luke and before the end of the fifteen days no scholar is obliged or can be forced to pay any fee even for the said time, unless he afterwards has continued to attend the classes of the doctor or reviewer. But when the fifteen days, beginning as above, are over, doctors and reviewers and other masters can take up their collection both in the morning and at noon regardless of any other statute, so, however, that scholars paying in the morning cannot be compelled to another payment at another time or for another hour in the same subject by one and the same doctor or master, and this morning collection may be made by each doctor or master only once a year. And we say the same of the collection made at noon. Declaring further that doctors or masters of logic for their salary and collection from the benches may have and receive from each scholar for one year forty solidi Bolognese, and more than the said forty solidi they may not receive from any scholar, under pain of ten pounds Bolognese for each person from whom it was received. And anyone may accuse and denounce it and be held in credence. And the accuser shall have a third of the fine. Moreover, for the collection to be made at noon they may lawfully have and receive per year from every scholar who has not paid the collection in the morning ten solidi Bolognese. Moreover, special reviewers may take twenty solidi Bolognese in winter and fifteen in summer, as much as reviewers in logic get. But to masters of grammar is paid a fee of thirty solidi per year by those who are not in lodgings. From lodgers they have and should have for their fee forty solidi Bolognese from each, while to reviewers in grammar is paid a fee of twenty solidi in winter and ten in summer.

But because it sometimes happens that some scholars enter after the collection, they decreed that such latecomers should pay a *pro rata* fee for the time spent to the doctor or reviewer, provided always that they have fifteen days after their arrival to try out the teaching and shall not be required to pay anything for this unless they continue under the same teacher afterwards, in which case payment shall be made as above. Moreover, the aforesaid holds good only in cases where there was no agreement as to a fixed fee, otherwise payment should be made as contracted, under penalty to anyone offending in any of the aforesaid cases of one hundred solidi Bolognese for each and every offense.

Also, since masters of grammar pay high rents for their lodgings, they decreed that every master of grammar who has sworn to obey the rector and keep the statutes of the university might effectually compel any scholar great or small, not a foreigner, who had slept three nights in their lodgings to pay them the whole fee for the entire time, even if he had transferred himself to another master or lodging, notwithstanding what is enacted above as to fifteen days trial, which we declare to apply to scholars who do not spend in the said schools fifteen days or three nights, if not foreigners. And this to avoid many enormous practices by which scholars often deceive. Moreover, doctors and reviewers who have not sworn, as directed above, by no means enjoy the benefit of this statute or any part of it, or any benefit of the university. Moreover, foreign scholars may make trial of the teaching of any doctor or reviewer for the space of fifteen days, as said above, even if they have passed the night in room or lodgings during that time, which time elapsed each may and shall be effectually compelled to payment of the fee for the entire year.

Also, since it happens that scholars change from one master to another, whence sometimes hard feelings arise, they decreed that any doctor or reviewer of whatever faculty should not dare to retain any scholar in his lodging or room or instruction or audience, unless he had first satisfied the master or reviewer with whom he first stayed as to what he was required to pay him. And this in case the person with whom he first stayed was a doctor or reviewer who had sworn to obey the rector and to keep the statutes of the university, and otherwise not, under pain of ten pounds Bolognese which offenders are required to pay, unless within four days after he has been admonished of the aforesaid he shall have expelled such a scholar from his classes and house or has satisfied the first master or reviewer. To prove, moreover, that anyone was a scholar of any master or reviewer the oath of the master or reviewer is sufficient and in the said case the oath shall be accepted as full proof.

Also, since it happens that a scholar sometimes leaves his bed or books for two years and does not pay the masters or their reviewers, they decreed that any master and reviewer after a complete year may freely sell both books and bed, having first lawfully cited the one who left them and notified the rector in whose presence or that of his deputy the said things should be seen and valued. And if anything is left above what is due, it should be deposited with the treasurer or depositary of the university. Moreover, it should be proclaimed by one of the general bedells through the schools, if anything is left over and whose the property was. And if the person to whom these things belonged or his proctor appears within a year, what is left over shall be restored to him, otherwise, when a year has elapsed, it shall go to the university. And if there was no property or not enough to satisfy the master or reviewer's fees or the scholar whose debtor he was, and he no longer attends or wishes to attend classes, any judge of whatever condition is required to render a summary account as to the said fee to each sworn master and reviewer without murmur and judicial red tape.

Also, since many from avarice, although they know Latin well enough, to avoid masters' fees attend the classes of reviewers, they decreed that no reviewer of grammar or any other dare retain any scholar speaking Latin or able to do so in their classes under pain of a hundred solidi for each one retained. And any master may force any of the said scholars to pay him, as if he had entered his classes, and anyone may inform on them or any one of them and he shall have a third of the penalty. Also, each of the aforesaid is obligated to pay the bedells' fees, as are those entering classes, which, if they do not pay, the reviewers who have kept them in their classrooms shall be required to pay both doctors and bedells out of their own money.

Also, that no aforesaid reviewer of grammar or general reviewer of any other subject be required to pay any fee to any master, but each is obligated to payment for room and collection according to the agreement made between them.

Also, that every master of grammar is required to enter twice a day, forsooth at mass of St. Peter and at small vespers, under penalty of ten solidi for each time, unless he was absent for just cause which may be proved by oath. Also, no master shall dare to receive anything from any reviewer directly or indirectly, openly or secretly, for acquiring expenses or profit to the same reviewer, under pain of ten pounds Bolognese, and anyone may accuse him openly or secretly and have a third of the fine. Also, that no master shall dare or presume, with a reviewer in his classrooms or lodgings, to take away or cause to be taken expenses from the said reviewer, under said penalty of ten pounds Bolognese. Also, they decreed that no contractual domestic or servitor of anyone be required to pay any fee to any doctor of physic, philosophy, logic or grammar, unless he wished to pay something of his own freewill, which is a matter for his discretion.

Reviewers, moreover, of whatever faculty are required daily at due hours to give alert and careful attention to their scholars and repeat to them and examine them and hear them in the accustomed way, under penalty of ten solidi Bolognese for every time they are negligent, of which the informer shall get a third, the university a third, and the rest go to the rector, faith having been made to the rector by one witness with the oath of the informer. Moreover, they wished the said statute to be precise and observed in perpetuity by whomsoever it affected under the penalties contained in the statute. Moreover, in every chapter where penalties are not specified, they should be understood to be ten pounds Bolognese for each offender with the same penalty for the rector who fails to execute the aforesaid. . . .

Since the laborer is worthy of his hire, they decreed that doctors lecturing in philosophy on the books named below, according to the method stated below, should receive pay from their scholars in this way, namely, 25 solidi Bolognese for the *Metaphysics*, for the *Physics* 25 solidi, for *De anima* 15, for *De generatione* 10, for *De celo* 15, for the *Meteorology* 15, and for each other book of *Parva naturalia* 5 solidi, except *De sensu et sensato* and *De sompno et vigilia*, for lectures on each of which they may receive 8 solidi. For lectures on the entire book *De animalibus,* 40 solidi. If he lectures only on *De genera-tione animalium,* 20 solidi; if *De partibus animalium,* 15; if *De hys-toriis,* 10. But if anyone lectures on the *Ethics,* 20; if on the *Politics,* 20; if on the *Rhetoric,* 20; if on the *Economics,* 5. If he is scholar or reviewer who lectures on the said books or any of them, for his salary and collection from his hearers he may receive half of the said fees for lectures on the said books. Further, that any scholar or reviewer who lectures on the *Posterior Analytics* may receive as his salary and fees ten solidi. He who lectures on the *Prior Analytics* may receive ten; he who lectures on *Elenchi,* ten; he who lectures on *Sex principia,*[1] five solidi. Also, that anyone lecturing on the aforesaid or any of the aforesaid is required to raise one question or determine one that has been moved for each lecture. . . .

We have decreed that all doctors lecturing in the science of medicine shall receive payment from their scholars in this way, namely from every scholar both for lecture fee and bench money together twenty solidi Bolognese, except that, if any scholar occupies the bench of the rector or the front benches, he shall be required to pay a florin. . . .

106

TEACHERS OF GRAMMAR EXCLUDED FROM EXAMINATIONS IN MEDICINE

Malagola, *Statuti,* rubric 48, p. 257.

Also, since it is disgraceful and improper that doctors of grammar be in the college of physicians and come to examine those who are to be promoted in medicine, they have decreed that the rector, together with a Wise Man and syndic of the university and councillors and doctors giving instruction, should go to the lord of the city or to him to whom this matter belongs and beg that special provision be made that no one who is not an M.D. may attend the examination of any candidate for promotion in medicine or vote at any ballot on any candidate in medi-cine. Also, that no one who is not regularly enrolled in the science in which anyone is up for promotion may be of the college of doctors examining in that subject, since no one can be a true judge of matters

---

[1] The work of Gilbert de la Porrée.

of which he is ignorant. Under penalty of one hundred solidi Bolognese to the rector, if he does not go within a month after publication of the statutes to obtain the aforesaid. But if it shall be otherwise, they have now decreed that no scholar up for promotion shall dare to pay any master who is of some college any amount of money for public or private examination against the said form under the said penalty.

107

TEXTS IN ARTS AND MEDICINE, BOLOGNA

Malagola, *Statuti*, rubric 68, pp. 274–76.

As the wording of the Statute is repetitious and tiresome, the texts lectured upon in successive years may be indicated more quickly and clearly by a diagram.

Lectures in Philosophy

Ordinary	Extraordinary

First Year

Physics, entire	*Generation and Corruption,* Bk. II
Generation and Corruption, Bk. I	*Sleep and Waking*
	Physiognomy of Aristotle

Second Year

Heaven and Universe	Averroes, *De substantia orbis*
Meteorology	*Memory and Reminiscence*
De sensu et sensato	*Inspiration and Respiration*

Third Year

De anima (except the errors of its first book)	*Metaphysics* (part of Bk. IV)
	Length and Shortness of Life
Metaphysics (Proemium only of Bk. I, and Bks. II, V–XII	*Cause of Movement of Animals*

Lectures in Medicine

Ordinary	Extraordinary

First Year

Ordinary	Extraordinary
Avicenna, *Canon*, Bk. I except the Anatomy and chapters on the seasons of the second fen, and only these chapters of the third fen: The Necessity of Death, Diseases of Infants, What to Eat and Drink, As to Water and Wine, Sleep and Waking *On Differences of Fevers* *Of a Bad State of Health* *Of Simple Medicine*, except Bk. VI *Critical Days*, Bk. I	*Canon*, Bk. IV, fen 2, and Bk. II *De interioribus*, except Bk. II *Regimen of Health* *Critical Days*, Bk. II *Aphorisms* of Hippocrates except the seventh Particula

Second Year

Ordinary	Extraordinary
Tegni of Galen *Prognostics* of Hippocrates, without commentary Hippocrates *On Acute Diseases*, without commentary and omitting Bk IV Avicenna, *De viribus cordis*, in part *On Accident and Disease* *On the Crisis* *Critical Days*, Bk. III *Fevers to Glauco*, Tract. I *De tabe* *On the Utility of Breathing*	*Avicenna*, Canon (portions noted as in other column under First Year) *On Differences of Fevers* *Of a Bad State of Health* *Canon*, Bk. IV, fen 2 *On Simple Medicine*, except Bk. VI *Critical Days*, Bk. I

Third Year

Ordinary	Extraordinary
Aphorisms, except Particula VII *Therapeutic*, Bks, VII–XIII Averroes, *Colliget*, in part	*Tegni* of Galen *Prognostics* of Hippocrates, without commentary

Ordinary	Extraordinary
Simple Medicines, in part	*On Acute Diseases,* without com-
On Natural Virtues, in part	mentary and omitting Bk. IV
Critical Days, Bk. II	*De viribus cordis,* in part
	On Accident and Disease
	On the Crisis
	Critical Days, Bk. III
	Fevers to Glauco, Tract. I
	On States of Health

Fourth Year

Avicenna, *Canon,* as under First Year	*Aphorisms,* except Particula VII
Canon, Bk. IV, fen 1 and Bk. II	*Therapeutic,* Bks. VII–XIII
De interioribus, except Bk. II	*Colliget,* in part
Regimen of Health, Bk. VI	*On Natural Virtues,* in part [1]
Hippocrates *On Nature*	

Lectures in Astrology

First Year

Algorismus on fractions and integers
Euclid, Geometry, Bk. I, with commentary of Campanus
Alfonsine Tables, with Canons
Theory of the Planets

Second Year

Sphere of Sacrobosco
Euclid, Bk. II
John de Lineriis, Canons on the Tables
Messahala on the astrolabe

Third Year

Alcabitius, *Introduction to Astrology*
Centiloquium of Ptolemy with commentary of Haly
Euclid, Bk. III
Treatise on the Quadrant

---

[1] Most of the foregoing medical texts are by Galen.

Fourth Year

Ptolemy, *Quadripartitus*, entire
(William of England), *On Urine Unseen*
Ptolemy, *Almagest*, Dictio tertia

108

ASTROLOGY AT BOLOGNA, 1405

THAT THE DOCTOR ELECTED TO A SALARY IN AS-TROLOGY SHOULD GIVE JUDGMENTS GRATIS AND ALSO IS REQUIRED TO DISPUTE

Malagola, *Statuti*, rubric 60, p. 264.

Further, they decreed, ordained, and established that the doctor chosen or to be chosen by the said university at a salary to lecture in astrology, be required to give judgments free to the scholars of the said university within a month after they were asked for, and also in particular to leave a judgment for the year in writing at the office of the bedells general, and also be required to lecture according to points, but only on feast days and in vacation, under penalty for each offense in each of the said cases of twenty solidi Bolognese.

Further, that the doctor elected to a salary in astrology be required and ought each year to dispute two questions in astrology and to determine them within eight days of the day of the said disputation, and that he also be required to dispute *de quolibet* at least once in astrology and to determine the said *quolibet*, as above, and to submit the said questions and said *quolibet* in writing at the office in a clear hand and on good sheets of membrane, not used before and in the larger size (?) within a fortnight after the determination. And the said questions shall be kept in the office so that there may be enough copies of them.

109

DISSECTION AT BOLOGNA

Malagola, *Statuti*, rubric 96, pp. 289–90.

Since the performance of dissection regards and pertains to the industry and advantage of scholars, and quarrels and rumors have often been customary in finding or searching for bodies from which or of which dissection should be made, they decreed and ordained that any doctor or scholar or anyone else shall not dare or presume to acquire for himself any dead body for such purpose of dissection, unless he has first obtained permission from the rector then in office. The rector, moreover, is held and required in giving permission to doctors and scholars to observe quality and order, when the said license is requested. Also, that not more than twenty persons may attend the dissection of a male; and not over thirty, the dissection of the corpse of a woman. And that no one may attend a dissection unless he has been a student of medicine for two whole years and is in his third year, even if he has attended classes at a forbidden time. And he who has once seen a dissection of a man cannot attend another the same year. He who has attended twice cannot attend again in Bologna except the dissection of a woman, which he may see once and no more, whether he has seen a man dissected or not.

Moreover, the said twenty or thirty who may attend and see a dissection are chosen and selected in the following manner; namely, in the anatomy of a man five from the nation of Lombards, four from the nation of Tuscans, four from the nation of Romans, three from the nation of Ultramontanes, and three of Bologna. And for the dissection of a woman there should be chosen eight from the nation of Lombards, seven from the nation of Tuscans, seven from the nation of Romans, five from the nation of Ultramontanes, and three of Bologna, except that the rector with one companion may attend any dissection, although that makes more than the aforesaid number and notwithstanding the rule that he who has seen a dissection once in a given year may not attend again that year. Moreover, it shall be in the choice of him who has the license from the rector to invite whom he will, so long as the terms of this statute are observed.

Also, that no one shall dare to request a dissection from the rector at the time of his election in S. Francesco under pain of five pounds Bolognese. And that the rector immediately after accepting office should have published through the schools to whom he has granted license for dissection, so that it may be known to all, with a penalty for the rector for failing to observe this and for not enforcing it of ten pounds Bolognese, and to each scholar who violates and offends against the aforesaid or any one of them, of one hundred solidi Bolognese.

Also, that any doctor who has been requested by scholars must hold a dissection in the way and form aforesaid, notwithstanding that he has done so already that year, and he shall have for his stipend one hundred solidi Bolognese. The said expenses and any others which may be incurred incidentally shall be divided equally among the scholars who were to attend, so, however, that for a dissection of a man not more than sixteen pounds Bolognese be spent and for that of a woman not over twenty, with the penalty to any doctor of one hundred solidi Bolognese. So, however, that the one who has so sworn and has made the expenditures, together with one associate whom he shall name, shall be wholly freed from the said expenses. And that the rector, before the dissection has begun, shall have summoned before him the scholar to whom he gave permission for the dissection, and shall require him to take oath that he will make the expenditures in good faith and without fraud and that he will lay them before the scholars witnessing the dissection, under penalty for the rector then holding office of ten pounds Bolognese.

110

SURGERY AT BOLOGNA, 1405

Malagola, *Statuti*, rubric 35, pp. 247–48.

Further, they decreed that the doctors lecturing on surgery ought to lecture in the following way: namely, that every year, when the university opened, they begin in the first course of lectures to read the Surgery of Bruno and, after finishing it, lecture on the Surgery of Galen. For the second course, lecture first on the Surgery of Avicenna and after it the seventh book of Almansor. Moreover, each doctor giving ordinary lectures in surgery should lecture in the afternoon at the nineteenth hour.

Further, they decreed that points in surgery should be determined by another of the doctors lecturing in surgery, namely, so many points as are assigned in other sciences.[1] And that each doctor giving lectures observe the points assigned and complete and cover them as assigned under penalty of twenty solidi Bolognese for each offense. Also, each doctor lecturing in surgery is held to dispute two questions in surgery, and even more, just as the doctors lecturing in medicine are held to do; and also he is held to give them in final form in good writing and on good paper to the office of the general bedells to be preserved there permanently and guarded and kept by the bedells. He ought to hold these disputations in the afternoon, unless some feast day occurs during the week on which he might dispute in the morning, provided a lecturer in medicine was not disputing then. Moreover, he is required to dispute only in surgery and in surgical terms, under pain contained in the statutes. Further, that no one shall presume to assist in any academic function, while the doctors of surgery are disputing, and that the rector and doctors lecturing in medicine shall be required to attend their disputations the same as others, and to be there from start to finish, and to take part in the arguing just as at other disputations, under pain of twenty solidi for each offender. Likewise, that each doctor lecturing in surgery shall be required to fulfill all the requirements of other doctors in other sciences. Moreover, they shall have for their labor and salary twenty solidi Bolognese from everyone attending their lectures in that subject, under penalty for each of the said doctors who offends in the aforesaid matters or any one of them of five pounds Bolognese in each of the said cases and for each offense.

[1] As this passage shows, a point (*punctum*) was a division of the text announced at the beginning of the course by the lecturer, or what he was required to cover within a certain time. In the next selection (111) the word point is used of a passage in the text, selected at random, upon which the candidate for a degree was given an oral examination or required to lecture.

III

ASSIGNMENT OF POINTS FOR EXAMINATION AT AVIGNON

FROM THE NEW STATUTES OF MARCH 12, 1407, PARAGRAPHS 13–17

Fournier, *Les statuts et privilèges,* II (1891), 377–78.

Also that, when a bachelor is admitted to examination by the lord bishop and on the day assigned to him for examination, the bachelor himself shall see that two acceptable persons are sent on behalf of the vicar of the lord bishop to all the doctors giving instruction in the faculty in which the examination is to occur. And should there be less than four giving instruction, then they should also be sent to other doctors of the same faculty not giving instruction to be named by the vicar, so that there may be at least four doctors of that faculty present at the assigning of points, at least if there are that many doctors of that faculty present in town, otherwise the vicar will have to be content with fewer. The messengers shall say to the said doctors on behalf of the vicar that they, on the next day after dawn at the accustomed hour, should present themselves at the palace or residence of the lord bishop for the assigning of points to the candidate according to the accustomed usage, and that the said doctors, unless lawfully impeded, shall by no means fail to come, otherwise they should know that they are *ipso facto* suspended by the rules laid down for the examination of the said licentiate. And let the bachelor beware that he does not presume in any way to commit fraud in order that easier points may be given him. And if he shall have been detected in such practice, then he shall be excluded by the lord bishop or his vicar from the degree in connection with which he committed fraud, or shall have the degree taken away, if he has already received it.

Also, we have decreed and do ordain that in assigning the said points this method be followed, namely, that the vicar of the lord bishop be very careful to choose for the said assigning the doctors in that faculty in whom he has most confidence that they will assign the bachelor good points, and that he take the book in which the points are to be assigned, open it, turn and re-turn the leaves, and inspect very carefully that there be not between the leaves straws or bits of paper or parchment or other marks by which one might open at points desired. And if he finds such, he shall remove them and order the points to be assigned from another part of the book. And afterwards he shall give the closed book to one of the doctors of the said faculty there present, to whom it shall seem to him most expedient, which doctor shall not turn the leaves more than three times but after three times or sooner he shall assign the decretal or decree or law that he has happened on to the bachelor as his point. Yet let the said doctor take care, as he fears to offend God and his own conscience, that he assign a good point which has good matter and also a good summary. And if the bishop's vicar knows that the contrary has been done, then, holding that point not assigned, he shall have the leaves turned again until a better point is assigned. And the same shall be observed in assigning the other point or at least care shall be taken that one of the two points has good matter and a good summary.

Also, that the doctors giving instruction who are present at the assigning of points may be able to leave to give their lectures in good season, we have decreed and do ordain that the bell which is wont to ring for the morning and ordinary lectures of the doctors should be rung immediately after the assigning of the said points and not before, and that he who is accustomed to ring the said bell shall be immediately advised on the part of the university bedell of the said expedition of points.

Also, we have decreed and do ordain that the vicar of the lord bishop, doctor presenting, and bachelor presented, and also the other doctors who should attend the examination, come for the examination to the episcopal palace or residence on the day assigned for this by the lord bishop at the beginning of the first striking of Vespers, or, if it is Lent, in the beginning of the striking of Compline. And that the harangue which the bachelor gives first be very brief, lest the principal performance be impeded by it, and that the bachelor in the case of each point first give an orderly summary. And if it is a point in the *Decretum*, he shall read through and declare the theme of the cause of the question and the questions of the cause itself, at least up to that question inclusive under which was the chapter assigned for the point, and he shall compose a well-ordered lecture so that one can follow his thought. And that, as is cautioned in the twelfth of the ancient statutes, each of the doctors arguing be content with two arguments or two questions and also two replies, if he wishes to reply, unless the presiding officer allows him to do otherwise.

Also, we have decreed that each doctor, after the withdrawal of the bachelor and the doctor presenting, shall write with his own hand and not by another on a ballot his approval or disapproval of the bachelor, and he shall deposit his ballot in his own handwriting in the hands of the vicar inside his cap, as is the custom, and he shall do this secretly so that no one can tell what he votes. And each doctor should take care that in writing an approval or disapproval of this sort he is mindful of the oath taken by himself at his doctorate, and that, as he fears to incur the crime of perjury and to offend his own conscience and feel finally divine vengeance, he shall not knowingly approve the unworthy or reject the worthy, and that under pretext of lecturing a while longer he approve no one whom he believes to be at the time unworthy of the grade of licentiate for obtaining it at the time, perhaps saying thus, "I approve but let him lecture two years more," because by this evasion he is not judged to be sufficiently excused from the aforesaid perjury, nor should he burden with the load of such lecturing him whom he believes worthy of promotion at the time.

112

ABSENCE FROM DISPUTATION, PARIS, 1409

MASTER JOHN BELARDUS WRITES TO THE FACULTY OF MEDICINE TO EXCUSE HIMSELF FOR NOT HAVING DISPUTED IN HIS TURN

Chartularium universitatis Parisiensis, IV, 169.

My reverend fathers, lords, and masters, because of the illness of my mistress, the dread lady constable, I am compelled by my lord, the dread lord constable, to remain here a season, wherefore I cannot dispute in my turn according to the laudable custom. I am very sorry and beg as humbly as I can that you deign to hold me excused and grant me dispensation that I may not lose my position but that the one following me dispute in my place, and I in his place by God's grace will dispute after Christmas. May the Most High preserve you happily and scrupulously. . . . November 30, 1409.

113

AN UNLICENSED WOMAN SURGEON, 1411

PERRETTA PETONNE, WHO PRACTICED SURGERY IN
RUE ST. DENIS, ALTHOUGH SHE HAD NOT BEEN
APPROVED BY THE PHYSICIANS AND SURGEONS,
IS PROSECUTED AT THE INSTANCE OF THE
MASTERS SURGEONS OF PARIS.
JANUARY 31, 1411

Chartularium universitatis Parisiensis, IV, 198–99.

At a previous hearing of 1410 before Parlement, Perretta had been asked
if she knew how to read and what the properties of medicinal herbs were.
She had replied that she worked "for God," and that it was unfair to prosecute her, when other women surgeons of Paris were left undisturbed.

When, at the request and instance of the masters and *jurati* of the
gild of surgeons of our town of Paris, an examiner of our Châtelet, by
command and precept of our prévôt of Paris or his locum tenens, visited the house of Perretta Petonne located in Grande rue St. Denis,
Paris, and found that the said Perretta—although she had been neither
examined nor approved in the aforesaid art, as the privileges and
statutes of that art, issued and confirmed by our predecessors, require
and state—engaging in that same art, had caused to be hung before
her said house or lodging a box or banner or sign after the manner
of a public surgeon, he had the same banner or sign removed and taken
to the said Châtelet. Further, on our behalf he forbade the said Perretta to engage in the said art and its practice, until she should have
been examined and approved in conformity with the said statutes and
privileges, and until the said prévôt should have given further orders in the matter. He enjoined the said Perretta to appear in person
before himself, our proctor, and the said masters and *jurati* to answer
such questions as they wished to put and to proceed further, should
this seem best.

This Perretta was subsequently, by another order of the said prévôt or of his locum tenens, led prisoner to the Châtelet and placed under arrest without bail being then granted. Then, when the aforesaid parties had been heard, their case *in statu quo* was postponed to be continued another day. It was further ordered and appointed by the said prévôt that in the meantime the said Perretta deposit her books on the said art of surgery at the office of the said prévôt to be examined by four physicians of Paris in the presence of the said examiner and the criminal clerk of the same prévôt, and that Perretta herself be examined by the said physicians in the presence of the said examiner and clerk and of two surgeons in whom both parties could trust. When this had been done and the said examiner had been informed as to the cures of the sick of which Perretta boasted and as to which the said masters and *jurati* wished to give him information to the contrary, the same physicians, examiner and clerk should report their findings to the said prévôt. And further the said Perretta should be released on bail, she having at last asked to go ahead in the said case according to the tenor of the said appointment, since everything was ready so far as she was concerned. On the contrary, the said masters and *jurati* asked that a delay be granted them to get a copy of the report of the said physicians, examiner and clerk, which, they said, they had sought before but had not yet succeeded in obtaining, the said Perretta opposing this. And having heard the parties, the said prévôt postponed the said case for another short day immediately following, whereupon the said Perretta, because she had many sick persons or patients under her care, who required essential remedies and visitation, demanded that permission be granted her to visit these sick persons and patients, the said prohibition notwithstanding. Which license the said prévôt was unwilling to concede fully to the said Perretta. . . .

With respect to the principal case, the court remitted and remits the said parties and the said prévôt to the fifteenth day of the month of February next, to proceed and act in the principal case as shall seem best. Further, it has forbidden and forbids the said Perretta, while this process is pending, to exercise the profession or act of surgery in any way, or to place, or cause or presume to place, on her house a box, banner or other sign of a surgeon or surgeoness. And without costs of the case of the said appeal.

114

VISITS TO FENCING SCHOOLS FORBIDDEN, HEIDELBERG, 1415

Eduard Winkelmann, *Urkundenbuch der Universität Heidelberg,* 1886, I, 106–7, No. 72.

The rector of the university, to the members of our university, all and single, we enjoin, strictly commanding, that no one of you shall presume to attend fencing schools or participate in their exercises, nor attempt to practice the art of fencing publicly or secretly, at least so far as teaching others and introducing them to this sort of art is concerned, under penalty of two florins and the greater penalty which the university may decide to establish for the future for transgressors of this sort.

Given in the year of the Lord 1415.

115

LEASE OF CLASSROOMS, PARIS, 1415

STATUTE OF THE FACULTY OF CANON LAW

Chartularium universitatis Parisiensis, IV, 302.

On September 19 the faculty, on petition of the holding corporation of the schools of the faculty, voted the following:

1. The faculty wished to preserve and maintain the corporation in its ancient liberties and franchises in accordance with the statutes of the faculty.

2. It voted that each new recipient of the doctorate should pay to the corporation of the schools at least eight solidi Parisian, as has heretofore been the custom.

Also, it voted that each person attending and hearing morning lectures should pay the corporation of the schools two Parisian solidi in the customary way.

Further, the said faculty voted regarding the lease of schools that, when the doctoral schools were filled, no schools should be hired or leases signed by the dean unless first the great schools and other schools pertaining to the said corporation, both inferior and superior, had been leased and filled. Moreover, it was the feeling of the faculty that students newly registering under doctors, whether in disputations or repetitions, should pay something for the repair of benches and pulpits.

Finally, the said faculty declared that by its dispensation made with regard to discourse or harangue it in no way derogated from the right of the corporation, nay it wished that those receiving such dispensation should make the customary payment to the corporation, since the faculty was not accustomed to issue dispensations to the prejudice of a third person.

On Thursday, September 26, the faculty of canon law, assembled after mass in St. John's, agreed and ordained that the dean of the said faculty should give no one a schedule to begin his lectures in canon law until the great schools were filled for every hour. Also, when these and the doctoral schools were filled, he should give no one a schedule until the upper schools above the second schools of the said faculty were also filled, as has been said.

Also, it was forbidden the bedell or sub-bedell of the said faculty to seat anyone to make discourse or harangue, even if he had been granted dispensation therefor, until the corporation should have received the two solidi which such an incipient owes the said corporation on occasion of his opening, under penalty of obliging themselves for such sums, if they did contrary.

Also, that a record of this deliberation be given the said corporation under seal of the dean and of other earlier deliberations relating to the said schools.

This deliberation was recorded by the lord prior of Prato in place of the dean, who was then occupied with public and general disputations, and he wrote it down on a certain schedule and signed it at the close with his own hand thus.

R. de Becco.

116

LECTURES AND REPETITIONS IN CANON LAW, 1416

ORDINANCE OF THE FACULTY OF CANON LAW

Chartularium universitatis Parisiensis, IV, 319.

Also, on June 26th, the faculty ordained who should lecture on decretals and also hold repetitions or preside, when a bachelor or licentiate was to respond. And, according to the tenor of the statutes starting with the younger members, Master Nicholas de Logia, prior de Pontibus, was ordered to lecture on the decretal *Firmiter* on Christmas eve; master Leonard de Passano, on the decretal *Omnis utriusque sexus* on the eve of Palm Sunday; master Ralph Roussell, on the decrees *Majores* and *Cum Marthe* on the eve of Pentecost; master Gerard Phaidetus, for the first repetition or presiding thereat to be held before Easter; while master Hervey Pouchard should make another repetition or preside thereat within the said time. Nevertheless, by this assignment of repetitions the older masters were not excluded, if they should wish to repeat or to preside, as has been said.

Also, on the said day, it was requested by action of the dean in the name of master John of Villanova that it please the faculty to reserve him a place for the embassy of the university to the Council of Constance, as he had been already chosen. Which was agreed to by all, none dissenting.

117

POSTPONEMENT OF ACADEMIC EXERCISES, PARIS, 1418

THE FACULTY OF MEDICINE, BECAUSE OF THE MISERY OF THE TIMES, POSTPONES THE ORDINARY DISPUTATIONS AND LECTURES OF THE FACULTY TILL AFTER THE FEAST OF KINGS

Chartularium universitatis Parisiensis, IV, 351–52.

On Saturday, the 22nd of October, the faculty was convoked by the bedell at St. Mathurin after faculty mass . . . to take action regarding the ordinary lectures and ordinary disputations of the teaching masters of the faculty. . . . It was there set forth that on account of the misery of the times due to wars, lack of victuals, failure of the crops, and prevailing pestilence, many masters, bachelors and scholars were absent from Paris, with the result that the university was stripped of the scholars and bachelors who were accustomed to attend the masters' lectures. Also, that the teaching masters, busy with practice because of the multitude of sick, were unable to devote themselves to teaching. Furthermore, that the faculty would seem to act too harshly to those under it, to whom it should be gracious, and to the absent bachelors, if on account of their excusable absence from Paris for the reasons aforesaid the time should be counted against them and to their prejudice. Finally, it was pointed out that in other faculties and nations of the university, our alma mater, ordinary lectures and disputations had been delayed and postponed for the causes aforesaid. For all which reasons our mother faculty, moved by the said considerations, did agree that it was its good pleasure that both lectures and disputations of the regents, only ordinary ones however, be postponed till after the feast of kings. Moreover, it voted that the same ordinary masters who began their lectures the first day should be continued in their functions by the faculty after the feast of kings. It was not its intention, however, that if any masters wish to hold extraordinary disputations, say on pastilles or other matters, that they should be in any way impeded by the present ordinance.

118

LAW ADVERTISING AT BOLOGNA

MSS Vatican Latin 3121, fol. 53r; 2028, fols. 153v–154v; and Vatican Palatine Latin 922, fol. 161r.[1]

The following very curious and flamboyant eulogy of two youthful graduates in law from the university of Bologna would seem self-inspired. It is found in most manuscripts of the huge fourteenth-century encyclopedia of Domenico Bandini of Arezzo, where it commonly occurs at the close of the eighth book on the planets, with whose subject matter it has no connection, being in every way an irrelevant interpolation. Bandini's encyclopedia was published posthumously by his son, Lorenzo, who states that he first submitted it to various competent authorities who urged him to make it public, whereupon he issued it at great expense as an act of filial piety. How our two young lawyers contrived to insert this puff of themselves in such a work remains a mystery. Perhaps they bribed the copyist: perhaps they themselves were engaged as copyists, not yet having a sufficient legal practice and ekeing out a livelihood by this means. Possibly they were friends of Lorenzo and acted with his connivance, although this would hardly seem respectful towards his father's memory. If not, he cannot have overseen the publication with the care which he implies, and later copyists who allowed the passage to stand would also appear to have been at fault. Domenico Bandini died in 1418.

Rejoice, Bologna, mother of laws, true nurse of every study, and of all philosophers the asylum, haven and sweet nest, because, though you have made many a happy harvest from the rich crop of jurists, never in our age have you given birth more happily than with Charles and Romeo. For they as sons of legal fullness uphold your candelabrum on the right and on the left, or, like the two major luminaries of the sky, shine from east to west. They are of most noble stock but far more illustrious in their virtuous characters. They have both been educated under the most glorious doctors. They were both examined together to the delight of the doctors and, no dissenting voice being raised, they received the doctorate from the council of examiners with the plaudits of the people and the presence of the city fathers. Now

---

[1] For the Latin text see my note, "Law Advertising in Medieval Manuscripts," *Political Science Quarterly*, 51 (June, 1936), 270–72.

they are most useful citizens. For Charles gives most praiseworthy law lectures for the commune, while Romeo, attending to public affairs, with marvelous ease and sense aids all in consultation. But since examples move more than words, he offers such stupendous miracles concerning himself that he degenerates from the virtue neither of his father nor his ancestors, just as shoots naturally are not diverse from their root.

119

TEXTS REQUIRED FOR A.B. DEGREE AT ERFURT, 1420

POINTS OF THE CONTENTS OF PRACTICALLY ALL THE BOOKS WHICH ARE LECTURED AND EXAMINED ON FOR THE BACHELOR'S DEGREE AT ERFURT, THAT IS, ACCORDING TO THE COLLECTION OF MASTER HERBORDUS DE LIPPIA PROMOTED AT ERFURT

MS Amplon. Q. 241, 1420 A.D., 200 leaves.

Fols. 1–17: Of the shorter edition of Donatus

fols. 17–28: also of the second part of the *Doctrinale* of Alexander of Villa Dei

fols. 28–41: also of the *Supposition of Terms* of Thomas Maulivelt

fols. 41–47: also of the treatise of Confusions and *Sinkathegreumata* of the same

fols. 48–51: also his treatise of Ampliations

fols. 51–52: also his treatise of Restrictions

fols. 52–55: also his treatise of Appellations

fol. 55: also his treatise of Alienations
    also his treatise of Remotions

fols. 55–64: also his treatise of Consequences, otherwise that of John Sutton of England. Incipit: "About the matter of consequences it is to be noted that argumentation is considered . . ."

fols. 64–79: also the treatise of Richard Biligam On the Proofs of Propositions. Incipit: "About the matter of Bilegam it is to be noted that concerning the subject of this notice . . ."

fols. 79–82: also the treatise of Obligations of Hollandrinus. Incipit: "About the matter of obligations note that . . ."

fols. 82–83: also the treatise of Insolubles of the same Hollandrinus. Incipit: "About the matter of insolubles note that the science of insolubles . . ."

fols. 83–98: also of the *Isagoge* of Porphyry

fols. 98–114: also of the *Predicamenta* of Aristotle

fols. 114–122: also of the *Peryermenia* of Aristotle

fols. 122–141: also of the books of *Prior Analytics* of Aristotle

fols. 141–154: also of the books of *Posterior Analytics* of Aristotle

fols. 154–162: also of the books of *Elenci* of Aristotle

fols. 162–187: also of the books of *Physics* of Aristotle

fols. 187–198: also of the books *Of the Soul* of Aristotle.

And so is an end to the points pertaining to the degree of bachelor in liberal arts finished and completed at Erfurt in 1420 A.D. by the hand of John Copes, alias Pettiken, of Schuttorpe.

fols. 199–200: [1] also of the treatise of the Material Sphere of John of Sacrobosco. Incipit: "About the opening of the Material Sphere it is to be noted that the science of the sphere . . . Explicit: . . . according to theologians is called hell."

It will thus be seen that the undergraduate curriculum at Erfurt was almost entirely devoted to dialectic, comprising seventeen texts in logic as against two in grammar and one each in physics, psychology, and perhaps astronomy.

120

PROVISION FOR TEACHING GREEK AND HEBREW AT PARIS, 1421, 1424, 1430

Chartularium universitatis Parisiensis, IV, 394–95, 430, 505.

Also, since by an ancient ordinance there should be in the university doctors of Hebrew and Greek, and at present there is only one Hebrew doctor who, because of the hard times, can hardly provide himself with decent food and clothing, it shall be explained to the Regent [2] that general provision be made for these. And since as a special provision

---

[1] The last two leaves are added in a later hand.   [2] Henry V of England.

the serene Regent ordered and arranged at Corbeil that a hundred francs be sent to the said doctor and master, Paul de Bona Fide, and of these he has received only fifty francs, his serenity should deign to order that the rest be sent to the said doctor. . . .

On March 14, 1424, Paul de Bonneffoy, master of Hebrew and Chaldean [1] at the university of Paris, testifies that he has received sixteen solidi of Paris from the faculty of theology.

In December, 1430, the French nation expressed the wish that provision be made from a sufficient benefice for some doctors of Greek, Hebrew, and Chaldean, so that those languages might be made accessible by them in the university of Paris.

121

OATHS REQUIRED OF APOTHECARIES, PARIS, 1422

Chartularium universitatis Parisiensis, IV, 406–7.

On the second day of the month of October, the faculty of medicine was called together according to custom by the bedell with a schedule at St. Mathurin concerning two articles. The first was to hear the oaths of the herbalists taken before the entire faculty. . . . All herbalists existing in Paris had been summoned and swore as follows:

First, they swore that they will have the *Synonyms* [1] in corrected form and the *Circa instans* of Platearius.

2. That they will have better weights just and true from the pound to the scruple.

3. That they will not put in their clysters any medicine which has lost its virtue or corrupted.

4. That they will not substitute one drug for another in any prescription except by permission of the master giving the prescription, but will adhere strictly to the prescription as given, and if they do not have any herb or drug listed in the prescription, they will refer the matter to the master who ordered it, that he may see about it.

5. That they will not give nor knowingly permit to be given any

---

[1] Meaning Aramaic or Syriac.
[1] The thirteenth-century work of Simon a Cordo of Genoa.

clyster or any other medicament, unless they have a special prescription for it from some master, nor will they take a recipe from his book except, by his special consent, a recipe which he has ordered beforehand.

6. That they will not receive prescriptions from any quack or from anyone else unless they know that he is a graduate of Paris or another university or is at least approved by the faculty of medicine of Paris.

7. That they will not employ a clerk unless he knows how to understand, speak and write Latin and French, and, before they engage him, he shall be required to take all the aforesaid oaths.

8. That they will cause all the aforesaid oaths to be inviolably observed to the best of their ability by their wives, messengers, clerks, and footmen.

122

ACADEMIC ITINERARY, 1422–1427

Codex Monacensis latinus 671, fol. 1r–v.

The following memorandum of the activities of a German student, Conrad Buitzruss, during the years 1422–1427 and from his fifteenth to twentieth year, covers both sides of the first leaf of a Latin manuscript in the Staatsbibliothek at Munich [1] which otherwise may be described as a book of magic. As far as I have been able to ascertain, it has not been printed nor its author noted in works dealing with the history of the university of Heidelberg, which he attended. Conrad's personal memorandum is prefaced by some verses reflecting upon the venality of the papal court which suggest on the one hand the similar satire of the Goliardic poets and *clerici vagantes* of the twelfth and thirteenth centuries, and on the other hand the German discontent at "German gold flying over the Alps," to which Luther gave more effective voice a century later.

> The curia wants marks; it empties purses and arks.
> If you have no marks, shun popes and patriarchs.
> If you have given marks and have filled up their arks,
> You will then be free, no matter how guilty;
> For the Roman stool seeks no sheep without wool.

[1] For the Latin text see my note, "A Personal Memorandum by Conrad Buitzruss," *Speculum*, IV (1929), 88–89.

In the year of the Lord 1422, I, Conrad Buitzruss, came to Heidelberg and I was fifteen years old and I was enrolled under master Dietmar, distinguished doctor of sacred canons and I deposited the entrance fee in the purse of master Henry de Gauda (Ghent?).

In the year of the Lord 1424, on the day of Augustus,[2] I was examined for the degree of bachelor in arts, and these were the examiners: master Hermann of Heydelsheim, dean at that time, master John Kraushein, master John Deriechen—and under him I straightway determined the subject for disputation, and the title of my question was this, Whether in good polity it is lawful to believe, practice, and study magic arts [3]—master Arnold of Tharen and master Rudolph of Brussels, and the number of those becoming bachelors was 26 and four were rejected.

Also, I spent in Heidelberg 166 florins and seventeen florins which I had by chance,[4] and I was there four years less six weeks. Sum total 200.[5]

Also, in 1426 A.D. on Monday in the feast of Paul died duke Rupert, son of duke Louis, count Palatine of the Rhine.

Also, in 1426 A.D. on Nicodemus day [6] I left Würzburg and on Friday in the morning about the tenth hour I reached Heidelberg.

In 1426 A.D. I left the university of Heidelberg on St. Bernard's day [7] and I reached Strasburg on the day of Saints Symphorien and Timothy.[8]

1427 on the Saturday before *Invocavit* I left Strasburg and on the Monday before the feast of pope Gregory I came to Heidelberg, and on the day of Ciryacus I left Heidelberg and reached Augsburg on the day of Benedict the abbot, and on the eve of the Annunciation I

[2] October 7.

[3] Fols. 2r–127r of our MS consist of Conrad's *Liber diversitatis*, or magic miscellany of materials which would no doubt be useful to him in dealing with this question. The *Liber diversitatis* is dated, at the close, July 30, 1424: "Finitus est ille liber sub anno domini 1424 in die tricesima mensis Iulii sole existente in 16° gradu leonis hora saturni indicione secunda de quo laudetur conditor conditorum et magister omnium astronomorum cum virgine maria que sit nobis misericors et pia. Amen."

Conrad might seem rather youthful to be dabbling in magic lore at the age of seventeen.

The remainder of the MS to fol. 182v, is in another hand and even more magical in character.

[4] Presumably, by gambling.

[5] Whether he refers to weeks or florins is hard to say.

[6] Wednesday, March 27.   [7] August 20.   [8] August 22 or 23.

arrived at Würzburg. And on St. Ambrose's day I departed from Würzburg toward Italy.[9]

123

ABSENCES OF PROFESSORS AT PADUA, 1424

Antonio Favaro, "Intorno alla vita ed alle opere di Prosdocimo de' Beldomandi matematico Padovano del secolo XV," *Bullettino di Bibliografia e di storia delle scienze matematiche e fisiche*, XII (1879), 31.

1424—Francis Foscari, by the grace of God, doge of Venice, etc., to the noble and wise men, Paul Corarius, by his command podestà, and John Navaterius, captain of Padua, and their faithful and chosen successors, greeting and affectionate regard.

It has recently been brought to our hearing that some of our doctors teaching in our university of Padua very frequently with your permission, and possibly without it, leave Padua for the purpose of transacting various private business of their own, deserting their lectures with the greatest annoyance and embarrassment to the students under their charge. We, indeed, taking such news very ill, give you instructions herewith that they shall devote themselves exclusively to their lectures. We write to your fidelity, together with our councils of requests and accounts; and we strictly and effectually order that you should assemble all our doctors who receive stipends at Padua and say to them and enjoin under that penalty which shall seem good to you, that hereafter they are, under no circumstances, to go outside the boundaries of Padua without your permission but are to remain in Padua and attend to their lectures. And to keep such matters under the control of your fidelity with our said councils of requests and accounts.

We write and enjoin that at the time at which they ought to lecture you shall not give such licenses to any of these doctors without our permission, under penalty of one hundred ducats for each of you in your own property and for each offense and for each licensed doctor, making the same requirement of our advocates who serve part time as of others.

[9] In other words, he left Strasburg, March 8, reached Heidelberg, March 10, left on March 16, reached Augsburg, March 21, and Würzburg, March 24, departing for Italy on April 4.

But we give you the liberty of giving the said license to said doctors of going outside the limits of Padua during the time of vacations. Nevertheless, care should be taken not to give these licenses too readily even in vacation time, since at that time their presence is useful. Moreover, do you cause these letters to be registered in the Records of Chancery for future memory.

Given at our ducal palace on the second of June the second Indiction, 1424.

1424—On Sunday, the eleventh of June, at Padua in the hall of the council concerning the custody of those salaried, there being convoked the doctors giving lectures, the rectors caused to be read publicly the said ducal letter and gave them orders as is contained above; directing and imposing a penalty on anyone who should offend against it, namely: loss of salary, first *pro rata* for days on which they are not scheduled to lecture, and double loss of salary for those days on which they are scheduled to lecture.

(There follow these signatures)

Jurists

The Rector
Renaldus de Camerino
Prosdocimo de Comitibus
Io. Franciscus de Capitibus
The Protonotary
Paulus de Dottis
Raphael Fulgosius

Raphael de Cumis
Marcus de Zacchis
Franciscus de Zenariis
Iacobus de Mussatis
Leonus de Lacara
Petrus de Frantia
Ioannes de Pensauro

Artists and Doctors

The Rector
Antonius Cermisoni
Galeatius de Sancta Sophia
Bartholomaeus de Montagnana
Stephanus de Doctoribus
Bonus à Flumine
Franciscus de Maso
Nicolaus de Cavazolis

Antonius de Asilo
Gaietanus
Ioannes Calderia
Ioannes Matthias de Feltria
Nicolaus de Andria
Prosdocimus de Beldomando
Marianus de Camerino
Iacobus de Languschis

124

TEACHING OF GRAMMAR AT TOULOUSE, APRIL 21, 1426

SETTLEMENT BY ARBITRATORS OF DISAGREEMENT AS TO LECTURES BETWEEN TEACHERS IN ARTS

Fournier, *Les statuts et privilèges,* I (1890), 770-71.

Since by the text of sacred canon, if we should destroy those things which were established of old by our predecessors, we could be called with justice not wholesome builders but overthrowers, witness the voice of truth saying, "Every kingdom divided against itself shall fall," and every science and law, if divided against itself, be destroyed, and similarly the ecclesiastical order is confounded, if its jurisdiction is not preserved. Wherefore we, Bernard, by divine pity bishop of Bazas and doctor of canon law, Arnaldus Roberti, professor of sacred theology, Andreas Sanxii and Bertrandus de Cluzello, canon and almoner of the metropolitan church of Toulouse, two doctors of canon law and teachers from our number who give ordinary lectures in the faculties mentioned of our venerable university of Toulouse, have been chosen judges, arbitrators and amicable reconcilers by our alma mater, the said university, with the express consent of those signed below, to settle and concord in a friendly way a debate long since arisen between the venerable and discreet men, masters Johannes Juvenis and Michael Belayci, masters in arts and teachers in the grammatical faculty in the said university on the one hand, and Louis Cardona, also a master of arts and lecturing in the logical faculty, on the other hand, over this matter. The said Cardona claims that he may lecture in grammar under color that he can lecture on *Priscian minor* according to the tenor of the statute of the same said university which opens, "Know all . . ." on leaf 8, even without license from the said masters teaching grammar, notwithstanding a certain other statute which begins, "Since by the ignorant . . ." at leaf 43 verso, which the said Cardona asserts is not to be understood of masters teaching logic but merely of schoolteachers, while the other two masters, Juvenis and Belhacii, assert the opposite and contrary, that neither Cardona himself nor any other master, licentiate, bachelor or even scholar in arts may lecture on grammar under color of the said *Priscian minor* either in the city or suburbs of Toulouse without seeking and obtaining their permission.

We, therefore, having fully seen and understood the reasons and motives in writings of both sides set before us, to the honor of God almighty and of the whole city, of the glorious Virgin mother, of our blessed lord Jesus Christ, and the whole court of the saints, also to the perpetual advantage and glory of the said university, to the utility, too, of the parties aforesaid and devout peace and lasting concord between them, for the information of the present generation and the perpetual memory of future ones, declare and ordain, pronounce, and also by tenor of the present papers in the presence of the said parties before us do judge as follows.

First, that between these parties there shall henceforth be, as there ought to be, good peace and concord and brotherly love, and there shall cease entirely and forever between them matter of strife with regard to this question.

Second, that the said Cardona or his representative by himself, or other qualified and sufficient person in his auditorium, vulgarly called "of logic," may lecture on the said *Priscian minor* according to the form of the statute which opens, "Know all . . . ," according to its commentaries and authentic readings and by questioning of the arts students in class, which is approved especially in this university, and elsewhere at least by no means condemned. And the said Cardona shall be required on oath to observe this as well for himself as for his reviewer, whom he may decide to appoint for this purpose.

Third, that such a reviewer shall not begin to lecture on *Priscian minor* under the said Cardona, nor shall anyone else teach grammar or things grammatical under color of the said lecture, until he has taken the accustomed personal oath to the rector of the university, the form of which is contained in the statute which begins, "Also that no reviewer . . . ," leaf 25 verso, inner column.

Fourth, that none of the masters teaching logic shall, either by himself or another, lecture explicitly on any of the books forbidden to be lectured on by others than the masters teaching grammar. These books are the *Doctrinale*, Ebrardus, Alexander and *Priscian major*, concerning which it is treated in the apostolic statute which opens,

"Also, since according to the usage . . . ," [1] leaf 25 verso, in the first column, and in the apostolic statute which begins, "Since by the ignorant . . . ," leaf 43 verso, in the first column, except by special license procured from the masters teaching in grammar themselves, since by the tenor of the statutes above mentioned it is clearly evident that the university at the time when the said statutes were published, forsooth in order that confusion might be avoided henceforth, wished that the masters teaching in the said two auditoriums of grammar and of logic should be content with lecturing there on certain designated books publicly in their separate classes. Elsewhere the canon has said, "I do myself an injury, if I disturb the rights of my brothers," and in another place, "I do not deem my honor increased where I know that my brothers have lost their honor," nor may the oaths which we have taken to observe the statute be transgressed, since they are in accord with reason.

Finally and in the fifth place, that such a reviewer or anyone else, of whatever state or condition he may be, may read the other books of grammar, provided the four mentioned are excepted, freely to whomsoever and go ahead in the city and suburb of Toulouse, with the proviso, however, that such before all will be required to recognize that their classes are in grammar and to make a friendly settlement as to salary with the masters giving instruction therein, so that frauds which might arise from the existence of many reviewers or instructors in grammar may be entirely avoided, nor matter be given for future dispute and strife. And the said statutes shall by no means be indirectly violated by anyone, but each shall be content with his limits in his own faculty, condemning no one to a part in the expense of a case of this sort. . . .

In 1489 one of the four teachers of grammar in the university complained to the rector that one of the teachers of logic and philosophy was giving private instruction in grammar in his house. The latter countercharged that the teacher of grammar was lecturing on books of logic in his classes and that conversely he himself had the right to teach grammar. The rector, citing the above settlement of 1426, decided that each must stick to his own subject. The teacher of grammar thanked him for his decision but the other appealed from it. Fournier, *Les statuts et privilèges*, I, 873–75.

[1] This statute of 1328 has been translated above, selection 68.

125

ASSIGNMENT OF POINTS FOR EXAMINATION IN THEOLOGY, MONTPELLIER, 1429

STATUTES OF THE FACULTY OF THEOLOGY

Fournier, *Les statuts et privilèges*, II (1891), 207.

We have decreed that, when lectures are completed and responsions made to questions as above directed, the bachelor shall be presented to the chancellor or his vicar by his master and by all the masters on behalf of the master under whom he lectured as a bachelor, to enter on private examination. And on that day points should be assigned in chapel in the episcopal residence in the presence of the chancellor or his vicar in the accustomed way and form, so that to the first bachelor to be examined shall be given points from the first and third books of the *Sentences*, to the second bachelor to be examined shall be given from the second and fourth books, and so on alternately points shall be assigned to bachelors for the future. Also the points shall be assigned in the morning about sunrise and the bachelor shall have to respond concerning them on the morrow about the hour of Vespers in the episcopal chapel. Also the bachelor should communicate his positions on both points to the chancellor or his vicar . . . and to each master who is to examine him he shall communicate the position on the point concerning which he has to respond to the same.

126

QUODLIBETA OF 1429 AND BEFORE

VARIOUS PHILOSOPHICAL QUESTIONS FROM A QUOD-
LIBETUM, OF WHICH THE AUTHOR SEEMS TO
HAVE BEEN URBAN DE MELLICO,[1] DISPUTED
AND DETERMINED FOR THE LICENSE IN
ARTS

MS Melk 6, 15th century, fols. 385–504.

At fol. 385 begin two questions disputed by Peter Pirchenwart in
1421: Whether it can be demonstrated from grounds evident in natural
light that there is one ruler of the universe? Whether in a well regulated state it is better that the community be governed by one or more
rulers?

At fol. 395, Simon de Asparn discusses whether every moral virtue
moderates the passions and directs the operations of appetite.

At fol. 403 follows a question debated in 1406 by John Hymel,
Whether the magisterial activities of philosophers are worthier and
more perfect than military arts?

At fol. 410 is another contribution from Simon de Asparn who questions the dictum of Aristotle that "All men by nature desire knowledge."

At fol. 414, John Angerer, Whether impetus is productive of local
motion?

At fol. 419, Andrea de Weitra, Whether solid bodies have the natural property of immediate contact in air or water?

At fol. 425, Stephen de Egenburga, Whether *habitus* is nobler than
the operation proceeding from it?

At fol. 429, Michael de Schriek, Whether the actions of material
substances are more related to their substantial forms than to their
qualities?

At fol. 437, Nicholas de Tulu, 1429 A.D., Whether seminal virtue is
the productive cause of substantial form?

---

[1] We are informed that master Urban de Mellico, bachelor of divinity, began to
dispute *de quolibet* in 1429 A.D.

At fol. 441, John of Salveden, 1429 A.D., Whether our external senses know their objects only in their presence?

At fol. 447, Whether flebotomy is more helpful in the first quarter of the moon than in any other, and more so in spring than at any other time of year?

At fol. 450, Paul of Giengen, Whether human felicity is the final cause of all human acts?

127

STUDENT RESPONSIBILITY

WHETHER THE HEARERS OF DIFFERENT MASTERS WHO HOLD DIFFERENT OPINIONS ARE EXCUSED FROM SIN, IF THEY SHARE THE OPINIONS OF THEIR OWN TEACHERS, WHEN THESE ARE NOT GOOD?

Antonino, *Summa*, III, 5, 2, 9.

Saint Thomas replies in *Quodlibeta*, If the different opinions of doctors of sacred scripture are not contrary to the faith or good morals, their auditors may follow either opinion without peril. . . . But in matters pertaining to the faith or good morals no one is excused if he follows the erroneous opinion of any master. For in such matters ignorance is no excuse. . . . For he who agrees with the opinion of any teacher against the manifest testimony of scripture or against what is publicly held by ecclesiastical authority cannot be excused from the vice of error: Monald, William and Hostiensis (Henry of Susa) agree.

There are some points which once were disputed among the doctors before they were determined by the church, and during that period a person could be excused who held either view. But after one of these had been settled and confirmed by the church, it would be heretical to hold the other. For example, before John XXII there were varied and conflicting opinions concerning the poverty of Christ, whether Christ and the Apostles held any movable property in common. But it was settled by John XXII himself, or rather by the church, that He had.

128

GETTING A DEGREE

Antonino, *Summa*, III, 5, 2, 2.

Wherefore, there is required a vigorous examination by some lecture or disputation in which he must answer arguments. And then he has to be approved or rejected by a ballot of the members of the college according as the majority vote. And by the chancellor or vice-chancellor of the university is given him license to receive the doctorate, either in theology or law or philosophy or medicine, and the power of occupying a chair, of lecturing in universities, disputing publicly, interpreting, glossing, and the like. Then the recipient of the degree, after making a brief speech in praise of the faculty, requests one of his promoters whom he names and who is present that the insignia of the doctorate may be given him. And that one rising, after commending the candidate's proficiency in the subject in which he is to receive the degree and commending the doctorate, gives him the insignia: namely, first a closed book that he may have that science close and familiar in mind and may keep it sealed from the unworthy and in such respects as it is not expedient to reveal. Second, he gives him an open book that he may teach others and make things plain. Third, he gives him a ring of espousal to that science. Fourth, a cap as a token of aureole or reward. Fifth, the kiss of peace.[1]

129

PROPOSED TRANSFER OF PROFESSOR AND STUDENTS FROM BOLOGNA TO FERRARA, 1430

Borsetti, *Historia almi Ferrariae gymnasii*, Ferrara, 1735, I, 29–30.

In the name of Christ, amen. In the year of His nativity 1430, eighth indiction, February 11.

---

[1] In connection with an oration on conferring the M.D. degree, in a manuscript of the fifteenth century, Wolfenbüttel 2841, fols. 234r, col. 1; 235v, col. 2, six slightly different insignia are conferred: first, a magisterial chair, and last, besides the closed, open book, finger ring, and kiss of peace, a paternal benediction instead of the cap.

All the said citizens [1] having gathered in the office of the twelve Wise Men of the city of Ferrara in the presence of the worshipful and eminent doctor of laws, Bartholinus de Barbalungis, judge of the said office of the twelve Wise Men, the same judge addressed these remarks to the said citizens.

"Distinguished doctors and prudent citizens, the famous doctor, Joannes de Finotis, has secretly written here to that noble and distinguished man, Jacobus Zilioli, that he is lecturing at Bologna before large classes, but that he does not wish to remain at Bologna and desires to come with many students to this our city of Ferrara, provided that the commune of Ferrara will merely provide classrooms for him."

To certify which statement he read with his own lips the letters of the aforesaid John which he held in his hands. He then said in conclusion that the greatest utility would be conferred on our commune by John's coming with the said throng of scholars through their purchase of victuals, lodgings, and other necessaries. He asked them, if they should see fit, that the commune of Ferrara assume the expense of the said classrooms in order that the said great advantage might follow.

Whereupon all the above-named citizens having weighed the matter carefully came to this decision, that the aforesaid John with his following be favorably received and this as speedily and promptly as might be, with the understanding however that the commune should not assume more than the expense of the classrooms.

130

THE DIGNITY OF A DEAN UPHELD, PARIS, 1431

MASTER JOHN FRANCISCI WHO ADDRESSED THE DEAN OF THE FACULTY OF CANON LAW WITHOUT REVERENCE IS REPROVED

Chartularium universitatis Parisiensis, IV, 531.

Also, on that day master John Francisci, master of arts and licentiate in canon law, aged sixty-six or thereabouts, was cited to appear before

---

[1] The names of sixteen men are listed.

the faculty because at a certain meeting of the university he had spoken to the abbot of St. Katherine of the Mount at Rouen, dean of our faculty, saying many words by way of reproof without any reverence, with cap and hat or cowl on his head and seated, contrary to the well-known custom of the university, by which those of the faculty of arts, whether masters or others, are not accustomed to speak seated but erect and standing, in distinction from the doctors and masters of the superior faculties who speak while seated. On which day master John Francisci appeared in person. And because these matters touched the said lord dean, I, Livinus Neuelinc, doctor of canon law, was deputed as an older man to speak to him and insinuate the feeling of the faculty which was to this effect: in view of the aforesaid reproof and transgression of his own oath twice taken, on receipt of the degrees of bachelor and licentiate, by which he swore to show reverence and honor to all doctors present and future, the faculty intended to proceed against him on acount of his deeds aforesaid in every possible and legal way to the end of obtaining due reparation.

John Francisci apologizing sought pardon, bending his knees thrice to the ground and weeping. In view of his penitence the faculty excused his offense.

131

VACATION OF THE MEDICAL FACULTY, PAVIA, 1433

AN ADDITION TO THE STATUTES OF THE COLLEGE OF PHYSICIANS

Codice diplomatico di università di Pavia, II (1913), 314-15.

Further they order and decree that when the time of the long vacation draws near, namely, from the feast of the most blessed Virgin occurring in the month of August, the college is free from duties and should be understood to be so until the beginning of term time, so that examinations, assemblies, and other activities be suspended, unless urgent necessity forces to the contrary, for example, the coming of some scholar from foreign parts who wished to have a case expedited, or some similar emergency. In which case their pleasure is that for doctors absent on vacation and only for such cause, their share of the money so received shall be kept by the prior or vice-prior or some one else, as it shall seem good to the prior to arrange.

132

HUMANISM AT PAVIA, 1434–1435

Codice diplomatico dell' università di Pavia, II, 333, 347.

I. LETTER OF THE DUKE OF MILAN, NOVEMBER 30, 1434

We have appointed the eminent and notable doctor, Guinifortus de Barziziis,[1] of Bergamo, to lecture publicly in our city of Milan on oratory and moral philosophy, according to the custom of institutions of higher learning, with an annual salary of four hundred florins, at thirty-two solidi the florin, to be paid by our chamber. We wish therefore that you arrange to pay him this stipend, so much per month in our city of Pavia, as is done with the other doctors of our university of Pavia, beginning next December.

II. PETITION OF STUDENTS AT PAVIA, MARCH 18, 1435

The greatest profit and honor, most illustrious prince, would accrue to this your renowned commune, if it had a learned man to lecture here ornately upon rhetoric and the outstanding works of the poets. For in this city there are many youths who are exceedingly eager to cultivate those studies which they call humanest, if they might have a wise preceptor of the art of oratory and the sweetness of sacred poesy. For could that be conveniently done, this republic of yours would indeed be made more learned and richer, and rendered more suitable for the safety of your state. Wherefore, most humane prince, since here in our midst is the eminent man, Baldassar Rasinus, most famous in the art of speaking, who from earliest years has devoted himself to humanistic studies with great éclat, whom your said commune desires greatly for his innumerable virtues to behold lecturing pub-

---

[1] Son of Gasparino da Barzizza.

licly, may your most pious lordship deign, in view of what has been said, to depute the said Baldassar to such a lectureship in sweetest poetry and rhetoric with a sufficient salary. This we doubt not we shall obtain in view of your singular kindness towards us all, since your lordship has ever been ready to make trial of anything that might redound to the advantage of this your republic. Our prayer is that God, best and greatest, may see fit long to prosper your estate.

133

A PROPOSAL FOR REFORM QUASHED, PARIS, 1434

THE FACULTY OF MEDICINE DECLARES THE RE-FORM OF THE UNIVERSITY ADVOCATED BY SOME TO BE UNNECESSARY, PROVIDED THE STATUTES ARE DULY OBSERVED

Chartularium universitatis Parisiensis, IV, 561.

On the eighth day of August of the same year the faculty was convened in St. Mathurin by schedule concerning two measures. The first contained that a reformation ought to be made by certain deans through the university in single faculties and nations, and, when made, laid before the university. . . .

As for the first point, it was unanimously agreed by the masters that reformation of the faculty is nothing but observance of its statutes, and it was voted that on the day set the university should be told that the faculty wishes to keep its statutes as it has done, and would that other faculties would do the same!

134

POSITION OF SURGEONS AT PARIS, 1436

THE UNIVERSITY OF PARIS REGARDS APPROVED
SURGEONS AS SWORN SCHOLARS OF THE
UNIVERSITY

Chartularium universitatis Parisiensis, IV, 594.

To all who shall inspect the present letters the rector and university of masters and scholars studying at Paris wish eternal salvation in the Lord. We make known that to us gathered solemnly to transact among ourselves difficult business the venerable man, John de Subfurno, master in arts and surgery, both in his own name and those of the discreet men, Dionysius Palluau, John Perricardi, Adam Martini, John Gileberti, Geoffrey Serre, Roger Ernoult, Dionysius de Lens, and Peter Peuple, masters of Paris approved in the science and art of surgery at Paris by those in charge of examinations and approbations, and true scholars in our university of Paris, set forth that, contrary to the public good, many quacks have arisen, not approved, and false or feigned surgeons, greatly disturbing and cheapening the venerable science of surgery with grave and horrid popular scandal and injury to the same. Which also seems to redound to the prejudice and no small detriment of the said petitioners, in view of the great and notable privileges conceded and bestowed by many kings of France upon the same petitioners and their predecessors in the said science of surgery, to wit, that no persons may practice surgery in the town or viscounty of Paris or exercise the function of a surgeon, unless they have been previously diligently examined and approved by the *jurati* of our lord the king in his Châtelet at Paris and the provost of the surgeons, or whatever they may be called, as he said was more fully set forth in their said privileges. The same master, John de Subfurno, begged in the name of those mentioned, that the aforesaid surgeons and others duly approved in the future in the art of surgery, be reputed scholars and enjoy their privileges, franchises, liberties, and immunities conceded to us or to be conceded, and that we aid them in this.

We, moreover, after mature and long deliberation over the aforesaid matters, held in the manner accustomed, have conceded and do concede the petition of the aforesaid surgeons, provided only that they attend the lectures of the masters at Paris teaching in the faculty of medicine, as is customary. In testimony of which thing we have directed that our great seal be affixed to the present letters. Given at Paris in our general congregation at St. Mathurin solemnly celebrated in the year of the Lord 1436, on the thirteenth day of the month of December.

135

UNIVERSITY LIBRARIES OF THE FIFTEENTH CENTURY

I. UNIVERSITY DECREE FOR THE USE OF BOOKS WILLED IT BY ELECTOR LOUIS III AND FOR ENTERING THE LIBRARY. HEIDELBERG, DECEMBER 8, 1438

Eduard Winkelmann, *Urkundenbuch der Universität Heidelberg,* 1886, I, 138–140, No. 98.

We, John Rybeisen of Brussels, master of arts, bachelor of holy canons, rector, and all the university of Heidelberg, to all and singular to whom the present letters may come, safety in Him who is true safety. Since to the glory of God and the increase of said university and the utility of those under its authority, the illustrious prince and lord Louis, count palatine of the Rhine, cupbearer of the Holy Roman Empire, prince elector and duke of Bavaria of happy memory, while he still lived among men, intent on laying up merits for his salvation, bequeathed and, by reason of death, gave and assigned to the said university and to the prebendaries of the church of the Holy Spirit, as is comprehended in letters and codicils above set forth more clearly, some books which he had collected at great expense from many places in the room of his castle at Heidelberg, forsooth, in theology, civil and canon law, and medicine and astronomy, which books the illustrious prince and lord Otto, count palatine of the Rhine, duke of Bavaria and tutor of the illustrious prince Louis, count palatine of the Rhine, cupbearer of the Holy Roman Empire, prince elector and duke of Bavaria, son of the said duke Louis, after the death of the same duke Louis of precious memory, according to his command and disposition, graciously handed over to us, the rector and university aforesaid, to keep, guard and use, as our letter, drawn up above and sealed, more fully declares, in which the said books are specified *seriatim* and are noted by their titles, and we, wishing that the last will and command of the said duke Louis of precious memory, as conceived by him concerning his books as aforesaid, should be exactly observed, and that the persons of the aforesaid university should edify and inform themselves more richly to the glory of God and to the spread of divine worship from the same, and yet they should remain uninjured and undisturbed forever at the university and church of the Holy Spirit of Heidelberg, have declared to be observed forever a method of preserving and safeguarding them in the custody or library, made and to be made, of the aforesaid university.

Forsooth, that to the library or room in which the aforesaid books for the time being are placed and enclosed, the following persons shall have keys and guard them diligently: the rector of the university, the seven salaried doctors, namely three theologians, three jurists, one physician, the regal dean of the church of the Holy Spirit, the dean of the faculty of arts, the priest and preacher of the town of Heidelberg, and other doctors—if any having domicile in the said university also wish to have keys of this sort—six masters of the college of arts and other masters who hold prebends through the aforesaid university.

That all and singular aforementioned, to whom keys are entrusted as aforesaid, shall promise in good faith and take corporal oath, that they will take and have diligent care concerning the said books while they are using the library.

When it happens that these, or any one of them, has access to the said books, and with them or any one of them, any person or persons who have not taken the oaths and do not have the said keys, has or have access, then that person who has taken the oath, with whom such person or such persons as have not taken the oath enter the library, shall give diligent attention and keep his eye on that person or those persons, lest they remove the books or any one of them offend in any way, nor shall the person who has taken the oath leave or depart from the aforesaid library unless the person or persons who have not taken the oath shall have gone out before him, and he shall carefully close and lock the library after himself and them.

No one of those taking the oath, as aforesaid, shall lend or give his key to any other person who has not taken the oath.

And when any one of those who have taken the oath shall enter the said library, he shall immediately close it after him and not allow it to stand open, without fraud and deceit in the things aforementioned or any one of them.

Furthermore, we wish an oath under the aforesaid form to be administered by the rector of the aforesaid university for the time being, so often as it happens that any one of the aforesaid positions is assumed anew, in the presence of four sworn persons of the four faculties, who, as often as it shall be convenient, we wish to be convoked by the rector to witness the administering of the oath.

And in order that the aforesaid ordinance and all and singular as aforesaid may remain forever unshaken and firm for us and our successors, we promise and profess in good faith that we wish the said books, all and singular included in the said libraries and there secured as aforesaid, to be preserved and forever remain under guard, nor any one of them to be loaned to any man outside the library of the said university, except to the count palatine then ruling, in the manner, however, and condition as is contained and specified in detail in the letter of the university in which the books are written with their titles, without any fraud and deceit whatever in all the aforesaid points.

In testimony and confirmation of which thing, in the presence of our rectorate and university aforesaid, we have caused to be affixed in common the seals of the venerable master John of Frankfurt, doctor of sacred theology, dean, and in the name of the same faculty, because the same faculty for the present has no seal of its own, of the faculty of law, of the venerable master Gerhard de Honkirchen, doctor in medicine, dean, and in the name of the same faculty, because the same faculty similarly for the present lacks its own seal, and of the faculty of arts.

II. DECREE CONCERNING THE LIBRARY OF THE FACULTY OF ARTS WHICH SHALL BE OBSERVED BY OATH. SEPTEMBER 12, 1454

Ibid., I, 173, No. 113.

On the twelfth day of September it was harmoniously agreed by the deputies of the faculty of arts:

1. If any book in the lower library of the faculty of arts exists in duplicate at least, it may be loaned to a master of this university and to no other person, for the time of his ordinary lecture or for one or two months, not however for purposes of daily use but in order to make a copy of it or to collate it with another copy.

2. If only one book is taken at a time, it may be loaned to the masters of our university for such time as is likely to be required to copy it and no longer, and let care be taken regarding this.

3. No book should be loaned outside the university without the consent of the entire faculty, concerning which further the master borrowing the book shall be warned not to transmit the book so borrowed outside the university, and if after this he shall have done so, he shall be suspended from privileges of the library for a year.

4. In all the aforesaid cases individual masters shall deposit with the librarian a sufficient security and a book of the same value as the book borrowed, with a receipt in their own handwriting which is to be left with the librarian for the time of the use of the book.

III. REGULATIONS OF 1412 AT OXFORD

Henry Anstey, *Munimenta Academica*, 1868, I, 263–266.

Since in course of time an importunate multitude of students would prejudice in various ways the books of the university, and the sound purpose of those wishing to make progress would be impeded by the excessive tumult of popular concourse, the university has ordained and decreed that no one henceforth shall study in the library of the university except degree-holders and members of religious orders after eight years in philosophy, an oath having first been taken by them before the chancellor in the presence of the librarian that they have spent eight years in this university, together with the oath which other graduates of the university will take, whose tenor is contained below in the next statute. Moreover, the sons of lords who have seats in the royal Parliament, since the university has decreed to them the privilege of entry of its special grace, should know that they are bound to the same oath to be administered under a similar form.

The university has further ordained that no bachelor not yet a master shall study there except in academic dress, bachelors of theology and licentiates of certain faculties excepted. But masters of grammar, so far as entry to the library is concerned, shall be required to conform in costume with the bachelors.

Also, for safer custody of the books the university has ordained and decreed that all graduates now in the university and any others permitted to enter the library by the terms of the statute, shall take personal oath before commissioners deputed to this by the chancellor before Christmas that, when they enter the common library of the university to study, they will treat in decent fashion the books which they inspect, doing no damage by erasures or removing leaves or quires. . . .

Also since, if there are not specific hours assigned for study in the common library, the life of the librarian will become an insupportable burden from many importunate demands upon him, while on the other hand by his laziness the happy impulse to study might often be frustrated, the university has ordained and decreed that the daily hours of study shall be before noon from nine to eleven, after noon from one to four, which hours the librarian shall be required faithfully to observe, Sundays and major feast days excepted, together with days when university masses and obsequies are chanted. Moreover, on those days when masses of the university are celebrated he shall have only the forenoon off, and when there are funerals, the afternoon only. And lest inclement restriction of residence cause such custodians to weary with lapse of time, the university has generously provided that during the long vacation he shall have a month off, but subject to limitation by the chancellor and proctors. Moreover, at other hours or times than those above mentioned no one shall be admitted, unless by chance there be some stranger, having with him a notable graduate, who wishes to visit the library. Then, moreover, it shall be licit for the librarian to open the library to those wishing to see it from sunrise to sunset, provided they are notable personages and a noisy crowd does not follow them.

IV. RUBRICS OF THE STATUTES OF THE LIBRARY
OF THE UNIVERSITY OF ANGERS, 1431

Fournier, *Les statuts et privilèges*, I (1890), 386–89.

1. There follow the statutes concerning the common library of the university of Angers and its custodian made in the year of the Lord 1431.

2. Of the oath to be taken by each new custodian of the library.

3. Of the general regimen and custody of the library and its books to be executed by their custodian.

4. Of the privileges which the custodian of the library shall enjoy.

5. To what persons the library shall be open and to whom not, and of its visitation and closing daily by the custodian.

6. At what hours of days on which lectures are given the library shall be closed and at what not.

7. At what hours of days on which lectures are not given and feast days and vacations the library shall be open and at what not.

8. On what feast days throughout the year the library shall be closed and not open.

9. On not drawing out chained books and volumes of the library without obtaining the permission in writing of the rector and college.

10. On visiting the library each year at the close of the university and checking up its inventory and putting it away with the keys of the reading desks in a chest.

11. On not whispering or making a noise or disturbance in the library and on excluding those doing this.

12. On preferring members of the teaching staff to all others and giving them the place in the library which they want.

13. On not bringing or keeping women in the library building as occasion for sin.

14. On not stealing anything from the library and to whom it is permitted to correct its books and to whom not.

15. On copying lectures and the charges therefor and conversion of them to the perpetual use of the library.

16. On charging for the books and quaternions of the library before they are loaned out and marking them with a sign manual.

17. To whom the unchained books and quaternions of the library

may be loaned and to whom not, and of the method of doing this and raising the salary of the custodian.

18. On demanding a fine from those who keep books or quaternions of the library more than thirty days.

19. Of the faculty granted the custodian of the library of selling for others and not for himself, and of his salary.

20. Of revealing in the college any infractions of these regulations by the custodian of the library.

136

CERTAIN REGULATIONS OF THE FACULTY OF MEDICINE, CAEN, 1439

Fournier, *Les statuts et privilèges*, III (1892), 167.

Also, in the school of medicine only medical books shall be lectured on except the books *De animalibus* and the fourth book of the *Meteorology*.

Also, that within fifteen days after the candidate's admission to the degree of bachelor he shall begin to lecture, and the book which he lectures on first shall conform to the books on which lectures should be given, and neither he nor others shall give rambling lectures but well assembled and orderly ones with expositions and questions, if he can find them, namely, the book of *Aphorisms* for 70 lectures, the *Tegni* for at least 50, the *Regimen of Acute Diseases* for 38 lectures, the *Prognostics* [1] for 36, the book of Johannitius [2] for 30, the entire *Viaticum* [3] for 70—and anyone wishing to lecture on the seventh book of the *Viaticum* for half of a course shall deliver at least 20 lectures —the *Universal Diets* for 34, *Particular Diets* of the same [4] for 26, the *Urines* of the same for 24, the *Urines* of Theophilus for 14, the *Urines* in verse of Egidius [5] for 20 lectures.

Also, the bachelor shall be required to come regularly to *quodlibet*

---

[1] The four texts thus far named are Hippocratic except the *Tegni* of Galen.

[2] Hunain ibn Ishak, Introduction to the *Tegni* of Galen.

[3] An Arabic work translated by Constantinus Africanus in the eleventh century.

[4] Isaac Judaeus or Israeli, translated by Constantinus Africanus.

[5] Gilles de Corbeil (c. 1140–1224).

disputations for two years from the beginning of each ordinary course till Lent, observing peace, tranquillity and the method of argumentation in disputations ordered by the faculty.

Also, he shall be required to practice at Caen for two summers with a master, not however of himself administering any medicine, digestive, laxative or comforting, nor visiting the sick at all except the first time, unless by special license of some master. If he shall do otherwise, he shall be deprived of every honor of the faculty.

137

FOUNDATION OF THE FRATERNITY OF ST. SEBASTIAN, AVIGNON, 1441

Fournier, *Les statuts et privilèges*, II (1891), 417.

Since ease of body is the root and source of many evils, while idleness of soul is known to be even more the most certain cause of epidemic, of exhaustion of the soil, and of deprivation of eternal glory, and since the students of the university of Avignon, giving nothing to charity, pouring out no prayers for the defunct faithful, doing nothing whatever to please God, have until now remained indifferent towards God, nay, what is a shame, after the wont of Epicureans, believing that pleasures of the body are blessedness, have continually practiced nefarious and incredible actions at the advent of each novice or what is vulgarly called the purgation of the Freshmen, and in consequence God, perchance angered, by means of epidemic has often scattered the same students in times past from the said university and has given occasion for their transferring themselves to another place: therefore the venerable men . . . (26 names follow), and many others beyond the number of two hundred studying at the said university of Avignon, to the praise of almighty God and of the blessed Sebastian, glorious martyr, moved by the divine spirit, have banded together to celebrate a new brotherhood. . . .

138

A STUDENT'S RECORD OF HIS ACADEMIC CAREER, PAVIA, 1441

Padre Ireneo Affò, *Memorie degli scrittori e letterati Parmigiani,* II, 1789, 166–68.

This personal record was jotted down in a manuscript of the *Questions on Perspective* of Blasius of Parma, who died in 1416 and whose son, Francesco Pelacani, was one of our student's promoters for his degree. This document, printed by Affò, has been overlooked in the recently published *Codice diplomatico* of the university of Pavia. Since *rotuli* of the professors of arts and medicine at Pavia are lacking for the years 1436–1439 inclusive and again for the year 1440–1441, during which years records of examinations for degrees and lists of examiners such as our student gives are likewise wanting, it will be seen that the information here given for the years 1438 and 1441 helps to bridge these gaps.

Note that I, Matheus de Capitaniis de Busti,[1] was examined in arts June 27, 1438, and I had for points, etc.,[2] and I was passed, no one dissenting, and immediately after the examination I received the doctorate.

The lord rector was master Bartholomeus de Maglanis of Savoy.[3]

Promoters, Doctors of Arts and Medicine

Master Johannes de Concorezio [4]

[1] For the most part I have left this and the other proper names of the document in the Latin form as reproduced by Affò.

[2] *Puncta,* i.e., the passages from texts on which he was examined. Whether these were stated in the MS and omitted by Affò I cannot say.

[3] The name does not seem to be included in the index to the *Codice diplomatico.*

[4] John of Concoregio's or Giovanni da Concorezzo's *Practica nova medicine* or *Lucidarium* and *Flos florum* was printed at Pavia, 1485, and at Venice several times during the sixteenth century. According to Tiraboschi's History of Italian Literature, John says at the end of his preface that he finished it in 1438 after thirty-four years of teaching in Bologna, other universities of Italy, and finally at Pavia. Elsewhere I have seen it stated that in his preface John says he began the work at Bologna in 1433 and completed it at Pavia in 1438 at the wish of his scholars. It is doubtless true that he was at Pavia when he completed the work, but it should not be inferred that he had spent most of his time at Bologna or other Italian universities, since his name appears in almost every extant roll of the faculty of Pavia from 1421 to 1448, during most of which time he gave the morning lecture in medicine. Argellati, *Biblio-*

Master Apollinaris de Cremona,[5] who gave me the insignia
Master Antonius de Bernardigio [6]
Master Franciscus Pelacanus of Parma,[7] son of the late Master
Blasius who composed this book

Examiners in the College, Doctors of Arts and Medicine

Master Santinus Folpertus,[8] sub-prior

---

theca scriptorum Mediolanensium, I, ii, 451, and II, ii, 1978, was therefore mistaken
in giving the date of his death as 1438, correcting his own previous misprint of 1488.
By 1448, however, his teaching career was about over, and in a rough draft for the
salary roll where he is put down to "lecture at pleasure," the heartless note is added
that he is "superfluous and does not lecture."

Argellati states that John was enrolled in the college of physicians of Milan in 1413,
and he obviously would have had some years of previous teaching before being called
to the ordinary professorship of medicine, with which his connection with Pavia
began in 1421. In Dallari's *Rotuli* for the university of Bologna the name of John of
Concoregio or Concorezzo does not seem to appear, despite the above-cited statements
indicating that he taught there.

One other work by John to be printed was his treatise on fevers which appeared at
Venice in 1521. Both it and the aforesaid *Lucidarium* were mentioned under John's
name by Tiraquellus (1480–1558) in the long list of medical men in the thirty-first
chapter of his *De nobilitate*. Argellati ascribed some five works to him, but they
appear to be reducible to these two.

[5] Apollinaris of Cremona, or Apollinare Offredi, taught natural philosophy at
Pavia from 1425 to 1440, and held an ordinary professorship of medicine from 1441
to 1448, which is as far as the *rotuli* published in the *Codice diplomatico* go. He was
then receiving the large salary of 800 florins a year. He was sub-prior of the college
of physicians in 1425.

[6] The name of Antonius de Bernadigio first appears in the faculty of Pavia as
teacher of logic in 1415–1417, and natural philosophy from 1417 to 1429. From
1425 to 1440 he also taught astrology. Meanwhile in 1430–1431 he advanced to the
afternoon lectures in medicine and in 1439–1440 to the morning or ordinary lectures
which he continued to give as a colleague of the aforesaid Apollinaris until the published *rotuli* cease in 1447–1448. In the preparatory draft for the roll of 1448–1449
his name, however, does not seem to appear.

[7] Francesco Pelacani of Parma received the doctorate in arts at Pavia in 1422 and
appears in the *rotuli* as teacher of logic from 1425 to 1434, when he combined it with
natural philosophy, a subject to which he then exclusively devoted himself until at
least 1448. It will be noted that a young instructor usually began with logic, passed
on to natural philosophy, and then advanced to various grades of medical professorships.

[8] Santino Folperti began to give afternoon lectures in medicine at Pavia in 1425,
unless his name appeared in rolls between 1422 and 1425 which we do not have, and
continued on the faculty there most of the time for the next quarter of a century.
Sometimes he gave extraordinary instead of afternoon lectures, sometimes his name
does not appear on the roll. In 1448 he was described as "useless and not lecturing."

Master Girardus Bernerius of Alessandria [9]
Master Johannes Martinus of Parma [10]
Master Johannes Nicola de Bennis [11]
Master Jacobus de Rippa [12]
Master Henricus Marzarius [13]
Master Johannes de Piro

Doctors of Arts only

Master Petrus de Clericis [14]
Master Luchinus Balbus [15]
Master Friar Henry of Sicily [16] of the Order of Preachers
Master Alexander of Bergamo [17]

[9] Gerardo Berneri of Alessandria also had been long connected with the faculty of arts and medicine at Pavia. We find his name as instructor in logic in 1415–1417, of moral philosophy from 1418 to 1422, as afternoon lecturer in medicine 1425–1427 and then as extraordinary professor of practice to 1434, when he became ordinary professor of practice. About 1443 his connection with that university seems to cease.

[10] Giammartino Garbazza had also been a professor of medicine at Pavia since 1425 and was still one in 1448. The Index to the *Codice diplomatico* lists separately as if three distinct personages: Giovanni Marco Ferrari da Parma, Giovanni Martino Ferrari da Parma, and Giovanni Martino Garbazzi da Parma, but I feel sure that these are simply three sections of the same career, and three variants of the same name.

[11] Gian Nicola Benni received his degree in arts in 1434 and is listed as an examiner of candidates for degrees in 1442 and 1443 and again mentioned in the *Codice diplomatico* in 1448. But his name does not appear in any *rotulus* as a salaried member of the faculty.

[12] The *Codice diplomatico*'s Index again makes two persons of Giacomo Ripa or Riva and Ripalta, but they seem to be the same. He appears in 1435–1436 as giving extraordinary lectures in natural philosophy and in 1439–1440 and 1441–1442 as afternoon lecturer in medicine and in 1446–1448 as extraordinary professor of the practice of medicine.

[13] This and the following name I do not find in the *Codice diplomatico*.

[14] Pietro Clerici was appointed to lecture on the *Pronostica* of Hippocrates at a salary of thirty florins in 1435, and his name appears in the *rotulus* for that year, but not in the next extant *rotulus* for 1439.

[15] The name of Luchinus de Balbis first appears in the *rotulus* for 1435–1436 as giving extraordinary lectures in natural philosophy. After 1439 he was teaching medicine.

[16] In the *Codice diplomatico* the earliest mention of Henry of Sicily is his presentation of a candidate for a degree on June 12, 1442, which our student's memorandum antedates by four years. Henry taught natural and moral philosophy from 1443 to 1446, and theology in 1446–1448.

[17] Alexander of Bergamo is not mentioned in the *Codice diplomatico* as attending an examination until 1443, and not as a salaried teacher of medicine until 1448.

Master Johannes de Pescina [18]
Master Paganinus Zerbus [19]
Master Pantaleo de Vercelis [20]
Master Johannes Antonius de Castronovo [21]

and several others whom I omit for sake of brevity, and this in the time of the most reverend father in Christ and Lord, lord Henricus de S. Alosio, by divine providence bishop of Pavia, and most worthy count, likewise well-deserved chancellor of the whole university. Amen.

Note that I, Matheus de Capitaniis de Busti, was examined in medicine, June 10, 1441, and I had as points, etc., and I was passed, no one dissenting, and immediately after the examination I received the degree but not the insignia, and I deposited thirty ducats as security for holding a public banquet.

The lord Rector was master Francischinus Acerbus [22] of Mantua.

Promoters, Doctors of Arts and Medicine

Required

Master Girardus Bernerius of Alessandria
Master Apollinaris Offredus of Cremona

Voluntary

Master Johannes de Concorezio
Master Antonius de Bernaregio
Master Tebaldus Madius de Salis [23]

Examiners in the College, Doctors of Arts and Medicine

Master Antonius Marsarius de Castronovo,[24] sub-prior

[18] Johannes de Pescina seems not to be mentioned in the *Codice.*
[19] The only mention of Paganino Zerbi is a ducal letter of 1441 implying that he had that year resigned his position as extraordinary lecturer in natural philosophy. The roll for that year is missing; he does not appear in that for 1439–1440.
[20] Pantaleo received his M.D. in 1440.
[21] Giovanni Antonio Guerra da Castelnuovo first appears in the *Codice diplomatico* as giving afternoon lectures in medicine in 1441–1442.
[22] Francesco Acerbi received his M.D. in 1441.
[23] Tebaldus gave an afternoon course in medicine 1418–1422, was extraordinary professor of practice from 1425 to 1442, and ordinary professor thereafter.
[24] Antonius Merzari of Castelnuovo was professor of surgery at Pavia in 1415–1422. After an interval his name appears again in the same position from 1439 to 1448.

Master Sirus de Rubeis [25]

Master Santinus de Folpertis

Master Franciscus Pelacanus

Master Johannes Matheus Ferrarius [26]

Master Johannes Martinus of Parma

Master Antonius de Terzago [27]

Master Antonius de Gambaloto [28]

Master Jacobus de Rippa

Master Luchinus Balbus

Master Nichola de Bennis

Master Albert of Mantua [29]

Master Johannes Antonius de Castronovo, and several others, etc. as above.

Note that I began to study November 3, 1433, and I completed my studies in arts and medicine June 10, 1441.

[25] Sirus de Rubeis was professor of surgery, 1425–1442.

[26] Giamatteo Ferrari da Grado has been treated of by a descendant: Dr. Maxime Ferrari, *Une chaire de médecine au XVe siècle et un professeur à l'université de Pavia de 1432 à 1472*, Paris, Alcan, 1899; summarized in English by Sir T. Clifford Allbutt, *Greek Medicine in Rome*, 1921, pp. 475–89. The *Codice diplomatico* shows him teaching logic, 1432–1436, giving extraordinary lectures in practice in 1439–1442, and occupying one of the ordinary chairs of medicine from 1443. In 1448 he is said to have been too ill to lecture. Various works by him appeared in one or more editions before 1500: see Arnold C. Klebs, *Incunabula scientifica et medica*, 1938, Nos. 392, 393, 394; Margaret B. Stillwell, *Incunabula in American Libraries*, 1940, F94, F95, F96.

[27] Antonius de Terzagho taught logic during the same years as Giamatteo Ferrari da Grado. After 1439 he seems to have divided his time between an ordinary professorship of medicine and astrology.

[28] The name of Iacobus de Gambolato (as it is there spelled) appears frequently in the rolls, first as teaching metaphysics and then medicine, but I did not notice that of an Antonius. The former is indexed in the *Codice* as Giacomo Farrari da Gambolo.

[29] Albert of Mantua, doctor of arts and sub-prior of the college of physicians, presented a candidate for a degree in 1442 and attended an examination in 1443, but his name does not appear in the salary rolls thus far published.

139

A CONTENTED DEAN OF THEOLOGY

FROM TWO LETTERS OF NOVEMBER 17, 1441, AND
FEBRUARY, 1442, BY GERARD MACHETI, DEAN
OF THE FACULTY OF THEOLOGY, PARIS

Chartularium universitatis Parisiensis, IV, 620.

We have been so educted to Paris, where I received your card of October third, that we could hardly leave it. I have found the city air favorable to my health, perhaps because I breathed it for many years or because it approaches my native place, so that the constellations are more temperate. There are found here supplies of wood against the winter cold, I have made hay for the use of the horses and have bought suitable bed-coverings at a high enough price, fearing to borrow from friends lest I incommode any of them by consuming others' property. I have found a nice house and pleasant garden. And lest I grow too lazy or empty days pass without fruit, I have decided to resume my lectures, long interrupted, with the regents in our faculty. And already our theology has induced a new zest, and the work is most agreeable which I carry on as dean, being the ranking senior officer. Those under the faculty are increasing, especially the seculars. The royal college alone flourishes here, the others lie uncared for and without students. Benefices are worth little, but food is cheap and excellent to my taste and bodily temperature. The wines are of wonderful flavor and nourish my joints and abound here from every place and region. . . . From Amboise.

I have been in Paris for some months, living quietly away from the tumult of the courtiers, and have resumed lecturing until spring. I seem to have renewed my youth to those pristine days when the university flourished, illumined by so many famous lights and marvelously adorned. In your absence I fill the office of dean of our faculty, but would that I had found you hale and hearty. I have had the professors meet at my house, since there was a division between the seculars and the mendicant friars which I pacified. I have found the condition of the air exactly suited to my health and have a very nice house, which I occupy by royal gift, surrounded by pleasant gardens with the water of fountains running with sweet murmur through the whole house and most agreeable garden, so that it seems to observers a sort of paradise in whose midst springs a fountain irrigating the earth's surface.

140

ACTION AT PARIS AGAINST SPECIAL PRIVILEGES FOR FRIARS

MARCH 24, SEPTEMBER 20, DECEMBER 11, 1442

Chartularium universitatis Parisiensis, IV, 626, 628–31.

Eugenius IV, at the petition of the generals and brothers Minor, Preachers, Eremites of St. Augustine and Carmelites, decreed that the brothers of these orders, who were sent to Paris, by their superiors having this power, to lecture there publicly on the Bible, should be admitted immediately and without delay regardless of regulations, if they were found qualified by deputies of the faculty of theology, but those sent to lecture on the *Sentences* "should be admitted with no delay of any time whatever, without lecturing on the Bible, without courses and without any equivalent for the courses"; but after they have become bachelors, each teacher of these orders shall present and should present one of the said bachelors to obtain the licentiate to the chancellor of Paris, and so presented he shall immediately be admitted to receive the licentiate, even if he has not completed the statutory period of five years, provided however he has responded twice in ordinary. These were the ancient customs in the faculty of theology observed from time immemorial, to which some of the faculty of theology had been opposed for many years of late. Given at Florence in the year of the Incarnation of the Lord 1441, March 24, the tenth year of our pontificate.

On September 20, 1442, the university being convoked in St. Bernard by the rector by reason of a bull directly contrary to the privileges of the university and especially to the statutes of the faculty of theology which the four Mendicant orders had obtained from the supreme pontiff, it was concluded by the French nation and agreed to by the other nations that all members of the said four orders, graduate or not graduate, should be deprived of the society of the university, and unanimously at the petition of the venerable faculty of theology, from all scholastic acts, until and when the said Mendicants should have obtained another new bull contrary word for word to that bull obtained by them from the supreme pontiff. Nay more, one nation willed with the other nations that when this new contrary bull was procured, the university would then have to see what should be done as to new incorporation of the said brothers. And the rector then in office sought public instruments of all these things.

On December 11, 1442, at the time of the proctorship of Odo de Credulio, licentiate in medicine, it was harmoniously agreed in St. Mathurin by the nations and faculties on account of the controversy risen in the venerable faculty of theology between the Mendicants and non-Mendicants on the occasion of a certain bull obtained by the said Mendicants directly contrary to the statutes of the faculty of theology and of the university and very derogatory to the same, that the following articles should be reduced to writing in the books of the nations, and that all masters of the four Mendicant orders, teaching or non-teaching, specially summoned for this with the bachelors in theology of the said orders in the sight of the university, should swear to observe these. And thus it was written in the schedule.

. . . For the security of the faculty the said friars, both masters and bachelors, will swear and promise in good faith . . . never to use the said bull recently obtained in the name of the four orders and that they will work to the best of their ability and stretch every nerve to induce their generals to seek the revocation or quashing of it in the register of the Roman curia and concerning the said quashing and annulment they will give assurance to the said faculty of theology before the next Exaltation of the Holy Cross.

And lest in the future any occasion of discord arise as to biblical bachelors and those to be presented of the same orders, the said faculty, assembled on the day aforesaid in St. Mathurin, has determined and concluded certain points in the form written below, agreeing substantially with the schedules exhibited by the same religious to the faculty, namely, that the students of the four orders who are sent to lecture on the *Sentences* should stay at Paris for three years before the said lectures, namely, for a year before they lecture on the Bible and for the year in which they lecture on the Bible, and for a third in which they prepare themselves to lecture on the *Sentences*, so that their views and characters may be tested. And if anyone chances to be sent by his superior to lecture on the *Sentences* who has not been trained and qualified to lecture on the Bible, he shall similarly be required to reside at Paris for three years before the said lecture on the *Sentences*, in the second or third of which years he shall be required to give two courses and fulfill the regulations of the faculty.

But if any foreigner, that is from outside the Gauls, has been assigned to the said lectures on the *Sentences*, he shall reside at Paris before the lectures on the *Sentences* for two years, so that those may be dealt with more gently who come from afar to the most celebrated university of Paris. The remaining space of time required by the papal statute for lecturing on the *Sentences* they shall acquire in schools or universities of their orders, in which according to the custom of each order there are lecturers, regents and bachelors engaged in lecturing on the *Sentences* ordinarily and responding as to ordinary questions, and in which students are accustomed to be assigned to theological exercises (which schools or convents of theirs outside of universities in the Gauls are designated and described by them to a certain number, but outside the Gauls they have not designated because they do not have certain information as to them), but so that out of reverence for this university of Paris two years in their said schools or universities shall count for one year.

Moreover, as to students presented the faculty concluded, conformably to the schedules given by the same religious, that henceforth and for the future a bachelor who has taken his degree in the past and resides at Paris shall be presented on the day of the licentiate ordinarily in presence of the faculty, preserving among the Friars Preachers the distinction between natives and foreigners; and the person thus presented shall have six months beyond others after which he shall be required to respond twice ordinarily, as is stated in the statute.

All which aforesaid the religious swore and promised to keep and to observe in the way above stated and so far as in them lies, and to procure and promote from their said generals, as above stated, the annulment of the said bull before the next feast of the Exaltation of the Holy Cross. When these things had been sworn and promised by the religious, the said faculty decreed and concluded to suspend the deprivation made about these, and it was suspended until the next feast, and similarly by the university. But if within this time it has not received satisfaction as to the said annulment, quashing and revocation, it decrees now as then that they will be deprived at the pleasure of the same faculty. And concerning all these matters an instrument was drawn up by master Michael Hebert, scribe of the university, and is preserved in the ark of the university.

141

STUDENT LIFE AT OLD HEIDELBERG

ADDITION TO THE STATUTES JUNE 23 TO JULY 2, 1442

Eduard Winkelmann, *Urkundenbuch der Universität Heidelberg*, I, 1886, p. 145, No. 100, in part.

No master or student shall presume to visit the public and ordinary gaming houses, especially on days of lectures and above all where the laity meet, under penalty of half a florin and the taking of this into account by the university in making promotions.

No one shall presume by day or night to engage in gaming or to sit or tarry by night or otherwise for any time in a brothel or house of prostitution, under penalty of a florin and under penalty that such persons shall be posted by the university as public procurers and as such to be punished according to statutes previously enacted against such.

Concerning dances at Lent or other time of year not being held by students in public and their not going about in unseemly fashion, wearing masks, and not engaging in jousts, the rector at that time always ought and has power to provide under heavy penalties.

All students are required to attend each week at least some lectures. Otherwise, besides statutes previously promulgated against such, which we wish to remain in their strength, the university intends to provide against these as it may see fit, and the rector at the time shall be required to take measures against them in accordance with his office.

If anyone is unwilling to give testimony on oath concerning the excesses of the students or for other reason, when he is required to do so by the rector, or if anyone who has been arrested shall run away, the rector may and should denounce him to the university for expulsion. . . .

142

REASONS FOR RE-ESTABLISHING A UNIVERSITY AT FERRARA

SIGNED BY JOANNES DE GUALENGIS, JUDGE OF THE BOARD OF TWELVE WISE MEN OF FERRARA, EIGHT WISE MEN, AND TWENTY-THREE CITIZENS, JANUARY 17, 1442 [1]

Borsetti, *Historia almi Ferrariae gymnasii*, I (1735), 47–49.

A supplication was directed to the illustrious and mighty prince, Leonello, marquis of Este etc. and our exceptional lord, from a number of the most respected and prudent citizens of Ferrara, in which they suggested to that prince an outstanding boon for this his city, that he reform its university and give to the shade of this school a true and living form. To which supplication the most prudent prince inclined a most friendly ear and bade our illustrious Joannes de Gualengis, judge of his board of twelve Wise Men, to assemble that board with other citizens of weight, take mature counsel, decide what should be done, and then report to him the decision of himself and the citizens summoned. Wherefore, in conformity to the command of the prince, the said Wise Men and citizens were called together. Joannes de Gualengis, the aforesaid judge, sagely explained the petition and the response of the prince, and then asked the advice of these Wise Men and citizens whether there should be a university in this

---

[1] Rashdall (1936) II, i, 54, writes: "There were Schools in all Faculties except Theology at Ferrara at least from about the middle of the thirteenth century, but the Studium did not become general till 1391. . . . Another unsuccessful attempt was made to renew the Studium in 1402: but the real resurrection of the University does not begin till 1430, when the movement for a restoration of the University originated with the city government . . . . after the more elaborate Reformation of 1442 the University rapidly became a flourishing Studium. . . ."

In 1438 had occurred the famous debate between Hugh of Siena, physician to the marquis, Niccolò d'Este, and the learned Greeks attending the council of Ferrara. But in 1439 the council had been transferred to Florence and Hugh had passed away.

town and whether it would pay the city. And these Wise Men and citizens, having heard the judge's polished statement, were all of this one mind: that a university be established in this city, which step would be of the greatest utility, praise and honor.

For, to begin with its utility, strangers will flock hither from various remote regions, and many scholars will stay here, live upon our bread and wine, and purchase of us clothing and other necessities for human existence, will leave their money in the city, and not depart hence without great gain to all of us. Moreover, our citizens who go elsewhere to acquire an education and take their money there, will have an academy at home where they can learn without expense, and our money will not fly away.[2] Besides, there are many excellent wits in this town of ours which remain undeveloped and lost, whether from the carelessness of their fathers or their own negligence or lack of money. These will be aroused by the presence of a university and the conveniences for study, and will be enabled to pursue their education without great expense. What praise, what honor there will be for our city, when the report shall spread through the whole world that we have our own seat of good disciplines and arts. Great indeed and one sought by every city, should opportunity offer. But since fortune, or rather God almighty himself, has furnished us the occasion in this time when other university cities are either shattered by wars or weakened by other ills that our city flourishes and lives in peace under the lead of our most wise and divine prince, what is there to persuade us that we defraud this our city in this matter of utility, praise, and honor? In view of which reasons and many others brought forward by the aforesaid as above assembled, it is decreed and established: That a university be set up in this city, and may it be a great success. And they chose the undersigned jurists and eminent citizens to cooperate with our prince in selecting Reformers of this university after the custom of other universities.

[2] An example of mercantilism in the fifteenth century.

143

ACADEMIC EXERCISES AT FERRARA

Montreal, McGill University, Osler Library, MS 7554, ff. 19v, 21v–22r.[1]

I. STATUTE 37, ON OPENING THE UNIVERSITY AND CELEBRATING OTHER FESTIVITIES

For the benefit of scholars wishing to study at Ferrara they decreed and ordained that each year the university should open immediately after the feast of St. Luke,[2] and that the rector and counselors should have no power to postpone the opening of the university. Nor in this matter at the petition of a doctor or other person could dispensation be made in any way even by the university. Adding further, that lecturers, whether ordinary or extraordinary, should observe only one holiday per week, unless it were a solemn feast or a solemn feast fell on a Thursday.[3] Nor at the request of anyone should they do the contrary, unless for just cause. They decreed that at the season of Lent vacations should be observed from the last Thursday before and through the entire first day of Quadragesima, inclusive. And Easter vacation should begin on Palm Sunday and lectures resume on the Monday following the Sunday after Easter. Also that every rector taking office before Christmas continue until the eve of St. Thomas.[4] Under penalty for each offender, if a student, of 20 solidi, and if a doctor or the rector, five pounds of Ferrara. And this for tossing straw about, or doing anything else to prevent the doctor from giving ordinary lectures. And that the university should adjourn every year at the end of August, adding this, that on the first of May each year they should take six days off to take medicine according to the usual practice.

[1] Also printed by Borsetti, *Historia almi Ferrariae gymnasii*, I (1735), 364 *et seq.*, but that work is no longer available to me.
[2] October 18.   [3] Presumably there were no lectures on Thursdays.
[4] Probably July 7 is meant.

II. STATUTE 46, WHEN THE DOCTORS
SHOULD LECTURE

They decreed further that doctors giving morning lectures, as well ordinary lectures in the science of medicine as in other liberal arts, should begin to lecture in the morning immediately after the bell rang for mass in the diocese of St. George, and should be required to lecture for two hours or at least for an hour and a half, under penalty of 40 solidi of Ferrara for each offending doctor and as much for the rector who fails to collect the same, if it has come to his notice and he has not demanded payment. Those giving extraordinary lectures on the practice of medicine should lecture for two hours after the bell of the diocese of Ferrara rings. Those lecturing at Nones should similarly begin immediately the bell of St. George rings for Nones, or at the twentieth hour.[5] Lecturers in surgery ought to lecture at the nineteenth hour. Extraordinary lectures in philosophy and ordinary lectures in medical practice begin at the twenty-first hour; ordinary lectures in philosophy at the twenty-second hour. Those lecturing on moral philosophy should do so at the twenty-second hour on every feast day and every day when ordinary lectures are not given. The lecturer in astronomy should lecture every feast day and every day that ordinary lectures are not given or in vacations at the twenty-first hour, and this should be understood for the period to Easter. But from Easter till vacations he shall lecture an hour earlier.

Also, they decreed that no one could concur [6] with a doctor lecturing on astrology, either in lecturing or disputation, unless he gave the identical lectures in the same science and no others, under penalty of 40 solidi of Ferrara for each offender and each offence. Further decreeing that, in the case of other salaried doctors giving lectures, anyone who could lecture according to the statutes could concur at the same hour by giving the same lectures in the same subject. Also, they decreed that no doctor of whatever faculty could have another lecture for him, unless he had to leave the city of Ferrara to attend some patient to whose bedside he had been summoned, or unless prevented by his own illness or some other emergency, such as a marriage or

---

[5] It would seem that the twenty-four hours of the day were reckoned from sunset to sunset.

[6] A *concurrens* was one lecturing on the same subject at the same hour as his colleague.

death in his family. And in that case he should notify beforehand the rector then holding office, and, if he did so, could be excused and not otherwise, under penalty for each lecture omitted or not delivered by himself of 10 solidi of Ferrara, and the person lecturing for him should suffer the same penalty. And if any one of the doctors giving lectures should not have completed his lectures up to the feast of St. Mary in August, he should incur the penalty of loss of a sixth of his salary, to be retained in the hands of the Reformers, unless he had a good excuse.

144

DECREE AGAINST IGNORANT SCHOOL TEACHERS, FERRARA, 1443

JOANNES DE GUALENGIS AND THE BOARD OF WISE MEN, JULY 11, 1443

Borsetti, *Historia almi Ferrariae gymnasii*, I (1735), 50.

There exists at this time in this city a seminary of evil learning and ignorance. Our citizens desire to instruct their sons and their adolescents in good letters, and they are sunk in I know not what pit from which they can never extricate themselves. That is, certain barbarous teachers—who, far from knowing, never even saw, any good literature —have invaded our city, opened schools, and professed grammar. Citizens ignorant of these men's ignorance entrust their sons to them to be educated. They want them to learn and to graduate learned, but they learn those things which later they must unlearn. Lest this calamity and pest progress further, they decree that no one take scholars to train, nor hold a school, unless first he shall have demonstrated that he is acquainted with good literature or has been approved by the board of the Twelve Wise as suited to open a school. If anyone shall dare to do different, let him be ejected from the city as a pestiferous beast.

145

STUDENT AMUSEMENTS AND MERRY-
MAKINGS AT FERRARA, 1444

Borsetti, *Historia almi Ferrariae gymnasii*, I, 52–53.

Even from the foundation of our university we believe it to have been the custom that the students each year divert themselves sometimes from the daily round of studies to jocund and boyish pursuits. They turned to games and gala-making, especially either at the recurrence of Bacchanalia or when the rectors of the university assumed the cap which was the insignia of their dignity. For then the nations of students, from the contribution which they demanded annually from the lecturers for that purpose, were wont to celebrate either by dances or jousting, fighting for a prize, or banquets, or some such rejoicing. In pursuance, therefore, of this custom, on January 9, 1444, on occasion of the assumption of his cap by the new rector, the students in arts in the house of Niccolò Pasetti which was located in the street of Santa Maria Novella held a noble banquet and public dances. Nay more, having set up in the same street a wooden image of a man, which we call in the vernacular Bamboccio, they tilted against it with spears and gave a prize to the victor with applause from all the banqueteers and spectators.

146

HIRING A TEACHER OF GRAMMAR, 1444

CONTRACT OF THE COMMUNE OF TREVISO WITH
PHILIP, PROFESSOR OF GRAMMAR

Augusto Serena, *La cultura umanistica a Treviso nel secolo decimo-
quinto*, Venice, 1912, pp. 330–33.

In the year of the Lord 1444, the twelfth of the Indiction, Monday, March 24th, at Treviso in audience of the lords provisors of Treviso, there being present the doctors of laws, Guido de Lano and Zanandrea de Ursinico, and the noble man, Paul Casalorcio, and many other nobles and citizens convoked especially for the purpose to be stated, and others. The honorable and distinguished lords provisors of the commune of Treviso, namely, John de Vonico, Matthew de Mutonibus, and ser Christopher del Busco, in their names and the names of the other provisors by authority and consent of the magnificent and generous man, Carulus Marinus, honorable podestà and captain of Treviso for the most illustrious ducal dominion of Venice, in conformity with the action taken in the council of the lords provisors of Treviso and the council of citizens summoned by mandate of the said lord podestà and captain on the 25th day of January last, hired the famous and distinguished professor of grammar, Philip of Regio, there present and agreeing to teach boys and youths in the city of Treviso grammar and to lecture on poesy and rhetoric to all wishing to attend. Which lords provisors in the name and place of the commune of Treviso on one side, and the said Philip on the other, made and contracted pacts and conventions together as is contained in the following paragraphs. Videlicet:

That the said Philip is hired and is understood to be hired for five years beginning the first day on which he begins to lecture, giving him for salary one hundred ducats per year at the rate of five pounds, fourteen solidi per ducat. Which salary he receives in this wise, namely, 370 pounds from the commune of Treviso collected in pence, 150 petty pounds from the school of St. Mary de Batutis of Treviso, and fifty pounds from the college of notaries of Treviso.

Also, the said master Philip shall have from the commune a suitable place for holding school.

Also, he shall receive his salary every six months and always in advance.

Also, in the case of the payment from the school of St. Mary de Batutis he shall have half in wheat and wine and the other half in cash.

Also, if during this time a pest breaks out in the city of Treviso, which God avert, the said master Philip may leave the city of Treviso and live where he pleases within Trevisan territory during the time that pest afflicts the city, receiving for that period half pay only.

Also, that the said master Philip shall be exempt from all taxes and forced labor, real and personal, to which the citizens of Treviso are subject.

Also, that the said commune shall be required four months before the end of the said contract to notify master Philip whether it wishes to reengage him or not, and the conditions which he will be expected to fulfill towards the said commune.

Also, that the said master Philip should beyond the above stated salary receive every year for each pupil the following payments, namely, from the table [1] to beginning Donatus half a ducat, from beginning Donatus to beginning articles one ducat, from that point to the beginning of second Latin a ducat and a half, and from that point on two ducats, not including among these pupils foreigners coming from outside Trevisan territory. However, parents of other scholars shall be free to make their own arrangements with the said master Philip.

Also, the said master Philip is required to have a suitable assistant, and more, if it should be expedient.

Also, the school of St. Mary de Batutis may give master Philip or send to his school up to the number of twelve scholars without paying any salary.

Also, the said master Philip is required on feast days to lecture publicly on the art of oratory and such authors as his audience desire. And that the notaries attending on feast days or other days need make no payment.

Which provisions all and every one, the said lords provisors on one hand and the said master Philip on the other. . . do solemnly promise each other to maintain and observe and not violate, under penalty of fifty ducats for each offense to be paid by the offending party to the injured.

And on no less grounds may the present contract hold good. And to observe the aforesaid, the said provisors pledge to master Philip all the goods of the said commune, and conversely the said master Philip pledges all his goods to the said lords provisors accepting for the said commune.

And the magnificent lord podestà and captain of Treviso has accepted and approved the aforesaid and interposed his authority and decree on them all.

I, William son of the late ser Peter de Sancto Zeno, a citizen and inhabitant of Treviso, public notary by imperial authority and notary

---

[1] That is, the hornbook or alphabet.

and chancellor of the new chancelry of the commune of Treviso and the lords provisors in the district of Treviso, was present at the aforesaid and recorded them at the command of the said lord podestà and captain and provisors.

147

ABUSES AT THE UNIVERSITY OF PARIS, 1444

Chartularium universitatis Parisiensis, IV, 643.

On September 25, 1444 A.D., which was a Friday, a meeting of the faculty of arts was called by the rector in St. Julien as to making a reformation in the said faculty. And it pleased the nation of France to proceed to the said reformation. And for this purpose it appointed the following deputies, namely, those venerable and discreet men, master Jean François and Yvo de Ponte, deans of the provinces of Sens and Tours, Egidius Houdebin, Johannes Solerius, Victor Textor and Darianus Petri, together with me the proctor, Stephanus Nicolaus. And the nation willed that the future rector be required to swear to put through the said reform to the best of his ability.

Points to be reformed. First, that the scholars go from one house to another. Second, they make great feasts whence great inconveniences follow. Third, some buy up scholars and have their touts. Fourth, some lecture on the text of all logic, physics or metaphysics within two or three days' time. Fifth, as to conclave, forsooth, that a third supervening cannot withdraw.

148

FERNANDO OF CORDOVA, BOY-WONDER, COMES TO TOWN, 1445

Launoy, *Regii Navarrae gymnasii Parisiensis historia*, 1667, I, 157–58.

In the year 1445 there came to the Collège de Navarre a certain youth of twenty summers who was past master of all good arts, as the most skilled masters of the university testified with one accord. He sang beautifully to the flute: he surpassed all in numbers, voice, modes and symphony. He was a painter and laid colors on images best of all. In military matters he was most expert: he swung a sword with both hands so well and mightily that none dared fight with him. No sooner did he espy his foe than he would leap at him with one spring from a distance of twenty or twenty-four feet. He was a master in arts, in medicine, in both laws, in theology. With us in the school of Navarre he engaged in disputation, although we numbered more than fifty of the most perfect masters. I omit three thousand others and more who attended the bout. So shrewdly and cumulatively did he reply to all the questions which were proposed that he surpassed the belief, if not of those present, certainly of those absent. Latin, Greek, Hebrew, Arabic and many more tongues he spoke in a most polished manner. He was a very skillful horseman. Nay more, if any man should live to be a hundred and pass days and sleepless nights without food and drink, he would never acquire the knowledge which that lad's mind embraced. And indeed he filled us with deep awe, for he knew more than human nature can bear. He argued four doctors of the church out of countenance, no one seemed comparable to him in wisdom, he was taken for antichrist. Such are the quotations of Stephen Paschal, book V of *Disquisitions*, chapter 23, from a history in manuscript made by an eye witness.

Of this adolescent John Trithemius writes thus in his Sponheim Chronicle: "But as we write this, we recall Ferrandus of Cordova, who in the year 1445, a young gilded knight of twenty, doctor of arts, medicine and sacred theology, came from Spain to France with eight horses and stupefied the entire university of Paris by his marvelous science. For he was most learned in every faculty of the scriptures, most honorable in life and conversation, not proud and arrogant like him (of whom we were just speaking) but very humble and full of reverence. He knew the whole Bible by heart, also Nicholas of Lyra,[1] the writings of St. Thomas Aquinas, Alexander of Hales, John the Scot, Bonaventura and many others in theology. Likewise the *Decretum* and all the books of both laws, and in medicine Avicenna, Galen, Hippocrates, and Aristotle and Albertus and all the books of philosophy and metaphysics and commentaries he remembered to the nail, as the saying is. Finally, he read, wrote and understood perfectly Hebrew, Greek,

[1] A fourteenth-century commentator on the Bible.

Latin, Arabic and Chaldean. Sent to Rome by the king of Castile as orator, he disputed in all the universities of France and Italy, conquering all and being himself overcome by no one on the slightest point. There was a diversity of opinion concerning him among the doctors of Paris, some accusing him of being a magician and full of the demon, others thinking the contrary. Nor were those lacking who deemed him antichrist because of his incredible knowledge of scriptures, in which he seemed to excel all mortals."

149

CONDEMNATION OF THE FEAST OF FOOLS, PARIS, MARCH 12, 1445

LETTER AND FOURTEEN CONCLUSIONS OF THE FACULTY OF THEOLOGY OF PARIS TO PRELATES OF THE CHURCHES AGAINST THE FEAST OF FOOLS CELEBRATED ON THE EIGHTH DAY OF THE LORD'S NATIVITY OR THE FIRST OF JANUARY IN CERTAIN CHURCHES

Chartularium universitatis Parisiensis, IV, 652 *et seq.*

To all the prelates of the churches and their venerable chapters wherever constituted, the humble faculty of sacred theology of the dear university of Paris sends honor and the respect due to Christian piety. Zeal for divine worship and the clamor of many of the faithful, likewise the querulous complaint of certain prelates, induce and impel us to state in a brief letter how much we abhor and how much we detest that rite of a certain festivity which its celebrants call the Feast of Fools. And although from the testimony of holy writ, both of the Old and New Testament, in which God has commanded that His temple and ministers should be kept free from all taint and wholly sanctified, it would be very easy to condemn such a travesty on festivals, in which priests and clergy pollute themselves within and without, and foul the temple and churches of God; nevertheless because the supporters of this thing try to protect themselves by the law of custom and on that ground pertinaciously resist their superiors, there is need of greater and keener repression and such that the sharpness of correction shall break and overcome the contumacy of such pertinacity. Wherefore, we will briefly and succinctly declare what we feel in this matter, to the end that prelates may the more zealously and boldly expel this pestiferous rite from their subordinates, even by cautery of hard punishment, if need be.

And first, what we think of its origin. This taint certainly came from the Gentiles, and this festivity is a relic of theirs, although it may be entitled the Feast of Fools by its advocates.

The faculty then demonstrate that the Gentiles were superstitious and worshiped statues dedicated to demons. Princes, "thinking to deify themselves," erected idols like themselves to be worshiped, and instituted feasts on certain months and days to themselves to be celebrated by games after the desires of the flesh, on which days the priests reveled before others.

So on the first of May, the feast of Venus and Priapus, so in February the feast of Pluto and Persephone, so on the first day of January the feast of foulest Janus. . . . Only the wicked tradition of foulest Janus on New Year's Day has lasted until now and even in churches, in sanctified places and indeed by persons consecrated to God, on the eighth day of the Nativity of the Saviour, on which they ought to be wholly devoted to holiness.

And, I ask, whether all Christians who had any sense would not call evil those priests and clerics whom they see at the time of the divine office masked, with monstrous faces, or in the clothing of women or panders, or leading choruses of actors, singing shameful songs in the choir, eating rich morsels at the altar rail near the celebrant of the mass, shaking dice there, censing with foul smoke from the leather of old shoes and parading through the whole church, dancing, not blushing at their shame, and then going through the town and public places in chariots and base vehicles to infamous spectacles, making shameful gesticulations with their bodies to excite the laughter of the bystanders and those accompanying thèm, and uttering most immodest and scurrilous words? And the same way with many other abominations, which the mind is ashamed to recall and dreads to recite, which, nevertheless, as we have learned by faithful relation, were done this year in many places. What faithful and intelligent person, I ask, would not judge these ecclesiastics impious and cruel with respect to the honor of God, the decency of the church, and their own reputation? . . .

"But," they say, "we do those things in jest and not seriously, as has been the custom from antiquity, in order that the folly innate in us may escape and evaporate once a year. Would not wineskins and casks often break asunder, if their bungholes were not occasionally opened? We indeed are old bottles and half-broken casks, wherefore the wine of wisdom, fermenting overmuch, which we retain under pressure through the whole year in the service of God, would flow forth to no purpose, if we did not occasionally recreate ourselves with games and follies. Therefore, there should sometimes be an opportunity for jests, to the end that we may thereafter return the fitter for retaining wisdom." They say this and similar things, even aged men, participants in evil days, seeking an excuse for their sins; furthermore, young men, always eager for novelties and sports, applaud such monstrosities that provoke laughter. But men solicitous for their salvation think very differently from this.

The faculty opposes at length sound evangelical doctrine and good sense to these excuses of the ecclesiastics who allege long-standing custom in their defense.

Wherefore, O reverend fathers and honored prelates, hear the law of God and the saints by whom God has wrought wonders on earth, that they should be to us for an example and testimony of His will. Do not listen to the sly voices of men who speak thus; "Our predecessors who were thought notable men allowed this feast. It is enough for us to live as they did." Beyond doubt that argument is of the devil and that persuasion infernal. For you do not know the fate of those predecessors, whether it was good or evil. Therefore, do you follow those whom God by miracles declared should be followed. Do you follow the saints . . . ; do you follow many glorious bishops . . . ; do you follow the holy canons of the supreme pontiffs and general councils condemning these pastimes as pests of souls; do you follow further grave and devout persons who cannot see this wicked spectacle without grief.

This, O celebrated fathers, we beseech; listen and stretch every nerve in your power to dissipate and destroy this conglomeration of impiety. Nor let anyone's exemption or privilege delay or move you, for since in these cases there is vehement suspicion of heretical depravity, exemption should be allowed no one. . . .

Therefore we conclude our epistle, with the injunction that the continuation or abolition of this pestiferous rite depends on you prelates. For it is not probable that the clergy themselves would be so insane and obstinate in this madness but that, if they found the face of the bishop rigid and not to be turned from punishment, with the assistance of inquisitors of the faith and the aid of the secular arm, they would yield or be broken. For they would fear prisons, they would fear losing their benefices, they would fear losing their reputation, and being driven from the holy altars. Therefore, we pray God the Father in his mercy, that he give you the spirit of strength against these diabolical ministers and all pestilent men. Amen.

The fourteen conclusions which follow are not reproduced here, since they do little but repeat at length the points already made in the letter.

150

VIA ANTIQUA AND VIA MODERNA AT HEIDELBERG

Eduard Winkelmann, *Urkundenbuch der Universität Heidelberg,* 1886, I, 165, 173–74, 193.

Via Antiqua, or the ancient way, was the teaching of the older schoolmen such as Albertus Magnus, Aegidius Romanus, Aquinas, and Duns Scotus. The modern way, or *Via Moderna,* was the teaching of William of Ockham and his successors. In some German universities of the fifteenth century only one of these ways was taught and the other prohibited, but in the following legislation at Heidelberg we find both schools of thought tolerated and maintained simultaneously but separately. In our later Selection 158, entitled "Defense of Nominalism," the ancients are described as realists, while various representatives of the *Via Moderna* are listed as nominalists.

I. THE RECTOR OF THE UNIVERSITY OF HEIDELBERG, SEPTEMBER 16, 1452

To the members of our university, all and single:

We enjoin strictly that no one cast reflections on the *Via Antiqua* or the *Via Moderna,* or the authors of either of them, or make any unfavorable remarks which might border on vituperation of either of the aforesaid methods and their authors, under pain of imposition of a penalty by us according to the seriousness of the offense. In the same way we'forbid anyone to hinder scholars by word or deed from freely hearing and attending lectures or disputations of any master belonging to the faculty, whether he be in the *Via Antiqua* or *Moderna.*

Given under the seal of our Rectorate, September 16, 1452.

II. THE DECREE OF THE FACULTY OF ARTS, JULY 14, 1455

It was decided that a scholar transferring from one *Via* to another ought to have all the requirements for the degree for which he is working according to the *Via* in which he wishes to be promoted. That is to say, a scholar transferring from the *Via Moderna* to the *Via Antiqua,* if he wishes to be promoted in the same, should attend those lectures, exercises and examinations which are customary for the ancients, as if he had never heard any in the *Via* of the moderns, so that the formalities of the *Via Moderna* are not accepted in lectures or exercises or time for those wishing to be promoted in the *Via Antiqua.* The same holds true if anyone should transfer from the *Via Antiqua* to the *Via Moderna,* and to this end is the decree which the faculty wishes to confirm, which also has been decided by the university, and in which, if anyone has any question to raise, he should petition the university, and not the faculty. Also, it was decided that no dispensation should be granted to any bachelor who has petitioned for such in this matter on the ground that, wishing to be promoted in the *Via Antiqua,* he has heard only the books of *Physics* and the *De Anima* in part, although he may have heard the books . . . required in the *Via Moderna.*

III. DECREE OF THE FACULTY OF ARTS, SEPTEMBER 28, 1481

The faculty of arts willed, decreed and ordered that these books of *Ethics,* as well as the other books, should be lectured on in both *Viae* by masters of the same who have completed two years of teaching, this however specially added, that, if in one *Via* no one of the masters should be found qualified to lecture on the said books, then in the same year in which the master was lacking the bachelors of that *Via* by virtue of this statute are required actually and in effect to attend the lectures of a master of the other *Via* in order to complete their book, and let these two books be read among the first, each in its *Via*, unless one lecturer wishes to yield to the other.

151

A CASE OF VIOLENCE AND ACADEMIC DISCIPLINE, MONTPELLIER, 1455

Fournier, *Les statuts et privilèges*, II, 233–34, No. 1156.

To all who shall inspect, see and hear the present letters, Jacobus Angeli, master in arts and medicine, and chancellor of the venerable university of medicine of Montpellier, everlasting greeting in the Lord.

We make known by these presents that to us, gathered with the reverend masters of arts and professors of medicine teaching in the said university, Deodatus Bassolus, Nicolaus Caresmel, Antonius Angeli, Nicolaus Cadier, Robertus de Leone, Adam Fumee, Johannes Hervei, Raphael Calveti . . . the aforesaid Johannes Hervei signified tearfully that recently and within a few days a certain Emericus Roberti, alias de Solo, persuaded by diabolical suggestion, had rashly laid violent hands on the same master, even unto lesion of his face and head and no little shedding of blood, and in other ways had insulted the same master and dealt with him shamefully both by atrocious verbal abuse and·offensive acts.

And while the same master by himself and his friends was avenging these injuries, as justice demanded, and prosecuting the same Emericus at law for reparation for the same, the aforesaid master Nicolaus Caresmel . . . had received the same insulting offender, nourished him in his own house, and defended him in his iniquity, supplying him with wine, favor, aid and advice, and, what is worse to hear, the said Caresmel did all he could to prevent the same culprit from atoning for such nefarious insults and execrable offenses . . . and rashly received the said Emericus in his classes publicly . . . although by tenor of the statutes of the said university . . . and the tenor of the privilege conceded . . . by the papal legate and confirmed by the apostolic see, every master is required, if another master has a lawsuit either with disciples and scholars . . . or even with other persons, to support the same master in pursuit of his right, aid him, and offer force, counsel and aid with all his strength, and, as long as the suit with disciple or scholar shall last, no other master may dare receive that scholar or disciple in his classes. . . .

Having heard this we, desirous in the first place, as is right and reasonable, to settle such quarrels of masters amicably without noise and formal judgment, as far as we can, have summarily questioned the same Caresmel as to the truth of the matter and whether he provided favors, counsel and aid to the same offender, de Solo, and received him contrary to the statutes in his classes, even after having been duly informed of an offense of this sort, and further had failed to give counsel and favor to the complaining master. . . .

Caresmel straightway replied that it had not been and was not his intention to violate the statutes and privileges mentioned of the said university, nor to attempt anything in any way against them. Nay more, with humble supplication making submission, he requested us and the aforesaid college that, after careful deliberation, we should treat in the present meeting and otherwise, as the force of the same statutes requires, concerning observing them inviolate and punish not merely Caresmel himself but any others infringing the same statutes and privileges. . . .

. . . We have ordered that the same Caresmel, who perhaps under rigorous judicial procedure and the tenor of the said statutes would have been suspended for five years or a long time, should be deprived merely for one and the first distribution of a circle of the university of the honor and emoluments of this circle,[1] saving his practice of medicine, which we wish to be reserved for him. We further ordain that the same Caresmel pay for one candle of new wax and six pounds' weight [2] in honor of God and the blessed virgin Mary, unless his true humility and condign reconciliation with those offended induces us to order otherwise in this affair and deal more mildly. . . .

---

[1] In speaking of the university of Padua, Rashdall, I (1936), 219, note 1, says, "These 'circuli' seem to have been informal disputations or discussions among the students presided over by a doctor."

[2] In the Statutes of the university of medicine of 1340, article 50, (Fournier, II, 73) bachelors being examined for the master's degree are required to furnish two candles of twelve pounds' weight for light. But when the examination is over, they can dispose of what remains of the candles as they choose.

152

DISPOSITION OF CLASSROOMS IN THE LAW SCHOOL, AVIGNON, 1461

Fournier, *Les statuts et privilèges*, III (1892), 663–64.

September 23, 1461. Since there was a contention as to the auditorium or new great schools—in which the late James of Orléans, doctor of laws, lectured for seven months and a half or thereabouts, and which were then vacant in consequence of the decease of the said reverend father James—between the reverend fathers, Peter of Supervilla and Matthew de Damianis, and me, Christopher Bottini, doctors, finally the contention was ended and settled by the reverend father in Christ and lord cardinal de Foix, vicar and legate *a latere*, with the goodwill and consent of the doctors of our dear university, namely, the reverend fathers, Pontius de Sadone, bishop of Vaison, and John Payer, bishop of Aurac, I, Christopher Bottini, primicerius, Oliver Nobletus, vicar and vice-chancellor, Antony Amelhotus, George de Garonis, Peter of Supervilla, Peter de Lassonia, William Maynerius, Louis de Faretis, Matthew Damianus, and Louis Meruli, doctors both of civil and canon law then present in the gallery of the apostolic palace of the present city of Avignon, as follows below in a certain paper written by the hand of the aforesaid William Maynerius at the dictation of the reverend father in Christ the cardinal himself.

Let two lecture in the morning in canon law, namely, the bishop of Aurac and Arnaud Guillelmus; two in civil law, Peter of Supervilla in the auditorium which once was that of Antony Virro, and Christopher Bottini in the new auditorium which was once that of James Guilhotus of Orléans.

At the hour of vespers let two lecture in canon law, namely, Louis Meruli in the auditorium of the bishop of Aurac and William Rayer, licentiate in canon law who will become a doctor, in the auditorium of Arnaldus Guillelmus, and he shall lecture either on the *Liber Sextus* or the *Clementines*. In civil law at the same hour shall lecture Matthew in the auditorium of Christopher and Peter de Lassonia in the auditorium of Peter of Supervilla. And they shall lecture on the *Infortiatum* and *New Digest*, and no one else shall lecture at that hour.

Also, the aforesaid lecturing extraordinarily shall be regarded as

ordinary lecturers in the office of the primicerius and also in the announcement made by the bedell.

Also, if the said Supervilla and Bottini withdraw or die, Lassonia
and Matthew shall be admitted, if they wish, to the ordinary lectures
in the said auditoriums.

Also, the said bishop of Aurac and Arnaud Guillelmus shall be
able to delegate to fit and sufficient persons admitted by the primicerius
and the college of doctors, so that all the classrooms are at the disposition of the said primicerius and doctors.

153

AN EXAMINER CHANGES HIS VOTE,
FERRARA, 1465

Giuseppe Pardi, *Lo studio di Ferrara nei secoli XV e XVI*, 1903,
p. 266.

January 16 at Ferrara in the episcopal palace in the room of the lord
vicar.

Before lord Francesco (de Fiesso), vicar of the lord bishop, there
appeared lord Antonius Maria de Benintendis, doctor of arts and medicine, and said that he recalled his adverse vote which he had cast in
the approbation . . . of Zacharia de Zambotis, and he now gave his
affirmative vote.

On hearing this, the said lord vicar, in view of all the votes of the
others which were favorable, imposed and decreed that there be inserted by me (the notary) in the privilege of the same lord Zacharia
these words: "by unanimous vote" (*ipsorum nemine discrepante*).

154

MAGIC BOOKS CONDEMNED, PARIS, 1466

Du Plessis d'Argentré, *Collectio judiciorum de novis erroribus*, 1755,
I, ii, 256.

On October 28, 1466 A.D., the dear university of Paris gathered at
St. Mathurin to hear the reading of certain letters sent by our sov-

ereign lord the king. The royal letters were read publicly before the university, and there were brought in some books of the magic art belonging to master Arnoldus the astronomer, large and small volumes to the number of 27 or 28. The royal letters enjoined upon the dear university of Paris, as the mother and foundation of studies of Gallic religion, to examine these books as to whether they were consonant with the Christian faith and sound Christian doctrine. And to that end solemn deputies were appointed from every faculty and nation.

On November 10 of the year already noted, a meeting of the university of Paris was held at the church of St. Mathurin concerning three matters. First was heard the careful report of the deputies to examine the books of the late M. Arnold Desmarets which the king had submitted to the university, and the dean of Paris recited in the name of all the deputies what had been done.

On November 12, 1466 A.D., the dear university of Paris was gathered at St. Mathurin concerning the report of the deputies as to the books submitted to the university by our sovereign lord the king. And there was read a minute made by them to the effect that books of this sort contain many superstitions, many manifest and horrible conjurations and invocations of demons, many concealed heresies and manifest idolatries. Wherefore, it seemed good to the university, as mother of all studies, that these books be condemned and communicated to no one, and it chose as ambassador to send to the king a man to be cherished with all celebrity, our lord the dean of Paris, master Thomas de Corcellis, or should he be unable, that reverend man, master John Aubein.

155

DECREE AS TO LECTURES AND DIS-
CIPLINE, HEIDELBERG, 1466

Eduard Winkelmann, *Urkundenbuch der Universität Heidelberg,*
1886, I, 183, No. 124.

On the day of the Dispersion of the Apostles,[1] a meeting being held of masters of the faculty of arts to hear the report made on oath by

---

[1] That is, Festum Divisionis XII Apostolorum, on July 15.

its deputies, it was decided that masters giving formal lectures on these books, forsooth *Ars vetus*, the books of the new logic, and the *Physics*, should so lecture, at least on the first two of these, that every scholar might be able to take down the gist of them and also make an interlinear gloss. The same course should be followed by those lecturing before bachelors, especially on books studied in the colleges, namely, *Heaven and Universe, Generation and Corruption*, and *On the Soul*, under pain of losing their board. Similarly, that every scholar in lectures on the aforesaid books should have his own text which he should gloss, if he knows how to write.[2] If he does not know how to write, he shall pay careful attention in other respects, lest he annoy or impede the master or masters or scholars by clamor or insolence. Nor shall anyone compel any Freshmen to sing, or throw filth at them, under penalty of being set back.

156

AN ACADEMIC BANQUET

Borsetti, *Historia almi Ferrariae gymnasii*, 1735, I, 68, from the statutes, about 1467.

It is the custom in the faculty of arts on the day of the candidate's public examination either to hold a banquet or to pay a certain sum of money in its place, as to which in this statute the masters of the college and bedell are answerable. If a banquet is held, the following convivial laws are proposed for observance, to wit: that the said banquet be a formal one, but without any superfluous frills; that it should be attended only by the masters, baccalaureates, *biblici*, lecturers, masters of students with their students, excluding others even if they are related by blood to the candidate receiving his degree; that if anyone other than the aforesaid intrudes at the banquet, he shall be ejected from the same as a parasite by the master of ceremonies; finally, that all attending shall conduct themselves properly and soberly and eat what is set before them with silence and modesty under the penalties constituted for doing otherwise in the present sanction.

[2] Perhaps the meaning is, to write the very abbreviated Latin script commonly found in the manuscripts of this period, with its many signs in addition to the mere letters of the alphabet.

157

BIBLE STUDY AT HEIDELBERG, 1469

ORDER OF LECTURING ON BOOKS OF THE BIBLE
BY DOCTORS OF THEOLOGY, DETERMINED BY
THE FACULTY OF THEOLOGY THERETO
ASSEMBLED, JULY 20, 1469

Eduard Winkelmann, *Urkundenbuch der Universität Heidelberg*,
1886, I, 184–85, no. 126, in part.

Because the foundation of the catholic faith and the Christian religion
is recognized to consist in the texts of holy canonical scripture, therefore to give opportunity to the masters and scholars of the faculty of
theology to study in the same more fervently, completely and perfectly, and especially in those which are known to be more important
than others, the said faculty of theology, having held mature deliberation on the subject, has enacted, decreed and ordained that henceforth
the following order of reading the books of the Bible shall be observed
by its masters, in order that their hearers may receive greater fruits
from their lectures.

Also, that the three doctors now receiving salaries as ordinary professors in theology, and in like wise their successors, shall so proceed and
be held to proceed and lecture, namely, that one of them shall lecture
on the Gospels, finishing these in twelve years. Another shall lecture
on the Pauline and other canonical Epistles, together with the Apoca-
lypse, completing them in the same number of years, namely twelve.
The third one of them shall read the books of Moses or the Pentateuch,
or the major and minor prophets, in like manner, completing them in
the same number of years, namely twelve.

Furthermore, if there shall be above the said three masters one master or more masters in theology who desire to concur with these three
in lecturing, then the first of such (additional masters) ought to read
in the Old Testament the books of Moses in case they are not being
read by one of the aforesaid three ordinary professors, but if they are,
then let him lecture on the major and minor prophets, completing them
in twelve years. Moreover, in case there is a fifth master, let him lecture
on the Psalter in the same number of years, namely twelve. If there

should be still a sixth master, let him read the Books of Job and Solomon in the same number of years. . . .[1]

158

DEFENSE OF NOMINALISM

Du Plessis d'Argentré, *Collectio judiciorum de novis erroribus*, 1755, I, ii, 286–88.

The problem of universals had been a chief concern of medieval dialecticians since the days of Abelard. Those who regarded such abstract and collective terms as dog, beauty, justice as mere handy names were called nominalists. They held that only individual dogs, beautiful objects, and just actions actually existed. The realists, on the other hand, regarded such general concepts as true substances, although perhaps of an incorporeal and spiritual nature.

The following defense of nominalism was offered in connection with the edict of March 1, 1473–1474, by which Louis XI forbade the teaching of nominalism at Paris. The royal edict said: "It has seemed to us that the doctrine of Aristotle and his commentator Averroes, of Albertus Magnus, of St. Thomas Aquinas, Aegidius Romanus, Alexander of Hales, Scotus, Bonaventura, and other realists ought to be taught in the faculties of arts and theology as more useful than that of the new doctors, Ockham, Gregory of Rimini, Buridan, Pierre d'Ailly, Marsilius (d'Inghen), Adam Dorp, Albert of Saxony and other nominalists." The king therefore ordered that realism alone was to be taught at Paris henceforth, where all must take oath to observe the edict under penalty of receiving no degree and of exile.

The edict, however, was not long enforced. Already in 1476 seven books of dialogues by Ockham were printed. In 1481 the king allowed nominalism to be taught once more, and in 1482 the books of nominalists which had been seized were restored to their owners. The defense of nominalism follows:

Those doctors are called nominalists who do not multiply things that are principally signified by terms according to the multiplication

---

[1] The long years spent in these lectures on portions of the Bible recall Aeneas Sylvius's tale that Thomas of Haselbach spent twenty-two years explaining the first chapter of Isaiah. This was somewhat exaggerated, since Thomas actually spent from 1428 to 1431 on four chapters and from 1428 to 1460 on sixteen. Similarly Henry of Hesse at the university of Vienna took thirteen years on the first four chapters of Genesis.

of terms. Realists, on the other hand, are those who contend that things are multiplied with the multiplication of terms. For instance, nominalists say that deity and wisdom are one and the same, but realists say that divine wisdom is divided from deity.

Also, nominalists are called those who apply diligence and study to know all the properties of terms from which depend the truth and falsity of speech, and without which there can be no perfect judgment of the truth and falsity of propositions. These properties are *suppositio, appellatio, ampliatio, restrictio, distributio exponibilis*.[1] In addition they know obligations and insolubles, the true foundations of argumentation and dialectic, and all their defects. Instructed in which matters, they readily recognize what is good and bad in any argument. But the realists neglect and despise all these things, saying, "We attend to things; we don't care about terms." Against whom master Jean Gerson says, "While you go to things neglecting terms, you fall into ignorance of the thing." So far he in his treatise on the *Magnificat*, and he adds that the said realists involve themselves in inexplicable difficulties, when they seek difficulty where there is merely logical difficulty.

Among the nominalists the first to be condemned is said to have been William Ockham, whom John XXII persecuted, first because the said William Ockham took opposite sides from the pope on the heresy of the souls of the blest, which the same pope said would not see God face to face before the day of final judgment, and similarly he said that the souls of the damned would not suffer in hell before that day. And the said Ockham compelled the same pope to revoke his heresy. And against the same heresy he wrote a most beautiful treatise in which he most lucidly dissolved all the errors of the said John XXII and all his adherents. Furthermore, he wrote another treatise in which he collected some errors of the same John XXII regarding this.

A second reason why John XXII persecuted Ockham was because in his *Dialogue* he defended the royal authority by holy scripture and the utterances of popes and general councils and doctors of the church, showing by a powerful line of argumentation that the king of France

---

[1] *Suppositio* is probably used here in the sense of placing or classifying the term with reference to the tree of Porphyry; *ampliatio*, of referring the particular to the universal; *restrictio*, of the converse process.

had his kingdom directly from God and not from the pope, nor was subject to the pope in temporal matters, nor could the pope at will depose the king of France, nor could the kingdom be passed from people to people, as Boniface VIII had seemed to dogmatize in a certain Decretal which he promulgated on this point, asserting that it was necessary to salvation to believe that every prince of this world was fully subject both in spiritual and temporal matters to the pope. And the Decretal opens, "Unam sanctam. . . ."

For these reasons John XXII bestowed many privileges upon the university of Paris that it might condemn this doctrine of Ockham's. Yet the said university was unwilling to condemn it. But the faculty of arts, overcome by importunity, made a statute in which it enjoined that the said doctrine should not be taught because it was not yet approved and examined. And later it instituted an oath by which all swore not to teach the said doctrine in cases where it was contrary to the faith. And in the same book are noted four respects in which it is asserted that Ockham erred, none of which, as is evident to one reading them, is contrary to the faith. And the first article is found in none of his writings. Nay, he frequently held the contrary both in his logic and his theology. And so there is an error of fact, which is intolerable.

Also, the same pope ordered one of the cardinals to examine Ockham's doctrine. But although he raised many objections against Ockham, yet they found nothing that they dared to condemn. Nor did any condemnation result of the articles examined by that cardinal.

Next we read that the nominalists were expelled from Bohemia at the time when the heretics wished to infect the kingdom of Bohemia with their heresies, as is learned from the history of pope Pius which he wrote concerning Bohemia, so that when the said heretics could not prevail in disputation, they secured from Abbisseslas, prince of Bohemia, that the university of Prag should be governed by Parisian usage. By which edict, as the same author states, the said nominalists were compelled to leave the city of Prag, and migrated to Leipzig and there founded a most solemn university. After their expulsion the heretics disseminated their heresies through the kingdom of Bohemia.

At that time God so provided for the faith of his church that, while the university of Bohemia was following the Parisian usage, he raised up such catholic doctors as Pierre d'Ailly, Jean Gerson, and many other most learned nominalists, who, assembling at the Council of

Constance, to which were cited the heretics, notably Jerome (of Prag) and John (Hus), defended the faith of Christ and in a forty days' public disputation so overcame and confounded the said heretics that they admitted that they had been conquered by the arguments of Pierre d'Ailly.

A third persecution of the nominalists was after the killing of the duke of Orléans. For because of the wars which then intervened there were scattered through various regions and provinces the most learned men of the university and most erudite in the path of nominalism, through whose doctrines the said university had so flourished that it might well be called the light of the world. After this dispersion certain Albertists came in who, with no one to resist, ejected the doctrine of the nominalists. But afterwards, when the English had been driven out and this university began to flourish once more, it was filled with most ingenious men by whom the said doctrine of the nominalists was resuscitated and resumed, and, whatever the rivals of this path and truth may say, thereby gathered increments of praise and glory for twenty years even to the present day, as manifestly appears to all who judge rightly unaffected by favor, envy, or hate the fruits of this erudition and how much utility there is in these doctrines.

The fourth persecution is made in these days, namely 1473. For which there are three chief reasons. The first is the praise and glory of those who sweat at this doctrine. The second reason is that those who are called nominalists so triumph over some persons and especially the Thomists in disputation that these can in no way resist them and hence try to get rid of them entirely. The third cause comes from a heresy concocted at the university of Louvain. For a certain teacher at Louvain composed a treatise in which he denied certitude and divine prescience concerning contingents, asserting that propositions concerning the contingent future, even contained in the Bible and set forth by Christ, were not true. This treatise, full of these heresies, the university of Louvain approved and sent its promoter to Paris to solicit the faculty of theology to approve the said treatise. When many doctors of the said faculty were favorable to him, and those especially who are intent on the extermination of the doctrine of nominalists, those who are called nominalists objected and opposed this strongly, fearing no peril for the defense of the faith, and they prevented the faculty of theology from approving the said treatise. Those who are called realists took this very hard and to the number of twenty-four subscribed to the said treatise and approved it.

Moreover, the author of this treatise was cited before the apostolic see being accused by master Henry de Zomeren, a doctor of Paris among the nominalists most learned, and having set out for Rome to defend himself, alleged his reasons, causes and motives, and produced in his justification the signatures of the twenty-four doctors of Paris, namely, Petrus de Vaucello, Rolandus le Couzich, Johannes Boucart, Guillelmus de Castroforti, Guillelmus Boville, Petrus Caros, Johannes Cossart, etc.

Their support notwithstanding, the said Louvain composer of the treatise was condemned and his treatise declared heretical. Because of which condemnation the said approvers of these heresies were moved with anger and hatred to disturb, molest, and harass the defenders of the faith.

Moreover, after these signatures had been obtained, a regent in arts at Paris from somewhere in Germany publicly sustained these Louvain heresies in the street of Straw, asserting that Christ could not be telling the truth when He said to Peter, Thou wilt deny me thrice. And when he was accused before the faculty of theology of having called Christ a liar, he was defended by the doctors who had approved the said heresies from Louvain.

As for that which is alleged against the nominalists, that their science is perverse and full of heresies, first it is replied that in those matters which concern nominalism and realism the position of the nominalists is always more in conformity with the faith and frequently approved by the church, while the position of the realists is precarious and reproved in many things by the church, as is plain in the matter of universals concerning the eternity of propositions and the multiplying of entities without cause.

It is answered in the second place that, in matters pertaining to nominalism and realism, the nominalists without comparison err less than others, and always for one error found in the doctrine of the nominalists, if any are found, four or five are shown in the doctrine of the realists. And the nominalists offer themselves to prove this.

Nevertheless we do not wish to say that the nominalists are wholly immune from errors. "For if we say that we have no sin, there is no truth in us." For neither can the Thomists assert this concerning St.

Thomas, against whom while still living many articles were drawn up at Paris, against whose errors in the name of the faculty of theology a treatise was composed and sent to Rome. Nor can the followers of the *Sentences* assert this of master Peter Lombard, since there are commonly listed against him twenty-six articles in which he is not to be followed. But we will say that among all doctors they erred least and followed the truth of the faith more integrally than others, which will be evident if the propositions against them are published. For it will be shown that many of them are contained in the doctrines of realism and that none or very few of them are erroneous.

159

A SALARY LIST, 1474

Borsetti, *Historia almi Ferrariae gymnasii*, 1735, I, 93–96.

List of salaries which this commune of Ferrara ought to pay on October 18, 1474, to all the doctors and scholars whose names are written below, who are lecturing and have lectured in this university of Ferrara, and to each of them for the amounts and quantity written below. To them and to each of them mentioned and listed for their salaries or stipends for having lectured in this dear university of Ferrara one whole year, beginning on the Feast of St. Luke of the month of October, 1473, and ending on the Feast of St. Luke of the present year 1474. And after the names of the doctors and scholars is given the amount for each, namely:

Canonists and Jurists	Lire
To magnificent Messer Giacomo de Argentina, rector of the said canonists and jurists, for his provision, according to custom	120
To Messer Alberto Trotto for the ordinary morning lecture in canon law three hundred and fifty lire	350
To Messer Filin Sandeo for the ordinary morning lecture in canon law three hundred and fifty lire	350
To Messer Domenego de Bertolin for the aforesaid ordinary lecture three hundred lire	300

To Messer Ludovico Pauluzo for the aforesaid ordinary lecture three hundred and fifty lire — 350

To Missier Antonio dai Liuti for lecturing on the *Liber Sextus* and *Clementines* one hundred and fifty lire — 150

To Missier Antonio di Vincenzi for the aforesaid lecture on the *Liber Sextus* and *Clementines* one hundred and fifty lire — 150

To Messer Antonio da Quieto d'Arzenta for lecturing on canon law on feast days thirty lire — 30

To Messer Augustin di Bonfrancischi for lecturing on civil law on feast days four hundred and fifty lire — 450

To Messer Zohane Maria Riminaldo for the ordinary morning lecture on civil law five hundred lire — 500

To Messer Ludovigo Bolognin for the said ordinary morning lecture six hundred lire — 600

To Messer Alberto di Vicenzi for the said lecture on civil law three hundred and fifty lire — 350

To Messer Zohane Sadoletto for the said lecture on civil law five hundred lire — 500

To Messer Boetio di Silvestri for the extraordinary lecture on civil law one hundred lire — 100

To Messer Federigo da Lugo for the said extraordinary lecture on civil law one hundred lire — 100

To Messer Cosma di Paxiti for lecturing on the *Institutes* one hundred and twenty-five lire — 125

To Messer Alphonso de Marcho Galeotto for lecturing on the said *Institutes* one hundred and twenty-five lire — 125

To Messer Hellia Bruza for lecturing on the *Ars notaria* sixty lire — 60

To Messer Zohane Andrea Torexella for the extraordinary lecture on civil law fifty lire — 50

To Messer Lodovigo da Valenza for the said extraordinary lecture on civil law fifty lire — 50

To Messer Nicolò da Pexaro for the said extraordinary lecture on civil law fifty lire — 50

To Messer Zohane Andrea d'Arzenta for lecturing on canon law on feast days twenty-five lire — 25

To Messer Michiel Costanzo for lecturing on civil law on feast days twenty-five lire — 25

Artists, Philosophers, and Physicians

To master Messer Ruberto di Girardin da Lendenara, rector
of the artists for his provision according to the custom   100

To master Frà Zohane da Ferrara of the Order of Preachers
for lecturing on the Bible on feast days   50

To M. Orazio di Zirondi for the ordinary morning lecture in
medicine   600

To M. Francesco Benzo for the aforesaid ordinary morning
lecture   800

To M. Girolamo da Castello for lecturing on the practice of
medicine   500

To M. Girolamo di Zirondi for the said lecture on the practice
of medicine   500

To M. Girolimo Nigrixollo for the morning lecture on medicine two hundred and fifty lire   250

To M. Zanfrancesco Sandeo for the aforesaid morning lecture
on medicine two hundred lire   200

To M. Mattio del Brun for the extraordinary lecture on the
practice of medicine one hundred and thirty lire   130

To Mr. Zacharia Zambotto for the aforesaid lecture on practice, as above, one hundred lire   100

To M. Baptista d'Arzenta for the aforesaid lecture on practice, as above, one hundred lire   100

To M. Ludovigo dai Carri for the ordinary lecture in physics
and metaphysics two hundred and fifty lire   250

To M. Nicolò de Girardin de Lendenara for the ordinary lecture in physics two hundred and fifty lire   250

To M. Antonio Benintendi for the ordinary lecture in physics
one hundred and fifty lire   150

To M. Antonio da Faenza for the aforesaid extraordinary
lecture in physics one hundred and thirty lire   130

To M. Bortolomio da Roma for lecturing on surgery one
hundred lire   100

To M. Zohane da Parma for the aforesaid lecture on surgery
one hundred lire   100

To M. Piedrobon del Avvogaro for lecturing on astrology two
hundred lire   200

To M. Nicolò da Lonigo da Vincenza for lecturing on moral
philosophy two hundred lire   200

To M. Jacomo de Piamonti for lecturing on logic in the morning one hundred and twenty lire   120

To M. Palmerin da Piaxenza for the aforesaid lecture on logic
in the morning one hundred lire   100

To M. Antonello dal Sagrà for lecturing on logic at noon one
hundred lire   100

To M. Zohanbaptista da Canan for the aforesaid lecture on
logic at noon fifty lire   50

To M. Corradin de Gilino for lecturing on medicine on feast
days twenty-five lire   25

To M. Francesco Camazarin for lecturing on logic on feast
days thirty lire   30

To M. Lucha da Ragusa for the aforesaid lecture on logic on
feast days twenty-eight lire   28

To M. Ludovigo Carbun for lecturing on rhetoric and Greek
four hundred and fifty lire   450

To M. Baptista Guarin for the aforesaid lecture on rhetoric
and Greek five hundred lire   500

To Don Baptista del Bello of the company of bell-ringers of
the diocese of Ferrara for ringing the bell   23

160

A LETTER FROM PLAGUE-STRICKEN AREZZO
TO A LAW STUDENT AT BOLOGNA

THE ABBOT JEROME ALIOTTI TO ANTONIO
DE GERIIS, 1479

Hieronymi Aliotti . . . Epistolae et Opuscula, Arezzo, 1769, ed.
G. M. Scarmalius, II, 137.

Ever festive and memorable to me has been the day of the most
blessed abbot Antony. But your most ornate letters which were delivered to me on that day rendered it even more joyful and festive
than usual. For you so apply yourself to the study of law that you

seem to imitate those ancient jurisconsults who combined knowledge of law with culture and to follow in their footsteps. As regards our city's calamity, it is incredible to state how many citizens, especially heads of families, have died of this pestilence. It was a deplorable spectacle, it is now again, to see at one and the same time the cruelty and truculence of foemen in the fields [1] and the wrath of God raging through the town. Your parents and brothers and sisters and little nephews are so far keeping well. Of the death of John Gerius I believe you have heard. The wind and cold of winter have been able to check the virulence of the pestilence in part, but we fear lest with the spring and summer it may revive and disseminate its poison once more. For it is now three years since this pest began to rage, so that we do not feel secure or even safe for the future. Besides, we are anxiously expecting a siege of the town, so that, implicated in so many and so harsh evils, I deem blest you and our other countrymen who are absent at this calamitous time. Since therefore it is not possible to write you any cheerful news, I have thought it well to be as brief as may be.

Farewell. At Arezzo, January 17, 1479.

161

LATIN TO BE USED RATHER THAN FRENCH, ORLÉANS, 1484

STATUTE OF THE PROCTOR OF THE GERMAN NATION

Fournier, *Les statuts et privilèges*, I (1890), 249.

Petrus Jacobi of Arlon (in the diocese of Trèves), bachelor of both laws, proctor of the most splendid German nation, summoned to court by the Picards because of a member of our nation whom they were plotting to claim as theirs, although by Hercules they had no legal remedy, I responded. Moreover, they tried (what will seem to learned men incredible to relate) to have me, who have had nothing to do with that language, set forth the defense of our nation in

---

[1] In connection with the wars of Sixtus IV against Florence.

the French tongue at a meeting and conference of most learned men, abandoning the Latin language, or else reply silently through an advocate contrary to every legal form. All which I brought to the attention of the meeting and obtained an interlocutory opinion of the lords that I should employ Latin. Wherefore, I urge and warn all proctors of our nation that, when occasion for this sort of nonsense arises, if they believe their case should be set forth to others, they shall not disgrace our dear nation, which often has offered potent prayers by most eloquent scholars, by preferring French to that milk of the Latin word, especially in the college of our dear university in which there is no one, at least in his right mind, who does not know that this should by no means be done.

The outcome is in doubt!

Petrus Jacobi of Arlon.

162

REGULATION OF THE BEJAUNIUM OR FRESHMAN PAYMENT, VALENCE

SECTION XVI OF THE UNIVERSITY STATUTES, 1490–1513

Fournier, *Les statuts et privilèges*, III (1892), 395.

In accordance with the tenor of statutes already published and in force we have decreed and do ordain that nobles maintaining the state of nobles and others with fat benefices, newly arrived at our university to study law, canons or other faculties, shall be required and ought to pay for their jocund advent three florins in current money, nor may more be demanded of them except what they may freely donate. Other nobles moderately well off shall be required and ought to pay two florins, but the rest one, and that within a month. But from the poor nothing shall be demanded. Which moneys are to be turned to relieving the burdens of the university, not to superfluous and harmful banquets, in which there is no acquisition of knowledge and from which many scandals arise. And from those frequent banquets it was once found that many and varied and nefarious scandals arose among the scholars, so that scholars newly arrived withdrew from the university because of the improper and insulting things which were said and done to them, when they could not pay so much money. All which we order to cease now and forever.

163

THE STUDENTS OF INGOLSTADT TO CONRAD CELTES

Latin text edited in *Serapeum*, 1870, p. 259, by Ant. Rutland.

Celtes (1459–1508), one of the younger German humanists or "poets," taught poetry and eloquence at Ingolstadt in 1492, 1494, and 1497.

By your long and incessant scoldings, with which you frequently consume half the hour, you force us to make some reply in the name of truth. You accuse us of madness and charge that we are stupid barbarians, and you call wild beasts those whose fees support you. . . . This we might have borne with better grace, but for the fact that you yourself abound in the faults of which you accuse us. For what of the fact that, while you carp about us, you yourself are so torpid from dissipation that in private conversation your drowsy head droops to your elbow like a figure eight. You touch on many points in questions, but you speak neither plain argument nor cultured speech nor elegant Latin expositions; nor do you observe true coherence and order of speaking. Yet you have at hand the motto, "He teaches clearly who understands clearly." Either you lack understanding—a shameful thing in a doctor—or you think us unworthy of your learning, which is incredible. For you certainly experience daily studious auditors, sometimes learned men, calculated to adorn you with great praise. Or you dislike the labor of lecturing, as we clearly comprehend, understand and see. In this one point you both derogate from your own reputation and seem to us all deficient. But now we have clearly expressed ourselves on that point. Wherefore, if you are ready and willing to vindicate the name and dignity of a preceptor and doctor, to fulfill your professorial duties, we will be more attentive. If first, as befits you, you clear yourself of the fault you impute to us, you will make us more diligent by your diligence, which has now long been lacking, if you can conquer and overcome your dislike of study and tardiness in work. If you do less, we shall have to take more stringent measures.

164

REGULATION OF SCHOOL TEACHERS, 1494

FROM THE STATUTES OF THE FACULTY OF ARTS, UNIVERSITY OF ANGERS

Fournier, *Les statuts et privilèges*, I (1890), 431–32.

And first it was decreed that one wishing to hold a school should be a master of arts, mature, prudent and discreet.

Also, it was decreed that every schoolteacher compel his scholars to speak Latin both at play and work, and especially in commonplaces.

Also, that no one be allowed to hold a school unless he has scholars who can dispute together and make a satisfactory exercise.

Also, that in every school disputations be held twice a week with daily reviews and other exercises.

Also, that in every school there be at least two teaching masters, one in logic and the other in philosophy, who in the aforesaid exercises and disputations may offer the scholars a model and guidance.

Also, that the headmaster accustom his scholars to rise and salute the masters and humbly obey them.

Also, that no teacher fraudulently steal away the scholars of another either by his own or another's action.

Also, that no breach of discipline be permitted among the scholars, but the teacher, without dissimulation in the sight of all, shall take note of offenders as the case requires.

Also, let teachers beware lest their scholars be truants or leave the house without permission, and see to it that they do not soil their clothing or books in untimely and superfluous feasting and games, but stay indoors especially as it grows dark.

Also, that on Sundays and holy days the teacher send them in order to low mass in the morning before breakfast and then to high mass and others, if the feast calls for this.

Also, that on the chief feasts of the year, and especially at Easter,

Pentecost, Assumption, All Saints, Christmas, and the beginning of Lent, he exhort and induce them to confess their sins and send them to church to confess.

Also, it was decreed that, when there shall be a sermon to the clergy in the faculty of theology, they shall be required to send them there in order by themselves or with some one of their masters, and likewise to solemn actions of the faculty of arts, and that on such occasions they shall be seated and walk two by two going and returning.

Also, it was decreed that scholars of this sort should not be sent to the fields without a master to lead them and bring them back, to keep them together and control them and keep an eye on them all, and they should go and return two by two especially through the town.

Also, that these teachers should not permit any scholar of theirs to undergo an examination for any degree, unless they believe him sufficiently prepared and able to obtain the degree, but should exhort and warn him not to subject himself to such an examination lest he chance to be failed and so brought into disrepute.

Also, it was decreed that in points not here specified we should follow the statutes of the university of Paris as far as possible.

Also, it was decreed that no teacher or instructor in arts or even in grammar may receive the scholars of another instructor or teacher, whether they are students in arts or even in grammar, for any reason without the consent of the headmaster of the house or school, which consent he shall be required to manifest to the person to whom the said scholar shall go by a note signed with the sign manual of the preceding master.

Also, it was decreed that no master or instructor should receive anyone as a student in grammar by making a deal for less than the usual price, which is twenty solidi of Tours, unless there be several of the same family or a case of evident poverty.

Also, it was decreed that no master of any school shall receive the guide or tutor of young students or those in arts, unless the tutor himself is studying in the faculty of arts or has the degree of master in the said faculty and is of its bosom.

Also, it was decreed that whoever of the teachers shall have done contrary to the aforesaid should *ipso facto* be deprived of all honor and emolument as a teacher.

165

LECTURE COURSE IN ETHICS

FROM THE NEW STATUTES OF THE FACULTY OF ARTS AT CAEN, 1495

Fournier, *Les statuts et privilèges*, III (1892), 255.

It has seemed best that the lectures in ethics should be given not by houses, because the faculty would lose the liberty of election, but duly by election by the masters, giving instruction or not, in the assembly of the same faculty duly convoked by the bedell and terminated by the dean, so however that no one henceforth be named, elected, assumed or established in the office of this lectureship except a master actually giving instruction and who has taught and completed two full courses in the said faculty and university, and has received the degree at least of bachelor in one of the higher faculties.

It is further decreed and ordained that no one henceforth shall be appointed to this position of lecturer in ethics for more than a year, so that he shall be able to exercise the said lectureship for a year only, in which year he shall be required to lecture in the public schools on five books of the *Ethics* and on feast days and those for extraordinary lectures at the seventh hour in the morning in winter, that is from the feast of St. Denis to Annunciation Sunday, but from the latter feast till the end at the sixth hour of the morning.

And the following lecturer shall cover the other five books, and so on alternately with the others who are installed in this office. Which lecturer for his stipend and pay shall receive seven solidi and a half from every scholar taking a degree for one year spent under him. And that scholars in the future may have greater reason and occasion for proficiency in moral philosophy, which is especially useful to youths, their respective teachers shall be required to go over the same books of moral philosophy with their scholars in their own house and to ensure in this way that the said scholars have heard the text of the moral philosophy with its commentary in their school or private houses before it is lectured on publicly by the public lecturer. And lest those teachers have nothing for their pains, they shall receive an extra two and a half solidi from each scholar of theirs. And thus they will have in all as much as the public lecturer, namely, seven solidi and a half. . . .

Writing a few years later, Pierre de Lesnauderie, a doctor of laws and syndic of the university, in his *Brief Compendium Concerning the University of Caen,* says (*ibid.,* p. 279):

There was in times past a general and public lecturer in ethics who was elected on the first day of lectures after Easter. And he continued his lectures for two years, receiving no small salary. But because of the excesses committed in this election it was abandoned and a new statute made that in each college some teacher of arts who had taken two courses and the degree in a higher faculty should give a special lecture to the scholars, from whom at the end of the course he should receive a moderate stipend for his labor. So nevertheless that lecturing in turn they take their scholars to the public schools and make the accustomed lecture there.[1]

166

INSPECTION OF UNIVERSITY BUILDINGS, HEIDELBERG, 1512

Eduard Winkelmann, *Urkundenbuch der Universität Heidelberg,* 1886, I, 208–9, No. 154.

The university willed that each year within a fortnight after the Feast of Passover the rector then in office should be required by order to visit the buildings of the university as specified below.

In each visitation there should be present the rector then in office and the dean of the faculty of arts, together with the person ranking next to the dean in the university council, also the bedell of the university should be required to attend with two workmen deputed for this purpose.

Further, the workmen in visiting the buildings should be required by oath faithfully to observe without deceit or fraud what needs to be done in the roof, walls, rain spouts and latrine, that they reveal

---

[1] For a similar situation at Paris see Robert Goulet, *Compendium of the University of Paris,* 1517, English translation by Robert Belle Burke, 1929, page 62: "The Abolition of the Public Lecturer on Ethics owing to the excesses and murders committed in the election of this officer who received no trifling stipends."

what they have observed and that they shall not accept drink in the building they visit so that all suspicion may be removed.

As for the salary to be given to the two workmen, it was decided that each year the rector of the university then in office should pay both from the treasury and should be obliged at the time of visitation to give each five solidi of Halle per day, even if the visit takes them only one hour.

Notice should be given of the time of visitation by the rector through the bedell two days beforehand to those who are to make the visit so that they may not excuse themselves through ignorance.

The bedell of the university shall be present at the visitation and make a faithful record in the university book of the statements of the workmen and others. For his labors he shall be given a quarter of a florin.

If he shall have neglected the inspection or minimized it, and at the end of a year shall not have obeyed the orders of the rector and his fellow deputies, he shall be subject to the penalty laid down by the university; also, saving the right of his successor, if he shall have died during the year, all complaint and action against him under pretext of preserving the building shall cease.

In the same session it was decreed that the following buildings should be visited, forsooth, the classrooms and auditoriums of the ordinary doctors of theology, law and of the college of medicine; of the three theologians, the house of the ordinary professor of Decretals, if he shall have a house from the faculty of law, the house of the ordinary lecturer on new laws and the ordinary lecturer in medicine opposite the monastery of the Franciscans and the house which is now in the possession of the licentiate, Johann Linke.

167

A WOOD FIRE FOR THE THEO-
LOGICAL STUDENTS

Launoy, *Regii Navarrae gymnasii Parisiensis historia*, 1667, I, 240–41.

In 1515 William Crassus, a canon and dean of Rouen, having noticed that the theological students of the College of Navarre had no supply of wood for the public fireplace during winter, provided the rent of certain islands in the Seine for the purchase of wood for a fire for all, immediately after dinner and supper, from the Kalends of November to the Easter holidays.

The fellows approach the fire, arrange themselves about it in a semicircle, and engage in familiar conversation. The time allowed for warming themselves is a half hour, which terminated, each withdraws to his cubicle and studies theology.

The sole obligation attached to the fellows was to recite for Crassus after dinner the 66th Psalm opening, *Deus misereatur,* and the prayer, *Retribuere digneris,* and after supper the 129th Psalm opening, *De profundis.*

168

DECREE CONCERNING QUODLIBET DISPUTATIONS, 1518

Eduard Winkelmann, *Urkundenbuch der Universität Heidelberg,*
1886, I, 211–12, No. 158.

The dean of the faculty of arts of the university of Heidelberg.

We order, strictly commanding the honorable masters, bachelors and other alumni of our same faculty, that no one of them henceforth, if about to respond in a quodlibetical disputation now imminent, shall propose or bring forward, as has often been the case in former years, questions of little importance which are also commonly called *facetiae* or "salts," shameful, lascivious and impudent, which by their allurements may attract or provoke the religious and innocent youth ignorant of sexual matters, or any others, to unseemly or illicit lust, under severest penalty to be inflicted by the faculty on each transgressor.

Given on August 24th 1518 under the seal of our deanship.

169

EDUCATION OF JOACHIM CUREUS AT WITTENBERG, PADUA AND BOLOGNA, 1554–1558

Narratio historica de vita et morte viri summi Ioach. Curei Freistad. Sil. philos. et medici clarissimi in inclyta urbe Glogoviensi scripta a V. Cl. Ioan. Ferinario Academiae Marpurg. professore historico Curei dum viveret familiarissimo, Lignicii edita sumtibus ampliss. V. dn. Ant. Schultzii ill. pr. Ligio-Breg. Consiliarii, A.c.MDCI, fol. (C 4) *et seq.,* reprinted by C. F. Heusingerus, *Comm. de J. Cureo summo saec. XVI medico theologo philosopho historico,* Marburg, 1853, p. 48 *et seq.*

On July 31, 1554, the degree of master of philosophy was publicly conferred on Cureus by the most illustrious and eminent dean of the philosophical college, Caspar Peucer, (a man justly most famous in church and state to all posterity and never praised enough), who proposed to him, when he was heard in private examination, a passage of Lucan from the colloquy of Pompey with the sailor, "Quae sit mensura aequoris in caelo?" [1] Also the 32nd proposition of the first book of Euclid. He then offered two writings to the examiners: the first in Latin, a history concerning the nature and examples of the virtues which are seen in bees; the other in Greek, a history of Sanseverino, prince of Naples not long before our time who, since he excelled in military virtue by employing an ingenious stratagem, escaped, as Pontano tells, the toils of the Arabs when he set out for the Holy Land. Melanchthon approved especially of this narration and said that the style resembled that of Xenophon, that most praiseworthy little Attic bee. . . .

While teaching school in his native town of Freistadt, Cureus prepared himself for subsequent medical studies by reading the *Philonium* of Valescus de Taranta and making an outline of the more recent works of Montanus and Fernel. In September, 1557, he set forth for Italy.

The best doctrine is that by word of mouth, and the living voice has

[1] *Pharsalia*, VIII, 168.

a latent energy, nor, as he said, is there a readier way of learning than to listen to artists. At Padua therefore, where there is a school well constituted from ancient times till now, he attached himself to the most eminent philosophers and medical men of that time who were there. Victor Trincavella of Venice, an old man of rare learning who, Cureus thought—and many others agreed with him—was the best medical man of all then living. He taught Avicenna on fevers, after that Rasis on affections of the head and thorax. In his extraordinary lectures he treated of worms and arthritis. His *concurrens*, that is, he who covered the same subjects at the same hour, was Antonius Francanzanus of Vicenza, also a learned man, but Trincavella had supreme skill in the humanities and perfect knowledge of the old medical writers, Greek and Arab. Francanzanus nevertheless, who drew young men to himself by a marvelously pleasant way of speaking, was the more popular. Two taught Theory in the morning at the same time, ordinary professors as they call them, Odus ab Odis [2] of Perugia, a talkative old man of an illustrious family who was *concurrens* to Montanus. Then there was Bassianus Landus of Piacenza, very well versed in the philosophy of Aristotle and in the books of Galen, ready in his Latin, and most attentive to method in his lectures. He succeeded his teacher Montanus and later was attacked by cutthroats and strangled. . . . Cureus expressed his debt to him for clever explanations of many matters, chiefly philosophical. At that time both of them taught the *Aphorisms* of Hippocrates and then the *Ars (parva)* of Galen. Next there were three *concurrentes* who were called ordinary professors of Practice. First was Aloisius Bellocatus of Brescia, very skilled in medical practice, physician of a large part of the city, a man of advanced years, humane and good. Second, Apelatus, also a good and learned man. Third, Hieronymus Cappivaccius, a youth who aspired to a higher place and solid erudition and was industrious. The Germans heard him with avidity. But our friend, looking at Practice from a correcter point of view, as I think, preferred Bellocatus as a most experienced physician. In the third place was the sole lecturer on tumors, surgery and botany, Gabriele Falloppia of Modena, ready, ingenious, industrious, and a very successful teacher and practitioner. Hardly anyone else in the university then was more helpful to the students, who were very fond indeed of him. About Advent the usual

[2] More commonly spelled Oddis.

lectures of the first quarter of the year ceased and anatomies were held until Christmas. That year therefore Falloppia was very busy. For he dissected seven human bodies and brutes of all sorts.

A certain Dominican taught theology, a man of great dignity, resourceful, ready and, as it appeared, not ignorant of truth. Sometimes he so qualified the conclusions of the students that in reality he denied and overthrew them. His *concurrens* was a Minorite of the college of St. Antony, very talkative. They lectured on the *Sentences*. Two monks, too, commented upon the *Metaphysics* of Aristotle, one a Dominican, a youth of great ability, a follower of St. Thomas like all of his Order. The other, Jacobinus Bargius, a Minorite of the Antonian college, a bent old man, dry, humble, talkative, very well versed in Aristotle and the writings of the Schoolmen, with a memory nothing short of miraculous, adroit in teaching, clear-headed and very facetious, a Scotist like all in that sect. Cureus attended his lectures assiduously not without profit and so became fairly familiar with scholasticism. But the chief of all the philosophers was Antonius Passerus of Genoa whom they called Jenoa. All Italy worshiped him as a god, and there was no auditorium more august than his, since the most noble and powerful men attended his lectures—bishops and counts in great number and among the first the Venetian nobility. He was then lecturing on Aristotle, *De anima*. Our hero said that he was indebted to him especially, because he was imbued by him with a knowledge of the true Aristotelian philosophy. Concurrent with him was Abracius, learned indeed but not his like. We have indulged in this reminiscence, neither useless nor unpleasing, so that young men fond of learning might know what Italian universities are like and under what doctors Joachim studied philosophy and medicine, in order that he might not easily yield to anyone in Germany.

At first Cureus did not relish Italian food and longed for German stove-heated rooms, for some days was very homesick, and finally clean broke down, sick in body and mind. But the lectures and Italian cleanliness soon restored him to health. On the sail to Padua he composed a poetical complaint on exile, suggested by the flight of Christ to Egypt. At Padua, before the lectures started, he wrote some Italian epigrams in Latin verses. Through the winter despite the cold he began to read the works of Galen and, along with his other exercises and classes, to review his medical reading of previous years.

Then, fired by a great desire to hear and learn, he visited Bologna, the mother of universities, where magnificent palaces of the nobility are to be seen on every hand, and the nobility itself is interested in the humanities and hospitable to foreigners. There then, too, he followed the courses of illustrious, successful and much experienced physicians, Benedictus Victorius of Faenza, quite an old man, Helidaeus Ferolinenses, who knew many good medicaments, and Aldrovandi,[3] a humane man, who was dean or prior, as they call it, of the medical college, a most zealous investigator of medicinal simples. On September 10, 1558, in the sacristy of the cathedral of St. Peter, the insignia of the doctorate in medicine were bestowed upon Cureus, in order that his ability and learning might receive their due reward, and that others might know that he was equipped to practice. The vice-chancellor was Ludovicus ab Armis, the celebrated jurisconsult. For the examination he gave out the second aphorism of the first book and a passage from the *Ars parva* of Galen on the differences in signs. He was pleased by the speech of Cureus which was planned in imitation of Melanchthon —brief, to the point, and interspersed with certain flowers and moral apothegms.

170

FALLOPPIA'S LECTURES OF 1557

Gabrielis Falloppii Mutinensis De medicatis aquis atque de fossilibus . . . ab Andrea Marcolino Fanestri medico ipsius discipulo amantissimo collectus . . . , Venetiis Ex officina Ludovici Avantii MDLXIX, fols. 85v, 124r–v, 176v.

Gabriele Falloppia has already been mentioned in the preceding selection. More famous as an anatomist, he is in this case found lecturing on the *materia medica* of Dioscorides at the university of Padua.

Last year we took up the explanation of the last part of the fifth book of Dioscorides in which the subject of metals is treated, and we divided, if you will remember, all those things which are generated in the bowels of the earth into two kinds, under one of which we said were contained all that spring forth from the earth and erupt by their

---

[3] Ulysse Aldrovandi, the noted naturalist, taught at Bologna for half a century from 1554 to 1605: see Dallari, *I rotuli*, Index.

own motion, under the other those which do not come forth of themselves but are mined by human art and industry. To the first head or kind are referred vapor, smoke, fire, water, and other liquids. And since there were two kinds of waters, one indeed water pure and simple, the other metallic and medicated, therefore we were compelled to treat at length of this second genus of waters and we finished with it, as you know. There remains another topic or genus, namely, what are mined by art from the bowels of earth which now, ye best of youths and ever dearest to me, I begin to treat for your sake and I think, God favoring, that I shall satisfy you in this matter.

Later on in the course of lectures, after a long discussion of the material cause of metals, Falloppia says to the class:

But since—listen please—there were some of you who said that I was dwelling too long on universals, therefore, if it is agreable to you, I will omit what remains about universals till another time and I will commence particulars. Do you want me to do this or not? [The class having apparently voted in the affirmative, Falloppia continues:] Tomorrow then I will take up cadmia with Dioscorides and when I have finished with particulars, if there is still time, I will complete the treatment of universals.

To this the posthumous editor adds: "What remained to cover concerning universals the most excellent Falloppia never treated further to my knowledge, nor was there time for it that year, nay he could not deal with all particulars, as he had planned, because of lack of time and the excessive heat."

Falloppia concluded the course with these words:

This is the place to speak of those things which act against poison by their entire substance, as is said of many things and among the rest of that horn of the Alicorn which is circulated and sold as the horn of that animal but falsely, since it is not horn but a kind of earth brought from Apulia, which however is good against poison. It would be the place to discuss this matter but perhaps we shall speak about it on another occasion. For it is time to put an end to our labors of this year, since not only the holidays but the excessive heat invite us to rest. Farewell and love me as you have thus far.

In the Gymnasium of Padua, July 20, 1557.

171

AMENITIES OF CLASSICAL CONTROVERSY IN THE SIXTEENTH CENTURY

CHARLES SIGONIUS'S BOOKS OF PADUAN DISPUTATIONS AGAINST FRANCIS ROBORTELLUS: BOOK I. SOME NOTICES AFFIXED TO THE DOORS OF PADUAN CLASSROOMS PERTAINING TO THE FOLLOWING DISPUTATION

Caroli Sigonii Opera Omnia, VI, 225–26, 231–32.

First come the notices of his courses by Robertellus, then some of the insulting comments thereon of Sigonius. Both were classical scholars of considerable reputation.

Franciscus Robortellus of Udine promises to set forth the system of the Latin language by a new method to his hearers so that they may easily and quickly learn a sure standard of speaking in Latin, for most true is that saying, He who does not learn rapidly, never learns. Wherefore he wants all to be prepared to receive so excellent a discipline and to listen attentively. But he will not begin this before he has commented on the places of the *Topics* which are eighteen, according to Cicero in the books *On the Orator,* the *Topics* and the *Divisions.* But whether this instruction ought to be given in extraordinary lectures publicly or privately we will decide later. Adieu, most noble and elect adolescents, and love your Robortellus who day and night thinks of naught else than how he may in any way promote your welfare. At Padua, the Ides of February, 1562.

Franciscus Robortellus of Udine who has explained the passage of the *Topics* on the basis of Cicero's second book *On the Orator,* today, in obedience to the edict of the gymnasiarchs [1] will begin to explain the first book *On the Orator* and first its preface: then presently he will dissert at length on the dialogue and it will not be foreign to the subject to refute certain inept and unlearned persons that they may learn hereafter to write more cautiously.

[1] That is, the university authorities.

Reply

To these remarks this inept and unlearned person has this to say: First he asks Robortellus, since he cannot conveniently be present to learn his charges nor absent much cares, that he deign to write out whatever he has found fault with in his writings. For he will respond briefly to them all as before with utmost diligence. Then he says that he is amazed that Robortellus, who has most disgracefully ignored being most justly criticized in six hundred passages five years ago, should dare to promise to make any accusation against another's erudition. . . .

Of so many errata noted by us many years ago and now again against Robortellus he finally has decided to defend one which I for his own sake would wish least of all. . . .

I hear that Robortellus is very offended that I have proved that he seems not ever to have learned the rudiments. I will therefore deal with him more gently hereafter, if he will cease being angry at me, and I shall content myself with those reprehensions only which contain some integral learning and praise of ancient doctrine, of which I promise to show most clearly that he is totally devoid.

172

THE SCHOLASTIC CAREER OF WOLF-GANG MEURER (1513–1585)

From the "Vita" by Bartholomaeus Waltherus, prefixed to the posthumous edition of Meurer's *Meteorologia*, Leipzig, 1587.

Meurer's father was a miner who in 1488 came from Bayreuth in the Upper Palatinate to Aldenberg, a town of Meissen near the Bohemian frontier, where by the art which he had learned from his father, a citizen of Giessen, he made a moderate fortune and in a short time took a leading place in the college of *jurati* for the mines and was esteemed by prince George of Saxony. Later his fortune was much diminished by a fire which consumed nearly the entire town. He had eleven children: seven girls, of whom two died in infancy while the others were married to miners; and four sons, of whom James succeeded to his father's occupation, George and John became theologians, while Wolfgang studied philosophy and medicine.

There shone forth in the first years of Wolfgang Meurer a remarkable native talent and a mind apt for higher pursuits than those of his father. Therefore he attended the local school eagerly, listened to the teachers attentively, and at home ruminated diligently on what he had heard. This literary leisure, while agreeable to him, began to annoy his father, who was accustomed to assiduous labors and those manual, so that he thought this constant association with books and papers brought with it a kind of laziness and avoidance of work. And undoubtedly his son Wolfgang would have been compelled to leave letters and go to the mines, had he not at the age of eleven—his father finally reluctantly allowing this—been sent to Pirna, where John Schadius then taught belles lettres, a man of high moral character and celebrated for erudition, as those times and regions went, since he knew Greek as well as Latin, a rare accomplishment in that illiterate age.

Besides his master's learning and diligence, Meurer used often to praise the liberality of the citizens of Pirna towards foreign students, which even to this day they do not allow to diminish especially in those cases where they feel that their kindness will not be misplaced.

From the school at Pirna he went to Dresden, attracted by the reputation of John Scheffelius, who then was head of the school there, and, later, made doctor of both laws at Leipzig, besides the consulate which he administered with distinction for several years, attained most ample honors at the university. For neither in that age was it held disgraceful that they should first be trained in schools who were later to ascend public pulpits in churches and universities, nay rather many great men freely confessed that this training had been a great help to them. Scheffelius, moreover, loved Meurer much, both because of his good talents and his diligence in study, and as a token of his esteem gave to his ardent disciple in the study of the Greek language a Greek manuscript of the New Testament, which Meurer for the lack of other Greek authors never let out of his hands then, and afterwards ever valued from piety towards God and gratitude to his teacher. But Meurer made so great progress in his study of Greek and was so well thought of by his master, that he put the mere boy over bigger pupils and placed him in charge of the section on Aesop's Fables, by his conduct of which he increased his own learning and further won the love of his master and the admiration of his fellow students.

Shortly afterwards he betook him to Leipzig as to a richer mart of letters where he reaped the first fruits of his studies. For by his abundant learning, combined with piety and modesty, he readily found friends and patrons, in especial the head of the monastery of St. Thomas, who thought so well of him that he had the younger monks trained in Greek by him alone. Not long after there became rector of the school of St. Thomas Caspar Borner, a man preeminent in humane studies and a credit to our literature. He was much pleased by Meurer's talent, learning and industry, so much so that he made him his associate in the work of teaching and assigned him the highest post after himself among his colleagues. And when Borner moved higher up he kept the same good opinion of Meurer. No less was the esteem of Meurer for Borner, whom he did not cease to love as a second father and to cherish as his supreme patron all the time of his life even when absent. This is shown by letters written from Italy in which he gave an account of his studies and expenditure of time and money and sought his advice in the most serious matters.

The time came when Meurer thought he ought to shake the dust of schoolteaching from his feet and go on to higher things. He inquired what would be taught in the university and mapped out his programme of studies accordingly. In consequence he acquired that stock of philosophical subjects which would suffice to win the first degree. For when to knowledge of facts he added the study of a pure and elegant style, he set out not unsuccessfully also to write verses and attained his objective at the age of eighteen, when Heinrich Godeschalck was dean.

And since the exercise of public disputations, prudently established by our ancestors, is conserved by grateful posterity [here] above many other universities of these regions, not to say above all, Meurer, now become a bachelor with the function of publicly presiding and conferring concerning the matter proposed by others, not merely attended the public lectures and disputations and listened diligently to others conferring, but also at home privately with his friends discussed their studies familiarly and disputed some questions. For this exercise, Saturday after supper was assigned each week when, someone presiding who had prepared for it, the others conferred quietly, partly to bring out the truth, partly to prepare themselves to be recruits for the future battle. This private industry of a few excited others and stimulated them to join them, by whom they were well received, until finally the narrow quarters compelled them to seek a larger meeting-place, and the authority of the master, to whom the oversight of the new college was committed, granted them the use of a public hall. The result was that, still others coming in, partly attracted by the novelty of it, partly by zeal for learning, what had hitherto been a voluntary matter was afterwards subjected to regulation and all were ordered to form colleges at that day and hour. These are still observed under the designation of evening disputations, but the hour has been changed, I don't know at whose suggestion.

When Meurer had trained himself for three years in this exercise ground of disputations and had completed the prescribed order of studies, he sought the highest degree in philosophy, which he easily gained from those rigid and severe censors of studies and morals. The same examiners recommended that the most ample senate of Leipzig bestow on their new master, who had not sought it or even hoped for it, the direction of the municipal school opened at St. Nicholas. This he ruled for six years with a large attendance of pupils, from whom came many distinguished men of all orders, whose work was fruitful not only in the churches, schools and public life of those regions but of others. Moreover, although this school is no less bound by the strictest rules of discipline and in it the rod is to be feared by the contumacious and negligent, yet it approaches academic freedom, since its rector is either a public professor of the university or at least one of the Council of the faculty of philosophy, since its pupils are immune from the burdens which other schoolboys have to bear, and there are many real students, of whom some are admitted to public lectures, some adorned with the bachelor's degree do not disdain when their masters teach to sit with the others—of whom we have found a great number enrolled among the pupils of Meurer. With what fidelity he fulfilled this office those can testify who are still living and who recall their years of adolescence and this training, and is shown by a book written by Meurer at the beginning of his term and set before his pupils but as yet unpublished, *On the Establishment of the Proper Method and Order of Studies*. Which it is to be wished might be daily thumbed by the studious, for then they would begin the curriculum with greater success and complete it more happily. For so long as for lack of advice they wander hither and thither through all kinds of subjects as in an extensive field of flowers, they are needy in the midst of abundance and often return home empty, of which shilly-shallying we know many very famous men have complained, who by their examples have warned others away from that desultory method of study.

While Meurer was carrying on here, as we have said, the fourth year after by unanimous consent and in strict accord with the statutes he was coopted into the number of colleagues of the Minor College of the Prince as successor to Caspar Borner, who was transferred to the Major College of the Princes, where the income is larger. And this succession was the first step towards another, when, after nine years, Meurer was promoted to the place of the dead Borner. And so Borner, whom at the start he had as an associate in schoolteaching, while he lived saw him as his successor in public honors with singular pleasure and dying hoped therefor with great desire.

Made sharer of this endowment, Meurer wished also to serve the university in public lectures, since he was aware that hitherto he had devoted his efforts chiefly to elementary and secondary teaching. For these incomes were not founded by the munificence of most illustrious princes and amplified by the labors of our predecessors to encourage sloth but to promote learning especial in the humane studies, for whose masters they were particularly destined. Therefore since he sought a place in the council of the university on liberal arts and was readily received, he tried to be an ornament to the most honorable college.

At that time this arrangement prevailed with regard to the teaching of philosophy, that those who were to give the public lectures should be chosen by lot each semester from the philosophical college. For since there were many members, while the professorial stipends were fewer in number and scanty in amount, and since all were held worthy of this office of teaching, this method was devised by our ancestors which allowed no one to go without that honor and emolument, unless God and fortune judged against him. Whether this frequent changing of professors was to the advantage of the students or not I do not now question, since this is not the place for it. I merely say this: that custom after a few years was changed, and those functions in which they were especially versed were delegated to certain members, until either they died or it seemed to our philosophical college best to make a change.

Under that regime Meurer lectured to the students in the university now on something from the *Parva Naturalia* of Aristotle, now from the *Metaphysics*, now from *De anima*. After a little, by the unanimous consent of the electors the office of dean was imposed on him, that he should govern all the courses in philosophy, which he did with the greatest fidelity and singular prudence. And since in preference to other parts of philosophy—not that he carelessly neglected or proudly scorned them—both for itself and its professional prospects he had given especial attention to that concerned with the obscurity of nature and its causes and effects and had further worked hard at the mathematical disciplines, on that foundation which he had now well laid of knowledge of both languages, of physical and mathematical science, he began to erect the medical art, in learning which he had as teachers in this university Heinrich Stromer, George Schiltelius, John Pfeilius, Sebastian Roth, and other famous medical men of that time, whom he both heard in public lectures and consulted privately. And after the first degree in medicine, Sebastian Roth presiding, he replied publicly to the contrary arguments in an extensive disputation on the soul and its faculties and he published a distinguished example of his progress in this branch of learning which Philip Melanchthon, who adorned this disputation with his presence and objections, did not hesitate to read and commend.

Since Meurer knew that the study of anatomy is of first importance to a physician, he not only busily thumbed anatomical books but also wished to be an eyewitness of nature. As often therefore as our Germans or foreigners, like Eustathius Quercetanus of France who happened to pass through Leipzig, or Apollonius Massa of Italy who stopped for some time in these regions and rendered medical services to a very illustrious personage, offered the chance of seeing the human body dissected, he attended eagerly both here and in neighboring towns and took careful notes on what was said by the dissector and by other physicians attending, as is shown by the notebook which he left filled with such observations.

As he proceeded with the study of medicine, the desire to visit Italy grew upon Meurer, since he knew it flowered with solid masters of every department of science. And so at his own expense he undertook the journey with Wolfgang Werter, Ulrich Mordisius, John Sprembergerus and George Fabricius. First he settled at Padua and there applied himself wholeheartedly to the art of medicine except for those hours which he spent on the humanities and philosophy, then taught by Lazarus Bonamicus and Antonius Ianua. Whomsoever, moreover, he thought he should hear, their goodwill he sought by the right method, reverence for teachers, love of letters, zeal for truth and right. Hence the most skilled anatomist of that time, summoned from the Low Countries to Italy, Andreas Vesalius of Brussels, called him his friend; the most excellent physician, John Baptista Montanus, treated him like a son; Montagnana, whenever he practiced medicine, had him at hand; the eminent doctor of the humanities, Lazarus Bonamicus, was on intimate terms with him; the others offered him all kindly offices in profusion.

Meurer was not content with touching the outskirts of Italy but with Werter and Fabricius traversed almost the entire peninsula. In this wandering he had as a companion Valerius Cordus, son of Euricius, with whom he scaled the mountain peaks in search of herbs. After he had been at Rome a while and won the hearts of Alphonsus Ferius, professor of surgery, Joseph Cinthius, the botanist, and Luca Gaurico, the most excellent astronomer, he set out for Naples, where among the philosophers he most esteemed Simon Portius, among medical men Brancaleone. Then he traveled to other parts of Italy and illustrious universities, heard their professors lecture, called at Bologna on Lodovico Buccaferreus the philosopher, at Ferrara on the physicians, Antonio Musa and Hieronymo Fracastoro, at Florence on Matthaeus Curtius, the physician, and Petrus Victorius, well known in philosophy and the humanities, and whatever was worth seeing, he studied most eagerly and noted most diligently. It would take too long to give particulars. Anyone interested may read the Italian travels of George Fabricius, whose companion Meurer was and who let him alone censor and emend his work.

It happened during those years which Meurer spent in Italy that Maurice, duke of Saxony, after the death of his brother Henry gave careful attention both to matters of government and a reform of the churches and schools of these regions and was especially concerned as to the university of Leipzig. Therefore he had Joachim Camerarius called from Tübingen as professor of both languages and from Wittenberg the most excellent mathematician George Joachim Rheticus. And inasmuch as there was still lacking an eminent expositor of the philosophy of Aristotle who would teach solidly and soberly that subject, made intricate by the thorny disputations of some and drawn from the lacunae of its interpreters rather than its true sources, Meurer though absent seemed worthy of the place and office above many other candidates. Therefore by public letters, by the advice of Philip Melanchthon, he was summoned from Italy by the philosophical college for this position. And although he was recalled in the middle of his course of study, yet he willingly obeyed and taught Aristotelian philosophy faithfully for 27 solid years, nor would he have left that post, had he not, by authority of the most ample College of Medicine, succeeded its dean who had just died. This office, although it requires a physician not only eminent in theory but renowned in practice, was laudably and adequately administered by Meurer for fourteen years. By his erudition, diligence and system in teaching, and perspicacity he far exceeded the expectations which the entire university had when it called him to this difficult administrative task. Daily the concourse of students grew to hear that eminent philosopher, and of many famous men in the university. Nay, the great Philip Melanchthon coming from Wittenberg was not infrequently seen with Joachim Camerarius approaching his lecture room and by his presence rendering the new professor, though commendable enough *per se*, still more acceptable to his audience and the entire university. For the illustrious esteem of great men for professors is a great help to students, especially adolescents deficient in judgment.

So the authority of Meurer daily waxed great among his colleagues who shortly judged him fit to control in place of the chancellor of the university, which is the peculiar office of the bishop of Merseburg, all promotions of those to be decorated with the highest degree in liberal arts—this by most clement concession of Augustus, duke of Saxony, at that time political administrator of that diocese, since the coadjutor of ecclesiastical affairs was George, prince of Anhalt. This was the occasion of learned men seeking his acquaintance not only from this locality but other parts of Germany. Of our own the chief were Caspar Borner whom he cherished as a father, Joachim Camerarius, John Pfeffinger, Alexander Alesius, Heinricus Salmuthus, Leonartus Badhorn, Victorinus Strigelius, whom he not merely loved in prosperity but also never deserted in adversity. At Wittenberg, Luther, Melanchthon, Justus Jonas, Peucer; at Zurich, Gesner; at Tübingen Fuchs and Scheck; at Strasburg, Sturm and Gerbel were his close friends. What shall I say of the Werters, the Naevii and brothers Fabricii? What of others most celebrated from other places, of whom not the least is George Agricola, most noble writer on mining? Time would fail to read the letters preserved among the heirs of the most distinguished men, in which they testify to their singular love towards our Meurer and highly laud his genius and erudition. Among foreigners the friendship that he at once contracted by his humanity and candor he retained most constantly and cherished most sacredly. Witnesses are letters of Paul Manutius of Venice, Apollonius and Nicolaus Massa, most excellent physicians, and Luca Gaurico, the Roman astronomer, who did not hesitate to give Meurer's letter to other learned men, and finally to the pope himself to read, because it drew so directly from, as he said, the Ciceronian spring.

But not to digress too far, I return to Meurer to whom the thirty-fifth year of his life had brought so much honor and authority. For although, on account of the besieging of the city and the contagion that followed it, he had withdrawn from Leipzig, together with certain other public professors and those the leading ones, yet when Caspar Borner succumbed to fate, he was though absent transferred from the Minor College of the Prince to the Major, which we have also said before, since soliciting and canvassing votes were not yet employed and were prohibited by the rules. When after that accession of honor he returned to public duties, he was made rector for the winter semester by unanimous vote, which important office he discharged faithfully and diligently, so that in the following years together with Joachim Camerarius he shared in most serious deliberations as to our republic of letters and stabilized, increased, amplified and adorned it by his work and advice.

These labors and public cares by no means impeded his private studies. For since he had devoted himself to medical studies in Germany and spent the flower of his youth on them in Italy, in the following year, which was his thirty-sixth, he was created doctor of medicine together with Blasius Thammuller and Balthasar Cleinius by public proclamation and coopted into the most ample College of Physicians. And although he was to be occupied for many years to come with teaching those subjects for whose sake he had been recalled from Italy, yet he kept religiously the faith given to both colleges, teaching philosophy and practicing medicine and, as occasion offered, examining the candidates in medicine to whom also by the most gracious concession of Michael, bishop of Merseburg, he bestowed the degrees high or low. So great, moreover, was his devotion to the university and to academic freedom, that he magnanimously spurned many opportunities to reach better paying positions. For when he was sometimes most kindly admonished by letters of some great man to choose the splendor of courts in preference to the cloistered life he had thus far led, he did not wish to change, since he was now his own master.

Waltherus goes on to tell of Meurer's marriage to Margarita Blasebalgius, with whom he lived 26 years and had six sons and three daughters, of whom there were still living Philip, a doctor of both laws, Christopher, professor of mathematics in the university of Leipzig and a candidate in medicine, John, a student of theology, and two daughters, one married to a senator of Leipzig, the other to a native of Freiberg. His wife died of the pestilence and he remained for the last ten years of his life a widower. Before her death he became a town senator, and, on the death of Martin Drembach, was made dean of the medical college and henceforth taught medicine instead of philosophy.

173

A JUDGMENT AGAINST A STUDENT REVERSED

Centuria Consiliorum clarissimi Iurisconsulti Elberti Leonini, Primarii iuris civilis Professoris in florente paulo ante Academia Louanensi et Cancellarii Ducatus Geldriae et Comitatus Zutphaniae, Antverpiae, Ex officina Christophori Plantini, MDLXXXIIII, p. 191.

Consilium 63

Summary

If a horse rented to a student receives any injury, this should not be charged to the student, if he is not to blame, even if there is evidence of some inexperience and carelessness on his part.

Unjust and to be reversed is the opinion of the magnificent lord rector, by which on August 12 of the present year he condemned the original defendant, now appealing, to pay for the horse in question and costs. For since it is established by his own allegation and the testimony of witnesses offered by him, that the said horse died of a lethal wound inflicted upon it, one should inquire as to the cause and author of that wound, who it is established was a servant of the inn at the sign of the Mirror in the town of Leewen, as is known from the deposition and testimony of the servant himself, also Leonard van Ortenburch the innkeeper, and Jaspar Reynes the blacksmith. For which reason the original plaintiff ought to summon the servant of said inn, not the appellant, who neither inflicted the wound nor admitted any fault leading to the injury which occurred. For the point raised as to his traveling too fast is remote from the cause of said wound, since the latter was inflicted not in order to make the horse go faster but when it was being led in the usual way and to improve its condition from the stable to water to drink, in the absence of and without the knowledge of the appellant, who should be excused if, as is the custom, he turned over the horse on reaching the inn to the care and treatment of the innkeeper and his groom, especially since it is a case of a hired horse for use of which pay is given or promised and of its being hired by a student in whom inexperience in horsemanship is presumptive. For these circumstances imply that not the most exacting care is required but such as the hirer is accustomed to give his own property. So if the horse receive any injury, either from unskillful riding or otherwise, the renter ought to stand for it, as Salicetus writes and decides in so many words, and he warns those who lend or rent their horses to students that they must accept the cost of any injury which may follow.

This being the case, the appellant should be free from risk as to the horse, which he took the precaution to have shod with sharp iron shoes when the lender had sent it out without sufficient protection of its hoofs against ice, and the appellant gave no cause for the said wound, which cannot be imputed to his fault. Yet this would be essential in order to concur in his condemnation, nor could any blame resulting from delay or haste or any other occasion suffice, but it must be a fault directly connected with the said accident, and the infliction of the wound itself have resulted from that fault as its immediate cause, which is not the fact.

Therefore, altering the terms of the condemnation, the appellant in this second instance is to be absolved, the adversary condemned in costs for this as well as the prior trial, in so far as additional testimony has been offered, saving to the same adversary or appealed his action against the said servant or groom or his master and innkeeper of the Mirror, who is held to answer for his household and employees, saving a better judgment.

174

STUDENT LIFE: PAST AND PRESENT

Steno Bielke, *Commentatio de academiis*, Tübingen, 1609, pp. 28–35.

Depart therefore from the classrooms, ye inept and unfit who have your brains in your heels and measure all virtue by strength of body . . . [Presently Bielke quotes the Italian proverb,] "Five hours of sleep for the traveler, six for the student, eight for the merchant, and eleven for all rogues," or, "Five for the student, six for the merchant, seven for the people, eight for the sluggard."

Nor are they to be excused who while they themselves snore and wallow in bed, order their servants to perform the vicarious task of writing and listening in the auditorium. . . . You sons of Venus who, as Luca de Penna says, *lex I, cap. de Stud. liber 11*, affect rooms overlooking the street to see the girls across the way or those who pass by, or who often appear in church principally on this account, that you may see the ladies! . . . although in many places the virgins are too gentle and tame and amiable and affable and tractable, and either give ready ear to the students or entice and anticipate in the matter of attentions. At Cologne and Tübingen, says Heinrich Hornmann in his *Commentary on the Line of Love*, chapter four on kissing, it is thought a great sin if a youth who meets a girl does not kiss and hug her. [Bielke, however, denies this in the case of Tübingen.] For public decency and the sanctity of the laws do not allow such prodigality of kisses.

Jacob Butrigarius and Baldus in *l. neque natales c. de Probat.* write that it is enough to prove a woman a prostitute if students visit her by day and night, without proving the commission of any sexual act, since, when a student talks with such an one, it is not to be presumed that he is repeating the Lord's Prayer, *secundum Baldum in d. l. neque natales*, Kirchman. *de virginitatis iure, c. 18*. And the same Baldus in *l. aedem C. locali* says that the leaser of a house to a student cannot evict him because he has brought prostitutes there and therefore injured the property, since this should have been presumed as a common occurrence. See also Pet. Rebuff. *de privil. universit. priv. 2 et privil. 21 et in comment. ad Auth. Habita* . . . [On this Bielke comments,] Such abuses prevail in Italy and other kingdoms of lascivious Venus: our Germany and Suevia are by the grace of God incapable of such petulance.

A student who sells his books unless forced to do so by inevitable necessity becomes infamous *ipso facto*, Petr. Rebuff. *Privil. 57*, like a soldier who has lost his arms in battle. . . .

And because these literary studies closely concern the honor of God and public utility, students may study even on feast days and in church: and Peter Rebuff affirms that he has seen many doctors intent on their books in church while vespers were being celebrated. He adds, however, that it would be more seemly and devout to pray in church and dismiss all other thoughts rather than to study . . . and he justly praises Jean Boerius, royal advocate in the parlement of Mombeliard, who on feast days never held consultations except with the poor.

It is also permissible for a student to expel from the house a smith who disturbs his studies: Bartolus et alii *in l. 2 in fi. ff. solit. matrim.* Iac. Benius *de privil. ICtor. priv. 69, num. 12*. And so at Mombeliard Peter Rebuff compelled a certain weaver who filled the neighborhood with songs and shoutings almost without cessation to change his lodgings, when, despite an injunction of the magistrates, he continued to make a terrible noise. Petr. Rebuff. *Scholar. privil. 3*.

Matthias Colerus evoked the same law at Jena against a certain cooper, who lived next door to him and used to get up at midnight and make so much noise in putting hoops on wine casks that the priest of Themis passed many sleepless nights and imperiled his health. But, having complained to the wine gild, an order was issued by the senate of Jena that it should compel the cooper either to leave that habitation and seek another or cease his labors in that neighborhood. Matth. Coler. *de processib. executiv. part. I, c.4, n.8*.

. . . And let the student be diligent in his first year, more diligent in the second, most diligent in the third, and even more diligent in the fourth, as Baldus says of the appellant. . . .

But let not the student try to teach himself before he has learned much, or he will learn late and badly. Nor without a guide and teacher should he enter a way which he has never known. . . . [Bielke adds that the self-taught are very rare.]

And the spoken word of the professor has some occult virtue that penetrates deeper into the mind of the hearer and makes a greater impression upon the memory than private reading. . . .

Wherefore Caccialupus inveighs severely against those hard-necked students who disdain the lecture hall and master's voice, saying that they do not deserve to be called scholars or to enjoy the privileges of scholars, nay rather should be punished as deceivers. Io. Neviz. *d.l.n.55.* And Peter Rebuff writes in *Comment. ad Auth. Habita* that it is a sure sign of a good scholar when he listens readily to all lectures, especially until he is endowed with knowledge: that on the contrary those are foolish students who are willing to attend only one or two lectures a day, for such will not acquire much subject matter but only enough for a couple of lectures. Once at Toulouse there was marvelous competition in occupying the benches of the lecture hall, since students would go to the university at the third hour after midnight or thereabouts to get the best seats. Sometimes they would send servants to keep the places, whom the other students would sometimes drive out, and so dire controversies arose between them and the masters of the servants when they finally arrived. Wherefore, the rule was made that vacant places should be reserved for their first occupants, and that no one else might take a place against the will of its original occupant, but with the proviso that an infrequent auditor should forfeit his place after a fortnight's absence. Petr. Rebuff. *Scholar. privil. 10.*

Far be, moreover, from our student that profane Italian custom, by which the students fill the auditorium more with petulant clamor, murmurs and tumult than with their presence and attention, and often are accustomed to injure the professor's feelings shamefully by loud laughter, whistling and disorder, and not merely to make a disturbance from the platform. . . .

But no wise man would advise that all students everywhere and without discrimination be strictly required to attend all public lectures: *vide Leges Illustr. Collegii,* ¶ *equidem p. 37.* And we have seen students of long standing who were already imbued with much learning take nothing more ill than to be asked in public assembly, as if they were novices and tyros, What lectures have they attended? What ones have they not attended? Why not? Where do they live? Where do they eat? How much do they drink? etc. . . .

At Paris the faculty of canon law passed the following legislation as to attending lectures: We decree that no one shall be regarded as a student of the faculty of canon law and enjoy the privileges and immunities of the university, unless he shall have attended classes at least twice or thrice a week and listened to lectures after the manner of scholars. Petr. Rebuff. *Schol. privil. 31.*

In Spain a student does not enjoy the privileges of scholars unless he hears two lectures daily, as may be seen in the Constitutions of Spaniards in the Agreement made with the university of Salamanca, 1492 A.D., Petrus Rebuffus. *Schol. privil. 141 et 165.* . . .

Eobanus Hessus had an audience of fifteen hundred when he lectured on the poets at Erfurt, says Herman Kirchner, *Oratio de fatal. Acad. dissipat.* And John Corrasius taught law at Toulouse to such a throng of auditors that sometimes four thousand students listened to the professor's voice. Geraud de Maynard *liv. 4, c.2, n.1 des notabl. et sing. questioni.*

175

LECTURES IN ASTRONOMY, 1642–1644

SYLLABUS OF LECTURES TO BE HELD IN THE UNIVERSITY OF BOLOGNA DURING THE FIRST TERM OF 1642 BY BROTHER BONAVENTURA CAVALIERI, PROFESSOR OF MATHEMATICS

Printed by Antonio Favaro, "Amici e corrispondenti di Galileo Galilei: XXXI. Bonaventura Cavalieri," *Atti del reale Istituto Veneto di scienze, lettere ed arti,* Anno academico 1914–1915—Tomo LXXIV— Parte seconda, p. 755 et seq., "Appendice. R. Archivio di stato in Bologna.—Reggimento. Serie di annue lezioni lette da diversi Lettori alli Scolari nello Studio pubblico di Bologna esibite di tempo in tempo agli Illustrissimi SS. Assunti di Studio." (For the years 1635–1699.)

November

5. Will be held the introductory lecture to the doctrine of the planets, and their sublime estate among the bodies of the universe will be shown.

7. Astronomy will be defined and divided into the doctrine of the sphere and the theory of the planets.

8. Further facts of the theory of the ten circles of the material sphere will be explained.

10. The accidents will be expounded which are connected with the aforesaid starry circles.

13. It will be explained what the Theory of the Planets is, what its object, what its divisions and what their order. Moreover, there will be shown to be three, that is to say, hypotheses, particular theories and the passions following the same.

14. The first hypothesis of theory will be set forth, namely: that the celestial movements are circular and regular.

15. The second hypothesis will be explained, forsooth: that there are two movements in the sky, that is to say, the daily movement and the movement proper to every planet.

17. The third hypothesis will be shown, namely: that the celestial movements, although they appear irregular, nevertheless will be reduced to regularity by means of eccentric circles and epicycles.

18. The fourth hypothesis will be declared concerning the construction of the universe according to the theory of Ptolemy.

19. A fifth hypothesis will be brought forth concerning the construction of the universe according to the theory of Copernicus.

22. A sixth hypothesis will be explained concerning the construction of the universe according to more recent astronomers and especially the theory of Tycho.

24. Views on particular theories that require explanation will be set forth, namely: what order will be followed, and it is proposed to explain five things: first, how many particular spheres or circles there are and their position; what are the periodic times of their movements; third, for what reason these movements are referred to the sun; fourth, what are the terms employed regarding them; fifth, how they are applied in theory by tables.

26. A beginning will be made of the theory of the sun according to

Ptolemy and the explanation of this will be adduced and his spheres will be described.

28. The periods of movements in the said spheres will be considered.

29. The terms employed in this theory by Ptolemy will be expounded.

December

1. The theory of the sun will be applied to his tables, in which connection will be considered epochs, or the roots of time and movements.

3. The doctrine concerning the equation of natural days will be unfolded.

4. The circles of the sun will be explained which constitute the Theory of the Planets according to the Copernican hypothesis.

5. The lecture will be concerning periods, terms and tables which are employed by Copernicus.

9. The circles of the sun will be considered which constitute the Theory of the Planets according to more recent astronomers, especially Tycho.

11. There will be set forth the theory of the movements, terms, and also tables.

12. There will be a dissertation concerning sun spots, and the doctrine of that theory will be related.

15. Reasons will be given why, immediately after the sun, the moon is discussed, and its spheres will be described according to the theory of Ptolemy.

17. The periods of the movements of the orbits of the moon will be set forth according to Ptolemy.

19. The analogy of the movements of the moon to the motion of the sun will be explained.

20. The *termini* of the Ptolemaic lunar theory will be expounded.

January, 1643

8. Will treat of the tables used in the same theory of the moon.

9. The circles constituting the theory of the moon according to Copernicus will be made public.

10. A lecture will be held concerning the periods of motion according to Copernicus and their analogy to the motion of the sun.

12. The circles according to more recent astronomers will be introduced and especially those of Tycho having to do with lunar theory.

14. Will discuss the periods and movements and their analogy to the motion of the sun.

16. The terms and tables of the same will be explained.

19. There will be disputation concerning spots on the moon and its phases and its light, primary as well as secondary, and the theory of the moon will be set forth.

22. The reason will be stated why, after the moon, we treat of the three superior planets, and of what sort the spheres are will be explained according to the theory of Ptolemy.

23. The periods of their movements will be examined.

24. The analogy of their movements with the motion of the sun will be explained.

26. Explanation of the terms customarily employed in this theory.

27. The composition of the tables according to Ptolemy will be declared.

28. The orbs and circles of the three superior planets and the periods of their movements and analogy to the sun, terms and tables will be discussed according to the Copernican hypothesis.

Close of the First Term.

For all of the preceding lectures the following authors may be examined, namely: for the Ptolemaic Theory, his *Almagest,* and the *Epitome* of Regiomontanus, with the *Theories* of Peurbach. For the Copernican, which is set forth merely as a hypothesis, you may read his work *On Revolutions of the Orbs,* corrected, the *Epitome* of *Copernican Astronomy* of Kepler after permission is obtained from the authorities, as well as his *Commentaries on the Star of Mars,* the *Rudolphian Tables* and the *Theory* of Maginus. For the views of Tycho and more recent astronomers, let the student go to the *Progymnasmata,* to the *Danish Astronomy* of Longomontanus and the *Theory and Tables* of Landsbergh. Which authors, indeed, are to be read through as classics, superior to other treatments of astronomy

SECOND TERM, 1643. PUBLIC LECTURES TO BE HELD BY
BROTHER BONAVENTURA CAVALIERI

February

19. The theory of the three superior planets will be discussed according to the more recent astronomers and the orbs and circles constituting them.

20. Of the planets and their movements and their analogy to the sun.

21. Of their terms and tables.

23. Of the two satellites of Saturn and the four planets of Jupiter.

24. Of the two inferior planets, namely: Venus and Mercury and their orbs according to Ptolemy.

27. Of their periods and their movements.

28. Of the analogy of their movements with the motion of the sun.

March

2. Of the terms customarily employed in their theory.

3. Of the composition of the tables according to Ptolemy.

4. Of their orbs and circles and periods of movements, their analogy to the sun, terms and tables according to Copernicus.

9. Of the same according to more recent astronomers.

10. Of the periods and movements of the same and their analogy to the motion of the sun.

11. Of terms and tables.

16. Of the theory of the eighth sphere according to Ptolemy.

17. Of names of circles, stars or images.

18. Of the same theory according to Copernicus.

23. Of the same according to more recent astronomers.

24. On observing and recognizing the stars in the sky.

26. On new stars.

28. On comets.

LECTURES TO BE HELD IN THE THIRD TERM OF THE
YEAR 1643 BY BROTHER BONAVENTURA CAVALIERI

April

13. Introduction to the third part of Theory in which is proposed to treat of passions of the planets and to what genera they reduce.

14. Of the first kind of passions, that is, concerning latitudes of planets in common.

15. How astronomers demonstrate that the sun is without latitude.

17. Of the latitude of the moon according to Ptolemy.

18. Of the latitude of the moon according to Copernicus.

20. Of the latitude of the moon according to Tycho and more recent astronomers.

21. Of the latitude of the three superior planets according to Ptolemy.

22. Of the latitude of the three superior planets according to Copernicus.

24. Of the latitude of the three superior planets according to Tycho and more recent astronomers.

27. Of the latitude of the two inferior planets according to Ptolemy.

28. Of the same according to Copernicus.

30. Of the same according to Tycho and more recent astronomers.

May

2. Of the table of latitudes.

4. Of the second kind of passions, which come to planets by reason of eccentrics and epicycles, that is to say, considering direct and retrograde movement and stationariness.

5. Of the third kind of passions which happen to stars from their status and position with relation to the sun.

7. Of the first aspect of the new moon.

21. Of the arc of vision of the stars.

22. Of the fourth kind of passions which happen to the planets in relation to one another, that is to say, concerning conjunction, sextile, quadrate and trinal aspect, and opposition.

23. Of the condition of these aspects and their influence on these inferiors.

27. Of the fifth and last kind of passions which happen to planets and especially to the luminaries with reference to the earth, and first considering mean, true and visible syzygies of the luminaries.

29. Concerning the apparent diameters of the planets.

30. Of parallax in genus.

June

2. Of the species of parallax.

6. Of eclipses of the luminaries and first of the cause of lunar eclipses.

8. Then concerning the quantity of the three bodies, sun, moon and earth, and a comparison of them.

9. Of the varieties of lunar eclipses.

10. Of the duration and quantity of lunar disappearances.

12. Of the cause of solar eclipses.

15. Of the variety of solar eclipses and their difference from lunar ones.

16. Of the time of the duration of an eclipse of the sun.

17. Why it cannot be universal for the whole world like a lunar eclipse.

19. In what way eclipses of the luminaries can be observed.

22. Concerning eclipses of the planets of Jupiter with Jupiter and one another.

23. Of the mutual occultation of the stars.

End of Lectures for the Third Term of the Year 1643.

SYLLABUS OF LECTURES TO BE HELD IN THE UNIVERSITY OF
BOLOGNA IN THE FIRST TERM (OF 1644), BY BROTHER
BONAVENTURA CAVALIERI, PROFESSOR OF MATHEMATICS

November

3. An introductory lecture to the astronomy of Ptolemy will be delivered.

5. The prohemium of the *Almagest* will be elucidated, and the principles of this doctrine will be revealed, and the first and second chapters of the first book will be explained.

6. The doctrine of the third chapter will be examined concerning the figure of the sky itself.

7. The doctrine of the same chapter about the quality of the sky.

9. The fourth chapter which concerns the figure of the earth will be laid open.

10. There will be disputed whether, in the earth, the center of gravity and the center of magnitude are the same.

13. The question will be whether the earth is in the middle of the universe, according to chapter 5.

14. There will be treated the insensible (sensible?) magnitude of the earth compared to the sky, according to chapter 6.

16. The celebrated question will be discussed whether the earth moves or is at rest, according to chapter 7.

17. The rest of the previous question will be finished.

18. It will be examined whether in the heavens there is a double difference of the first movements as chapter 8 teaches.

20. Will treat of the regularity and irregularity of the celestial movements.

24. The question will be discussed whether any circles should be introduced by astronomers into the mundane and material sphere, and following this, the question will be raised concerning circles of the material sphere as follows:

26. Where in the material sphere it is suitable to place the horizon.

27. Whether it is suitable to place the meridian in the same.

28. The equator.

December

1. The ecliptic and zodiac.

3. The two coluri.

4. Whether there are many circles in the material or mundane sphere thus far conceived by astronomers.

9. We shall treat of the importance of trigonometry and its extreme necessity for the pursuit of astronomy, on which occasion it will be explained what the arc was for Ptolemy and the ancients and the chord, for Ptolemy treats of chords through the whole of chapter 9 in which he teaches how to find them.

11. The contributions of the later writers to trigonometric calculation will be set forth.

12. The rule of three will be treated and applied to tables of chords and of sines.

14. The nature and importance of logarithms will be explained.

15. There will be a lecture considering the axioms of plain trigonometry.

17. The axioms of spherical trigonometry will be set forth and the propositions of Ptolemy which will be of service to the same.

14. We shall discuss the observation of the arc which is between the tropics according to chapter 2, or according to the maximum obliquity of the sun or zodiac.

19. Considering the construction of a table of the declination of the sun or ecliptic.

January

8. Of the use of the same table.

9. How to construct a table of right ascensions.

11. Of the use of right ascension.

12. Of the very easy calculation of the declination and right ascension by logarithms.

13. Of certain general rules concerning declinations and right ascensions of the points of the ecliptic.

15. Shows how declinations of the stars can be obtained by observation.

16. Expounds how right ascensions of the same may be observed.

18. It will be shown how, given the arc of the ecliptic, the rest of its right ascension of which one *terminus* is known, can be found.

19. We shall disclose the method of finding the point of the ecliptic terminating in each quarter the arc which is highest in its right ascension.

End of the First Term

LECTURES TO BE HELD BY BROTHER BONAVENTURA CAVALIERI, PROFESSOR OF MATHEMATICS, IN THE SECOND AND THIRD TERMS OF 1644

February

11. The first chapter of the second book of the *Almagest* will be explained, which is about the position of the universal earth which is inhabited by us, and some points will be taken up about chapter 2.

12. The general division of the earth will be discussed, and for a given region the altitude of its pole will be investigated according to chapter 3.

13. It will be shown how it is to be found to whom and when and how many days the sun appears in the zenith, according to chapter 4.

15. The shadow of the sun will be discussed according to chapter 5.

16. It will be disputed whether the face of the earth has been

rightly divided up by astronomers and geographers, in connection with the fifth chapter.

17. Four properties of the regions will be expounded by single parallels, namely: 1st, the longitude of the greatest day, 2nd, the latitude, 3rd when the sun becomes vertical for the given place, 4th and last, the quality of shadows at noon according to same 6th chapter.

19. Will treat of the ascensions and declinations of the signs according to chapters 7 and 8.

20. Of the use of the same according to chapter 9.

23. Also of the use of same in making directions.

24. Concerning spherical angles and the arcs which are made by the ecliptic with the horizon, meridian and each vertical circle, according to chapters 10, 11, and 12, and thus the doctrine of the second book is finished.

26. A transition will be made to the third book, and, in place of the preface, the method will be given of observing the movement of the equinox.

27. There will be a lecture on the magnitude of the time of the year, according to chapters 1 and 2.

29. Will be an explanation of the mean and true movements among astronomers according to the same chapter 2.

March

2. It will be disputed whether in the heavens eccentric circles and epicycles are to be conceded.

3. It will be shown how appearances in the heavens can be saved by eccentrics and epicycles, according to chapter 3.

5. Will discuss the method of finding the eccentric of the sun according to chapter 4.

8. Concerning solar *prostaphereses*.

9. Of epochs and finding the place of mean motion of the sun for a given time according to chapter 8.

10. Of computation of solar movement according to chapter 9.

14. Of the inequality of natural days according to chapter 9.

15. Of the movement of the sun about its own center and its spots.

16. Of sun time, and the third book is finished.

April

4. It will be expounded by what observation the accidents of the moon are to be examined according to the first chapter of the 4th book of the *Almagest*.

5. Will treat of the periodic times of the moon according to chapter 2.

6. Of the actual movements of the moon according to its parts, according to chapters 3 and 4.

8. It will be shown that, if you consider the moon by itself, it gives the appearance of both eccentric and epicycle, according to chapter 5.

9. Will set forth a demonstration of the first and simple lunar inequalities according to chapter 6.

11. Will treat of the emendation of the movements of mean longitude and inequality of the moon according to chapter 7.

12. Concerning the places of equal motion of longitude and inequality of the moon in the time of *Habenassari* (Nebuchadnezzar?).

13. Of emendations of mean motions of latitude of the moon and of their places in the first year of Habenassari, according to chapter 9.

15. The table will be explained of the first and simple lunar inequality according to chapter 10.

16. Will treat of the difference between Ptolemy and Hipparchus in the quantity of lunar inequality according to chapter 11, and the fourth book will be finished.

18. At the beginning of the fifth book, will treat of the Astrolabe, according to the first chapter.

19. Concerning the supposition which pertains to the second inequality of the moon, according to chapter 2.

20. Of the quantity of the same inequality which appears according to the distance of the moon from the sun, according to chapter 3.

22. Concerning the proportion of the lunar eccentric circle according to chapter 4.

26. Of the declination of the lunar epicycle according to chapter 5.

27. Will show how, by lines from the periodic movements, the true movement of the moon is found, according to chapter 6.

28. Will expound the table of lunar inequality according to chapters 7 and 8.

30. Will treat of universal lunar calculus according to chapter 9.

May

11. Will make plain that no difference, to amount to anything, is made by conjunctions and oppositions with regard to the eccentric circle of the moon, according to chapter 10.

12. Will treat of the aspects of the diversity of the moon according to chapter 11.

14. Of the construction of the instrument to record the diversity of aspect according to chapter 12.

18. Lunar distances will be demonstrated according to chapters 13 and 14.

19. Will treat of the quantity of the diameters of the sun and of the moon and of the shadows which are seen in conjunction and opposition.

21. Of the distance of the sun and those matters which are demonstrated with this according to chapter 15.

23. Of the size of the sun, moon and earth according to chapter 16.

28. Of the table of aspects according to chapter 16.

30. Of the discerning the diversity of aspects according to chapter 19 which is the last of book five.

31. In beginning book six, we will treat of opposition of the luminaries according to chapter 1.

June

2. It will be shown how tables of mean conjunctions and oppositions are to be constructed according to chapter 2.

3. Will treat of the synods and full moon according to chapter 3.

4. It will be made plain how one ought to consider both periodic and true conjunctions and oppositions according to chapter 4.

6. Will treat of the ecliptic *termini* of the luminaries according to chapter 5.

7. Of the distance of the ecliptic months according to chapter 6.

8. Of the tables of the Egyptians according to chapter 7 and 8.

10. Of the computation of lunar eclipses according to chapter 9.

14. Of the computation of solar eclipses according to chapter 10.

15. Of the inclinations which are made by solar eclipses according to chapter 12.

17. Inquiry will be made concerning inclination according to chapter 12, and book six will be finished.

18. In beginning book seven it will be shown that the fixed stars always maintain the same relative positions, according to the first chapter.

21. Will show that the sphere of the fixed stars progresses according to the succession of the signs according to chapter 2.

22. Will demonstrate that the same sphere of the fixed stars is moved according to the succession of the signs about the poles of the ecliptic according to chapter 3.

23. A method will be declared for describing the fixed stars and indicating constellations on a solid sphere according to chapters 4 and 5 and the same constellations will be enumerated.

End of the Lectures for the Third Term.

176

CATALOGUE OF LECTURES AND EXERCISES WHICH THE PROFESSORS OF THE UNIVERSITY OF HESSE-SCHAUMBURG WILL HOLD NEXT SEMESTER FROM MICHAELMAS 1654 TO EASTER 1655

October 1 . . . by Peter Lucius, university printer.

John Henichius, doctor of sacred theology, after in the summer past he has finished the first part of moral aphorisms and has exercised his hearers in homiletics, has it in mind, for the sake of those who delight in the study of ecclesiastical antiquities, to survey and confute briefly the chief heresies by which once the mysteries of the Christian religion were opposed.

Dr. Henry Martin Eccard, if God wills and in so far as the public office which he still holds permits, will continue to explain the articles of faith and to have and hold public disputations, which finished, he will revert to the interpretation of Genesis.

Dr. Peter Musaeus will engage, if God is good, in private explanation of theological passages and solution of leading controversies. Moreover, the philosophical disciplines, logic and metaphysic, which last semester he expounded privately, he will henceforth teach publicly; and he will proceed to hold public metaphysical disputations, worked out for the profit of studious youth according to the number of respondents; nor will he fail in guidance to those who wish to train themselves in disputation privately whether in theology or in philosophy.

Dr. David Pestel, by the favor of the divine will, will labor publicly to unravel and solve the skein of judicial procedure, following the guiding thread of the most noble â Rosbach; and within private walls having reviewed the *Institutes* he will subject to examination the disputations thereon written by lord Ludelius Altorphinus, his predecessor.

Dr. Christoph Joachim Bucholtz, professor of the *Code*, will undertake to explain publicly singular matters of law from the *Code;* and at the same time he will open a private college [1] of practice in which one may make a start in practice.

Dr. John Martin Brandes, professor of the *Pandects*, will pursue the subject of public judgments, lecturing publicly from the 48th book of the *Digest.* Privately, having dismissed the college on the *Institutes*, he will open another or a lecture course or a disputation, as may suit the needs of those cultivating jurisprudence.

Bernhard Schultze, doctor and professor of public law, will publicly expound the compendium of public law written by the most noble Lampadius concerning the Roman-German state; and he will continue to subject to public examination the dissertations of Bernhard Sutholt, in which the universal law of institutions is explained from its foundations; and within private walls he will endeavor to finish the *Pandects* of Matthaeus Wesenbechius with the *Animadversions* of Reinard Bachovius; and having finished reading Grotius on the law of war and peace, he will open another college for students of jurisprudence.

Dr. Rodoger Timpler, professor of medicine, when the course which he has started in general pathology is finished, will come by God's

---

[1] That is, a seminar.

gift to special pathology, and first the explanation of internal disorders; and at the same time, he has whispered to the gentlemen students, he will open a private college of chemistry.

Master Reinhard König, professor of history and politics, will treat and resolve publicly the more illustrious political matters from both sides. Having now completed some private colleges, he will open one of history and will institute private discourses concerning the nature and constitution of histories, their importance, necessity and utility, also enjoyment; with what judgment historians are to be read, in what order, and who of them is more delectable. And if it so pleases his hearers, these discourses will be printed with political additions.

Master Gerard Bodin, professor of eloquence and the Hebrew language, will lecture publicly on those matters which seem to pertain to the third part of rhetoric, namely elocution. Privately he will have two colleges in Hebrew, one of grammar, the other Biblical and textual.

Master Arnold Redeker, professor of morals and poetry, perhaps as a consequence of his recent long illness expresses himself in a complicated sentence which can hardly be translated clearly but of which the gist is that he will lecture publicly on Aristotle's Nicomachean Ethics and Poetics, and privately will teach moral doctrine from an epitome.

Master John Stille, professor of mathematics and physics, after he has finished the Spherical Precepts of Stierius, will add some points about erecting *sciatherici* and *themates coeli*,[2] passed over dry-shod by that author but not to be rejected in another more roomy place. Afterwards, Providence permitting, he will enter the vast field of Theories of the Planets according to the hypotheses concerning the system of the world both of Ptolemy and Copernicus, follower of the pristine Pythagoreans. Privately he will open a college of geometry to give more ready access to the course in military architecture which will begin next summer. And if any students wish to dispute in physics, he will offer material on the principles of physics from the mind of the Aristotelians.

[2] Sundials and horoscopes.

APPENDIX I

DE COMMENDATIONE CLERI

Vatic. Palat. lat. 1252, fols. 99r–109v.

In this appendix the generally approved method in editing Latin texts is followed: namely, that words or letters not found in the MS but which in the judgment of the editor should be in the text are enclosed in claw-hammer brackets —< >, while words or letters found in the MS which in the judgment of the editor should not be in the text are enclosed in square brackets—[ ]. The foliation of the MS is indicated within parentheses.

Si dormiatis inter medios cleros penne columbe deargentate et posteriora dorsi eius in pallore auri. In hiis verbis, si quis altius ea perspexerit, spiritus domini per os propheticum tanquam per tubam altisonat auream felicis cleri benedictionem. Quoniam et si clericos quo ad statum recipimus scolasticum congrua sunt hec verba laudibus eorum. Si etiam quo ad ritum militantis ecclesie conveniunt apertissime clericali decori. Quid enim est dormire inter medios cleros quam ipsos quiescere in medio extremitatum omnium agibilium humanorum. Omnis enim virtus humana in medio duarum consistit malitiarum sicut in monosticis [1] oportunitatibus elucidavi. Et qui a vitiis non abstinent, quamvis omnes noverint scripturas, medii clerici non sunt sed extremi, non enim virtuosi sunt sed potius malitiosi. Et extremorum siquidem duo sunt genera scilicet clerus deficiens et clericus habundans. Clerus enim a medio deficiens est ille qui labores studiorum abhorret sed in apparentiis scientiarum altius gloriatur qui modus catinus asseritur. Catus etenim piscem amat sed flumina fugit atque in ritibus ecclesie militantis sunt nonnulle qui celos ascendere cupiunt sed terrenas blandities non postponunt. Clerus autem habundans a medio est qui nimis accuit ingenium suum et altius quam viribus queat volare desiderat. Quibus apostolus ait, Non debemus plus sapere quam oportet sed ad sobrietatem id est ad convenientem mensuram. Sunt etiam quidam in actibus ecclesie militantis excedentes volentes exercitia corporis desiderio mentis coequare. Cum spiritus quidem promptus sit, caro autem infirma. Aut certe dici potest quod clerus deficiens in statu scolastico est hic qui naturas plurium abnegat rerum quemadmodum frater Wilhelmus de Octhan anglicus atque sui sequaces qui tam relationes quam situs habitus ubi quando asseruntur preter animam res indistinctas a rebus absolutis atque quantitatem eandem cum substantia rem affirmant. Motus etiam in quibus

[1] Monasticis?

actiones rerum et passiones firmantur dicunt res indistinctas a permanentibus rebus. Illi autem in statu scolastico habundant a medio qui quedam preter animam fingunt conceptibilia que ipsi res esse abnegant sed modos intrinsecos rerum aut certe rerum formalitates depingunt et in deo hii talium formalitatum ponunt pluralitatem preter hoc quod summa simplicitas collatur in eo. Et deficientes quidem clerici nausigraphi dici potuerunt eo quod nauseam pretendant in scripturis rerum aut nature distincte asscriptarum. Dicitur enim nausigraphus a nausea et grahos quod est scriptura. Habundantes autem pleographi dicantur a pleos quod est supervacuum quasi supervacua scribentes unde etiam pleonasmus dicitur superflua dictionis additio ut dicendo ego omne loquebar. (fol. 99v)

Clerici vero proprie dicti sunt qui a medio virtutum non exorbitant nec a centro veritatis ad circumferentias inanes declinant. Nam in medio subsistere sanior est usus. Hii sunt felicissimi virorum quibus hoc solis proprium est ut hominum regant universum. Sunt quasi dii in humanis corporibus hospitati in quorum scolis spiritus domini habitat et exaltatur deus in cordibus eorum, quoniam hii sunt medium divinum ex participatione gratie dei in quo deus deorum deos id est magistros sapientiarum diiudicat propheta dicente, Deus stetit in synagoga deorum: in medio autem deos diiudicat. Et iterum, Ego dixi dei estis et filii excelsi omnes. Deus enim quamvis omnia cognoscat uberiori tamen gratia felicem clerum in medio omnium discernit virtutum. Dico clerum qui mortificavit omnia desideria sua in hoc seculo et qui sibi deum pro sorte et hereditate sua accepit aut qui de sorte atque parte est domini. Nam sicut ait Papyas, Cleros idem est quod sors vel hereditas: inde clerici dicuuntur quia dominus est sors et hereditas eorum. Ergo qui bona huius mundi extra deum desiderant et preter deum amant quippe clerici non sunt eo quod hereditas non sit dominus illorum neque pars hereditatis. Quilibet enim verus clerus spiritus dei vim possidet et in eodem spiritu sicut olim propheta flagrantibus perorat labiis dicens, Dominus pars hereditatis mee et calicis mei: tu es qui restitues hereditatem meam michi. Eiusdem denique felicis hominis ut comprehensoris in patria deus est tota hereditas et ipsius ut viatoris in hac vita est tanquam pars hereditatis. Quia nemo hic plene divina fruitur bonitate sicud in patria sed quasi partialiter quoniam diminute.

Potest etiam clerus dici a cleos quod est gloria et ros rorum quasi ros glorie humane aut quia generis humani gloria roscida et fructifera est clerus benedictus. Sicut enim ros celi terram impregnat et fecundat floribus et herbis atque generaliter vegetabilibus nascentibus ex terra, ita procul dubio clerus felix virtutibus et sapientia genus humanum depingit et ornat atque coronat gloria celesti et honore dulcedinis divine quam siquidem dulcedinem bonitatis dei clerus aliis hominibus dispensat domino largiente. Aut dicitur clerus a cleus quod est mons altus et ros rorum quasi mons domini altus et roscidus. Dicitur enim clerus mons altus ex apice seu celsitudine speculationis et contemplationis divine atque mons roscidus quo ad doctrine sancte fertilitatem et bonorum operum ubertatem. Vel dicitur clerus a cleus quod est ascensus et ros rorum quasi ascensus roridus id est ascensus fructifer in deum. Isti namque sunt lux mundi et lucerne ac lampades quibus ecclesia dei tanquam serenissimis radiis illuminatur. Ecce clerus ascensus est atque mens coagulatus fortitudinis et perseverantie firmitate. Sicut scriptum est, Qui perseveraverit usque in finem salvus erit. Mons pinguis felicum operum fructificatione ut sibi dicatur, De fructu operum tuorum satiabitur terra. Iste utique mons est de quo propheta dicit, Mons in quo beneplacitum est deo habitare, in eo etenim dominus habitabit in finem.

Convenio vos inquam O layci quare non dormitis. Cur non quiescitis inter medios cleros? Non intuemini quod intus habent? Sed exteriora eorum corroditis preter id quod intrinsecus latet in ipsis et sic testam non nucleum iudicatis. Non dormitis in<ter> hos sed ad ipsos exterius vos convertitis molestiis atque nauseante suspicione ut quidem suspicamini montes coagulatos. (fol. 100r) Quare tanquam fere arundinis dilaceratis illos vos milites temporales inquam quorum motus ab arundine exeunt que vento vane glorie agitatur. Arundines vos dico apparentie vane que intus nil habent nisi aerem inflationis et superbie inanis. Ve vobis infelicibus feris exercentibus ferocitatem inhumanam in patriominium Christi quod inter vos dividitis tanquam spolia et rapinas. Sed non minus peccati habet congregatio taurorum in vaccis populorum qui se tanquam domesticos ecclesie dei et advocatos ecclesiasticarum asserunt personarum sed oves lactiferas quales sunt fructus et obventiones ecclesiarum disgregant quasi thauri lascivientes et in usus suos convertunt spoliantes ecclesiam dei ut excludant viros ecclesiasticos qui probati sunt argumento puritatis et dissertionis divine. Domine deus meus increpa feras arundinis corripe thauros insanientes dissipa gentes que bella volunt contra ecclesiam tuam. Non enim dormiunt inter cleros tuos sed motibus iniquis eosdem inquietant nescientes illos esse fotores et pastores sponse tue immaculate columbe tue benedicte, columbe inquam simplicitatis turturis pulchritudinis cuius vox primo audita est in terra nostra per unigenitum tuum ewangelizantem nobis verbum patris verbum veritatis verbum pacis et felicitatis eterne. In terra dico quam ex castis clausulis induit virginis benedicte in terra nostre humanitatis.

Penne columbe illius deargentate sunt argento facundie divinorum eloquiorum quibus dulcissime volat ritus ecclesie inter animas fidelium Christi. Iste sunt penne quibus volant ewangelizantes verbum dei. Penne utique altivole que divina humanis conportant celos transcendunt et principem porrigunt celorum. Qui dulciloquia ecclesie cuius caput Christus est audire desideret attendat cantica Salomonis et certe si bene sapuerit dulcedinem eorum dicet cum propheta, Quam dulcia faucibus meis eloquia tua super mel ori meo. O vere benedicta et deliciosa Christi columba nam et posteriora dorsi eius in pallore auri. Dorsum spina est ossea transiens per totum corpus animalis habens sibi costas annexas quasi sustentamentum corporis totius. Incedit autem hec spina nodose et articulatim a summo usque deorsum. Quid igitur aliud est dorsum ecclesie sustenans eam quam fides catholica? Est enim fides articulata et nodosa articulis et nodis que in symbolo Christiano ponuntur atque huic adherent coste id est scripturarum appendentie et quedam additiones quas ecclesia dei addidit que certe sunt de fidei integritate et sustentant substantiam ecclesie Christi. Posteriora dorsi sunt postrema et ultimata fidei sustentamenta sine quibus fides esset mortua et absque medulla vivacitatis sicut sunt karitas in sapientia dei et sapientia in karitate opera karitativa et karitas operosa. Sine hiis etenim fides est in divinum anime mortue nil decoris habens in oculis Dei. Et testis est michi in hiis vas electionis quia non mentior. Si lingwis inquit hominum atque angelorum loquar karitatem autem non habuero factus sum sicut es sonans et cymbalum tynnens. Hec siquidem postrema fidei fulcimenta in que ultimate omnia bona fidei resolvuntur quamvis prima sint fundatione atque vigore et maioritate quia maior horum est karitas sunt tamen ultima resolutione. Simile huius videmus (fol. 100v) in principiis domus materialis nam que prima sunt domus principia via compositionis quemadmodum fundamenta sunt ultima via resolutionis. Sunt autem hec posteriora fidei orthodoxe pulcherrima et pallore auri quemadmodum amicta. Nam sicut aurum super omnia est metalla nitore atque nobilitate et ex natura sua cor hominis confortans sic revera karitas omnia et singula confortat opera pietatis. Qui ergo dormit extra cleros dei extra Christi ecclesiam dormit non siquidem dormitione quietis et salutis sed mortis dormitione non mortis temporalis sed mortis eterne. Et sic infideles dormiunt extra prespiteros Christi dormiunt utique per bonorum operum cessationes quomodo nichil recte fidei operantur. Alii vero sunt infra ecclesiam et inter cleros a quibus ecclesie recipiunt sacramenta sed non dormiunt inter cleros id est non quiescunt quiete ipsos felicitante nec cuiquam eorum poterit dici, Si dormit salvus erit, sed potius dormiunt tanquam patientes lytargum aut aliam egritudinem qua dormitur sicut sunt qui semen iusquiami gustaverunt aut quos ypnapis serpens momordit. Est enim ypnapis serpens ut dicit Solynus de genere aspidis quem etiam Iheronimus et hystoria Romanorum aspidem vocant qui quos mordet sompno interimit, quia veneno suo inmittit sompnum qui nullo impulsu poterit averti. Semen iusquiami comedunt qui infra Christi ecclesiam nomen acceperunt Christianum sed non est in eis aliqua scintilla karitatis ymmo frigent frigore invidie ac odii algore ut nec proximum diligant nec dominum ament creatorem suum.

Sic enim frigiditas iusquiami id est terrene vanitatis congelavit eos in duritiem lapideam. Est namque herba hec ex natura sua frigidissima secundum phisicorum assertiones atque cum hoc momordit eos ypnapis serpens et intoxicavit animas eorum. Serpens inquam malitie dyabolus nostre humane propaginis inimicus ut incessanter dormiant dormitione qua clauditur ratio serena ad sola bona inclinata quamvis sensualiter vigilent tanquam bestie et animalia bruta. Hii sunt quos accidia nichil sinit divini operis operari sed quasi in omnibus byrriana pigritia torpent, quibus si matutino sydere dicitur, Surge byrria, Byrria surge, non surgunt hii sed brachia scalpunt et pedes in longum distendunt capita sua huc et illuc volutando. Malunt enim in lectis suis stercere quam divinis laudibus invigilare.

Sunt etiam alii homines qui non tam a bonis cessant operibus quam etiam continua sollicitudine ecclesiam Christi et pastores ecclesiarum inquietantes, quamvis nomen habeant Christianum. Et hii infra ecclesiam non tam preter ecclesiam quam contra ecclesiam vigilant die noctuque ut matrem suam sacrosanctam exhereditent dotibus suis et exterminent eam sibi ipsis nichilominus in confusionem et in supplicium sempiternum. Que prochdolor tyrannides in nonnullis Alamanie partibus nostris temporibus adeo inolevit ut non solum patrimonium Christi vilibus diripiatur tyrannis sed etiam libertas ecclesiastica in servitutem penitus redigatur. Isti non dormiunt inter cleros benedictos nec dei vivi in cuius iudicio sunt fovent columbam sed potius eisdem insidiantur similes cuidam generi draconum quod ipsis columbis naturaliter insidiatur. (fol. 101r) Legimus enim in naturalibus quod in oriente quedam arbor est que greca lingwa paradyzum dicitur latine vero quasi circa dexteram appellatur. Illius siquidem arboris fructus dulcis est in quo columbe mira quadam delectatione delectantur atque umbra et ramis eius ab eisdem insidiantibus draconibus proteguntur. Quoniam huiusmodi dracones hec naturaliter horrent in tantum ut umbra illius arboris timeant attingi. Quapropter sedentibus columbis in hac arbore dracones a longinquo insidiantur eis atque diligenter respiciunt si ulla earum arborem hanc deserat et in sortem ipsis cedat. Ista etiam dracones venando columbas illudunt calliditate quod si umbra fuerit parte dextra insidiantur sinistra et econverso aut si antrorsum insidiantur retrorsum et vice versa.

Sic felicissima Christi columba ecclesia sancta dei non aliud subsidium habet nisi arborem benedictam lignum sancte crucis cuius fructus dulcissimus flores eius super omnia aromata redolentiores folia eius latissima ad refrigerandum estuantes autem calore propter quid ipsa eadem columba in die passionis Christi speciales laudes medullariter ympnizat sic dulciter canens, Crux fidelis inter omnes arbor una nobilis nulla silva talem profert fronde flore germine, ffructus enim huius tam ammirabilis quam venerabilis arboris Christus est. Quo non est fructus dulcior nec sanior sed ut dicam laudabilior in celo et in terra. Quem qui manducaverit vivet in eternum. Flores eius fructum hunc in circuitu ornantes undique amici Christi sunt utpote martires rubro colore sue passionis virgines candore sue puritatis confessores fiolatico colore sue contritionis et doctores ewangelici ceruleo seu aureo sue venerabilis informationis. Et frondes denique ipsius seu folia delicie sunt bonitatis divine scilicet misericordia pietas largitas vel karitas et universaliter divitie sapientie dei quibus ab insidiantibus inimicis ecclesia Christi defenditur et in seculum defendetur. Si etenim quandoque a malis patitur in ruinam permittitur illorum non tamen in ecclesie durabile detrimentum. O iniqui dracones quorum dux dyabolus est quo usque tendunt insidie vestre? Estimo quod non nisi ad proprium interitum vestrum. Non potestis sustinere columbam avem simplicem et innocuam cum tamen ingratas opupas atque nocuos coradulos sustineatis. Ista siquidem avis sine felle est. Secundum Bedam puro grano vescitur, nulli nocet, morticinio non vivit, super aquas libenter requiescit ut sitim restringat et advenientis accipitris umbram perspiciat in aquis, atque gemitum pro cantu habet. Intuere queso et respice diligenter has columbe proprietates et videbis quantum decenter congruunt ecclesie Christi quoniam ecclesia fel amaritudinis et fraudis non habet. Cunctis etenim vult prodesse et nulli obesse ad instar dilecti sui qui Christus est unigen tus dei. Puro grano vescitur quia de decimis vivit et aliis donationibus que in pios usus convertuntur. Sunt etenim hec vescibilia pura quia sine contractibus iniquitatis fieri debent. Non vivit morticinio, id est lucris quibus mortalis macula contrahatur. Super aquas sapientie scientie fortitudinis consilii intellectus et aliorum spiritus sancti donorum libenter requiescit, scriptura de ipsa dicente, Vidi speciosam sicut columbam descendentem (fol. 101v) desuper rivos aquarum quas siquidem aquas Christus promisit discipulis suis et omnibus in eum credentibus se daturum unde et Samarithane dixit, Qui bibit aquam quam ego do fiet in eo fons aque salientis in vitam eternam. Istas aquas bibit ecclesia ad satisfaciendum siti karitatis in deum pro modulo divine fruitionis in hac vita que tamen tenuis est et quasi equivoce dicta ad eam que est in patria fruitionem. Bibit etiam illas aquas ad restringendum sitim carnalium desideriorum quoniam ubi spiritus domini adest carnis abest illecebra. Etiam in hiis aquis munit se Christi columba contra sibi adversantis accipitris id est dyaboli insidias et carnis atque mundi huius vana desideria et inanes promissiones. Ecclesia militans gemitum pro cantu habet quoniam presente sibi sponso qui ubique est tamquam absente sibi caret in comparatione ad eas delicias quibus ipsum in patria comprehendet. Et propter hanc absentiam dilecti languet amore ipsius unde et ad hanc intentionem gemitus sui ipsa in Canticis ait, Nunciate dilecto quia amore langueo.

Ex habitis itaque liquet quod dormientes inter medios cleros dormitione salutis dormiunt sub alis columbe atque sponse brachiis, sponse inquam dei omnium utique pulcherrime mulierum cuius clerici sunt rectores et dispensatores divitiarum suarum. Qui siquidem clerici pastores et prelati populorum argentum possident divine facundie qui et nectar bibunt celestium eloquiorum et nichilominus aurum id est lumen habent ecclesie quod feliciter distribuunt in singulos prout capaces sunt eiusdem. Sed qualiter argento et auro utantur magistri et discipuli in domibus scolasticis in hoc tractatu apparebit, quoniam scientie liberales que in eloquentiam finaliter ordinantur congrue poterunt argento comparari, quales sunt grammatica rethorica et loyca et trivium nuncupantur. Alie vero scientie que in agnitionem veritatis finaliter deputantur sicut sunt arysmetica musica geometria et astronomia cetere quoque sub hiis conprehense conparantur rationabiliter auro. Quapropter scolastica disciplina que prelatos ecclesie parit atque nutrit quousque in annos suarum maturitatum merito columba dicitur pennis argenteis mirabiliter pennata quo ad scientias triviales et certe posteriora dorsi eius in pallore auri quo ad habitus quadruviales.

Si ergo vos O filioli mei filioli inquam septennes apti literarum mancipationi quiescatis inter medios cleros id est doctores venerabiles scolasticos virtuosos atque nutriamini ab eisdem, sub alis militabitis columbe benedicte sub brachiis omnium virtutum nutriatis atque sub clamide phylosophie scolastice que est amata sapientia omnium bonorum magistra cuius mirabiles utique sunt delectationes firmitate et puritate. Scolastica tamen disciplina quasi nutrix est ecclesie militantis et pullus columbe dici poterit eo quod educet ac nutriat parvulos in ecclesia dei pastores preficiendos.

Si vero inter sophistas dormieritis graculum pro intersignio feretis vestre vanitatis. Est etenim graculus avis que crebras quasi unius figure continuat voces. Sic errophyli non aliud virtutis aut bonitatis accipiunt quam quod inaniter garriunt tota die. Dicitur autem errophylus ab errore et phylos (fol. 102r) quod est amor quasi amator errorum. Et sunt omnes tales qui potius in dictis suis amant singularitatem quam quod proferant veritatem quasi rara non tamen vera altitudinem arguant ingeniorum aput eos. Dorsum autem vere columbe scolastice est habitus primorum principiorum naturaliter venientium ad habentem per que ultimatim omnia scibilia solidantur sicut sunt enunciationes hec kathegorice, Ens est ens, Aliquid est aliquid, Res est res, atque iste conditionales: Si ens est aliquid est, et econtrario, Si aliquid est ens est, Si res est aliquid est. Similiter et iste disiunctive: Omne conceptibile aut est ens aut non ens, De quolibet esse vel non esse et de nullo eorum ambo. Coste vero huius dorsi possunt dici prima scientiarum specialium principia. Quia quelibet scientia suis propriis gaudet et principiis primis. Posteriora vero dorsi huius sunt lumina spiritus sancti atque virtus intellectus agentis nam hiis irradiantibus in animam rationalem ex parte intellectus possibilis recipiuntur in eo conceptibilia prima et in eorum virtute intellectus speculativus ducitur in posteriora tamquam in luminibus humanarum cognitionum. Unde ad hanc intentionem illustris vir Linconiensis primo Posteriorum ait, Non solum doctor exterius in aure sonans docet nec solum littera visa docet sed ille verus doctor qui interius mentem illuminat et veritatem demonstrat.

Quapropter de domibus scolasticis nunc magis speculariter videamus, quia secundum promissum a principio ordinem hic tertius liber meus yconomicus de regimine domorum rimabitur divinarum. Et ratio in hiis postulat primo venari qualiter prelati qui presunt domibus divinis et universaliter ecclesiastice persone in scolastica nutriantur disciplina et mox subiungere oportebit qualiter in scolis sufficienter nutriti et officiis ecclesiasticis postea preficiendi et prefecti se debeant habere.

CAPITULUM SECUNDUM. PONENS DOMUS SCOLASTICE DESCRIPTIONEM

Scolastica domus est communicatio persone docentis hominis et eorum qui ab illo discunt in mansorio sollicitudinis literarum. Dico communicatio ad differentiam unius domus hominis quia communicatio proprie est plurium hominum. Igitur heremita solitarius manens in tecto suo domum scolasticam non constituit. Et dico persone ad differentiam brutorum animalium que licet saltem gregalia in uno mansorio sibi mutuo communicent opera sua tamen non sunt corpora personalia eo quod persona in proposito sit rationabilis creatura individua essentia et sic apum communicatio excluditur que siquidem carent ratione. Dico etiam docentis et eorum qui discunt ad differentiam aliarum communicationum in domo sicut est communicatio viri ad uxorem et domini ad servum et huiusmodi. Atque dico in mansorio ad differentiam domus materialis que scola dicitur in qua disciplina scolastica exercetur. Hec enim domus ex lapidibus et lignis fabricata non est communicatio personarum docentis et discipulorum sed potius latibulum in quo dicta communicatio se exercitat operibus suis. Dico etiam sollicitudinis literarum ad differentiam communicantium personarum ad invicem sine sollicitudine aut si cum sollicitudine non tamen literarum sed potius aliarum occupationum. Et propter hoc non proprie sunt domus scolastice ubi aut doctor non est sollicitus erudiendo (102v) aut discipuli in capiendo. Dicitur enim scola a scolon quod est sollicitudo eo quod tam magister quam discipulus sollicitudinem ut oportet debeat habere, hic quidem in dispensando illi autem in recipiendo. Nec domus scolastica proprie dicitur ubi circa alia quam circa scientias literarum occupatur, sicut est sollicitudo circa dimicandi agilitatem cuius receptaculum proprie gympnasium dicitur quamvis propter quandam harum occupationum similitudinem unum interdum pro altero transsumatur. Si quis etiam subtiliter inspexerit non sine ratione in priori particula pluraliter dixi et eorum qui ab illo discunt quoniam eruditio unius ab uno scolasticam non proprie constituit domum. Nos enim in proposito eam personarum communicationem domum usitamus que cum quadam sit solempnitate et discipulorum distincta graduatione sicut infra patebit. Et preterea relative ab illo scilicet homine docente dicebam ad differentiam spiritus dei et intellectus agentis quibus aliqui latenter quasi per seipsos inveniendo addiscunt scientias sibi novas. Atque etiam per hoc scripturarum elementa renoventur quibus tanquam ab homine mortuo seu depicto instruimur et docemur. Non est autem homo mortuus homo nisi equivoce sic neque spiritus sanctus homo est nec intellectus agens homo est sed hii duo principes potius sunt humane compositionis.

CAPITULUM TERTIUM. DE DISTINCTIONE DOMUS SCOLASTICE

Scolasticarum autem domorum quatuor sunt genera, quia sunt scole artistarum medicorum iuristarum et theologorum. Sic enim distinguit eas mater nostra venerabilis universitas Parysiensis que hiis quatuor facultatibus distincta loca discernit auditoriorum atque distinctos habitus dispensat dominis earum. Artiste namque prope Secanam flumen in vico straminum cuius in extremis stramina marginibus venduntur artes percolunt liberales. Et hii in cappis nigris atque rotundis de nobili bruneto aut subtili persyto subducto quoque vario incedunt frequentantes kathedras ordinariarum lectionum in aurora diei. Nominantur autem artiste a septem liberalibus artibus et sub hiis comprehensis, quorum siquidem facultas non est nisi subtilium ingeniorum grosse namque ruditates earum artes aut apices attingere nequibunt. Congruus est hic habitus phylosophie liberalis dominis quia nigri coloris natura visum est congregare. Oportet namque interne visionis eum congregare vires qui tam subtilia rerum volumina perspicaciter appetit intueri atque totius machine universi tam principiorum differentias quam etiam principiatorum alietates funditus speculari. Rotunditatis vero plus quam thalarum spericitas gyrum denotat creati orbis quem hii sui capacitate cerebri claudere videntur metientes astrorum qualitates ventorum varios volatus naturas quoque animalium et plantarum mineralium virtutes atque omnium metherologycarum impressionum originationes. Unde et birreti testella qua caput suum philosophus coronat capacitatem sui cerebri atque sue mentis hyatum figurat. Fflos autem birreti morum significat decorem liberalium scientiarum comitantium thesauros. Quia perfectus non est philosophus quem non omnis virtus humana bonis moribus perornat. Aurum in digitis quo antiquitus ornabantur artium magistri mentis sapientiam significabat atque gemma in auro excellentiam sapientis ad communes homines connotabat, quia sapiens est naturaliter dominus rudium populorum. Attamen vetustas olim phylosophie dominis pallia indulserat rotunda nichilominus (103r) antrorsum patula et vario subducta que siquidem de scarleto fiebant optimo rubro flammata colore et pallii rotunditas idem quod in cappa sperica connotaverat. Sed flammeus hoc innuerat fervor ut hii super omnes homines ferverent ad rimandum mirabilium mundi humanitus agnitiones. Nichil etenim quondam exteriorum veri phylosophi sollicitaverant utilitatum sed totus laborum suorum in hoc finis congre < g > atus est ut originum et rerum originatarum agnoscerent veritatem. Et propter huius finis unitatem latitudo omnium liberalium scientiarum una scilicet artistarum dicitur facultas.

Hinc vero medici in domibus suarum habitationum morantes suos venerabiliter auditoribus elucidant anforysmos. Et guadent hii cappis ordinariis de bruneto siquidem lucidiori quam artiste magisque rubore nubente quasi colorato cerusio quodam colore cerusi maturati ut in vicinitate coloris huius ad verum brunetum facultatum harum adinvicem connotetur connexio, quoniam inanis est medicus qui loycam ignorat aut qui ad naturalem philosophiam non habet recursum. Cerusius etiam color cum sit nigredo declinans in ruborem turbationem significat egritudinum commixtam bone spei ad medicum fixione. Nisi enim quis eger esset medicum non sitiret nec medicum infirmus appeteret si non per illum iuvari speraret.

Post hos iuristarum se vigent eruditici, quibus chnobernelli vicus Parysius deputatur qui et vicus dicitur asinorum. Isti cappis gaudent scolasticis de scarleto igniti siquidem ruboris quoniam color rubeus mentis flagrantiam significat. Ffervent etenim hii circa humani generis tranquillitatem atque infinitis se immiscent questionibus ad compescendum materias litium et reprimendum conatus innumeros litigatorum. Aut ideo eis color hic indultus est tam patule apparicionis quia circa res publicas humane sollicitantur moralitatis.

Supreme vero omnium scolarum cathedre in claustris religiosorum atque in domo Sorbone aliisque collegiis benedictis feliciter statuuntur ad legendum libros theologicos et mirabilia divinarum scripturarum disserendum. Reverendi quoque theologice profunditatis magistri cappis induuntur sui ordinis si viri sint religiosi aut cuiuscumque simplicis actu seu humilis coloris si clerici sint seculares ad connotandum huius scientie humilem atque innocuam in se predicationem. Et sicut medici a phisicis derivantur, sic canoniste a theologis oriuntur quia sacri canones plerumque conclusiones sunt divinorum eloquiorum sicut patet decreta patrum diligenter intuenti.

Alia quoque divisio scolarum dari poterit ut dicatur quod scolarum alia est autentica alia vero leninoma. Et autentica est cuius studia privilegiis apostolicis imperialibus quoque libertatibus sunt laudabiliter fundata sicut scole Parysienses Bononienses Paduenses et Oxonienses. Leninoma autem scola est que levis nominis est carens privilegiis principum mundi sicut in Theutonia scole sunt Erfordenses Viennenses et huiusmodi. Et siquidem differentia magna est in illis quoniam in autenticis milites fiunt et domini scientiarum coronantur ut tam vestibus quam libertatibus gaudeant specialibus atque reverentiis singularibus reverantur non minus a principibus laycis et clericis quam a vulgo, atque tales magistri et domini sunt scientiarum laudabiliter intytulati. In leninomis vero quamvis magistri nutriantur re non cum privilegiata tytulatione ex quo sequitur quod magistri nomen est equivocum ad plura. Est enim aliquis magister tytulo et re, alius vero magister re sed non tytulo, (103v) et tertius magister tytulo sed non re, quartus autem est magister nec tytulo nec re sed sola nominatione. Magister tytulo et re propriissime dicitur magister quoniam hic habitus scientiarum possidet et cum hoc tytulo gaudet meritis condignis acquisito atque libertatibus principum privilegiato. Dicitur autem tytulus a tytan quod est sol quia sicut sol orbem corporeum lumine suo decorat sic verus tytulus intytulatum laudabiliter perornat. Sed magister dicitur quasi ter magis aliis prelatus utpote ingenio mentis habitu rationis et virtutum operatione, quorum si unum deficit non est hic bonus magister. Qualiter autem verus magister tytulum suum obtineat infra patebit. Magister re sed non tytulo est qui thesauros scientiarum habet atque virtutum possidet hereditatem sed tytulum non accepit privilegiatum. Et hic similis est nobili viro strennuo atque in armis laudabili qui nondum privilegio utitur militari. Sed magister tytulo et non re est qui precibus aut pretio symoniace ingreditur ad solam magistratus intytulationem rebus scientiarum ad tantum tytulum carens. Iste viro timido comparatur qui numquam actum bellicum exercuit nec exercebit attamen militie tytulum accepit ut sericeis appareat in divinis et in digitis suis splendeat auro. Est autem magister nec re nec tytulo sed sola nominatione qui nec res scientiarum notabiles possidet nec tytulum in scolis sibi usurpavit [2] privilegiatis sed aliquo eventu nomen accepit magistri ut quia notarius domini aut causidicus in foro contentioso.

CAPITULUM QUARTUM. DE PERSONIS ET COMMUNICATIONE PERSONARUM IN DOMO

In domo scolastica leninoma artistarum quatuor sunt persone ad minus necessarie videlicet magister discipulus pedagogus et accusator. Magister est paterfamilias atque dominus scolastice domus cui singule persone in eadem communicantes domo reverenter obedire tenentur. Sed discipulus est filius atque heres magistri cui pater sue mentis thesaurum venerabiliter dispensat vel saltem desiderat dispensare. Pedagogus vero est ductor pueri scolastici et in scola ipsius vicemagister. Illum autem accusatorem dicimus

[2] Usurpant in the MS.

qui scolarium excessus pernotat et ipsorum exorbitaciones magistro accusat. Dictarum quatuor personarum tres sunt communicationes: videlicet magistri cum discipulis tanquam patris cum heredibus, et magistri cum vicemagistris et accusatore tanquam domini cum servis, atque communicatio servorum cum filiis venerabilis magistratus. Nos enim in hac domo divina communicationem viri hominis ad uxorem hominem non habemus sicut in domo temporali, verumtamen non est magister sine magistra nec poeta sine musa. Legictima etenim phylosophi socia est omnium deliciarum precipua in hac vita domina ipsa phylosophia que iubente domino est omnium virtutum magistra, quoniam simpliciter sumendo nomen phylosophie ipsa se ad omnes extendit sapientias ab humana specie possessas et tam divinitus quam humanitus acquisitas. Dicitur enim phylosophia quasi amata sapientia quapropter artista philosophus est medicus etiam quidam philosophus est naturalis inmediate a ramis incipiens rerum naturalium quarundam radices autem earum physico dimictit. Iurista philosophus est a phylosophia quadam morali, quoniam erudicio iuridica morali scientie subalternatur, ut ait Iohannes Monachi super decretalium sexto. Theologus philosophus est a phylosophia divina. Sed quoniam artiste de omnibus loquuntur materiis iam enunciatorum philosophorum ut pote de generatione hominis et eius natura atque partibus ipsius, sicut patet in libris Arystotilis de generacionibus animalium, et in hoc (104r) conveniunt cum medicis, loquuntur etiam de moribus hominum et de regimine domorum et civitatum imperantes homines virtuose vivere sicut liquet ethicos intuenti libros et yconomicos atque politicos egregii Aristotilis et in hoc conveniunt cum iuristis. Similiter de deo disputant et numero atque naturis intelligenciarum ut patet in libris methaphysice et in hoc cum theologis conveniunt, igitur artista verus authonomasice et per excellentiam philosophus nominatur.

Regrediendo igitur ad propositum dicamus quod vera uxor uniuscuiusque philosophi est sua phylosophia ex qua ipse parit libros sibi similes secundum formas et habitus anime sue et quod eius discipuli sunt quodammodo filii eius. Ffamilia vero ipsius sunt vicemagistri ac custodes scolarum qui secundum imperium magistri scolares instruunt et ab illicitis cohercent. Et plures oportuni sunt in scolis leninomis artistarum ministri quam in aliis eo quod heredes earum sint teneriores atque plurium differenciarum, quapropter tam in moribus quam scientiis capescendis pluribus tutoribus egent. In scolis autem artistarum autenticis tantum tres requiruntur persone preter balivos [3] scolarum clavigeros et preter predones seu pedellos qui magistrorum lecturas et disputaciones intimant communitati. Est namque in scola autentica magister bachalarius et discipuli. Quid autem sit magister aut discipulus dictum est prius sed bachalarius est archyscolaris qui loco magistri lectiones cursorias

[3] Maigne d'Arnis gives *balivus* as equivalent to *bajulus*.

legit atque qui arguendo et respondendo scolas doctorum perambulat nondum tamen lauream accepit milicie doctoralis sed nichilominus vicinus est ad magisterii gradum. Et dicitur bachalarius a baca quod est gemma et lar domus quasi gemma in domo scolastica. Aut dicitur bacalarius a bachalo quod est liber pater et lar ignis quasi ignis ardens liberi patris id est magistri, qui siquidem ignis illuminat domum scolasticam magistratus. Vel dicitur bachalarius non per a sed per v a baculo quod est sustentamentum vitis aut hominis, quoniam bacularius quodammodo sustenat magistrum. Sive per a dicitur bacalarius a baca quod est fructus lauri et lar laris quod est casa vel domus quasi fructus lauri in scolastica domo. Nam ut dicit Ysidorus laurus est arbor a ver<b>o laudis sic dicta quoniam ipsa olim in signum laudis capita militum et victorum coronabantur, unde apud veteres laudea dicebatur. Et asserunt naturales phylosophi quod hec arbor fulmine celi fulminari non possit. Ffolia numquam deponit et sunt odorifera multum habentque vim confortandi ex aromaticitate plurimam quoque operantur efficaciam medicine, unde arbor hec congrue doctorem significat qui mundanarum fulmine non leditur adversitatum nec concupiscenciarum aduritur ardore sicut ceteri homines sed in omni statu variabilis fortune viret foliis bonorum morum et aromatibus virtutum redolet bene. Illius fructus iam maturatus baca est id est archiscolaris qui bacalarius dicitur et vicino tempore ad magisterium aptus.

In aliquibus tamen studiis sicut Bononie loco bacalarii sumitur repititor precipue in iuridica facultate que viget ibidem. Et ille post lecturam doctoris ceteris repetit eandem lectionem qui voluerint audire. Sed hic modus Parysius non servatur. Bacalarii quodam vestitu gaudent angelico Parysius qui cappa rugata dicitur eo quod hic habitus rugis seu plicis subtilibus plenus sit a scapulis quousque ad talos, non sine ratione plenitudinem involutarum significans speculationum quibus bacalarius habundat. Habet etiam hoc indumentum alas duas thalares ad significandum volatum speculatoris tam sensuum efficacia quam lumine racionis. Nemo etenim ingeniosus est speculator in hac vita sine virium materialium anime (104v) efficacia et anime rationalis claritate. Aut poterunt hec due ale intellectus possibilis significare capacitatem et intellectus agentis activitatem, quia hiis binis alis volat speculator in apicem intellectus speculativi quem apicem phylosophi nominant intellectum adeptum, ut patet per Averoym tertio de anima. Iste igitur sunt persone quibus opus est in scolastica domo et quarum ad invicem quasi angelice sunt communicaciones sicut infra patebit.

CAPITULUM QUINTUM. DE CONDICIONIBUS MAGISTRI IN ARTIBUS

Oportet autem nos incipere a disciplina magistrorum in artibus tamquam a venerabili nutrice cuius regimine non prelibato ut oportet nemo humano studio ad cathedras aliarum facultatum assumetur. Unde qui facultatem deridet artium aut rusticus est quia literas non novit aut uterum detestatur in quo formatus est, ubera maledicit que suit, panem abnegat cottidianum, recusat spiraculum quo in aliis noticiis spirat, et quod sibi necessarium est tamquam vitandum turpiter blasphemat. Dicamus ergo quod magister in artibus regens cathedram in scolis autenticis et precipue Parysius ubi hec facultas ab antiquo possedit singulares prerogativas in se viii debet laudabilia congregare quorum primum est ut studio se doceat, secundum ut lecturas suas fructuose continuet, tertium ut ordinate procedat, quartum ut plus amet veritatem quam quod preferat singularitatem, quintum ut fidei catholice non oblatret, sextum ut sit morigerosus, septimum ut caveat de necessariis ad victum, et octavum ut symonia causas abhorreat promociones. Racio primi est quia qui sine previsione pronunciat non eque bene ac si previdisset enarrat, unde doctores qui studere negant ut ingeniosi videantur pocius ingenia sua scolaribus subtrahunt quam quod ea dispensentur eisdem. Ratio secundi est quoniam lector non continuans auditorium suum marcidat et ingratas reddit animas auditorum, unde ocia aut extraneos motus doctor postponat alias auditorium suum potius evacuat quam fecundet. Nec fructuose continuat quamvis non interpolet lectiones qui dispendiis innititur laborans mare in Danubium transffundere. Sed nec fertiliter continuat qui codices deputato tempori non come$<$n$>$titur ut cum temporibus ab universitate statutis salubriter finiantur. Ratio tertii est quoniam ordo in libris est cuiuslibet scientie secundum ordinem rerum congestarum in eis. Verumtamen ordo est doctrine facilioribus incipere et notioribus nobis atque sic procedere in nobis difficiliora et occultiora. Quapropter non ordinaria procedit doctrina que a prioribus in ordine nature ad posteriora eorum progreditur docendo sicut fecerat Plato sed potius Arystotelicus servandus est processus a posterioribus secundum naturam ad priora eundo. Ratio quarti est qui in omnibus singularis esse laborat potius sui ipsius fore nititur quam quod veridicus esse censeatur. Et sic contra ingenia omnium laborans ab omnibus est detestandus potius quam laudandus. Nemo etenim sibi ad omnia ingenium sufficiens habet sed veri speculatoris est plurima ab aliis mendicare et nonnulla per se ipsum invenire. Ratio quinti est quia qui fidei catholice oblatrat deum creatorem suum inhonestat, fantasmata sua divinis prefert miraculis, archana dei iudicat que penitus ignorat et siquidem stultiora asserit atque prudentiora philipendit. Dices forsitan michi quod nil tibi de miraculis dei cum de naturis rerum disseras. Et quid ego dicam? Certe mi$<$r$>$acula dei disputas cum mente tua ipsius revolvis creaturas. Nonne omnia in mira sapientia princeps universe mundi (105r) machine stabilivit? Et si solito nobis cursu fundavit singula ipse sua omnipotentia quodlibet eorum extra naturam suam poterit mirificare. Ratio sexti est quia philosophus non morigerosus moribus bonis non siquidem legalis est phi-

losophus sed potius adulter. Lex etenim philosophie est virtuose vivere munde
agere et vere sapere in singulis rebus, quapropter speculator inquit [4] vivens
aut immunda operans vel non vera sapiens potius errophilus quam philosophus intytulatur, repudiat namque hic philosophiam libello repudii turpi et
iniquo. Ratio septimi est quoniam turpe est tanti nominis reverentiam degere
ut platearum aspectus hanc lacerato derideat opytogio aut mensam mendi-
cet ingeniorum tanta honestas. Laudabilius est archyscolarem in ymo gradu
codri miseriis codriare quam in apice tante anilicie turpiter mendicare. Octavum est ex hac prodiens ratione quia magister scolarem indignum pro-
movens ad magisterii culmen prece aut pretio corruptus tanti nominis verti-
cem inhonestat, asinum loco ursini phalerat, symeam pro homine coronat,
atque rusticum pro milite honorat. Infelix est atque ingratus sapientie miles
qui ex favore fatuum antenectat magistratu solempni quasi sapientem quia
detrahit honori proprio qui alienis dat honorem suum. Alieni ab honore ho-
nesti viri sunt hii qui indigni sunt illo honore. Sicut enim timiditas dignum
non acceptat militem sed fortitudine approbatur omnis qui vere est militandus,
sic ignorantia venerabilem non admittit magistrum ymmo scientiarum
laudabili experientia reverenter archiscolarium quilibet est magistrandus.

CAPITULUM SEXTUM. OSTENDENS QUOD VERUS PHILOSOPHUS CIGNO COMPARATUR

Conditiones iam dicte verum philosophum cigno comparant secundum
veterum assertationes unde legitur in historiis de vita philosophorum quod
cum quadam in aurora Socrates in scholis suis lectionem inchoare proponeret
atque subditis ut moris est nova petentibus ille sompnium quod nocte viderat
revelaret, Platonem nondum literis mancipatum in specie cigni vidisse re-
fertur, quia Socrates in sompniis viderat cignum stantem in gremio suo
atque de gremio ipsius super portam volare achademiorum apud Athenas et
ibidem collum suum protendere ultra celos. Adhuc Socrate sompnium hunc
referente ecce pater Platonis filiolum scolis adduxerat et ipsum fidei Socratis
commendavit de quo mox Socrates quasi ore prophetaverat prophetico et
ait, Ecce cignus qui archana celorum penetrabit manifestans. Vere prophe-
tice locutus est Socrates de Platone quia, ut recitat beatus Augustinus in
libro confessionum, Plato totum hoc ewangelium de verbo dei incarnato
suis in libris exoravit quasi ad eandem penitus verborum monetam quod
Iohannes ewangelista scribit dicens, In principio erat verbum etc. quousque
ad eum locum, Fuit homo missus a deo. Sed numquid eadem prima pars
ewangelii generationem dei filii a deo patre propriissime cantat. Ita est.
Et quis aut quantus vel ut dicam qualis philosophorum hec archana celorum
attigerat preter Platonem? Nemo umquam. Bene igitur Plato in sompnis

[4] Inique or iniquiter would seem intended.

apparuit Socrati tamquam cignus qui capit anime humane intellectum scilicet speculativum ultra celos protenderat in divinam generationem. (105v)

Cignus enim avis est al<b>as habens plumas sed pedes nigros, cum uno pede natat et cum alio se regit veli modo, ut dicunt philosophi, parum comedit secundum magnitudinem corporis sui, fortitudinem habet in alis, dulci voce sonorat, natat in aquis puris, longum habet collum. Sic et perfectus philosophus vere sapientie candidus amator, albus est morum candore et virtutum puritate. Dulciter canit quoniam studiose docet fructuose continuat et viridice pronuntiat scibilia mundi. Fortitudinem habet in alis quibus volat in speculabilibus scilicet intellectum possibilem et intellectum agentum. Nigros pedes habet quibus securus navigat in undis humane fragilitatis utpote patientiam et humilitatem. Quorum pede altero viz. patientia secat undas et adversitatum vincit invasiones [5] sed pede reliquo puta humilitate regit se veli modo in flatibus et detractionibus superborum. Sunt autem hii pedes nigri quia despecti apud vulgum communitatis. Communes etenim homines modicum patientie possident et humilitatis. Parum comedit philosophus id est in paucis ad hanc vitam necessariis contentatur. Non enim querit esse dominator terre et maris sed ut habeat aliquem decoquentem sibi olera sua et vere hoc valde parum est respectu magnitudinis sue, quoniam altitudo scientiarum suarum iure naturali postulat eum esse dominum omnium insipientium et communium populorum. Desiderat etiam verus philosophus natare in aquis puris id est speculari aquas sapientiarum et scientiarum cum puritate et abstinentia ab illecebris mundi. Longum collum habet quia vim habet rationis erectam in altitudines speculationum.

CAPITULUM SEPTIMUM. DE RECTORE PUERORUM SCOLASTICORUM

Qualiter autem magister artium in scolis non autenticis sed leninomis se habere debeat circa scolares et archyscolares videamus. Et primo circa scolares ubi plerumque non magister in artibus regit sed rector puerorum sine tytulo nominatur qui tamen quandoque magister est re quamvis careat tytulo, quandoque vero nostris temporibus nec magister re nec tytulo sed vaniglorius ductor. Oportet igitur verum puerorum rectorem aspicere diligenter singulorum conditiones, nam septennis ut plurimum infantia dicitur, ad inbuendum et a primordiis receptionis. Quatuor sunt in novitiis huiusmodi consideranda viz. aeris qualitas corporis integritas nature complexio atque ingenii dispositio. Dico autem aeris intuendam esse qualitatem quia membrorum teneritas de facili frigore percutitur aut calore penetratur unde conveniens est citra veris medium infantulos disciplinabiles litteris alligare atque cautius dicendo expedit in eadem domo duas esse puerorum mansiones

[5] Invausiones in the MS.

unam viz. estivali calori convenienter reluctantem et suis aperturis respicientem ad aquilonem que in estate scolarium turbas recipiat cum aeris refrigerio quodam, aliam vero cautius munitam que tempore brumali brunis ardentibus calefieri valeat secundum consuetudinem regionis et iste modus in pluribus locis borealibus servatur. Alii vero scolas faciunt declives quadam cum depressione subterranea tabulis abietivis aut pineis delectabiliter parietata qui tempore estus fervoribus renititur et hyemis ingruente sevicie algoribus obstat. Etiam amictus varietas in hiis est sollicitanda ut scilicet hyeme pueri hyrtis induantur induviis et planioribus in estate. Est etiam pueri litterandi a principio sue mancipationis intuenda membrorum suorum integritas tam ex parte quantitatis continue quam discrete quam etiam partium corporee dispositionis. Dico autem quantitatis continue ut nullum organorum ipsius naturalium molem congrue magnitudinis excedat vel deficiat (106r) ab ea ut pote ne manus aut pes vel caput deviet a rectitudine extensionis. Et dico quantitatis discrete ne viz. aliquod eorum substantialiter desit quemadmodum pueri sine brachiis aut pedibus inveniuntur aut ne numero superfluetur sicut in ermoforditis membra sexualia vel sicut monstra sunt bicipita que duo capita habent et ventrem unum aut certe excedentes in numero digitorum vel peditorum et huiusmodi. Dico etiam partim corporee dispositionis quia gibbosi aut loripedes seu monoculi vel grandibus infirmitatibus infecti velut epilentici leprosi et consimiles tam venerabili non sunt litterarum dotandi nobilitate, quoniam notabiliter vitiati corpore nec kathedras ornant scolasticas nec divino congruunt sacerdotio propter scandala vitanda sed nec in scolis commode amittuntur propter puerorum lasciviam in eosdem cachinantem et conturbantem sollicitudinem eorum. Egrotantes insuper morbis contagiosis alios inficere possent scolares. Nature vero complexio est in pueris scolasticis pernotanda, quoniam non est omnibus complexionibus eadem mensura scolastice discipline sicut nec est omnibus eadem meta cibandi et potandi. Sangwinei namque mansueti sunt atque pacifici inter turmulas societatum et ingeniose capacitatis qui quasi ludendo et sine advertentia magna notabiliter capere videntur, sed lascivia hos ut plurimum seducit. Colerici vero partim minus capaces sed tenacius et firmius retinentes qui veluti furientes alios diversis motibus inquietant, saliunt enim tamquam hynuli caprarum, et raro in eisdem reperiuntur locis, quapropter inconstantia deluduntur nisi deus eis amorem dederit discipline. Et siquidem fleumatici pigri atque sompnolenti tardioris sunt capascentie et facilis oblivionis propter habundantem in eis humiditatem unde oportet illos quadam frequentia sollicitare ut ingenio calescantur. Melancolici autem silicine duriciei maximo labore capiunt atque non delebili memoria servant et horum obtusitas diligentia studii permovitur. Primi ergo auxiliandi sunt debita correctione ut eorum lascivia reprimatur. Secundi custodibus scolarum et accusatoribus sunt minandi ut insolentia sedetur in eis. Tertii vero et quarti repetitionibus sunt muniendi qui crebra eis subveniant lectionum reciprocatione nam sibi ipsis metunt qui aliis proficiunt atque qui alium docet seipsum instruit. Sed ingenii dispositio in discipline processu apud pueros velociter experitur. Reperiuntur enim in eodem genere compositionis quidam acuti alii acutiores et tertii acutissimi eorum. Sic etiam obtusi et obtusiores atque durissimi quasi ingenii desperati. Et hec varietas ex elementorum graduali provenit latitudine quam nemo physicorum seu etiam medicorum punctaliter concipere potest, concurrentibus in hiis differentiis astrorum variis aspectibus et quasi viribus innumeris eorum in puerorum conceptione formatione et nativitate que super corpora humana influunt occultas quodammodo affectiones ex quibus humana ingenia secundum plus et minus ingrossantur aut subtiliantur quoniam ut ars testatur physionomie anime secuntur corpora in dispositionibus suis. Sic ergo rector puerorum eos dirigat ut timidos verbis corrigat frivolos virgis magistret atque unicuique secundum suas exigentias dona disposet litterarum. Nec semper scolares libris inminere tenentur et tabulis pugillaribus sed dandum est intervallum studiis quandoque atque ludis congruis inhyandum ut spiritus exaltentur et sanguis sublimetur ludi delectatione. Sic etenim puerorum ingenia subtiliantur (106v) et recreantur tediis scolasticis prius fatigati.

CAPITULUM OCTAVUM. DE GRADUALI PROCESSIONE IN ORDINE SCIENTIARUM

Specialius autem descendendo dicamus quod cum septennes primum gramata proferre didicerint et figuras noverint elementorum atque eadem orthographice componere sciverint in sillabas et sillabas in dictiones congregari oportunum est ut ethymologice insistant interpretationi tam scilicet dictionum significationibus quam partium proprietatibus quas modernorum perspicatitas modos significandi nominat obnixius inmorantes et cum medullam sumpserint in hiis dyasintheticis orationum constructionibus innitantur. Nec est inconveniens illa mixtim edoceri quoniam alterum alterius amminiculo gaudet. Interea vero commisceri operi oportet rerum moralium atque poetice deductionis codicellos in quibus tam fructus virtutum quam bonorum morum fertilitas carpitur et rethorice venustatis vestigia in eisdem reperiuntur. Talis autem in hiis processus primo scolastico maturatur septennio quousque in finem quartidecimi anni scolaris, tunc enim eluscescere incipit lumen rationis in eo atque hinc convenit dyalectice proponere involutiones acutis et hiis melioribus cum incidentiis rethorice pulchritudinum. Nichilominus quandoque de facilioribus aliarum scientiarum ysagogis aliquos [6] congerendo libellos. Consuevit etenim practica musice pariter cum lactifera

---

[6] Aliquis in the MS.

concurrere grammatica in scolarium educatione necnon ars algoristica practice deserviens arismetice. Similiter et tractatus de speris celestibus introductorius in astronomiam cum dyalecticis atque rethoricis desertionibus concurrunt. Hinc autem a vicesimoprimo anno angeli scolastici universaliter solidiora capiunt ut pote scientiam naturalem in sua latitudine ambiendo methaphysicam audiendo Euclidis descriptiones speculando quousque in finem tertii septenii literarum. Et sic in vicesimo octavo anno aptus est archiscolaris cathedre magistratus. Sed potuerunt hec tria septennia scolastica in quinquennia succingi in acutioribus ingeniis et excellenter acutis. Difficile tamen est qualicumque ingenio humano tot et tanta taliaque in hiis annorum funditus capere clausuris. Cui autem data est desuper ingeniorum tanta capacitas longe amplioribus mensuris sibi laudabiliter metietur. Qui vero ad sacram festinat paginam aut qui ius appetit canonicum sufficit ut trivium possideat ad eloquentiam divinarum scripturarum intelligendam. Et hic cum artes audit seculares scolas theologicas nichilominus accedat seu cathedras iuristarum frequenter quousque tenacitatem sibi in artibus hiis acceperit sufficientem. Sed quanto profectior in artibus tanto laudabilior theologus erit quia solius theologi est disputare de quolibet et noscere universa ut invisibilia dei per ea que visibilia sunt in creaturis lutulencius valeat declarare. Sacre namque scripture de omnibus rebus universi faciunt rememorationem. Medico vero est opus saltem trivii et naturalis scientie atque astronomie notitia forsitan aliqualis quam tamen si perfecte haberet cautius utique mederetur.

CAPITULUM NONUM. SOLVENS QUEDAM DUBIA CIRCA DICTA

(107r) Oritur tamen questio ex dictis an liceat clerico christiano quod studeat artes seculares. Et videtur quod non. Legitur enim de beato Iheronimo quod cum librum legeret Cyceronis ab angelo correctus est eo quod vir Christianus paganorum figmentis intenderet. Et preterea ratione cognititur non esse libris gentilium insudandum per virum Christianum quoniam rationes eorum fidei catholice contrariantur. Ratiocinatus est enim Aristotiles VIII Physicorum et primo Celi mundum fuisse ab eterno et non dandum esse primum hominem sicut nec postremum. Sed illud contrariatur expresse huic quod creditur de creatione ut patet in libro geneseos Moysi. Iterum autem Averrois iii° de anima probat esse animam rationalem individuam in omnibus hominibus que singulis eorum tanquam unus nauta pluribus navibus approprietur. Et vere hoc nobis manifeste abnegat vitam eternam in deliciis paradysi atque supplicium indeficiens hiis qui tartareis penis iusto dei iudicio deputantur. Quare sequitur non esse fas pueros christianos in hiis vanitatibus erudiri. Quia que consuevimus agilius mentem nostram agitant et habenant. Concordat etiam huic quod alii de filio prodigo scribunt comparando eum qui siliquas porcorum manducaverat atque hiis ventrem suum replere concupiverat eis qui gentilium insistunt documentis et mentam suam farciri affectant eisdem. Sic etiam Origenes per cinifes et ranas quibus Egiptii percussi sunt vanam dyalecticorum garrulitatem et sophistica intelligit argumenta. Iterum autem Iheronimus ad Damasum de prodigo filio sic dicit. Sacerdotes dei obmissis ewangeliis et prophetiis videmus comedias legere amatoria buculitorum versuum verba cantare tenere Virgilium in manibus et id quod in pueris est causa necessitatis crimen facere voluptatis. Atque iterum, Nonne nobis videtur in vanitate sensus et obscuritate mentis ingredi qui diebus et noctibus in dyalectica arte torquetur? Qui physicus perscrutator oculos trans celos levat et ultra profundum terrarum etiam abyssi ad quoddam inane dimergitur? Qui iambum fervet qui tantam metrorum silvam in suo studiosus corde distinguit et congerit. Videretur ergo aliquibus ex hiis libros gentilium philosophorum a nobis non esse legendos nec poetarum poesibus immorandum.

CAPITULUM DECIMUM. ARGUENS AD OPPOSITUM

In contrarium nichilominus arguitur, Quoniam in libris secularium scientiarum innumera ultilia reperiri nulli dubium est sed quare utilia legere prohiberemur? Sunt etenim in eis veritates que dona dei sunt. Unde Ysidorus in libro de summo bono, Multum mundo, inquit, philosophi predicant in dimensione temporum cursuque syderum ac discussione elementorum et tamen hec non nisi a deo habuerunt. Et si in dictis eorum aliqua nonnumquam sunt erronea licet ea legere nos ut vitemus. Unde Ambrosius super Lucam: Legimus aliqua ne negli<g>antur, legimus ne ignoremus, legimus non ut teneamus sed ut repudiemus. Exhortatur etiam nos ad idem quod Beda super libro Regum scribit dicens: Turbat acumen legentium et deficere cogit qui eos a legendis secularibus libris omnimodis estimat prohibendos. In quibus si qua inventa sunt utilia quasi sua sumere licet alioquin Moyses et Daniel sapientia et literis Egyptiorum Caldeorumque non paterentur erudiri quorum tamen superstitiones simul et delicias horrebant. Nec ipse magister gentium scilicet Paulus aliquot versus poetarum suis scripturis indidisset vel dictis supple<visset> si legi non deberent. Ad id etiam accedit quod asserit Gratianus in decretis dicens, Legitur quod precepit dominus filiis Israhel ut spoliarent Egiptios auro et argento moraliter (fol. 107v) instruens ut sive aurum sapientie sive argentum eloquentie aput poetas invenerimus in usum salutifere eruditionis vertamus. In Levitico etiam primitias mellis id est dulcedinem humane eloquentie domino iubemur offerre. Magi quoque tria munera obtulerunt domino in quibus nonnulli tres partes philosophie intelligi volunt. Hec Gratianus. Et intelligit per tres partes philosophie sermocinalem philosophiam que in trivio consistit atque realem philosophiam que quadrivium respicit et alias scientias sub quadriviis comprehensas ut supra deduxeram. Tertia quoque pars philosophie est philosophia moralis que in genere ethica dicitur tres habens partes principales ut patuit supra. Corroborat etiam propositum nostrum hoc quod Iheronimus scribit super epistolam ad Tytum. Si quis, inquit, grammaticam artem noverit vel dyalecticam ut recta rationem loquendi habeat et inter vera et falsa diiudicet non improbamus. Geometria autem et arismetica et musica habent in sua scientia veritatem. Sed non est scientia illa pietatis. Scientia autem pietatis est nosse legere scripturas intelligere prophetas in ewangelio credere apostolos non ignorare. Gramaticorum autem doctrina potest etiam proficere ad vitam dum fuerit in meliores usus assumpta. Suple < re > sic etiam est de omnibus aliis scientiis gentium et caldeorum que liberales nominantur.

CAPITULUM XI. SOLVENS DICTAM QUESTIONEM

Ad solvendum autem dictam questionem diligenter perpendendi sunt fines gratia quorum in hiis aut in aliis scientiis laboramus. Quidam enim student propter solum scire et in illo adeo delectantur ut nil aliud felicitatis aut utilitatis sibi vel aliis inde amministrent. Et qui sic seculares legunt scientias detestandi sunt quia non fructificant in vitam eternam. Quibus dicit Ysidorus in libro de summo bono: Philosophi gentium non sicut oportet deum querentes in angelos inciderunt prevaricatores factusque est illis mediator ad mortem dyabolus sicut nobis ad vitam Christus. Et iterum: Ideo prohibentur christianis figmenta inanium fabularum quia mentem excecant ad incentiva libidinum. Et post dicit: Quidam plus meditari delectantur gentilium dicta propter tinientem et ornatum sermonem quam scripturam sanctam propter eloquium humile. Sed quid prodest in mundanis doctrinis proficere et inanescere in divinis, caduca sequi figmenta, et celestia fastidire misteria? Cavendi sunt tales libri et propter amorem sanctarum scripturarum vitandi. Suple (?) gratia talis finis legendi. Quidam vero sic student mundanas scientias precipue ut sciantur et istorum finis est vana gloria. Quibus Ysidorus ait: Nichil aliud agit amor humane seu mundane scientie nisi extollere laudibus hominem. Nam quanto maiora fuerint literature studia, tanto animus arrogantie fastu inflatus maiori intumescit iactantia. Ecce illi quasi nichil divine admittunt veritatis, quin ipsum dentibus derideant canine subsannationis atque quod verum esse intelligunt fastu superbie quasi non sit eorum inventio nullatenus admittunt. Quibus iterum Ysidorus ait: Philosophi mundi utique deum cognoverunt sed quia displicuit illis humilitas Christi in invio transiverunt non in via. Ideoque evanescentes gloriam dei in mendacium mutaverunt ac rectitudinem vie relinquentes in anfractus inciderunt errorem. Sunt quoque tertii studentes scientias ut lucrentur et hos avaritia magistrat. Qui si terrenos apices ab initio possiderent raro scripturarum volumina revolverent aut studerent. Sic autem artes liberales nostris temporibus non amantur (fol. 108r) nisi quantum subtiliant ad possessiones aliarum scientiarum. Crudus etenim artista nisi aliis scientiis digestus sit quasi semper mendicus apud nos reperitur. Quod attendens versificator ait: Esurit ars, decreta tument, lex ipsa superbit, pontificat Moyses, thalamos medicina subintrat. Quarti vero student ut edificentur ad intelligendum ea que sunt fidei et sapiendum illa que in felicitatem ducunt humanam. Et sic scientias mundanas licet nos legere sicut probant rationes et auctoritates ad oppositum questionis superius inducte. Omnium etenim scientiarum subtilitas in divinis eloquiis vestigia sua pingit et describit unde Cassiodorus in expositione Psalterii dicit: Omnis splendor rethorice eloquentie omnis modus poetice locutionis quelibet varietas decoris pronuntiationis a divinis scripturis sumpsit exordium. Atque cum hoc consonat quod Ambrosius dicit super Epistola Colocensium. Omnis inquit ratio superne scientie vel terrene creature in eo est qui est caput earum et auctor ut qui hunc novit nichil ultra querat. Quia hec est perfecta virtus et sapientia quidquid alibi queritur hic perfecte inveniatur. Quinti vero student scientias non solum ut edificentur sed ut alios edificent et hos magistrat karitas atque dilectio proximi. Istis valde licitum est legere scientias gentilium ut maledica eorum detestari valeant et utilia que in eis invenerunt ad usum sacre eruditionis tanquam felices viri convertere possint unde Iheronimus super Epistolam ad Tytum ait: Quomodo si quispiam adversum mathematicos velit scribere imperitus matheseos risui pateat et adversus philosophos disputans si ignorat dogmata philosophorum. Discant ergo ea mente doctrinam caldaicam qua et Moyses omnem sapientiam Egiptiorum didicerat. Et iterum dicit: Si quando cogimur literarum secularium recordari et aliqua ex hiis disserere que olim obmisimus non nostre est voluntatis sed ut ita dicam gravissime necessitatis ut probemus ea que a sanctis prophetis ante secula multa predicta sunt tam grecorum quam latinorum et aliorum gentilium literis contineri. Ex hiis elucescere possunt ad quas intentiones patres divinarum scripturarum liberales inhibuerint artes gentilium magistrorum et ad quas commendaverint easdem. Quia non est illis inhyandum tanquam voluptuosis ut ea que sunt fidei delectamenta deserantur.

CAPITULUM XII. QUALITER RECTORES SCOLARUM IN TRIVIO ERRANT

Ex synodo etiam Eugenii pape percipitur omnis cura et diligentia haberi ut magistri et doctores constituantur qui studia litterarum liberaliumque artium dogmata assidue doceant. Quia ut eadem sancta synodus asserit in hiis maxime divina manifestantur atque declarantur mandata. Sed huic nostris temporibus in plerisque locis Theutonie cura minima subministrat quoniam scolarum rectoribus ut deceret minime providetur nec eorum promotionibus ab episcopis intenditur ut oporteret. Quapropter ab hac sollicitudine illuminati viri apostatare coguntur et aliis statibus minorari. Surguntque miseri quidam qui se numquam dignos noverunt discipulos et quod penitus nesciunt docere presumunt atque, quod condolendo refero, tales nobilibus ingeniis potius seductores quam doctores preficiuntur. Gramaticam indignis molestant derisibus affirmantes quod nulla partium orationis constructio est transitiva quomodo Appollonius grecus Pryscianus quoque latinus et ante hunc Donatus Romanus alias orationum transitivas alias [7] vero intransitivas construebant. Asserunt enim quod nichil transeat nisi pedes habeat. (108v) Quapropter aqua non transit in fluviis secundum eos neque venti volant quoniam alas non habent. Nec poterit dici quod una partium orationis regat aliam secundum modorum significandi proportiones quia intellectus humanus omnes partes orationis regit et dirigit. Proprietates enim partium orationis nichil sunt ut dicunt. Tandem fraudem in pueris hii faciunt tantam ut nec gramatice loqui sciant nec quod locuntur intelligant. Sed ut corvi crocitantes et graculi garrientes dictiones barbarisant et orationes turpiter soloctizant. Quia tamen ignorantiam propriam ignorant elatis frontibus magistraliter incedunt et paucissima cognoscentes de quolibet disputant plene. Rethoricam eloquentiam adeo sua cecitate postergant ut nec flores verborum nec colores sententiarum capiant sed flores in pratis crescere et colores varios pictores componere et pulchre variare ad instar nature affirmant. Qualiter hii dulciloquia sacrarum interpretentur scripturarum quevis ratio disposita noscit. Nec est dubium hereses ex hiis innumeras pululare. Scriptura etenim sacra non semel uterum virginalem virgam notat et filium inde conceptum florem appellat. Et si de virtute sermonis iste orationes false sunt sequitur rethoricam in pulcherrimis speciebus transsumptionis nullam ad orationes habere virtutem et sic rethorica quasi evanuit tota. Loycam autem se scire divulgant cum duodena vocatorum insolubilium aut obligationum senarium pauperem siliore grandibus impresserunt visibus cecitati. Negant hii quaslibet consequentias tam ratione materie congruas quia naturas rerum penitus ignorant quam etiam ratione forme convenientes quoniam ad latitudinem loyce minime pervenerunt. Quid plura tantus error est in hiis auctus ut etiam senum canicies non abhorreat hiis vilibus insudare. Et hoc facit errophylie comoditas et vere phylosophie gravitas augariosa. Facilius est etenim in singulis errare quam veritatis attingere metas. Quapropter diurnus fit magister qui errophylat trigennarius autem qui phylosophisat.

[7] Alios in the MS.

CAPITULUM XIII. QUALITER ALIQUI MAGISTRI IN ARTIBUS NIMIS EXTOLLUNT PHYLOSO-PHIAM GENTILIUM

Alii vero realem sic amant philosophiam gentilium similiter et moralem ut dicant omnes scientias preter necessarias excepta gentilium philosophica disciplina alias autem non dicant necessarias nisi in hominum consuetudine. Error est quoniam theologica necessario est scientia in salutem generis humani omnibus scientiis humanis que mirabilia dei predicat et de moribus hominum in vitam eternam felicitantibus disputat. Sic etiam scientia sacrorum canonum necessaria est ad bene vivere in fide orthodoxa tanquam beatissima omnium moralium scientiarum. Dicunt etiam quod nulla questio disputabilis sit per rationem quam philosophus gentium nutritus doctrinis non debeat disputare atque determinare, quia rationes accipiuntur a rebus, phylosophia autem humana habet omnes res considerare secundum diversas sui partes. Errant quia principia theologie que divinitus est sanctissimis hominibus inspirata a phylosophis humanitus phylosophantibus sunt incognita. Et per consequens solus theologus immorans eisdem et ea tamquam vera presupponens questiones theologicas disputare habet ac determinare. Licet autem philosophus gentilis omnes res consideret, non tamen omnibus realibus modis neque deo possibilibus viis, negant enim philosophi humani miracula dei que supernaturaliter ef<f>luunt a plenitudine divine bonitatis. (fol. 109r)

Asserunt nichilominus quod possibile vel impossibile simpliciter id est omnibus modis sit possibile vel impossibile secundum phylosophiam. Et male quoniam impossibile phylosophie humane que lumine nature est acquisita est possibile phylosophie divine que divino spiramine ad nos pervenit et ex miraculis dei nobis illuxit. Quomodo enim humanus philosophus deum incarnari acciperet aut accidentia panis sine subiecto esse in sacramento altaris? Ego nescio etiam secundum gentium phylosophiam quod ingenium dei maioris est capacitatis sine comparatione quocumque ingenio humano. Numquid igitur deus innumera potest ex ingenio suo que totum latent ingenium humanum? Noli ergo dicere nichil possibile apud dominum nisi quod tu comprehendere poteris humana ratione, unde Ysidorus in libro de summo bono, Ideo libri sancti simplici sermone conscripti sunt, inquit, ut non in sapientia verbi sed in ostensione spiritus homines ad fidem perducerent. Nam si a dyalectici acuminis versutia aut rethorice artis eloquentia editi essent, nequaquam putaretur fides Christi in dei virtute sed eloquentie humane argumentis existere et sic nullatenus crederemus ad fidem divino inspiramine provocari sed potius verborum subduci calliditate. Affirmant insuper nonnulli humane cultores phylosophie quod sapientes mundi sint phylosophi tantum. Error est, quoniam ut dicit Ysidorus ubi supra, Omnis secularis doctrina spumantibus verbis resonans ac se per eloquentie tumorem attollens per doctrinam simplicem et humilem Christianam evacuata est sicut scriptum est, Nonne stultam fecit deus sapientiam huius mundi fastidiosis atque loquacibus? Longe igitur sapientiores sunt divinis immorantes miraculis quam sapientiis innitentes humanis. Ad tantam etiam ascendunt pertinaciam ut dicant non esse excellentiorem statum quam vacare phylosophie. Error est quoniam nemo excellentior quam qui deo amicior, nemo autem deo amicior quam qui in deum fervidior quam qui deo obedientior et gratia dei refertior invenitur. Quapropter eos maiores cognoscimus atque in studiis letiores qui spiritu sancto revelante aliqua didicerint quam qui humanis doctrinis inbuuntur, unde Ysidorus ubi prius c. de spiritu sancto dicit, Credo equidem quod magnam letitiam sentit qui aliquid revelante dei spiritu didicit.

CAPITULUM XIIII. DE ERRORIBUS QUORUNDAM ARTISTARUM CUIUS PRIMA PARS EST DE ERRORIBUS CIRCA DEUM

Ut autem magis in specie cognoscas errores precipuos propter quos philosophi detestantur inanes, noscas omnes articulos subnotatos maturo consilio atque perspicaci collatione Parysius a magistris sacre pagine esse refutatos tamquam fidei catholice inimicos. Primus est quod deus non est trinus et unus, quoniam Trinitas non constat cum summa simplicitate. Ubi enim est pluralitas realis ibi est additio et compositio, exemplum de acervo lapidum. Error est quem incidit abbas Ioachim et reprobatus de summa trinitate et fide catholica primo decretalium. Nec motivum valet quoniam plures lapides non sunt una substantia indivisa sicut sunt tres persone in divinis. Nemo etenim humana disputatione trinitatem sanctem hanc atque individuam in summa simplicitate divina gurgitare poterit tanquam gurges sic humanis pedibus transeundus. Sed quod nobis veritas plena gratia retulit simpliciter credere convenit hiis qui divinis claruerunt miraculis quorum nemo rationem naturalem poterit assignare. (109v)

APPENDIX II

FOUNDATION AND LOCATION OF COLLEGES AT PARIS IN THE LATER MIDDLE AGES

In the second half of the eighteenth century the university of Paris was no longer the intellectual and social force that it had once been. It was to be snuffed out entirely for a time by the French Revolution. Nevertheless, on the eve of that event the buildings which once had been or still were occupied by its various colleges were among the chief landmarks [1] and points of interest in the Latin quarter. Students in the arts had long since ceased to throng the Street of Straw or law students the *Clausum Brunelli*. Instruction had gradually been transferred to the colleges; many of them in their turn had become *sans exercise* [2] or had been joined to the Collège Royale or the Collège de Louis le Grand. But most of them remained as impressive memorials. Originally intended to house poor students, they now vied with the hôtels of the rich and noble, as well as with churches and monastic establishments, as places of public interest and general importance, of long duration and venerable standing in time, and as having come sooner or later to occupy considerable space in plots of land or in groups of buildings. A century later all this was altered, and Rashdall wrote in 1895:

It is with a melancholy feeling that the dweller in Oxford quadrangles wanders through the old Quartier Latin of the Mother University and finds scarcely anything left to remind him of the historic Colleges and Schools and Convents which once occupied the sites now covered by dirty slums or trim boulevards.[3]

In the first volume of the *Chartularium Universitatis Parisiensis* documents connected with the foundation of colleges were included and have been utilized in Rashdall's work, which I shall henceforth cite in the revised edition of 1936 by Powicke and Emden. But in the subsequent volumes of the *Chartularium* and *Auctarium* documents about the colleges were omitted. It was explained in the second volume of the *Chartularium* that they would appear separately as the second part of that volume, but it has never been published. For the fourteenth and fifteenth centuries, therefore, or more precisely from the year 1286 on, the treatment of the Parisian colleges in Rashdall reduces to little more than a chronological table of their foundations.[4] This table does not always seem quite accurate, and one object of this appendix is to point out some discrepancies between it and the

---

[1] On the title pages of sixteenth- and seventeenth-century books the place of printing or sale in Paris was often indicated as near such-and-such a college. Thus on the title page of Gaffarel's *Abdita divinae Cabalae mysteria* we read: "Parisiis ex typographia Hieronymi Blageari via Carmelitana prope D. Hilarium a regione Collegii Longobardorum." For other examples see my *History of Magic and Experimental Science*, V, 148–49, 155, 296, 464; VI, 10, 324, 343–44.

[2] That is to say, were purely residential and held no classes.

[3] Hastings Rashdall, *The Universities of Europe in the Middle Ages*, 1895, I, 513–14.

[4] At pp. 536–39 of the first volume of the 1936 edition. Except for additional footnotes the list is little altered from that in the original edition of 1895, I, 514–17.

accounts of the several colleges given by Jaillot in his topographical work on Paris published late in the eighteenth century.[5] Jaillot had usually examined the available documents and often expressed disagreement with the historians of the city and university of Paris who had preceded him. In view of this rather sharp criticism of the statements made by others, he was not always as careful as he might have been in his own assertions and sometimes contradicts or corrects himself in different parts of his work. For the period covered by the first volume of the *Chartularium* its documentation is fuller and more reliable than his, but after it fails us, his suggestions may be of some importance until the documents themselves, so far as still extant, are published in full.

Use has also been made of the more recent and pretentious *Topographie historique du vieux Paris* (henceforth cited as THdVP) of Berty and Tisserand, of which volume V (1887), "Région occidentale de l'université," and volume VI (1897), "Région centrale de l'université," dealt with various colleges and included among their "Appendices et pièces justificatives" a number of documents concerning these (V, 625–52; VI, 439–587), most of which, however, were of late date. The seventh volume, which was to have been devoted to the eastern region of the university, seems never to have appeared. This work seldom cites Jaillot except to criticize him, yet repeats traditions which he had shown to be erroneous and omits important data which he gives. It also lacks an index, so that I shall indicate in footnotes where its discussions of certain colleges may be found.

Besides the standard work of Quicherat on the Collège de Sainte-Barbe [6] and a few more recent monographs, the histories of various individual colleges have been made the subject of investigation by pupils of l'Ecole des Chartes. But most of these have been published only in brief outline in *Les Positions des Thèses*, of which, however, we shall make some use. Some new information is also supplied by the *Registre des causes civiles de l'officialité de Paris, 1384–1387*, published in 1919 by Joseph Petit, in which a number of the colleges figure (henceforth cited as Petit).

On the accompanying plan of late medieval Paris south of the Seine and enclosed by the wall of Philip Augustus the approximate location of some fifty-seven colleges founded before 1500 is indicated by the Arabic numerals

[5] I have used the edition of 1782: *Recherches critiques, historiques et topographiques sur la ville de Paris, depuis ses commencemens connus jusqu'a présent; Avec le Plan de chaque Quartier:* Par le Sieur Jaillot, Géographe Ordinaire du Roi, de l'Académie Royale des Sciences & Belles-Lettres d'Angers. A Paris, Chez Le Boucher, Libraire, quai de Gêvres, au coin de la traverse, près du pont Notre-Dame, MDCCLXXXII. 20 parts bound in five vols.

[6] J. Quicherat, *Histoire de Sainte-Barbe, collège, communauté, institution*, 3 vols., Paris, 1860, 1862, 1864.

from 1 to 57. As each college is mentioned in the text, its number on the plan will be added in parentheses. Certain churches and convents have been designated by capital letters from A to P. It should be remembered that many changes in the topography of the region and in the names of streets have taken place, not only since but before the year 1500, so that the plan is at best only a rough approximation for any given date.[7]

It should also be kept in mind that considerable latitude may be exercised in selecting a precise date for the foundation of a college. One may take either the time when the donor made provision for such an establishment in his last will and testament, or the year when his executors got around to putting his instructions into effect. One may note the time when a donor first made financial provision for the support of a group of a certain number of poor scholars, or one may prefer the date when a building of their own was provided for them. The year of purchase or transfer of real estate for such a purpose may be given as that of the foundation, or the year when the institution was first actually in operation. Jaillot usually makes it clear in each case which of such alternatives he is accepting as the date of founding; the brief chronological table in Rashdall generally fails to supply this information.

The Collège des Cholets (28), for which Rashdall gives 1295 as the date of foundation, was already in existence in 1292 according to the manuscript annals of Sainte-Geneviève, Jaillot (XVII, 47) assures us.[8] Indeed, already in 1289 it had been agreed to build a chapel to atone for an attack upon students, resulting in the death of one of them, by the attendants of cardinal Jean Cholet, papal legate.[9] The college faced the chapel of Saint-Symphorien des Vignes across a street of the same name, which was later changed to Rue des Cholets after the college situated on it. The colleges of Montaigu and Sainte-Barbe in the course of time extended their holdings to reach this street.

The Collège du Cardinal Le Moine (45) is dated from 1301 in Rashdall, but Jaillot (XVI, 154) placed its foundation in 1302,[10] because it was in

---

[7] The plan of the Latin quarter published in the original edition of Rashdall, I, 271, was omitted in the edition of 1936 as "out of date." It indicated scarcely any streets and only forty-two colleges.

[8] Amand Rastoul, "Le Collège des Cholets," Ecole Nationale des Chartres, *Positions des Thèses*, 1899, p. 124, gives yet a third year, 1294, as the date of foundation. This abstract is cited in a bibliography in Rashdall, I (1936), 498, but the author's name is misspelled "Rastorel," and the abstract was apparently not utilized in compiling the chronological list of foundations of colleges at Paris. THdVP VI, 72–73, is inadequate.

[9] *Chartularium universitatis Parisiensis*, II, 34, 37; documents 560, 563.

[10] Charles Jourdain, "Le Collège du Cardinal Lemoine," *Mémoires de la Société de l'Histoire de Paris et de l'Ile-de-France*, III (1870), 42–81, remarks at page 48:

that year that the cardinal purchased the house, chapel and cemetery of the Augustinians "au Chardonnet" (*Cardinetum, les clos du Chardonnet*), because the statute of foundation was drawn up May 1, 1302, and approved May 4 by Boniface VIII, before he sent the cardinal to France, and because early in 1303 Lemoine increased the endowment of the college by two houses in Brie, which he gave to the poor masters and scholars studying at Paris "dans la Maison du Chardonnet"—that is, the house purchased from the Augustinians in the previous year. This college was situated in Rue Saint-Victor a little inside Porte Saint-Victor.

Different, although located not far away, was "le Collège du Chardonnet" or "le Collège des Bernardins" (46), which Stephen Lexington, abbot of Clairvaux, had founded for members of the Cistercian Order back in 1246.[11]

In the same general neighborhood was the large Collège de Navarre (40), founded in 1304, as Jaillot and Rashdall both agree. Farther off, in Rue de la Harpe or de Saint-Cosme et Saint-Damien, was the Collège de Bayeux (10), founded in 1309, another date as to which there is no dispute.[12]

Rashdall dates the foundation of a college by Gui de Laon and Raoul des Presles in 1314. Jaillot (XVI, 59) admitted that this date was given in an inscription on the college gate, but insisted that the college was actually founded in January, 1313. Later (XVII, 30) he recognized that this was according to the old style of beginning the year at Easter and hence 1314 by our dating from January first. Gui de Laon gave houses in Rue Saint-Hilaire (later Rue des Carmes) and between it and Rue du Clos-Bruneau (Rue Saint-Jean de Beauvais) and one hundred livres for en-

---

"date qui ne doit pas être reculée jusqu'en 1296 comme l'ont cru Corrozet et Sauval, ni retardée jusqu'en 1304 comme le veut Dubois, ni même jusqu'en 1303 selon le sentiment de l'abbé Lebeuf, mais fixée à l'année 1302, comme l'a très-bien vu Jaillot."

[11] *Histoire littéraire de la France*, XIX, 13; Jaillot XVI, 10–14; Rashdall I (1936), 506, 536.

[12] THdVP VI, 189, "1308 (vieux style)." In Jaillot's "Plan du Quartier Saint-André des Arcs," however, the positions of the colleges of Bayeux and Narbonne should be reversed. That Bayeux lay south of Narbonne on the east side of the street is shown by the tapestry of 1520, the so-called plan of Saint-Victor of 1555, by THdVP VI, 177, and by Jaillot's own text (XVIII, 74–79) which takes up Le Palais des Thermes, Le Collège de Séez, Le Collège de Narbonne, and Le Collège de Bayeux in that order, and states that three houses called *les Marmousets* across the street from the Collège de Bayeux were acquired by the Collège de Harcourt. Evidently they lay between it and the Collège de Justice, which was almost directly opposite that of Bayeux. THdVP V, 418, knows only one *Maison des Marmousets*. The Plan de la Caille of 1714 errs in placing the Collège de Séez opposite the Collège de Justice south of Narbonne and Bayeux.

dowment, while Raoul de Presles contributed two hundred livres. According to Jaillot, when the two colleges were separated in 1323, that of Laon occupied the property facing Rue du Clos-Bruneau (22) and leased the property on Rue Saint-Hilaire to the Collège de Soissons or de Presles (23). After 1339 the Collège de Laon moved into l'Hôtel du Lion d'Or, which Gérard de Montaigu had left to it in Rue de la Montagne Sainte-Geneviève (30), where the Collège de Dace or of Denmark (29), founded in 1275, lay between it and the convent of the Carmelites (I), who had moved to this site early in the fourteenth century. The site abandoned by the Collège de Laon was acquired on June 29, 1365, by Jean de Dormans for the college which he founded five years later (22). Henri Cahen more specifically locates the Collège de Laon at first in "la maison aux images" between Rue des Carmes and Rue Saint-Jean de Beauvais, whence it moved in 1340 to "l'hôtel du Lion d'Or" between Rue des Carmes and Rue de la Montagne Sainte-Geneviève.[13] After 1375 the Maison des trois Singes, adjoining that of the Gold Lion, was added to the Collège de Laon, as was in 1388 the Collège de Maclou (31), which had been founded about 1323 by Raoul Rousselet, bishop of Laon.[14] The Collège de Dace, which had fallen into ruin, was also annexed to that of Laon in 1430 (Jaillot: XVI, 64–65).

Jaillot (XVII, 221–25) and Rashdall agree that the Collège des Aicelins (37) dates from 1314, when, by his will of December 13, Gilles Aycelin, archbishop of Rouen, left houses in Rue des Sept Voies and Rue de Saint-Symphorien for that purpose. But, as against Rashdall's statement that it was restored in 1388 by Pierre Aicelin de Montaigu, bishop of Nevers and Laon and cardinal, Jaillot dates the cardinal's will of November 7, 1387, but dates its acceptance by his nephew and heir, Louis Aycelin de Montaigu de Listenois, on condition that the college henceforth bear the name of Montaigu and that the arms of that house be engraved over the main gate, only on January 18, 1392, and the college statutes on July 25, 1402. The Collège de Montaigu, as it was thereafter known, soon fell again into disrepair. It became an institution of note only when Jean Standonc assumed the principalship on May 12, 1483. Of its subsequent tiffs with the neighboring Collège de Sainte-Barbe over the unsanitary condition of Rue Saint-Symphorien or des Chiens, which ran between the two

---

[13] Henri Cahen, "Le Collège de Laon à Paris," *Positions des Thèses*, 1906, pp. 27–34.

[14] Rashdall I (1936), 538: "Jacques Rousselet, archdeacon of Reims, executor of Raoul Rousselet, bishop of Laon." Cahen, *op. cit.*, does not name the college, merely remarking, "Un collège particulier fondé par l'évêque Raoul Rousselot est réuni à celui de Laon en 1388." The Index to Rashdall also spells the name Rousselot, but Chevalier and Eubel spell it Rousselet.

colleges, and over the garden of the Collège de Montaigu which Sainte-Barbe coveted, Quicherat has given amusing accounts.[15]

Rashdall and Jaillot (XVIII, 76–78) agree that the archbishop of Narbonne instituted the college of that name in 1317, Jaillot adding the detail that it was established in his house in Rue de la Harpe (11), where it lay on the east side of the street south of the Collège de Séez and north of that of Bayeux.[16]

The names of the colleges of Linköping and of Skara, listed by Rashdall, are not found in Jaillot's index. Probably all trace of them had disappeared by his time.

For the Collège de Cornouailles [17] (21) Jaillot (XVII, 193–95) gives, like Rashdall, the date 1321, but argues (XVII, 113–15) that the fact that it accepted the offer of the Collège du Plessis (26) to lodge its five *boursiers* shows that the latter college was also in existence in 1321 and not founded in 1322, the date accepted by Rashdall.[18] The Collège du Plessis, with 20 *boursiers* in grammar, 10 in philosophy, and 10 in canon law and theology, was a large establishment which extended from Rue Saint-Jacques to Rue Chartière. The Collège de Cornouailles acquired a house of its own *in vico Plastri* (Rue du Plâtre) only in 1380.

The foundation of the Collège de Maclou (31) in 1323, to which we have already referred, seems not to be mentioned by Jaillot. For the Collège de Tréguier (53), founded for eight *boursiers*, Rashdall and Jaillot (XVII, 178) agree on the date 1325.[19] It was situated on the south side of Place Cambrai, until Marie de' Medici purchased it in 1610 to make way for a college for the royal professors (Jaillot XVII, 184), now the Collège de France. The adjoining Collège de Cambrai (25), founded in 1348, shared the same fate.[20]

Jaillot (XVI, 173–74) would date the foundation of the Collège des Ecossais (52) in 1323, when David, bishop of Moray, placed four Scottish students in the aforesaid Collège du Cardinal le Moine, rather than in 1326, as Rashdall does, in which year the bishop with royal sanction acquired real estate at Brie-comte-Robert, some twenty miles from Paris, for the permanent support of these students. Jaillot (XVII, 175) further points out that after 1333 the four Scottish students were moved from the Col-

---

[15] *Histoire de Sainte-Barbe*, I (1860), 144–49; II (1862), 15–21.

[16] THdVP VI, 186, for further details.

[17] Cornouailles here means Basse-Bretagne (*Cornu Galliae*) or the diocese of Quimper, not Cornwall in England. In Petit, col. 247, it is called *collegii Corisopitensis* (Collège de Quimper).

[18] And THdVP V, 417; but VI, 265, "En l'an 1322 (vieux style)."

[19] THdVP VI, 283–96, with an extract from the founder's will at p. 506.

[20] ThdVP VI, 286.

lège du Cardinal le Moine to Rue des Amandiers. After 1665 a new house
was built for the Collège des Ecossais in Rue des Fossés Saint-Victor.

For the foundation of the Collège du Marmoutier (27) Jaillot (XVII,
113–18) and Rashdall agree on the year 1329,[21] but the former seems the
more accurate in regarding "de Saint-Martin du Mont" as an alternative
name for the Collège du Plessis (26) rather than for the Collège du Marmoutier.[22] These two colleges were situated somewhat to the north of
the Collège des Cholets (28), between which and Marmoutier intervened
l'Hôtel de Langres or "la Cours de Langres," which the Jesuits acquired
in 1564 and turned into the Collège de Clermont.

Rashdall has 1332 for the foundation of the Collège de Bourgogne (4)
by queen Jeanne de Bourgogne, while Jaillot (XVIII, 55–57) dates her
will on February 15, 1329, old style, or 1330 by our calendar, the establishment of the college opposite the Franciscan convent in Rue des Cordeliers in 1331, and papal approval on June 28, 1334.[23] Provision was made
for twenty poor scholars from the Burgundies in logic and natural philosophy.[24]

The Collège d'Arras (44) is another dated by Rashdall in 1332, whereas
Jaillot (XVI, 6–7) notes that the act of foundation of the Collège du
Marmoutier of January 28, 1329, states that it was in the neighborhood
of Rue de la Charrière (Chartière) and of the gardens of the scholars of
Arras. This would, however, make the gardens a long way from the Collège d'Arras, whose location is stated in a deliberation of the chapter of the
abbey of Saint-Vaast of November 28, 1332. This refers to a house in Paris
in vico Murorum, a street which opened off Rue Saint-Victor opposite the
Collège du Cardinal le Moine near Porte Saint-Victor, "for the use and
support of poor scholars coming from the city or diocese of Arras and studying at Paris in the said house."

For the founding of the Collège de Tours (6) the year 1334 is given
in Rashdall, but Jaillot (XVIII, 123–25) found "dans les Archives de
S. Germain-des-Prés" a previous donation by the founder, Etienne de
Bourgueil, archbishop of Tours, in 1330. THdVP V, 569, without citing
Jaillot, also accepts the date 1330 on the basis of a note without indica-
tion of source found among Berty's papers. The Collège de Tours was
on Rue Serpente, where was also situated the "domus scolarium de Suecia"
or Collège de Suesse or of Upsala, founded in 1291.[25]

Jaillot (XVII, 33) likewise thought that scholars might have been re-

---

[21] As does THdVP VI, 269.   [22] THdVP VI, 266 is in agreement with Jaillot.
[23] THdVP V, 321–26 more vaguely dates this foundation between 1330 and 1332.
[24] THdVP V, 323.
[25] Rashdall I (1936), 537, note 2, correcting "ante 1280" of the chronological table.

siding in the Collège des Lombards (54), which Rashdall dates of 1334, as early as 1330, since in the Act of Foundation of February 27, 1333–1334, Ghini gave to Italian scholars "a certain house which the said scholars at present occupy." [26] It was on Rue Saint-Hilaire (Rue des Carmes).

The Collège de Lisieux, founded in 1336 by the bishop of that place for 24 *boursiers* in the Faculty of Arts (Jaillot XVII, 170–73; THdVP VI, 126–29; Rashdall I, 538), at first rented a house for that purpose in the little Rue des Prêtres Saint-Séverin (50), which ran in front of the west façade of that church (B) from Rue Saint-Séverin on the north side of the church to Rue de la Parcheminerie. All three streets still bear the same names. Rashdall says that this college was absorbed in the Collège de Torchi, "founded (1414) by Guill. d'Estouteville, bishop of Lisieux, Estond [27] d'Estouteville, abbot of Fécamp, and their brother, seigneur de Torchi." Jaillot makes it plain that only the will of the bishop was of December 8, 1414, that of the abbé, his executor, being of October 18, 1422. These testaments show that the institution was now being called "le Collège de Torchi," that houses for it had been purchased near the monastery of Ste. Geneviève in Rue Saint-Etienne des Grès (43), and that twelve *boursiers* in theology were to be added to the twenty-four in arts.

For the Collège d'Hubant or de l'Ave Maria (39) either 1336 or 1339 is suggested in Rashdall as the date of foundation.[28] Jaillot (XVII, 100–101) dates on August 9, 1336 the foundation by Jean d'Hubant, Président aux Enquêtes, of four *bourses* for poor scholars, and in February, 1339, the consent of the abbot and prior of Sainte-Geneviève and the grand master of the Collège de Navarre to execute the foundation. The college was located in a house with an image of the Virgin, under which were the words, "Ave Maria," situated near the conjunction of Rue de la Montagne Sainte-Geneviève and Rue des Amandiers (*vicus amigdalorum*).

The date, 1341, given in Rashdall for the foundation of the Collège du Cardinal Bertrand, otherwise known as the Collège d'Autun (20), was likewise preferred by Jaillot (XVIII, 13–14) to 1337, which some had suggested.[29] Jaillot further distinguished 1341 as the year when was passed the contract of foundation for a principal, chaplain and fifteen *boursiers*, of whom five should be students in theology, five in canon law, and five in philosophy. But the cardinal had already in 1336 formed the plan for this establishment and towards that end bought some houses adjoining

---

[26] In 1385 it was designated as "scolarium collegii Ytalicorum de Caritate Beate Marie": Petit 143, where the footnote seems incorrect in placing the Collège des Lombards in "rue du Mont-Saint-Hilaire," which did not extend to it. See THdVP VI, 335–39.

[27] Estoud in Jaillot.   [28] THdVP V, 417, gives 1339.

[29] THdVP V, 126 follows Félibien in adopting this date.

his own in Rue Saint-André des Arcs opposite the church of that name (A). He had had them amortized by the king in December, 1338, and by the abbot of Saint-Germain in 1339 on October 25, and had obtained a papal bull of December 12, 1339.[30] In 1398 Oudard de Moulins increased the number of *boursiers* by three, making six each in theology, law and philosophy.

The Collège de Chanac (47) or de Saint-Michel is dated 1343, with a question mark, by Rashdall. Jaillot (XVI, 18–19) was even less certain, of previously suggested dates rejecting 1402 as at least half a century too late, and questioning 1342, when Guillaume de Chanac ceased to be bishop of Paris and became patriarch of Alexandria. He died on May 3, 1348, and the terms of his will set aside his house in Rue de Bièvre near the Seine to serve as a college for ten or twelve *boursiers*. But Jaillot suggested that this was a design not yet executed, and that he does not seem to have made adequate provision for the support of that many scholars.

As to the existence before 1348 of the Collège des Allemands (55) in Rue du Murier and the foundation in that year of the Collège des Trois Evêques or de Cambrai (25) in Place Cambrai Jaillot (XVI, 107–8; XVII, 179–81) and Rashdall are in substantial agreement.[31] But the former does not assign any definite date to the Collège de Maître Clément (56), as Rashdall does,[32] and he professes ignorance (XVI, 22–23) as to the date of the Collège de Tournai (42), for which Rashdall gives "circa 1350." It was situated in Rue Clopin near the colleges of Boncourt and Navarre and had once served as a town residence for the bishops of Tournai.[33]

On the other hand, Jaillot (XVIII, 107) states explicitly that the Collège Mignon (2) on Rue Mignon (earlier called *vicus Stuffarum*), for which Rashdall gives the vague date, "ante 1353," was founded in 1343 by Jean Mignon, archdeacon of Blois in the church of Chartres and master of accounts at Paris, for twelve scholars, and that he acquired some houses for that purpose. Jaillot goes on to say, however, that Mignon died in 1345

[30] The brief abstract of a thesis on the Collège d'Autun by A. Hughes, *Positions des Thèses* (1885), 89–91, gave no date of foundation. The revised abstract, *ibid.*, (1886), 90, gives 1341 as the date but adds, "Le pape Benoît XII confirme, le 10 décembre 1339, la foundation par une bulle."

[31] THdVP VI, 286–88.

[32] Rashdall and THdVP VI, 143 give 1349 as the time of foundation. The name of the college does not appear in Jaillot's index, but at XVIII, 65 he notes that in 1370 for lack of funds it was incorporated with the Collège de Maître Gervais. Previously it had been located in Rue Hautefeuille.

[33] The Collège des Lombards was also sometimes called of Tournai: Petit 429, "in domo sua in collegio de Tornaco alias Lombardorum in vico sancti Ylarii," but was in a quite different location.

without having put his project into effect, and that his executors did nothing for eight years thereafter, until the complaints of the university led king John in July, 1353, to order Robert Mignon, brother and executor of the deceased, to purchase before Christmas "28 livres parisis de rente amortie" for the twelve scholars and to surrender to them the house which his brother had occupied or another of equal value, with fifteen beds and bedding, and to construct a fully equipped chapel.[34] The three extra beds may have been for a principal, chaplain, and assistant master.

The foundation of the Collège de Boncour (41) by Pierre Bécond, chevalier, is dated in 1353 by Rashdall. Jaillot (XVI, 21) mentions letters of Pierre de Bécoud of September, 1353 with reference to the college but dates the *Acte de Fondation* on November 18, 1357. This college faced that of Navarre across Rue Clopin.

Conversely, the foundation of the Collège de Justice (13) by Jean de Justice, chanter of Bayeux and canon of Paris, for twelve *boursiers* in philosophy and medicine, is placed by Rashdall in 1358, while Jaillot (XVIII, 84–86) declares that l'abbé Lebeuf and M. Piganiol erred in deferring its foundation to November 15, 1358. Jean de Justice died in 1353, after having acquired houses for a college, and his executors fulfilled his intention by an "Acte d'amortissement de ces maisons" of July 11, 1354. Jaillot's conclusion is that this *Acte* either immediately preceded or immediately followed the foundation of the college, which was situated on the west side of Rue de la Harpe about opposite the Collège de Bayeux.[35]

The Collège de Boissi or Boissy (1) is listed under the year 1359 in Rashdall [36] but Jaillot (XVIII, 16–19) places its foundation in 1358, when the *Acte* of foundation for six poor scholars was dated June 1, although its ratification by the university is of March 7, 1359.[37] The college was

[34] So also THdVP V, 483.

[35] THdVP V, 417–18, adds nothing new.

[36] THdVP V, 287 says it was founded in 1356.

[37] THdVP V, 288, has "7 mars 1358," but perhaps failed to remember that this was in the old style of dating. These same two dates of June 1, 1358, and March 7, 1359, are distinguished by Georges Crépy, "Etude historique sur le collège de Boissy de l'université de Paris (1358–1764)," *Positions des Thèses* (1904), 15–22, who adds the date of Godefroy's testament, 3 novembre 1353, to which Jaillot referred but did not specify, but does not give the date of his death, which Jaillot stated as August 20, 1354. Both Crépy and Jaillot agree that this testament provided that the residue of the estate should go to the poor of Paris and of Boissi-le-Sec (Jaillot adds the qualification, "si ses Exécuteurs ne jugoient pas à propos d'en disposer autrement"), but that his nephew, Etienne Vldé, canon of Laon (Jaillot adds, "& de S. Germain-l'Auxerrois, & les autres Exécuteurs testamentaires de Geoffroi"), applied it to the foundation of a college. The Crépy abstract is listed bibliographically in Rashdall (I, 498) but apparently was not utilized in revising the list of colleges.

situated on Rue du Cimitière Saint-André which ran south of the church of that name.

For the foundation of the Collège de la Marche (48) the year 1363 is given in Rashdall, both in the chronological list and previously at p. 506, where it is stated that "the single 'Bursar' or foundationer," who was found quartered in "the ruined and dilapidated buildings" of the College of Constantinople, "was persuaded to make over its property to the founders of the Collège de la Marche." Jaillot (XVI, 52–54) gives a different account. According to it, Jean de la Marche in 1362 rented the College of Constantinople (49), then situated in le cul-de-sac d'Amboise near Place Maubert, on the understanding that the cost of the lease, ten livres a year, be employed on repairs which were urgent and considerable. Of this arrangement the university approved by letters of July 19, 1362, and the college therewith took the name of "la petite Marche," since it had only one *boursier* when Jean leased it. Jaillot, however, did not regard Jean de la Marche as the founder of the Collège de la Marche, which, he says, recognized two founders, Guillaume de la Marche and Beuve de Winville. Guillaume, a nephew of Jean, after the latter's death obtained a continuance of the lease for an annual payment of twenty livres, of which fourteen went for "les cens et rentes" with which this college was charged, and six to support poor scholars. These conditions were set forth in university letters of April 22, 1374. When Guillaume died in 1420, he left most of his property for the support of a principal, proctor and six *boursiers*. His executor, Beuve de Winville, in the same year purchased houses on Monte Sainte-Geneviève from nuns of Senlis and built the college there in Rue de la Montagne Sainte-Geneviève, where the scholars of "la petite Marche" were now united with a new chaplain and six new *boursiers*. The patriarch of Constantinople and the bishop of Paris approved these arrangements, and the institution came to be called "le Collège de la Marche-Winville," while an inscription on its gate suggested yet another date, 1402, for its foundation.[38]

For the following dates Jaillot and Rashdall are in agreement.[39] The Collège de Vendôme (3) was already in existence in 1367 at the southern end of *vicus Galgani*, later Rue de l'Eperon (Jaillot XVIII, 63). In 1370 the colleges of Dormans-Beauvais (Jaillot XVII, 167–70) and of Master Gervais were founded: the former (22) in houses once occupied by the

[38] Pierre Lévy, "Histoire de collège de la Marche et de Winville en l'université de Paris," *Positions des Thèses* (1921), 71–77, similarly says, "le Collège fonctionne dès 1402." Otherwise his account of its foundation seems roughly identical with Jaillot's. Lévy's abstract is cited in the bibliography in Rashdall at I, 498, but apparently was not used.

[39] See also THdVP V, 479; VI, 103, 141–47: V, 531.

Collège de Laon, the latter (7) in houses in Rue de Foin, now completely obliterated by the Boulevard Saint-Germain, and Rue Erembourg de Brie (Jaillot XVIII, 63–65). The Collège de Dainville (8), west of Rue de la Harpe between Rue Pierre Sarrasin and Rue des Cordeliers or Saint-Cosme, was founded April 19, 1380 for twelve *boursiers*, six from the diocese of Arras and six from that of Noyon. At the angle of the building on the corner of Rue de la Harpe and Rue des Cordeliers were sculptured figures of kings John and Charles V, and of the founders presenting the principal and *boursiers* to the Virgin (Jaillot XVIII, 60–61).

Jaillot has been accused by Raoul Busquet [40] of dating the foundation of the Collège de Fortet (38) on April 29, 1397. Busquet cites "Jaillot, *Recherches critiques, historiques et topographiques sur Paris*, 5 vols., 1775. *Quartier Saint-Benoît* (t. III)." In the edition of 1782 which I have used, where "XVII. Quartier Saint-Benoît," is in Vol. IV, at pp. 225–27, Jaillot distinguishes August 12, 1391, as the date of Fortet's testament; April 24, 1394, as that of his death; and adds, "ainsi l'on ne peut pas dire que ce Collège ait été fondé en 1391, ni en 1393." He does not explicitly deny that it was founded in 1394; rather he refers to an *Acte* of May 8 of that year. He does, however, give the impression that the house in Rue des Cordeliers, which the testator had suggested for the college, was never accepted by his executors for that purpose, whereas Busquet has shown that extensive repairs were made in it with this end in view, and that it was actually occupied by the *boursiers* until the new building in Rue des Sept Voies was acquired in 1397, when Jaillot dated the contract of acquisition on February 28, not April 29 as stated by Busquet. Jaillot dated the statutes of the college on April 10, 1397, while Busquet put them in 1396, perhaps overlooking the fact that the year 1396 (*vieux style*) ran from April 2, 1396, to April 22, 1397, at Paris.

The Collège du Tou or de Tulleio (33), which seems to have been already in existence in 1387 [41] or even 1342 [42] and not merely in 1393, as Lebeuf suggested, Jaillot (XVII, 40) would locate in Rue des Sept Voies rather than Rue Chartière. If the "Plan du Collège Ste. Barbe et de ses environs vers 1480," published by Quicherat as the frontispiece to his first volume, is correct, and if a "Collège de Toul" there shown is meant for

[40] "Etude historique sur le Collège de Fortet (1394–1784)," *Mémoires de la Société de l'histoire de Paris et de l'Ile de France*, 33 (1906), 245, note 1.

[41] Petit 458, "collegii du Touil"; 462, "domus de Tullio." But there seems to be no ground for his saying that the Collège du Tou was "réuni vers 1423 à celui de Cornouailles." He perhaps misread Lebeuf's statement that "un docteur breton le joignit, vers ce tems là (1423) aux collèges de Tréguier et de Cornouailles, dans la distribution de ses aumônes" (quoted THdVP VI, 123).

[42] THdVP VI, 123, "dans un titre faisant partie des archives de Saint-Marcel."

the Collège du Tou, this institution was rather placed on the east side of the short Rue de Chaudron, which ran halfway between and parallel to Rue Chartière and Rue des Sept Voies.

The Collège de Tonnerre (24), whose *Acte d'amortissement* is dated December 3, 1406, was located towards the south end of Rue du Clos-Bruneau near the little Rue Saint-Jean de Latran (Jaillot XVII, 173–74).[43]

For the Collège de Reims (35), Jaillot (XVII, 227–28) and Rashdall prefer the date 1409, when the founder, Gui de Roye, archbishop of Reims, died, to 1412, when the college purchased l'Hôtel de Bourgogne, located slightly to the south-east of the Collège de Tonnerre, of which we have just been speaking.[44] In the Burgundian troubles of 1418 the Collège de Reims was almost destroyed and remained abandoned until 1443, when it was restored by Charles VII, who united to it another ruined college, that of Rethel (18), which had hitherto been located in Rue des Poirées.[45]

The Collège de Donjon was founded, according to Rashdall, in 1412 by Olivier de Donjon and afterwards was united with the College de Tréguier. Jaillot (XVII, 178), on the contrary, says that Olivier Doujon [46] in 1412 merely founded six new *bourses* in the Collège de Tréguier, then located, as we have seen, on Place Cambrai (53).

Rashdall lists as founded before 1421 both the Collège de Thori (Torchi?), which is not included in Jaillot's index and whose location seems unknown, and the Collège de Karembert or de Léon (34), of which Jaillot (XVII, 178–79) says that he could not find when or by whom it was founded. He dated its union with the Collège de Tréguier in 1575. Previously it had been situated at the corner of Rue des Sept Voies and Rue du Four, with the Collège de Reims to the south, the church of Saint-Hilaire to the north, and the Collège de Toul to the west. It was already in existence in 1386, when it brought suit before the Official of Paris.[47]

The Collège de Séez (9) is represented by Rashdall as founded in 1428 by Grégoire l'Anglais, bishop of Séez. Jaillot (XVIII, 75–76) notes that in 1763 the magistrate who was charged with rendering an account to Parlement of the state of the colleges at Paris complained of the inexacti-

---

[43] THdVP VI, 94.

[44] THdVP VI, 398, retains the date 1399, rejected by Jaillot, for the formation of the community of scholars. *Ibid.*, 562, for the contract of 1412.

[45] THdVP VI, 543–46 for documents concerning Rethel's incorporation.

[46] The name is also so spelled in the civil register of the Official of Paris in 1386. Petit 103, adds: "Olivier Doujon, docteur en décret, fonda en 1410 six bourses au collège de Tréguier (Du Boulay, *Historia Universitatis Parisiensis*, t. V, p. 909)."

[47] Petit 338. In the footnote Tréguier or Léon is confused with Laon.

tude of a *Mémoire* which had been submitted to him concerning this college. It recorded that the college was founded in 1427 [48] (February 24, old style) by a bishop, Grégoire Langlois. But inasmuch as the prelate in question had passed away, back in 1404, Jaillot regarded it as more proper to name as the founder Jean Langlois, executor of his uncle's will.

Of the five remaining colleges in the Rashdall list three do not appear in Jaillot's index: namely, the Collège de Lorris, the Collège d'Aubusson, and the Collège de Boucard.

The Collège de Sainte-Barbe (36) is said by Rashdall to have been founded in 1460 by Geoffroy Lenormant, who taught grammar school boys at the Collège de Navarre. Jaillot (XVII, 39, 214–15) puts the *Acte* of foundation as late as 1556, but dates from 1430 the formation of a group of teachers by Jean Hubert, doctor of canon law, out of which the college developed. In this Jaillot seems mistaken. Hubert appears merely to have purchased property which later belonged to the Collège de Sainte-Barbe but which remained in private hands for some time after his death. The Collège de Sainte-Barbe originated rather, as Quicherat has shown, [49] in a decree of Parlement of April 18, 1460, which forbade the brothers Lenormant to conduct a grammar school for profit as an annex to the Collège de Navarre, as they had been doing. In consequence Geoffroy acquired l'Hôtel de Chalon, which became the Collège de Sainte-Barbe, and transferred his pupils thither. As time went on, various adjoining pieces of property were added to the college.

Concerning the Collège de Coquerel or Coqueret [50] (32) Rashdall offers somewhat conflicting information. In his table 1463 is given as the date of foundation and Nicolas de Coquerel as the founder. But at I, 532, we are told that in 1463 the Collège de Coquerel "was found to have no bursar and to be full of workmen and their families who had occupied the empty rooms," which would seem to imply that the college had been in existence long enough to deteriorate sadly. March 7, 1463, however, appears to have been the date of the founder's will.

Henry Token, writing in the middle of the fifteenth century, listed and located the following twenty colleges: Navarre, Sorbonne, Cholets, Boncourt, Ave Maria, Reims, Lombards, Cardinal le Moine, Beauvais, Cambrai or Trois Evêques, Arras, Bons-Enfants, Cluny, Dainville, Narbonne, Dace, Maître Gervaise, Justice, Harcourt and Trésorier. He gave the di-

[48] THdVP VI, 181, also gives 1427 as the year of foundation.
[49] *Histoire de Sainte-Barbe*, I (1860), 3–9.
[50] Rashdall adheres to the former spelling; Jaillot (XVII, 39) employs both, "Nicole Couquerel (ou plutôt Coqueret)"; Quicherat, I, 17, writes, "Coquerel ou Coqueret," while his Plan has the form, Coqueret.

mensions in feet for the following colleges or classrooms: Navarre, 70 x 34; Sorbonne, 56 x 35; Lombards, 40 x 40; Cholets, 49 x 27; "scole iuristarum in vico Brunelli," 93 x 44, 68 x 28, and 51 x 36.[51]

It is remarkable that only three new colleges are recorded at Paris for the second half of the fifteenth century, and that of these two developed out of private grammar schools run for profit rather than originated in pious and philanthropical donations. The period of most frequent foundation seems to have been the first half of the fourteenth century, when a new college is known to have been opened on an average of every second year.

[51] Wolfenbüttel MS. Helmstedt 139b, fols. 47v, 48r, 336r: noted by P. Lehmann, "Mitteilungen aus Handschriften," IV (1933), 51, *Sitzungsberichte d. Bayer. Akad. d. Wiss., Philos.-hist. Abt.* (1929), Heft 1.

KEY
THE COLLEGES LISTED ALPHABETICALLY

THE COLLEGES LISTED NUMERICALLY

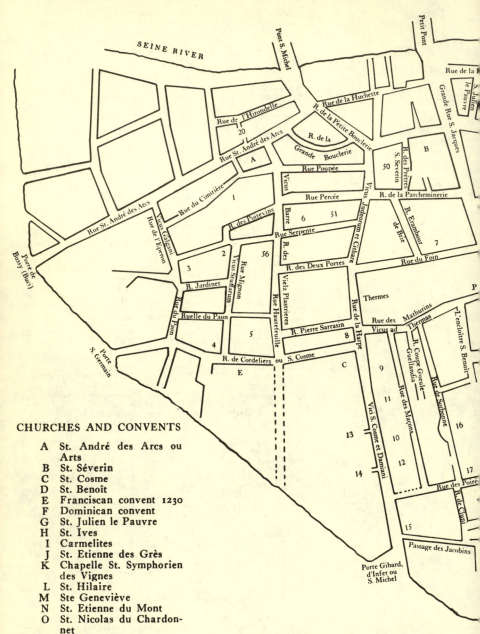

CHURCHES AND CONVENTS

A   St. André des Arcs ou
    Arts
B   St. Séverin
C   St. Cosme
D   St. Benoît
E   Franciscan convent 1230
F   Dominican convent
G   St. Julien le Pauvre
H   St. Ives
I   Carmelites
J   St. Etienne des Grès
K   Chapelle St. Symphorien
    des Vignes
L   St. Hilaire
M   Ste Geneviève
N   St. Etienne du Mont
O   St. Nicolas du Chardon-
    net
P   St. Mathurin

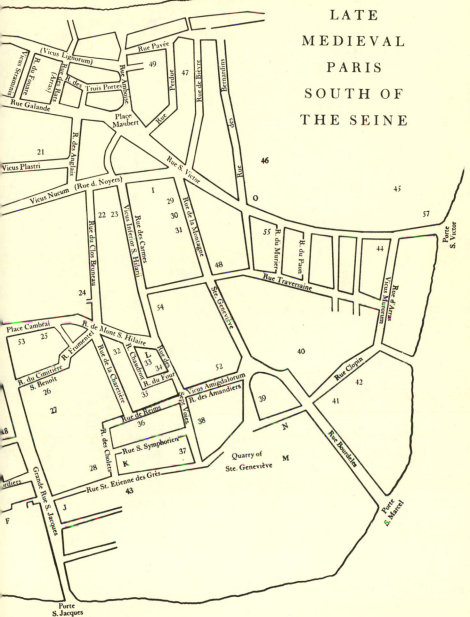

NE RIVER

LATE
MEDIEVAL
PARIS
SOUTH OF
THE SEINE

(Vicus Lignorum)
Rue Pavée
Vicus Straminis
R. du Foure
Rue des Rats
(Arras)
Rue Amboise
Rue Perdue
Rue des
Trois Portes
49
47
Rue de Bièvre
Rue des Bernardins
Rue Galande
Place
Maubert
Rue S. Victor
Rue des
46
R. des Anglais
21
Vicus Plastri
45
Vicus Nucum (Rue d. Noyers)
O
57
1
29
Rue de la Montagne
Porte
S. Victor
22 23
Rue des Carmes
Vicus Inferior S. Hilarii
30
31
55
R. du Murier
R. du Paon
44
Rue du Clos Bruneau
48
Ste. Geneviève
Rue Traversaine
Vicus Murorum
Rue d'Arras
24
54
Place Cambrai
R. de Mont S. Hilaire
40
Rue Clopin
53 25
R. Frumentel
32
R. Chaudcor
L
33
34
52
42
R. du Cimitière
S. Benoit
26
Rue de la Charetière
R. du Four
35
Vicus Amigdalorum
R. des Amandiers
39
41
Rue Bourdelles
27
Rue de Reims
36
38
N
ordiers
Rue S. Symphorien
37
Quarry of
Ste. Geneviève
M
48
28
K
Grande Rue S. Jacques
Rue St. Etienne des Grès
43
Porte
S. Marcel
F
J

Porte
S. Jacques

INDEX